ROMANTIC NATURAL HISTORIES

NEW RIVERSIDE EDITIONS
Series Editor for the British Volumes
Alan Richardson, Boston College

WILLIAM WORDSWORTH,
CHARLES DARWIN, AND OTHERS

Romantic Natural Histories

Selected Texts with Introduction

Edited by

Ashton Nichols

DICKINSON COLLEGE

Houghton Mifflin Company
BOSTON • NEW YORK

Once more, for Kim.
And I more pleasure in your praise.

Sponsoring Editor: Michael Gillespie
Associate Editor: Bruce Cantley
Editorial Assistant: Lisa Minter
Project Editor: Jane Lee
Editorial Assistant: Talia Kingsbury
Production/Design Assistant: Bethany Schlegel
Manufacturing Manager: Florence Cadran
Marketing Manager: Cindy Graff Cohen
Marketing Assistant: Sarah Donelson

Cover image: © Stefano Bianchetti/CORBIS

Library of Congress Control Number: 2003107917
ISBN: 0-618-31767-8
1 2 3 4 5 6 7 8 9-MP-07 06 05 04 03

CONTENTS

ABOUT THIS SERIES
Alan Richardson

The Riverside imprint, stamped on a book's spine or printed on its title page, carries a special aura for anyone who loves and values books. As well it might: by the middle of the nineteenth century, Houghton Mifflin had already established the Riverside Edition as an important presence in American publishing. The Riverside series of British poets brought trustworthy editions of Milton and Wordsworth, Spenser and Pope, and (then) lesser-known writers like Herbert, Vaughan, and Keats to a growing nation of readers. There was both a Riverside Shakespeare and a Riverside Chaucer by the century's end, titles that would be revived and recreated as the authoritative editions of the late twentieth century. Riverside Editions of writers like Emerson, Hawthorne, Longfellow, and Thoreau helped establish the first canon of American literature. Early in the twentieth century, the Cambridge editions published by Houghton Mifflin at the Riverside Press made the complete works of dozens of British and American poets widely available in single-volume editions that can still be found in libraries and homes throughout the United States and beyond.

The Riverside Editions of the 1950s and 1960s brought attractive, affordable, and carefully edited versions of a range of British and American titles into the thriving new market for serious paperback literature. Prepared by leading scholars and critics of the time, the Riversides rapidly became known for their lively introductions, reliable texts, and lucid annotation. Though aimed primarily at the college market, the series was also created (as one editor put) with the "general reader's private library" in mind. These were paperbacks to hold onto and read again, and many a "private" library was seeded with the colorful spines of Riverside Editions kept long after graduation.

Houghton Mifflin's New Riverside Editions now bring the combination of high editorial values and wide popular appeal long associated with the Riverside imprint into line with the changing needs and desires of twenty-first-century students and general readers. Inaugurated in 2000 with the first set of American titles under the general editorship of Paul Lauter, the New Riversides reflect both the changing canons of literature in English and the greater emphases on historical and cultural context that have helped a new generation of critics to extend and reenliven literary studies. The series not only is concerned with keeping the classic works of British and American literature alive, but also grows out of the excitement that a broader range of literary texts and cultural reference points has brought to the classroom. Works by formerly marginalized authors, including women writers and writers of color, will find a place in the series along with titles from the traditional canons that a succession of Riverside imprints helped establish beginning a century and a half ago. New Riverside titles will reflect the recent surge of interest in the connections among literary activity, historical change, and social and political issues, including slavery, abolition, and the construction of "race"; gender relations and the history of sexuality; the rise of the British Empire and of nationalism on both sides of the Atlantic; and changing conceptions of nature and of human beings.

The New Riverside Editions respond to recent changes in literary studies not only in the range of titles but also in the design of individual volumes. Issues and debates crucial to a book's author and original audience find voice in selections from contemporary writings of many kinds as well as in early reactions and reviews. Some volumes will place contemporary writers into dialogue, as with the pairing of Irish national tales by Maria Edgeworth and Sydney Owenson or of vampire stories by Bram Stoker and Sheridan Le Fanu. Other volumes provide alternative ways of constructing literary tradition, juxtaposing Mary Shelley's *Frankenstein* with H. G. Wells's *Island of Dr. Moreau*, or Byron's *The Giaour*, an "Eastern Tale" in verse, with Frances Sheridan's *Nourjahad* and William Beckford's *Vathek*, its most important predecessors in Orientalist prose fiction. Chronologies, selections from major criticism, notes on textual history, and bibliographies will allow readers to go beyond the text and explore a given writer or issue in greater depth. Seasoned critics will find fresh new contexts and juxtapositions, and general readers will find intriguing new material to read alongside familiar titles in an attractive format.

Houghton Mifflin's New Riverside Editions maintain the values of reliability and readability that have marked the Riverside name for well over a

century. Each volume also provides something new—often unexpected—
and each in a distinctive way. Freed from the predictable monotony and
rigidity of a set template, editors can build their volumes around the special opportunities presented by a given title or set of related works. We
hope that the resulting blend of innovative scholarship, creative format,
and high production values will help the Riverside imprint continue to
thrive well into the new century.

A poetic scientist or a scientific poet? The natural historian with the quill pen beneath the tree appears to be a poet and a scientist as he gazes at a hermit (on the right) and contemplates the peaceable kingdom that surrounds him: lion, peacock, oxen, goat, deer, wild boar, rooster, dog, rabbit, even a toad by his foot. Frontispiece to *The New Museum of Natural History* (Edinburgh: Oliver and Boyd, 1810).

INTRODUCTION
Ashton Nichols

From poison trees and fearful tigers, to sensitive plants and melodious nightingales, the discourse of natural history played a crucial role in the development of Romantic nature writing. The current surge of interest in ecocriticism reminds us that our contemporary concern for the natural world has its roots in the nature writing and natural history of the past three centuries. The writings of poets, novelists, and natural historians from 1750 to 1859 suggest the extent to which eighteenth- and nineteenth-century science connected to a wider Romantic sensibility. Romantic natural histories link "animated nature" with what Samuel Taylor Coleridge will call "the one Life within us and abroad" (*Poems*, 1796) and Charles Darwin will later describe by saying that "all the organic beings which have ever lived on this earth may be descended from some one primordial form" (*Origin of Species*, 1859). An emphasis on nature writing and natural history in the century before Charles Darwin's *Origin of Species* — not only in scientific works but also in poetry, prose fiction, essays, and letters — reveals an emerging sense of connections among humans, animals, and all living organisms on the planet. Insofar as the radical split between science and art has been a post-Romantic phenomenon, a renewed understanding of Romantic natural histories becomes an essential precursor to any current romantic (or literary) ecology.

Romantic Natural Histories gathers works of natural science and natural history together with well-known works of literature — and more obscure nature writing — by well-known literary figures. The goal of this collection is to remind us how complex and multifarious the concept of "nature" was to a group of writers we now identify as nature writers. At the same time, this collection of texts and images also suggests just how much figurative and imaginative thought went into the natural science of the pre-Darwinian era.

Romantic literature has often been discussed as though it stood in direct opposition to the scientific materialism of its age. John Keats is cited for his claim that Isaac Newton destroyed the poetry of the rainbow, while William Blake satirizes both classical atomism and Newtonian physics. William Wordsworth criticizes those who would murder to dissect, and Lord Byron poetically parodies the scientific spirit of his age: "Galvanism has set some corpses grinning" (*Don Juan* 1, 130). But this apparent poetic hostility is countered by a consistent interest in and comment on natural science in countless poems and prose narratives of the Romantic period. Wordsworth, in perhaps his most famous passage linking science and poetry, claims that "If the labours of Men of Science should ever create any material revolution, direct or indirect, in our condition, and in the impressions which we habitually receive, the Poet will sleep then no more than at present, but he will be ready to follow the steps of the Man of Science, not only in those general indirect effects, but he will be at his side, carrying sensation into the midst of the objects of Science itself. The remotest discoveries of the Chemist, the Botanist, or Mineralogist, will be as proper objects of the Poet's art as any upon which it can be employed" (Preface to *Lyrical Ballads,* Gill 606–07). Likewise, Coleridge's notebooks and marginalia are full of reflections on experimental and observational science: zoology, chemistry, electricity, and galvanism. Percy Shelley experimented with chemicals and electric machines in his rooms at Oxford. By 1818, Mary Shelley describes her fictional Victor Frankenstein as a powerful scientist who uncovers the secret of life and offers his desire to create a "new species" as a prime motivation for the unhallowed experiments that lead him to produce a "monster."

"Natural history" is also a complex category with less than clearly defined boundaries. The phrase is related to "natural philosophy" (which we now call "science"). But the systematic study of plants and animals also came to be associated with the popular treatment of these subjects, not merely a rigorously scientific practice. Likewise, collections of flora and fauna by amateurs and children were described as natural history, as were beautiful illustrations of botanical and entomological specimens that reached their zenith in ornately bound Victorian volumes. The laboratory experiments of Joseph Priestley and Sir Humphry Davy may seem far removed from the natural observations of Gilbert White and John Leonard Knapp, but the discourse of natural philosophy came to include the study of nature in all of its forms. Likewise, the language of science developed important connections with the language of poetry in ways that this anthology is organized to illuminate. The premise of *Romantic Natural Histories* is that the development of natural history, and related developments in experimental science, had a greater impact on the literature of the period, particularly poetry, than has been fully recognized. Romantic nature writing owed an important debt to scientific observation and to the analysis of natural processes during this same period. In a similar way, natural science from 1750 to 1859 relied more directly on literary images and on figurative thinking than we might at first imagine. A brief survey of the historical background will help establish a context for the selections of Romantic natural history that follow.

For the ancient world, mythology suggested powerful interconnections among the natural, the human, and the imaginary. Gods were like humans, humans were like animals, animals were like plants, plants were like humans, and vice versa. Spontaneous generation, parthenogenesis by fire, and impregnation by bulls, swans, and showers of gold were all reminders of permeable boundaries between living and nonliving, animate and inanimate, spiritual and material. Many plants and animals were sacred to the ancients for precisely this reason. A butterfly might be believed to *be* the soul of a deceased person, but more importantly, the soul might be imagined figuratively as being *like* a butterfly. A plant might have powerful medicinal uses, but it could also be identified with a specific god or goddess. The power of animals could be invoked for practical reasons (hunting) or spiritual purposes (rituals and sacrifices). Thus the image of a massive bull might concurrently be associated with human food, the story of the Minotaur, and the power of Zeus. Aristotle (384–322 B.C.) was perhaps the first systematic natural historian. He described over five hundred species; in fact, roughly one quarter of Aristotle's known work refers to zoology. Pliny the Elder's *Naturalis historia* was dedicated to Titus in 77 A.D. and included over three dozen "books" ranging through information on astronomy, geography, human biology, zoology, botany, medical botany, metallurgy, and geology. Pliny claimed that his work drew on one hundred earlier authors and included 20,000 facts of nature. His texts present a fascinating mix of careful observations and subsequently supported scientific facts interlaced with myths, false reports, exaggerations, and fanciful stories. The work became a standard source for classical knowledge about the natural world.

During the Middle Ages, natural history was a complex combination of accurate reportage, misinformation, and complete fabrication. Dragons vied with pythons for space in the pages of manuscripts and bestiaries, while herbals listed cures that were sometimes effective and more often farfetched. Travelers reported ten-foot lizards (komodo dragons) on islands in the South Seas, but such accurate reports appeared alongside accounts of many-headed hydras like the one that had been killed by Hercules. Medical botany was seen to be as bogus as legend when its cures did not work and as suspect as witchcraft when they did. Plants that could relieve physical symptoms immediately (digitalis, the opium poppy) seemed like magic well into the modern era. Whole areas of rational inquiry into the workings of nature were also off limits for religious reasons. Those who delved too far into the mysteries of creation were branded lunatics, sorcerers, or godless heathens. Scientific inquiry often seemed too close to spiritual activity or magic to be accepted by the wider society. The Renaissance, by contrast, came to be characterized by a new spirit of curiosity and discovery. Once the Earth was "removed" from the center of the universe by Nicolaus Copernicus, many other ideas about the natural world were likewise subject to complete revision. Wider understanding accompanied new discoveries in fields ranging from geology and botany to anatomy and physiology. While Andreas Vesalius was producing remarkably accurate anatomical drawings, and William Harvey was describing the circulation of the blood, however, confusion and debate flourished around a wide range of scientific questions.

In many cases, empirical observations came into direct conflict with religious beliefs. What was the connection (if any) between the Biblical flood and fossil remains? Was the world as it now appeared unchanged since ancient times? Were all human beings members of the same species (monogenesis) or descendants of different original types (polygenesis)? What accounted for monsters if the divine natural system otherwise operated with such predictable regularity? Were freaks of nature part of God's plan or merely mysteries that had to be accepted as beyond the realm of human knowing? How did people whose ideas of wild animals were based on foxes and field mice react when the first rhinoceros or elephant was removed from its crate in London or Venice? How could poisons from some plants kill, while tonics from the identical plants saved lives? Anxieties like these plagued scientists and nonscientists for centuries because of unquestioned theological assumptions, insufficient physical evidence, and the absence of any rigorously experimental methodology. At the same time, voyages of exploration and discovery were collecting astonishing creatures from distant lands and seas, as well as plants of remarkable usefulness and variety. News of hitherto unknown human societies suggested that fully developed cultures might exist that had nothing to do with the history, the religions, or the societies of Europe. Diversity in natural and social spheres produced a growing sense that the world was much wider and much more complex than it had seemed to earlier observers.

By the 1700s, revolutionary thinking was not only the province of philosophers, political theorists, and religious reformers. Natural philosophers, botanical collectors, physicians, and amateur naturalists were all engaged in radically new ways of organizing ideas about the nonhuman world. During these years, natural historians constituted a varied but often interrelated group of researchers. Joseph Kastner has called this loose affiliation of scientists perhaps "the eighteenth century's most pervasive and influential intellectual group"; they "were found all the way from Siberia to South America, and by their incessant correspondence, they kept information and ideas moving through all the civilized world. John Amman, the English physician working in St. Petersburg, might send a report on Russian rhubarb to Johann Jakob Dillenius, the German botanist working in England, who would pass the information on to Albrecht von Haller, the argumentative plant physiologist of Göttingen, who would inform Isaac Lawson, the physician general of the British Army in Flanders, who would tell it to one of the de Jussieu brothers in Paris, who might suggest to Sir Hans Sloane in London that he pass the information on to Patrick Browne in Jamaica" (19–20).

Likewise, Thomas Jefferson received tropical varieties of plants for his gardens at Monticello while he was sending mammoth bones to Paris for inclusion in the natural history museum organized by the Comte de Buffon. A related aspect of eighteenth-century natural science was the ongoing discovery of countless new species, many of which seemed as strange as monsters or mythical beasts. The South Carolina physician Alexander Garden, for example, described a new amphibian to Carolus Linnaeus, a snakelike creature with only two front legs and feathery gills behind its head. *Siren lacertina* Linnaeus called it, creating a new class of amphibian— the mud iguana or mudpuppy—in the process. Garden also presented Linnaeus with a three-foot long amphibian that appeared to be a watery serpent, except for its four feet, each of which had two toes: the two-toed conger eel (Kastner 76). In Britain, Thomas Pennant and later Thomas Bewick were classifying and illustrating species new and old, while in Europe, Buffon, Jean-Baptiste de Lamarck, and Alexander von Humboldt were offering theological, evolutionary, or materialist explanations for the elaborate diversity of all living things.

At the same time, chemical, electrical, and physical scientists were rapidly changing human understanding of the natural world, not only for specialists but for the general public. Benjamin Franklin, Joseph Priestley, Humphry Davy, Luigi Galvani, Alessandro Volta, and others explored connections between chemical properties and organic motion, electric impulses and chemical reactions, poisons and prescriptions, and oxygen and oxygenated blood. This experimental science was closely related to natural history insofar as it examined physical objects of the material world with an eye to understanding their composition, operations, and relations to one another. Like Galvani in Bologna, Priestley in Birmingham experimented on living and dead animals in order to better understand the operations of electricity and its connection to living systems. Meanwhile, Davy was experimenting with the chemistry of gases while inventing a safe miner's headlamp and observing the activity of electric fish. He was also writing poetry during these years and corresponding about his scientific discoveries with Coleridge. Likewise, Erasmus Darwin wrote heroic couplets while performing botanical experiments on "sensitive" plants.

What does all of this have to do with Romantic literature and a wider Romantic discourse? By the time Mary Shelley (1818) claimed that a "new species" might bless a completely human creator for its existence, Romantic poets and writers were hinting at the biological connectedness of all living things, even without the precise scientific details that would allow them to explain such links. When Coleridge refers to the "one Life within us and abroad, / Which meets all motion and becomes its soul, / A light in sound, a sound-like power in light" ("The Eolian Harp," ll.26–29), he is clearly imagining a naturalized version of divine unity. Erasmus Darwin would have probably called Coleridge's "one Life" a "vegetative" energy that pervades and links all living things, "all objects of all thought / And rolls through all things" as Wordsworth would add in "Tintern Abbey" (ll.102–03). In "The Eolian Harp," Coleridge imagines "all of animated nature" as "organic Harps diversely fram'd," and he refers to the animating principle of this organic unity as "Plastic and vast." The phrase "animate nature" was used by natural historians to distinguish those aspects of creation that were responsible for their own motion (anima: breath, wind) from inanimate (spiritless) objects. "Animate nature" also hinted at some unifying vital principle that separated living from nonliving things. But even the barrier between living and dead matter was appearing to be more and more permeable.

By 1818, Mary Shelley had penned a famous sentence that offered a natural historical explanation for Victor Frankenstein's desire to create a unique sort of living being: "A new species would bless me as its creator and source; many happy and excellent natures would owe their being to me." The line appears in the original 1818 edition of the novel and unaltered in the revised version of 1831. In Charles Robinson's facsimile edition of the manuscript, *species* appears to have been Mary Shelley's third word choice after *creation* and *existence* (1: 85). Much recent scholarship has emphasized Mary Shelley's biography and state of mind during the Frankenstein summer. Additional work on the novel has analyzed the scientific advances of the era. Both Galvani and Volta were experimenting with electric impulses and muscular contractions during the 1790s, as was Giovanni Aldini in the early 1800s. Less attention has been given to an equally important question: what precisely did Mary Shelley think the word *species* meant in 1818, and how did her sense of the concept of species relate to the wider concept of Romantic natural histories?

Of course, as this *Frankenstein* example suggests, the dramatically expanding discourse of natural science provided poets, writers, painters, and illustrators (and the general public) with powerful images and food for the imagination. In addition, the two-cultures separation we now often assume between the sciences and the arts simply did not exist before the twentieth century. As early as 1776, the natural historian Thomas Pennant, in the Preface to *British Zoology*, made this connection:

> Descriptive poetry is still more indebted to natural knowledge, than either painting or sculpture: the poet has the whole creation for his range; nor can his art exist without borrowing metaphors, allusions, or descriptions from the face of nature, which is the only fund of great ideas. The depths of the seas, the internal caverns of the earth, and the planetary system are out of the painter's reach; but can supply the poet with the sublimest conceptions: nor is the knowledge of animals and vegetables less requisite, while his creative pen adds life and motion to every object. (xiii)

Thus Wordsworth read Erasmus Darwin and used his psychological theories in lyric poems. Meanwhile, this same Darwin (Charles's grandfather) was writing in heroic couplets—book-length poems of botanical observations. Wordsworth then criticized Erasmus Darwin for his stilted and artificial diction. Humphry Davy and Joseph Priestley penned poems and theological essays while discovering chemical processes and oxygen, and Coleridge and Anna Barbauld sent poetic requests and scientific letters to these two natural philosophers. Percy Shelley experimented with chemical and electric equipment in his rooms at Oxford. Mary Shelley was listening to Shelley and Byron talk about the Italian electrical scientist Luigi Galvani on the night she conceived Frankenstein's monster. Coleridge sought poetically and philosophically for "one Life within us and abroad" that might unify the seemingly disparate elements of creation. Blake thought not only that "The Catterpiller on the Leaf / Repeats to thee thy Mother's grief," but that "A Robin Red breast in a Cage / Puts all Heaven in a Rage." Galvanic nerve responses, luminous plankton, sensitive plants (*mimosa*), poison trees (*bohun upas*), intelligence in animals, and sexuality in plants: ideas and images like these fostered poetic reflection and scientific lyricism throughout the century before Charles Darwin's *On the Origin of Species* (1859).

Nature, once understood as a reflection of the mind of God, gradually came to be seen as a reflection of the minds of humans. Such an increasingly psychological emphasis—nature reflects the inner states of individual human beings—is countered by an increasing tendency to see nature as alien, cold, and mechanistic, even at the same time that it is being touted as a source of aesthetic pleasure and emotional satisfaction. Natural history moves concurrently in several directions: the experimental and investigative (medicine, experimental science, field geology), the instructional and educational (poems for children, natural history as a pleasing pastime), and the socially uplifting (a Rousseauistic return to nature might cure the ills of society). In all of these cases, the standard of judgement is a purely human standard: what can nature do for humans, what can nature teach mankind, how does nature reflect a continuity or connection with human activity, desires, and concerns? This tendency also prepares the way for many of our own twenty-first-century attitudes. If we could fully understand nature (astronomy, theoretical physics, cognitive science), we now assume we might be able to solve many intractable human problems. Likewise, our personal attitudes toward nature seem to be based on our sense of how nature can be good for us and our fellow humans. Global warming is "bad" because of its impact on human society. Or do we just care about rising sea levels because they threaten our cities and summer houses? Preservation of a species is "good," since more species seem to equal "better" nature, at least in human terms. The loss of a species—whatever that species's natural status—is aesthetically and socially distressing to me, and to people who feel the way I do. But does it matter that the dinosaurs are gone? Is the extinct dodo bird an ethical loss?

Romanticism thus inaugurates a new brand of naturalistic anthropocentrism, the consequences of which are still with us in many ways. At the same time, somewhat ironically, the rise of the mechanistic model of nature since 1700 creates a concurrent and disturbing sense of the natural world as somehow separate from human concerns. This unsettling possibility, that nature is finally unrelated to human values, also derives from our post-Darwinian sense that one species does not matter to nature more than another species, that even the existence of *homo sapiens* is not a precondition for any other aspect of natural process. Nature, in this sense, could not care less about you or me. Shelley's "Mont Blanc" is a meditation on just such anxieties about the relationship between the category of "nature" and its apparent separation from human life. The vastness of nature, linked to Romantic ideas about the sublime, also leads in two conflicting directions, toward nature worship on the one hand (because of nature's power, magnitude, and inclusiveness) and at the same time toward a proto-existentialist fear and trembling (because nature is incomprehensible: too vast, too all-encompassing, too unknowable). In the nineteenth century, we should recall, it was the poet Alfred, Lord Tennyson, who noted (nine years before Darwin) that the natural "type" (the species) is all important; the individual matters little if at all. Nature, in this evolutionary sense, comes to be seen as valuable for its own sake, independent of human causes or concerns. What happens to humans is just one aspect of what happens in the wider natural world. Of course, the twentieth century will be the century during which the effects of humans on the natural world—oil wells, synthetic chemicals, nuclear power—come to seem increasingly powerful and destructive.

Yet ever since Carolus Linnaeus initiated the modern practice of cataloging species, European naturalists followed suit by collecting, displaying, researching, and writing about the details of the natural world. Human history became part of the wider category of natural history once Oliver Goldsmith (like Buffon before him) included a chapter "Of the Varieties of the Human Race" at the start of the section of *Animate Nature* entitled "A History of Animals." While natural historians were describing human beings as a species of animal, Julien Offray de La Mettrie was writing essays "to Serve as the Natural History of Man" entitled *L'Homme machine* (*Man a Machine,* 1747), and the even more suggestively titled *L'Homme plante* (*Man a Plant,* 1748) in which he argued that "the principal parts of men and plants are the same" (77). This idea of an organic unity linking all living things directly challenged the hierarchy of the Great Chain of Being, replacing it with a more dynamic, less-stratified model of organic order. This same concern about boundaries between humans and other animals, between plants and animals, and between living and nonliving things gradually emerged as central to the debate between vitalists and mechanists in the nineteenth century. Was a human being merely a complex machine? Was there any such thing as a soul? Might the idea of the self merely replace the idea of the soul? These and similar questions forced rethinking of a number of basic terms: *human, nature, animal, plant, soul, spirit,* and *self.*

Even with growing concern for accurate science, the state of natural historical knowledge by 1800 can sometimes look like a chaotic amalgam of mythology, half-knowledge, and limited observation: spontaneous generation, living mastodons, and man-apes were all being described as distinct possibilities well into the nineteenth century. While there was much wildly speculative thinking in the natural sciences, there were also a number of powerful ideas that came increasingly to be supported by observational evidence. Among the most significant of these was the idea that species might not be as distinct as earlier naturalists had supposed. In addition, the understanding of hybridization was receiving widespread attention. Not only horse breeders but also pigeon fanciers, vintners, and agriculturalists were, selectively and systematically, breeding and crossbreeding animals and plants. At the same time, botanists and naturalists were speculating on the causes of variation within living types, as is clearly evident in even a brief sampling of titles: Samuel Collins, *Paradise Retriev'd; plainly and fully demonstrating the most beautiful, durable and beneficial method of managing and improving fruit trees* (1717); Anonymous, *A Philosophical Essay on Fecundation; or, an impartial inquiry into the first rudiments of progression and perfection of animal generation, particularly of the human species* (1742); James Parsons, *Philosophical Observations on the analogy between the propagation of animals and that of vegetables* (1752); Archibald Cochrane, *A Treatise shewing the intimate connection that subsists between agriculture and chemistry* (1795); and John Sanders Sebright, *The Art of Improving the Breeds of Domestic Animals* (1809).

John Ray had, as early as the second half of the 1600s, defined a species as a "group of individuals that breed among themselves, so that 'one species does not grow from the seed of another species'" (Chambers 8). Linnaeus, who classified and named many of the world's known plants and animals, formulated "Observations" in the first edition of his *Systema Naturae* (1735) that clarified the species issue beyond debate: "there are no new species (1); as like always gives birth to like (2); as one in each species was at the beginning of the progeny (3), it is necessary to attribute this progenitorial unity to some Omnipotent and Omniscient Being, namely God, whose work is called Creation. This is confirmed by the mechanism, the laws, principles, constitutions and sensations in every living individual" (Chambers 18). By 1760, Linnaeus was willing to consider the possibility that "new species" might be "produced by hybrid generation," but he was not willing to follow this insight to its logical conclusions: "whether all these species be the offspring of time; whether, in the beginning of all things, the Creator limited the number of future species, I dare not presume to determine" (*Dissertation* 55–56). Of course, it is precisely the earlier Linnaen premise that "like always gives birth to like" that will come to be radically questioned by the time that Mary Shelley can imagine Victor Frankenstein creating "a new species."

The first complete English translation of the Comte de Buffon's *Natural History* echoes the traditional view of species as it was still understood in 1792: species are "ancient" and "permanent," "always the same," organized in a divine, and rigid, hierarchy. "Of these unities the human species is to be placed in the first rank; all the others, from the elephant to the mite, from the cedar to the hyssop, belong to the second and third orders" (Barr 10: 342). Buffon's effort to argue for the fixity of species is complicated by a question that he has difficulty answering: "What purposes then are served by this immense train of generations, this profusion of germs, many thousands of which are abortive for the one that is brought to life?" (10: 347). Although Buffon wants to argue for "fixed" and "constant" species, he is forced to acknowledge that nature often produces "failures," "abortions," and "monsters." These failed representatives of supposedly stable "types" pose continuing problems for Buffon's definition of species. In fact, Buffon anticipates Darwin—and famous lines by Tennyson—when he notes that "individuals are of no estimation in the universe; it is species alone that are existences in nature" (10: 342).

The solution to the problem of variety in Buffon's account is not variation of stable species (hybridization) but the production of what he calls "varieties": "the figure of each species is an impression, in which the principal characters are so strongly engraven as never to be effaced; but the accessory parts and shades are so greatly varied that no two individuals have a perfect resemblance to each other; and in all species there are a number of varieties" (10: 353). So species are fixed, but varieties within species are not. This distinction is comparable to current debates among evolutionary biologists about the status of subspecies. The test case for Buffon is, interestingly, our own; the human species, he says, is "fixed and constant," and yet "in all species there are a number of varieties. The human species, which has such superior pretensions, varies from white to black, from small to great, &c. The Laplander, the Patagonian, the Hottentot, the European, the American, and the Negro, though the offspring of the same parents, have by no means the resemblance of brothers" (10: 353). Buffon needs a way to explain variation, but he also needs to argue for the absolute stability of each species. As a solution he offers a theory of "varieties"—actually an attempt to explain human races—which clearly undermines the rigid boundary between species.

Erasmus Darwin takes Buffon's troubling question and turns it into a new way of thinking about natural order and biological unity. The earlier Darwin is clearly the natural historian most directly responsible for many of the ideas that made their way into a wide range of Romantic literature. He is referred to in the introduction to Mary Shelley's 1831 *Frankenstein* (1831, x), was praised by Coleridge as having "a greater range of knowledge than any man in Europe" (Barber 210), and was used by Wordsworth in "Goody Blake and Harry Gill" (*Wordsworth*, Gill 688). Erasmus Darwin's capacious and synthetic mind worked consistently to question the notion of immutable species. He not only personified and humanized the sexual life of plants in "Loves of the Plants," for which he was parodied and reviled but also anticipated the outlines of his grandson's theory of evolution by half a century. In his *Phytologia* (1800), Erasmus Darwin described the "muscles, nerves and brains of vegetables," concluding that plants have sensations and volition, "though in a much inferior degree than even the cold-blooded animals" (133). In *The Temple of Nature* (1803), he describes the Lycoperdon tuber, a plant that "never rises above the earth, is propagated without seeds by its roots only, and seems to require no light. Perhaps many other fungi are generated without seed by their roots only, and without light, and approach on the last account to animal nature" (48).

Darwin also argues, in *Zoonomia* (1794), that nature is full of complex forms of variation and metamorphosis within the lives of single creatures as well as types. He cites caterpillars changing into butterflies, tadpoles into frogs, the "feminine boy" into the "bearded man," and the "infant girl" into the "lactescent woman" as examples of dynamic and mysterious changes in individuals (*Zoonomia* 2: 500). He also marvels at "great changes introduced into various animals by artificial or accidental cultivation, as in horses" (2: 500). This line of thinking allows him to conclude that "all animals have a similar origin, viz. from a single living filament" and that "it is not impossible but the great variety of species of animals, which now tenant the earth, may have had their origin from the mixture of a few natural orders" (2: 498–99). He even goes so far as to cite David Hume's claim that "the world itself might have been generated, rather than created," with the resulting conclusion that all organisms would then derive not only from earlier organisms but ultimately from inorganic substances (2: 509).

Darwin offers an image that will dominate the thinking of the next two centuries when, in an additional note to *The Temple of Nature,* he imagines life as originating in the ancient seas: "all vegetables and animals now existing were originally derived from the smallest microscopic ones, formed by spontaneous vitality" ("Reproduction" 38). This speculation leads to the most often quoted lines in *The Temple of Nature:*

> Organic Life beneath the shoreless waves
> Was born and nurs'd in Ocean's pearly caves;
> First forms minute, unseen by spheric glass,
> Move on the mud, or pierce the watery mass;
> 5 These, as successive generations bloom,
> New powers acquire, and larger limbs assume;
> Whence countless groups of vegetation spring,
> And breathing realms of fin, and feet, and wing. (1, 295–302)

Darwin argues that sexual selection is far superior to asexual reproduction precisely because it introduces hybrid variation and mutability into individuals, which can be passed on and altered in subsequent generations.

Beyond the challenges posed to Judeo-Christian thinking by such speculations on the part of naturalists, the species debate was fostered by the astonishing proliferation of known biological forms in a relatively short span of time. In 1735, Linnaeus listed 4,162 distinct species in his *Systema Naturae*. By 1898, one Victorian classifier had counted 415,600 (Barber 65). Historian Lynn Barber notes a "species obsession" among the natural historians of the first half of the nineteenth century. This obsession was based partly on the desire to expand Linnaeus's classification to include all forms of life on Earth, and partly on the dramatic results of exploratory voyages that were bringing hitherto unknown creatures back to Europe from Asia, Africa, and the New World: display cases filled with gigantic insects, piles of bird and animal skins, living rhinoceroses and crocodiles, and an astonishing array of bones and fossils. We need only imagine a crowd on the London docks witnessing a living rhinoceros arriving in England, or the looks on the faces of Londoners examining an Ichthyosaur skeleton, to appreciate European amazement at species diversity and variation during the century before Charles Darwin.

Desmond King-Hele points to Denis Diderot, De Maillet, Johann Wolfgang von Goethe, and Maupertuis as also contributing evidence for the variability of species between 1740 and 1790 (*Romantic Poets* 66). In all such cases, however, naturalists lacked a coherent explanation for the differences, we might now say the mutations, they were describing. In addition, work on hybrids was carried on primarily among agriculturalists. Natural historians acknowledged the varieties produced by crossbreeding, but they had little systematic understanding of the processes at work in reproduction, much less in reproductive variation. Among other important contributors to the protoevolutionary thinking of the Romantic era we should add Thomas Malthus (*Essay on the Principle of Population,* 1798), Jean-Baptiste de Lamarck (*Philosophie Zoologique,* 1809), J. C. Prichard (*Researches into the Physical History of Mankind,* 1813), W. C. Wells (*An Essay on Dew,* 1818), and Charles Lyell (*Principles of Geology,* 1830–33). All of these authors, in different ways, attributed biological change in living individuals to a hybridizing principle of some sort, or they suggested that natural change has been misunderstood because of the difficulty of assessing minor incremental changes over vast periods of historic and geologic time.

Equally important to Romantic ideas about natural history was the suggestion that emotion, specifically pleasure and pain, might not be restricted to the human realm. Pleasure in the natural world was a concept that linked Romantic poetry and Romantic science in significant ways. Pleasure located in the nonhuman world and pleasure taken by humans in the natural world are concepts that commingle in a whole range of Romantic metaphors and rhetorical practices, anthropocentric and otherwise. In fact, the apparent anthropocentrism of much eighteenth- and early-nineteenth-century scientific and poetic thinking turns out to be much more centered in the nonhuman world than we might think. Discussions of plant and animal "pleasure" in the works of Erasmus Darwin and in those of Georges Louis Leclerc, Comte de Buffon (often by way of Oliver Goldsmith, who introduced many of Buffon's ideas to a British audience) can be directly linked, for example, to the use of "pleasure" in poems by Wordsworth, Coleridge, Shelley, and Keats. This link between the poetic and the scientific in Romantic natural history also reveals aspects of our current cultural sense of the interrelatedness of human and nonhuman nature. The question is not whether animals (much less plants) experience pleasure and pain. The questions are: why are plants and animals described in terms of these categories, and how do the human categories of pain and pleasure connect to physiological processes in other organic beings?

Where does this Romantic talk about the heart's filling with pleasure like dancing daffodils or a bird's being described as a "world of delight" come from? It comes, to cite one obvious source, from an otherwise hardnosed medical practitioner and experimental scientist like Erasmus Darwin. Here is Darwin, in one of his characteristic (and often controversial) descriptions of the love life of plants:

> Hence on green leaves the sexual Pleasures dwell,
> And Loves and Beauties crowd the blossom's bell;
> The wakeful Anther in his silken bed
> O'er the pleas'd Stigma bows his waxen head;
> 5 With meeting lips, and mingling smiles, they sup
> Ambrosial dew-drops from the nectar'd cup;
> Or buoy'd in air the plumy Lover springs,
> And seeks his panting bride on Hymen-wings.
>   (*Temple of Nature* 2, 263–70)

Darwin was roundly criticized, as had been Linnaeus before him, for this tendency to sexualize the life of plants. For Darwin, however, these erotic descriptions of plant love (and plant lust) were an analogue for human sexuality and an accurate description of the way flowers actually worked. Indeed, almost all of Darwin's claims about plant sexuality were based on direct observation. He often expanded his poetic rhapsodies on the sex life of plants with prose footnotes that ascribe a wide range of intentionality and emotion to the plant kingdom: "The vegetable passion of love is agreeably seen in the flower of the parnassia, in which the males alternately approach and recede from the female; and in the flower of nigella, or devil in the bush, in which the tall females bend down to their dwarf husbands. But I was this morning surprised to observe [. . .] the manifest adultery of several females of the plant Collinsonia, who had bent themselves into contact with the males of other flowers of the same plant in their vicinity, neglectful of their own" ("Economy of Vegetatian" 4, 121n.). Claims like these about plant life consistently suggest that willfulness, intention, and pleasure all extend—albeit in diminished forms—from humans to animals to plants, and even beyond.

More important for the ethos of this volume than Darwin's specific descriptions of the sexual life of plants are his views, most clearly summarized in the poetry and footnotes of *The Temple of Nature* (1803), about natural pleasures. In this work, Darwin clearly describes pleasure in any part of animate creation as an aspect of pleasure extending through the whole of the terrestrial biosphere: "From the innumerable births of the larger insects, and the spontaneous productions of the microscopic ones, every part of organic matter from the recrements of dead vegetable or animal bodies, on or near the surface of the earth, becomes again presently reanimated; which by increasing the number and quantity of living organisms, though many of them exist but for a short time, adds to the sum total of terrestrial happiness" (160n.). Pleasure in the entire biotic realm is increased not only by the prolific reproduction of *insects* (the word means "small creatures" to Darwin) and microscopic organisms but by the death and organic regeneration of larger creatures: "The sum total of the happiness of organized nature is probably increased rather than diminished, when one large old animal dies, and is converted into many thousand young ones; which are produced or supported with their numerous progeny by the same organic matter" (162n.).

Darwin also notes that the Pythagorean belief in the transmigration of souls derives merely from the organic and "perpetual transmigration of matter from one body to another, of all vegetables and animals, during their lives, as well as after their deaths" (163n.). This chemical and organic movement of elements through the bodies of living creatures leads, over eons, to a unified and complete "system of morality and benevolence, as all creatures thus became related to each other" (164n.) in terms of the matter that composes them. What Darwin calls the "felicity of organic life" is a function of the "happiness and misery of [all] organic beings"; this felicity, he says, depends ultimately on "the actions of the organs of sense" and on "the fibres which perform locomotion" (165n.). Every living thing, Darwin concludes, is subject to "immediate sources" of "pains and pleasures," the encouragement or avoidance of which might "increase the sum total of organic happiness" (166n.). Pain and pleasure, he argues, are entirely a function of the expansion and contraction of nerve and muscle fibers of sensation, organic elements that exist in all living things, albeit in a variety of forms and intensities. All emotional responses—pleasure, pain, happiness, and sadness — are thus based solely on the motion of material parts of each life form.

Finally, and perhaps most dramatically, Darwin's understanding of geology leads him to conclude that the planet itself is a record of the pleasures of earlier ages of animate beings: "Not only the vast calcareous provinces [. . .] and also whatever rests upon them [. . .] clay, marl, sand, and coal [. . .] gave the pleasure of life to the animals and vegetables, which formed them; and thus constitute monuments of the past happiness of those organized beings. But as those remains of former life are not again totally decomposed [. . .] they supply more copious food to the successions of new animal or vegetable beings on their surface [. . .] and hence the quantity or number of organized bodies, and their improvement in size, as well as their happiness, has been continually increasing, along with the solid parts of the globe" (166n.) — more dry land over eons, more living things century upon century, more happiness produced from millennium to millennium. At this point, Darwin even breaks down the boundary between organic and inorganic as part of his wider economy of nature, what we might now call his ecology. Material processes, compounds, and elements — which he always describes in fundamentally chemical terms (clay, sand, coal, heat, oxygen, hydrogen, carbon, phosphorus) — compose, decompose, and recompose, first into inorganic, then into organic, and ultimately into animate creatures, including human beings.

Darwin also argues that the plant and animal kingdoms are connected by the possibility of sensation. In *Zoonomia*, he describes "Vegetable Animation": "The fibres of the vegetable world, as well as those of the animal, are excitable into a variety of motions by irritations of external objects. This appears particularly in the mimosa or sensitive plant, whose leaves contract on the slightest injury" (1: 101). But the "fibres" responsible for sensation are also related to pleasure: "when pleasure or pain affect the animal system, many of its motions both muscular and sensual are brought into action [. . . .] The general tendency of these motions is to arrest [i.e., stabilize] and to possess the pleasure, or to dislodge or avoid the pain" (1: 45). The conclusion Darwin draws is obvious: "the individuals of the vegetable world may be considered as inferior or less perfect animals" (1: 102).

The belief that sensation might spread through all of animate creation was widely discussed in Europe and America throughout the eighteenth century by natural scientists, natural theologians, and poets, among others. As Christoph Irmscher has written recently, this was an age "that ascribed sensitivity, even souls, to plants" (31). But as Erasmus Darwin suggested, the point was not merely that plants might have souls, but that souls might turn out to be nothing more than complex combinations of material (i.e., muscular, nervous, or electrochemical) motions. Indeed, the barrier between plants and animals attracted so much attention precisely because it held out the possibility that all sensation (and even emotion) might eventually be explicable in purely material, physical terms. John Bartram, writing to Benjamin Rush in Philadelphia, noted that there was much to be learned about "sensation" in plants, even though many animals were already known to be "endowed with most of our [that is, human] faculties & pashions & [. . .] intelect [sic]" (Irmscher 690).

Georges Louis Leclerc, Comte de Buffon, describes many of the animals he catalogs in terms of human passions and intellect. Buffon's marmot "delights in the regions of ice and snow" (System 121). His elephant is "susceptible of gratitude, and capable of strong attachment" (152) and "loves the society of his equals" (153). If "vindictive," the pachyderm "is no less grateful" (159). Numerous writers were willing to extend pleasure even into the realm of lower life forms. A 1792 compilation by several natural historians of insects includes comments such as the following: each insect, no matter how small or seemingly insignificant, is "adapted for procuring its particular pleasures" (Buffon, *History of Insects* 2); indeed, every insect, like every creature, "was formed for itself, and each allowed to seize as great a quantity of happiness from the universal stock [. . .] each was formed to make the happiness of each" (6). "The butterfly, to enjoy life, needs no other food but the dews of heaven" (75), and "it is impossible to express the fond attachment which the working ants shew to their rising progeny" (125). Animals, of course, had been connected to human sensation and emotional response since ancient history: loyal dogs, sagacious elephants, wily foxes, and diligent ants. What was new by 1790 was the sense that these were not just rhetorical comparisons of behavior between human and animal realms but that such observationally supported comparisons reflected a deeper—and organic—unity of all living things.

Eighteenth-century talk about emotion and sensation in lower life forms was also related to an underlying philosophical monism, well articulated by Goethe. In "The Experiment as Mediator between Subject and Object" (1792) Goethe offers a holistic critique of "living Nature" that was designed to counter the fragmentary quality of empirical science: "Nothing happens in living Nature that does not bear some relation to the whole. The empirical evidence may seem quite isolated, we may view our experiments as mere isolated facts, but this is not to say that they are, in fact, isolated. The question is: how can we find the connection between these phenomena, these events?" (80). Likewise, Goethe is willing to include "joy and pain" among the categories that are applicable to any "organism":

"Basic characteristic of an individual organism: to divide, to unite, to merge into the universal, to abide in the particular, to transform itself, to define itself, and, as living things tend to appear under a thousand conditions, to arise and vanish, to solidify and melt, to freeze and flow, to expand and contract [. . . .] Genesis and decay, creation and destruction, birth and death, joy and pain, all are interwoven with equal effect and weight; thus even the most isolated event always presents itself as an image and metaphor for the most universal" (52). So while observational science is suggesting that expansion, contraction, attraction, and repulsion of tiny parts are physical properties of all living (and perhaps nonliving) things, the metaphysic of Romantic science argues that characteristics found in one part of nature are likely to exist throughout the entire natural system, albeit in differing, modified—reduced or expanded—forms.

Oliver Goldsmith, whose *History of the Earth and Animated Nature* was drawn largely from Buffon and other European naturalists, restrains himself from extending sensation into the realm of the inorganic, but he too indicates how widespread was the belief in common elements pervading the germ plasm, a unity behind the dazzling variety that characterized the animate world. He notes that the prevalence of invisible living creatures, animals and plants too small to see, has led "some late philosophers into an opinion, that all nature was animated, that every, even the most inert mass of matter, was endued with life and sensation, but wanted organs to make those sensations perceptible to the observer" (4: 322). The link between human and animal pleasure thus reaches well into the plant kingdom by the 1790s, producing a view well summarized by Buffon himself: "it is impossible to finish our short review of nature without observing the wonderful harmony and connection that subsists between all the different branches" (178). Pleasure described in one part of nature reflects the possibility, indeed the likelihood, of pleasure spread throughout all of nature.

In addition, of course, numerous debates were breaking out about the status of human beings in relation to the rest of nature. One of the most widely discussed was the so-called vitalist debate between the London doctors John Abernethy and William Lawrence. Abernethy took the "spiritualist" side of the argument, claiming that life in humans and, by extension, in other creatures could not be explained solely through reference to the physical properties of material substances. Lawrence, by contrast, argued for a completely materialist explanation of all organic organisms and processes. Lawrence's *Lectures on Physiology, Zoology, and the Natural History of Man* (1819) set forth the view that nerves and the brain could provide a physical explanation for everything that passed for soul and spirit in humans. Lawrence was also Percy Shelley's personal physician and one of the first experimental scientists in England to use the term *biologist* (OED).

What followed from the vitalist debate was a new realization: if human life and activity could be described in completely material terms, we would certainly need to refine and redefine our relationship to the rest of the natural world.

With Charles Darwin's *On the Origin of Species* (1859) came a unified system and the beginnings of an explanation for scientific and poetic ideas that had been partial, rudimentary, and undeveloped before his work. Not until the chaos theory of our own era, and emphasis by current scientists on the randomness of nature, have we reconnected natural science quite so completely with the possibility of imaginative wonder. Biology in the nineteenth century may not appear to determine destiny—as it so often does at our own cultural moment—but this anthology of Romantic natural histories will also help us to understand how the "Nature" of Newton, Linnaeus, and Wordsworth becomes the "nature" of Stephen Hawking, Stephen Jay Gould, and Annie Dillard. Romantic natural histories, like those included in this volume, help us to recall the extent to which science and art were not seen as distinct for most of human history. In addition, reflection on the contexts of both of these realms of human activity (What poems were scientists reading and writing? What sciences were poets and prose writers studying?) should also reveal the origins of some of our own cultural assumptions about the place of humans in the non-human world.

The point of this anthology is not that Romantic writers were good scientists or that their literary images always derived from accurate information. Sensitive plants, poison trees, and new species, however, indicate a pervasive paradigm shift, away from a nature that was static and unchanging toward a nature characterized by dynamic links among all living things. Such a view is, of course, much closer to our own contemporary claim that nature is not here for us but that we are part of a vast web of genetic links and animate interrelatedness. In addition, the linking of these usually disparate authors should remind us of the extent to which all scientific thinking relies on metaphors, analogies, and other forms of figurative comparison most often associated with the imaginative realm. In this sense, Copernicus had first to imagine the sun at the center of the solar system, since there was no clear empirical evidence to support such a claim; the sun still appears to circle the earth. Likewise Charles Darwin had to imagine—and he often uses the words *imagine* and *consider*—that animals might be linked in the ways that his theory describes.

Romantic natural histories produced in the years between Erasmus Darwin and Charles Darwin deserve more scholarly attention than they have hitherto received, in part because they help us to understand the sources of our own thinking. Current emphasis on ecocriticism and literary ecology does not arise solely from a contemporary "Green" sense of the interdependence between organisms and their environments; it derives as well from earlier Romantic thinkers. In the century before Charles Darwin, a wide range of scientists and imaginative writers saw human beings as organisms with important connections to the wider natural world. These same connections, we have come to understand, have profound implications for all life on the planet we share with the rest of animate nature.

A NOTE ON THE TEXTS
Ashton Nichols

A work that includes as many authors as this anthology produces complex choices about the selection of editions. In most cases, I have reproduced the earliest available editions of literary or scientific works. In other instances, I have used an edition (the 1802 Gilbert White, for example) that includes more than one work that I am reprinting. Works of natural history went through complicated publication histories. The first edition of White's *The Natural History and Antiquities of Selborne,* for example, was published by Benjamin White and Son in London in December of 1788 (but the title page reads 1789). In 1802, William Markwick collected White's *The Natural History of Selborne* along with *A Naturalist's Calendar and Observations on Various Parts of Nature,* other works by White that had first been collected by John Aikin in 1795. While not always relying on the earliest or most fully "corrected" editions, I have employed editions that include supplementary materials or revisions that help to establish the links between poetry and science that this volume is designed to suggest. In addition, I have tended toward editions that would have been available, or most likely to have been read, by other authors in this collection. The details of these editions and sources can be found at the start of each reprinted text as well as in the Works Cited. In some cases, I describe additional details about these textual choices in my introductory material for individual authors. I have ordered the works to suggest the sorts of connections that exist between these scientific and literary texts. So John Aikin precedes his sister, Anna Barbauld, whose letter is a response to his essay on natural history and poetry, and Giovanni Aldini appears before Mary Shelley, whose novel he is likely to have influenced.

In the case of literary works, I have favored later works over earlier works when they contained particularly suggestive links between natural history and poetic texts or prose fiction; for example, the fourth edition of Anna

Barbauld's *Poems* (1774) presents the plight of the captive mouse with even more sympathy for the hapless creature than earlier editions. I often lean toward earlier editions of works by Wordsworth, Coleridge, and Keats, in which the impressions of natural scenes and creatures often seem at their most vivid. In other cases, I have chosen from the earliest published editions of poems, as in the cases of Percy Shelley, Tennyson, and John Clare.

The publishing history of works of natural history is at least as complex as that of poets and prose writers of this period. Volumes were reprinted, bound together, reissued without title pages, expurgated, and issued in virtually dozens of versions during the nineteenth century. In some instances, authors like Oliver Goldsmith and Thomas Bewick used quoted extracts from earlier works as parts of their own volumes, collaborated with other writers, or included long extracts from earlier authors without always providing accurate citations. In both natural history and literary texts, I have nonetheless sought the most carefully corrected and accurate editions. I have also checked early editions against modern scholarly editions whenever possible. In a few cases, such as those of Charlotte Smith and John Leonard Knapp, I have used later editions in order to suggest the decades during which a particular work was popular or to remind readers of the transatlantic crossings experienced be certain texts.

In my own introduction to each author, I provide citations only for those quotations not included in the primary materials that follow. All of the works quoted or described in my introductions can be found in the Works Cited. The bibliography, For Further Reading, includes a wide range of texts, from the seventeenth century to the present day, that help to establish the sorts of links among literary works, natural history, and natural philosophy that *Romantic Natural Histories* is designed to highlight.

A note about the Latin translations. I am extremely grateful to my colleague Christopher Francese for his careful help with accurate translations and corrections of original Latin quotes. In some cases, the natural historians and poets were quoting Latin from memory or relying on inaccurate sources for their originals. In these instances, the inaccurate Latin source is noted in the footnote, which then provides a correct English translation.

My own introductory essay includes several paragraphs taken directly (or modified only slightly) from work that has been previously published elsewhere. I am grateful to *The Wordsworth Circle* for permission to reprint brief selections from "The Anxiety of Species: Toward a Romantic Natural History" 28.3 (1997), 130–36. I am also grateful to the *Romantic Praxis* series for permission to reprint similar brief selections from "The Loves of Plants and Animals: Romantic Science and the Pleasures of Nature," *Romanticism & Ecology*, ed. James McKusick (November 2001), reprinted by permission of the *Romantic Circles Website*.

My own textual editing has been light, in order to preserve as much of the sense of these originals as is possible in a modern reprinting. I have modernized confusing or ambiguous spelling (but not all archaic spellings), clarified numerous grammatical and punctuation errors that appeared in early editions, and replaced confusing printers marks and long Ss(f).

I am grateful to numerous librarians at the British Library, the Library of Congress, and the Natural History Museum in London, and in the archives and special collections department of the Waidner-Spahr Library at Dickinson College, for help in the gathering and reproduction of this wide range of material. I appreciate assistance from Jim Gerencser and Pierce Bounds in the preparation of illustrations for this volume. Thanks finally to Kelly Hoak for her painstaking work transcribing eye-straining early documents. This volume would not have been possible without the patience and assistance of all of these individuals.

CHRONOLOGY: 1750–1859

1750   Thomas Gray writes "Elegy Written in a Country Churchyard"; J. T. Mayer draws a "Map of the Moon."

1751   Carolus Linnaeus, *Philosophia botanica.*

1752   Thomas Chatterton b. (d. 1770); Benjamin Franklin invents lightning conductor.

1753   Linnaeus, *Species plantorum;* charter granted to British Museum.

1757   William Blake b. (d. 1827); John Dyer, "The Fleece."

1759   Robert Burns b. (d. 1796); Franz Aepinus, *Tentamen theoriae electricitas et magnetismi.*

1760   Kew Botanical Gardens open; John Hunter develops comparative anatomy.

1763   J. G. Kölreuter (Germany) studies fertilization of plants by animal pollen carriers.

1767   Joseph Priestley, *The History and Present State of Electircity.*

1768   Captain James Cook (ret. 1771) sails to Pacific; P. S. Pallas, *On the Transit of Venus.*

1769   G. L. Cuvier b. (d. 1832); Alexander von Humboldt b. (d. 1859).

1770   William Wordsworth b. (d. 1850).

1771   *Encyclopedia Britannica,* first edition; Luigi Galvani (Bologna) records "animal" electricity.

1772   Samuel Taylor Coleridge b. (d. 1834); Ernest Rutherford and Priestley discover nitrogen; John Walsh experiments on electric torpedo fish.

1774 Johann Wolfgang von Goethe, *The Sorrows of Werther;* Robert Southey b. (d. 1843); Oliver Goldsmith, *An History of the Earth and Animated Nature;* Priestley discovers oxygen.

1775 Captain Cook returns from second voyage; J. C. Fabricius, *Systema entomologiae;* digitalis (foxglove) used to treat dropsy.

1776 America declares independence (based on natural rights).

1777 Priestley, *Disquisition Relating to Matter and Spirit;* John Aikin, *An Essay on the Application of Natural History to Poetry.*

1778 G. L. L. Buffon, *Époques de la Nature;* F. A. Mesmer exhibits "animal magnetism" (later called hypnosis) for health.

1779 David Hume, *Dialogues Concerning Natural Religion;* Captain Cook murdered in South Pacific; Lazzaro Spallanzani proves semen necessary for fertilization.

1781 Jean-Jacques Rousseau, *Confessions;* Sir John Herschel discovers Uranus; Felice Fontana describes brain cells.

1784 Bernardin de Saint-Pierre, *Études de la Nature;* Goethe discovers intermaxillary jaw bone.

1785 Thomas de Quincey b. (d. 1859); Domenico Salsano develops seismograph to measure earthquakes.

1786 Buffon, *Histoire naturelle des oiseaux;* first ascent of Mont Blanc; Herschel, *Catalogue of Nebulae;* Linnaeus, *Dissertation on the Sexes of Plants* (English translation).

1788 Lord Byron (George Gordon) b. (d. 1824); Pierre-Simon Laplace, *Laws of the Planetary System;* James Hutton, *New Theory of the Earth.*

1789 French Revolution begins; William Blake, *Songs of Innocence;* Erasmus Darwin, *The Botanic Garden* (–1791).

1791 Michael Faraday b. (d. 1867); William Bartram, *Travels through North and South Carolina;* Luigi Galvani describes electric stimulation of nerves; Buffon's *Natural History* (English translation).

1792 Percy Bysshe Shelley b. (d. 1822); Mary Wollstonecraft, *Vindication of the Rights of Women.*

1793 John Clare b. (d. 1864).

1794 Blake, *Songs of Experience;* Erasmus Darwin, *Zoonomia; or, the laws of Organic Life.*

1795 John Keats b. (d. 1821); Mungo Park explores Niger River.

1796   G. L. C. Cuvier develops comparative zoology; Edward Jenner vaccinates against smallpox.

1797   Fredrich Wilhelm Joseph von Schelling, *Ideen zu einer Philosophie der Natur*; Thomas Bewick, *British Birds*; Jean-Baptiste de Lamarck, *Memoires de physique et d'histoire naturelle.*

1798   Wordsworth and Coleridge, *Lyrical Ballads*; Thomas Malthus, *An Essay on the Principle of Population.*

1799   Preserved mammoth discovered in Siberia; Rosetta stone discovered in Egypt.

1800   Sir Humphry Davy, *Researches, Chemical and Philosophical*; F. G. Gall (Germany) develops phrenology; Royal College of Surgeons founded in London; Alessandro Volta develops wet-cell battery; Alexander von Humboldt explores South America.

1801   Linnaeus, *Elements of Natural History*; M. F. X. Bichat, *Anatomie générale*; Robert Fulton (United States) develops first submarine in Brest.

1802   William Paley, *Natural Theology: or, Evidences of the Existence and Attributes of the Deity, Collected from the Appearances of Nature*; John Dalton introduces atomic theory; Gottfried Treviranus coins term *biology.*

1803   Ralph Waldo Emerson b. (d. 1882); Lamarck, *Recherches sur l'organisation des corps vivants*; Giovanni Aldini attempts to revive corpses using electricity.

1807   Byron, *Hours of Idleness*; Wordsworth, "Ode: Intimations of Immortality"; von Humboldt and Aimé Bonpland, *Voyage aux régions équinoxiales.*

1808   Goethe, *Faust*, (part I); F. J. Gall publishes on phrenology.

1809   Alfred, Lord Tennyson b. (d. 1892); Charles Darwin b. (d. 1882); Lamarck, *Système des animaux sans vertèbres*; Luigi Rolando stimulates brain cortex with galvanic current.

1810   Franz Joseph Gall and Johann Gasper Spurzheim, *Anatomie et physiologie du système nerveux.*

1811   Jane Austen, *Sense and Sensibility*; Charles Bell, *New Idea of the Anatomy of the Brain.*

1812   Byron, *Childe Harold's Pilgrimage*; Baron Georges Cuvier, *Recherches sur les ossements fossiles de quadrupèdes*; Davy, *Elements of Chemical Philosophy*; Robert Browning b. (d. 1889).

1813 Shelley, *Queen Mab*.

1814 Wordsworth, *The Excursion;* Jöns Berzelius, *Theory of Chemical Proportions and the Chemical Action of Electricity*.

1815 Wordsworth, "The White Doe of Rylstone"; Lamarck, *Histoire naturelle des animaux*.

1816 Charlotte Brontë b. (d. 1855); Shelley, "Alastor"; Coleridge, "Kubla Khan" (written 1797); René Laënnec develops stethoscope; Frankenstein "summer" (Shelleys and Byron in Geneva).

1817 Byron, "Manfred"; Henry David Thoreau b. (d. 1862).

1818 Byron, *Don Juan;* Keats, *Endymion;* Mary Wollstonecraft Shelley, *Frankenstein;* Friedrich Wilhelm Bessel catalogues 3,222 stars; first successful human blood transfusion.

1819 Keats, *Hyperion;* Shelley, *The Cenci;* Hans C. Oersted (Denmark) discovers electromagnetism.

1820 Keats, "Ode to a Nightingale"; Shelley, *Prometheus Unbound;* Thomas Brown, *Lectures on the Philosophy of the Human Mind;* galvanometer invented to measure electric current through a conductor; whale ship *Essex* rammed and sunk by a sperm whale in South Pacific.

1821 Keats dies of tuberculosis; Shelley, "Adonais"; Michael Faraday discovers electromagnetic rotation.

1822 Shelley drowns in a storm off Viareggio.

1824 Byron dies of fever in Greece; J. L. Prevost and Jean Baptiste Dumas prove sperm necessary for fertilization.

1826 Leopoldo Nobili invents galvanometer.

1827 J. J. Audubon, *Birds of North America;* Karl von Baer, *Epistola de Ova Mammalium et Hominis Generis;* London University chartered.

1829 Tennyson, "Timbuctoo"; James Smithson founds Smithsonian Institution, Washington, D.C.; James Mill, *Analysis of the Human Mind;* William Burke hanged for murdering to dissect.

1830 Emily Dickinson b. (d. 1886); William Cobbett, *Rural Rides;* Robert Brown (Scotland) discovers cell nucleus; Cuvier and E. G. Saint-Hilaire debate "unity of plan" in organic structures; Charles Lyell, *Principles of Geology*.

1831 Charles Darwin sails on H. M. S. *Beagle* voyage (–1836); James Clark Ross determines location of magnetic North Pole.

1833   William Whewell coins the term *scientist.*

1834   C. L. von Buch, *Theory of Volcanism;* Charles Babbage invents first computer ("analytical engine"), assisted by Byron's daughter, Ada Lovelace.

1835   Wordsworth, *Poems;* Browning, "Paracelsus"; Halley's comet reappears.

1836   Emerson, *Nature;* Asa Gray, *Elements of Botany.*

1842   Matthew F. Maury (United States) develops oceanography; J. R. von Mayer, *On the Forces of Inanimate Nature;* Crawford Long uses ether on humans.

1844   Horace Wells uses nitrous oxide for a tooth extraction; Robert Chambers, *Vestiges of the Natural History of Creation.*

1846   Herman Melville, *Typee;* H. von Mohl describes protoplasm.

1847   Charlotte Brontë, *Jane Eyre;* Emily Brontë; *Wuthering Heights;* I. T. Semmelweis (Hungary) establishes link between maternal mortality and infection.

1848   Alfred Russell Wallace sails to Amazonia (−1852).

1850   Tennyson, *In Memoriam;* Wordsworth dies; H. von Helmholtz measures speed of nervous impulses; E. Du Bois-Reymond invents galvanometer for nerves.

1851   Melville, *Moby Dick* (based on the sinking of the *Essex* in 1820); Helmzoltz develops ophthalmoscope.

1852   Herbert Spencer coins term *evolution* in *The Development Hypothesis.*

1854   Thoreau, *Walden; or, Life in the Woods.*

1855   Browning, *Men and Women;* Henry Wadsworth Longfellow, *Song of Hiawatha;* Walt Whitman, *Leaves of Grass;* Herbert Spencer, *Principles of Psychology.*

1857   Louis Pasteur proves that fermentation is biological.

1858   William Morris, *Defence of Guinevere and Other Poems;* T. H. Huxley, *The Theory of Vertebrate Skulls;* Charles Darwin and Alfred Wallace present their findings to Linnaean Society.

1859   Thomas de Quincey dies; Leigh Hunt dies; Charles Darwin publishes *On the Origin of Species by Means of Natural Selection,* which concludes "There is grandeur in this view of life."

Gilbert White (1720–1793)

W ithout Gilbert White, natural history would not have developed as it has over the past two centuries. *The Natural History and Antiquities of Selborne* became the first widely distributed, and most widely read, work in English on the subject. Educated at Oriel College, Oxford, White was an ordained minister who never wandered far from his small village in Hampshire. He began his journal in 1751, publishing his gardening remarks as *Calendar of Flora and the Garden* in 1765. This work was followed by *The Naturalist's Journal,* in which he ranged well beyond the flowers surrounding his own house and sought to present a more comprehensive view of the natural world in his neighborhood. He described himself as a "faunist" and claimed that his goal was to record "the life and conversation of animals." After almost two decades of observation and record keeping, he published *The Natural History of Selborne* in 1788. The volume included letters to his friends (Thomas Pennant and Daines Barrington) on various natural history subjects. The book was a resounding success from its first appearance and has gone through dozens of editions down to the present day. Wordsworth, Coleridge, Charles Darwin, Virginia Woolf, and W. H. Auden, among many others, have recorded their debts to White's careful visual record keeping, his profound sense of the richness of the ordinary natural objects around him, and his willingness to ascribe various levels of perception and feeling to the animal kingdom.

White's work was significant for its attention to the details of his surroundings, his observational skills, and his casual yet engaging prose style. In addition, White often gives the objects of his scrutiny a value for their own sake. He does not always present the natural world solely in terms of its significance to human beings. Nature may provoke powerful responses in White, but his version of nature does not seem to be here only for the benefit of human beings. In addition, he consistently combines personal observation with scientific curiosity. He does not accept colloquial thinking about topics such as migration or hibernation at face value. Rather, White presents personally observed facts and direct evidence to support his claims about the living world around him. He also embodies a powerfully protoecological sense of the interrelatedness and interdependence of animals, insects, plants, and even inorganic substances. White takes a methodical approach to his record keeping and queries about particular species, but he also employs lyrical observation, figurative imagery, and rhetorical flourishes that are occasionally worthy of a poet.

The selections that follow include extracts from *The Natural History of Selborne* as well as details from White's *Naturalist's Calendar* and observations extracted from his notebooks (by W. Markwick). Also included are several poems composed by White that were included in various editions of his works.

From The Natural History of Selborne

FROM LETTER VIII
[*To Thomas Pennant*]

Within the present limits of the forest are three considerable lakes, Hogmer, Cranmer, and Wolmer; all of which are stocked with carp, tench, eels, and perch: but the fish do not thrive well, because the water is hungry, and the bottoms are a naked sand.

A circumstance respecting these ponds, though by no means peculiar to them, I cannot pass over in silence; and that is, that instinct by which in summer all the kine, whether oxen, cows, calves, or heifers, retire constantly to the water during the hotter hours; where, being more exempt from flies, and inhaling the coolness of that element, some belly deep, and some only to mid-leg, they ruminate and solace themselves from about ten

From Gilbert White, *The Works in Natural History of the Late Gilbert White, comprising The Natural History of Selborne; The Naturalist's Calendar; and miscellaneous observations.* London: J. White, 1802.

in the morning till four in the afternoon, and then return to their feeding. During this great proportion of the day they drop much dung, in which insects nestle; and so supply food for the fish, which would be poorly subsisted but from this contingency. Thus Nature, who is a great economist, converts the recreation of one animal to the support of another! Thomson, who was a nice observer of natural occurrences, did not let this pleasing circumstance escape him. He says, in his *Summer,*

A various group the herds and flocks compose:
. . . on the grassy bank
Some ruminating lie; while others stand
Half in the flood, and, often bending, sip
5   The circling surface.

Wolmer-pond, so called, I suppose, for eminence sake, is a vast lake for this part of the world, containing, in its whole circumference, 2,646 yards, or very near a mile and an half. The length of the north west and opposite side is about 704 yards, and the breadth of the south-west end about 456 yards. This measurement, which I caused to be made with good exactness, gives an area of about sixty-six acres, exclusive of a large irregular arm at the north-east corner, which we did not take into the reckoning.

On the face of this expanse of waters, and perfectly secure from fowlers, lie all day long, in the winter season, vast flocks of ducks, teals, and wigeons, of various denominations; where they preen and solace, and rest themselves, till towards sun-set, when they issue forth in little parties (for in their natural state they are all birds of the night) to feed in the brooks and meadows, returning again with the dawn of the morning. Had this lake an arm or two more, and were it planted round with thick covert (for now it is perfectly naked), it might make a valuable decoy.[. . .]

FROM LETTER XXIII
[*To the Same*]

Selborne, Feb. 28, 1769.

Dear Sir,

It is not improbable that the Guernsey lizard and our green lizards may be specifically the same; all that I know is, that, when some years ago many Guernsey lizards were turned loose in Pembroke college garden, in the university of Oxford, they lived a great while, and seemed to enjoy themselves very well, but never bred. Whether this circumstance will prove any thing either way I shall not pretend to say.

I return you thanks for your account of Cressi-hall; but recollect, not without regret, that in June 1746 I was visiting for a week together at Spalding, without ever being told that such a curiosity was just at hand. Pray send me word in your next what sort of tree it is that contains such a quantity of herons' nests; and whether the heronry consists of a whole grove or wood, or only of a few trees.

It gave me satisfaction to find we accorded so well about the *caprimulgus:*[1] all I contended for was to prove that it often chatters sitting as well as flying; and therefore the noise was voluntary, and from organic impulse, and not from the resistance of the air against the hollow of its mouth and throat.

If ever I saw any thing like actual migration, it was last Michaelmas-day. I was travelling, and out early in the morning: at first there was a vast fog; but, by the time that I was got seven or eight miles from home towards the coast, the sun broke out into a delicate warm day. We were then on a large heath or common, and I could discern, as the mist began to break away, great numbers of swallows (*hirundines rusticae*) clustering on the stunted shrubs and bushes, as if they had roosted there all night. As soon as the air became clear and pleasant they all were on the wing at once; and, by a placid and easy flight, proceeded on southward towards the sea: after this I did not see any more flocks, only now and then a straggler.

I cannot agree with those persons that assert that the swallow kind disappear some and some gradually, as they come, for the bulk of them seem to withdraw at once: only some stragglers stay behind a long while, and do never, there is the greatest reason to believe, leave this island. Swallows seem to lay themselves up, and to come forth in a warm day, as bats do continually of a warm evening, after they have disappeared for weeks. For a very respectable gentleman assured me that, as he was walking with some friends under Merton-wall on a remarkably hot noon, either in the last week in December or the first week in January, he espied three or four swallows huddled together on the moulding of one of the windows of that college. I have frequently remarked that swallows are seen later at Oxford than elsewhere: is it owing to the vast massy buildings of that place, to the many waters round it, or to what else?

When I used to rise in a morning last autumn, and see the swallows and martins clustering on the chimnies and thatch of the neighbouring cottages, I could not help being touched with a secret delight, mixed with some degree of mortification: with delight, to observe with how much ardour and punctuality those poor little birds obeyed the strong impulse to-

---

[1] Nightjar or whippoorwill. [Ed.]

wards migration, or hiding, imprinted on their minds by their great Creator; and with some degree of mortification, when I reflected that, after all our pains and inquiries, we are yet not quite certain to what regions they do migrate; and are still farther embarrassed to find that some do not actually migrate at all.

These reflections made so strong an impression on my imagination, that they became productive of a composition that may perhaps amuse you for a quarter of an hour when next I have the honour of writing to you.

From Letter XXIV
[*To the Same*]

Selborne, May 29, 1769.

Dear Sir,

The *scarabeus fullo*[2] I know very well, having seen it in collections; but have never been able to discover one wild in its natural state. Mr. Banks told me he thought it might be found on the seacoast.

On the thirteenth of April I went to the sheep-down, where the ringousels have been observed to make their appearance at spring and fall, in their way perhaps to north or south; and was much pleased to see three birds about the usual spot. We shot a cock and a hen; they were plump and in high condition. The hen had but very small rudiments of eggs within her, which proves they are late breeders; whereas those species of the thrush kind that remain with us the whole year have fledged young before that time. In their crops was nothing very distinguishable, but somewhat that seemed like blades of vegetables nearly digested. In autumn they feed on haws and yew-berries, and in the spring on ivy-berries. I dressed one of these birds, and found it juicy and well flavoured. It is remarkable that they make but a few days stay in their spring visit, but rest near a fortnight at Michaelmas. These birds, from the observations of three springs and two autumns, are most punctual in their return; and exhibit a new migration unnoticed by the writers, who supposed they never were to be seen in any of the southern counties.

One of my neighbours lately brought me a new *salicaria,* which at first I suspected might have proved your willow-lark, but, on a nicer examination, it answered much better to the description of that species which you shot at Revesby, in Lincolnshire. My bird I describe thus: "It is a size less than the grasshopper-lark; the head, back, and coverts of the wings, of a

---

[2] Dung beetle. [Ed.]

dusky brown, without those dark spots of the grasshopper-lark; over each eye is a milkwhite stroke; the chin and throat are white, and the under parts of a yellowish white; the rump is tawny, and the feathers of the tail sharp-pointed; the bill is dusky and sharp, and the legs are dusky; the hinder claw long and crooked." The person that shot it says that it sung so like a reed-sparrow that he took it for one; and that it sings all night: but this account merits further inquiry. For my part, I suspect it is a second sort of *locustella*, hinted at by Dr. Derham in Ray's *Letters:* see p. 108. He also procured me a grasshopper-lark.

The question that you put with regard to those genera of animals that are peculiar to America, viz. how they came there, and whence? is too puzzling for me to answer; and yet so obvious as often to have struck me with wonder. If one looks into the writers on that subject little satisfaction is to be found. Ingenious men will readily advance plausible arguments to support whatever theory they shall choose to maintain; but then the mis-fortune is, every one's hypothesis is each as good as another's, since they are all founded on conjecture. The late writers of this sort, in whom may be seen all the arguments of those that have gone before, as I remember, stock America from the western coast of Africa and the south of Europe; and then break down the Isthmus that bridged over the Atlantic. But this is making use of a violent piece of machinery: it is a difficulty worthy of the interposition of a god! *"Incredulus odi."*

THE NATURALIST'S SUMMER-EVENING WALK
[*To Thomas Pennant, Esquire*]

> . . . *equidem credo, quia sit divinitus illis*
> *Ingenium.* — Virgil. Georgics.[3]

When day declining sheds a milder gleam,
What time the may-fly[4] haunts the pool or stream;
When the still owl skims round the grassy mead,
What time the timorous hare limps forth to feed;

---

[3] "I suppose, because they have some god given talent." Expressed as a negative in the original: "not, I suppose, because they have . . ." *Georgics* 1.415–16. [Ed.]

[4] The angler's may-fly, the *ephemera vulgata Linn.* comes forth from its aurelia state, and emerges out of the water about six in the evening, and dies about eleven at night, deter-mining the date of its fly state in about five or six hours. They usually begin to appear about the 4th of June, and continue in succession for near a fortnight. See Swammer-dam, Derham, Scopoli, etc.

5 Then be the time to steal adown the vale,
    And listen to the vagrant cuckoo's tale;[5]
    To hear the clamorous curlew[6] call his mate,
    Or the soft quail his tender pain relate;
    To see the swallow sweep the dark'ning plain
10 Belated, to support her infant train;
    To mark the swift in rapid giddy ring
    Dash round the steeple, unsubdu'd of wing:
    Amusive birds! Say where your hid retreat
    When the frost rages and the tempests beat;
15 Whence your return, by such nice instinct led,
    When spring, soft season, lifts her bloomy head?
    Such baffled searches mock man's prying pride,
    The GOD of NATURE is your secret guide!
        While deep'ning shades obscure the face of day
20 To yonder bench leaf-shelter'd let us stray,
    'Till blended objects fail the swimming sight,
    And all the fading landscape sinks in night;
    To hear the drowsy dor[7] come brushing by
    With buzzing wing, or the shrill cricket cry;[8]
25 To see the feeding bat glance through the wood;
    To catch the distant falling of the flood;
    While o'er the cliff th' awaken'd churl-owl hung
    Through the still gloom protracts his chattering song;
    While high in air, and pois'd upon his wings,
30 Unseen, the soft enamour'd woodlark sings:[9]
    These, NATURE's works, the curious mind employ,
    Inspire a soothing melancholy joy:
    As fancy warms, a pleasing kind of pain
    Steals o'er the cheek, and thrills the creeping vein!
35   Each rural sight, each sound, each smell, combine;
    The tinkling sheep-bell, or the breath of kine;
    The new-mown hay that scents the swelling breeze,

---

[5] Vagrant cuckoo; so called because, being tied down by no incubation or attendance about the nutrition of its young, it wanders without control.

[6] *Charadrius œdicnemus.*

[7] Bumble bee. [Ed.]

[8] *Gryllus campestris.*

[9] In hot summer nights woodlarks soar to a prodigious height and hang singing in the air.

Or cottage-chimney smoking through the trees.
    The chilling night-dews fall: away, retire;
40 For see, the glow-worm lights her amorous fire![10]
Thus, ere night's veil had half obscur'd the sky,
Th' impatient damsel hung her lamp on high:
True to the signal, by love's meteor led,
Leander hasten'd to his Hero's bed.[11]

I am, etc.

. . .

FROM LETTER XL
[*To the Same*]

Selborne, Sept. 2, 1774.

Dear Sir,

Before your letter arrived, and of my own accord, I had been remarking and comparing the tails of the male and female swallow, and this ere any young broods appeared; so that there was no danger of confounding the dams with their *pulli:*[12] and besides, as they were then always in pairs, and busied in the employ of nidification,[13] there could be no room for mistaking the sexes, nor the individuals of different chimnies the one for the other. From all my observations, it constantly appeared that each sex has the long feathers in its tail that give it that forked shape; with this difference, that they are longer in the tail of the male than in that of the female.

Nightingales, when their young first come abroad, and are helpless, make a plaintive and jarring noise; and also a snapping or cracking, pursuing people along the hedges as they walk: these last sounds seem intended for menace and defiance.

The grasshopper-lark chirps all night in the height of summer.

Swans turn white the second year, and breed the third.

Weasels prey on moles, as appears by their being sometimes caught in mole-traps.

---

[10] The light of the female glow-worm (as she often crawls up the stalk of a grass to make herself more conspicuous) is a signal to the male, which is a slender dusky *scarabœus.*

[11] See the story of Hero and Leander.

[12] Young birds. [Ed.]

[13] Nest building. [Ed.]

Sparrow-hawks sometimes breed in old crows' nests, and the kestrel in churches and ruins.

There are supposed to be two sorts of eels in the island of Ely. The threads sometimes discovered in eels are perhaps their young: the generation of eels is very dark and mysterious.

Hen-harriers breed on the ground, and seem never to settle on trees.

When redstarts shake their tails they move them horizontally, as dogs do when they fawn: the tail of a wagtail, when in motion, bobs up and down like that of a jaded horse.

Hedge-sparrows have a remarkable flirt with their wings in breeding-time; as soon as frosty mornings come they make a very piping plaintive noise.

Many birds which become silent about Midsummer reassume their notes again in September; as the thrush, blackbird, woodlark, willow-wren, etc.; hence August is by much the most mute month, the spring, summer and autumn through. Are birds induced to sing again because the temperament of autumn resembles that of spring?

Linnaeus ranges plants geographically; palms inhabit the tropics, grasses the temperate zones, and mosses and lichens the polar circles; no doubt animals may be classed in the same manner with propriety.

House-sparrows build under eaves in the spring; as the weather becomes hotter they get out for coolness, and nest in plum-trees and apple-trees. These birds have been known sometimes to build in rooks' nests, and sometimes in the forks of boughs under rooks' nests.

As my neighbour was housing a rick he observed that his dogs devoured all the little red mice that they could catch, but rejected the common mice; and that his cats ate the common mice, refusing the red.

Red-breasts sing all through the spring, summer, and autumn. The reason that they are called autumn songsters is, because in the two first seasons their voices are drowned and lost in the general chorus; in the latter their song becomes distinguishable. Many songsters of the autumn seem to be the young cock red-breasts of that year: notwithstanding the prejudices in their favour, they do much mischief in gardens to the summer-fruits.[14]

The titmouse, which early in February begins to make two quaint notes, like the whetting of a saw, is the marsh titmouse: the great titmouse sings with three cheerful joyous notes, and begins about the same time.

Wrens sing all the winter through, frost excepted.

---

[14]They eat also the berries of the ivy, the honeysuckle, and the *euonymus europaeus,* or spindle-tree.

House-martins came remarkably late this year both in Hampshire and Devonshire: is this circumstance for or against either hiding or migration?

Most birds drink sipping at intervals; but pigeons take a long continued draught, like quadrupeds.

Notwithstanding what I have said in a former letter, no grey crows were ever known to breed on Dartmoor; it was my mistake.

The appearance and flying of the *scarabœus solstitialis,* or fernchafer, commence with the month of July, and cease about the end of it. These scarabs are the constant food of *caprimulgi,* or fern owls, through that period. They abound on the chalky downs and in some sandy districts, but not in the clays.

In the garden of the Black-bear inn in the town of Reading is a stream or canal running under the stables and out into the fields on the other side of the road: in this water are many carps, which lie rolling about in sight, being fed by travellers, who amuse themselves by tossing them bread: but as soon as the weather grows at all severe these fishes are no longer seen, because they retire under the stables, where they remain till the return of spring. Do they lie in a torpid state? If they do not, how are they supported?

The note of the white-throat, which is continually repeated, and often attended with odd gesticulations on the wing, is harsh and displeasing. These birds seem of a pugnacious disposition; for they sing with an erected crest and attitudes of rivalry and defiance; are shy and wild in breeding-time, avoiding neighbourhoods, and haunting lonely lanes and commons; nay even the very tops of the Sussex-downs, where there are bushes and covert; but in July and August they bring their broods into gardens and orchards, and make great havock among the summer-fruits.

The black-cap has in common a full, sweet, deep, loud, and wild pipe; yet that strain is of short continuance, and his motions are desultory; but when that bird sits calmly and engages in song in earnest, he pours forth very sweet, but inward melody, and expresses great variety of soft and gentle modulations, superior perhaps to those of any of our warblers, the nightingale excepted.

Black-caps mostly haunt orchards and gardens; while they warble their throats are wonderfully distended.

The song of the redstart is superior, though somewhat like that of the white-throat: some birds have a few more notes than others. Sitting very placidly on the top of a tall tree in a village, the cock sings from morning to night: he affects neighbourhoods, and avoids solitude, and loves to build in orchards and about houses; with us he perches on the vane of a tall maypole.

The fly-catcher is of all our summer birds the most mute and the most familiar; it also appears the last of any. It builds in a vine, or a sweetbriar, against the wall of an house, or in the hole of a wall, or on the end of a beam or plate, and often close to the post of a door where people are going in and out all day long. This bird does not make the least pretension to song, but uses a little inward wailing note when it thinks its young in danger from cats or other annoyances: it breeds but once, and retires early.

Selborne parish alone can and has exhibited at times more than half the birds that are ever seen in all Sweden; the former has produced more than one hundred and twenty species, the latter only two hundred and twenty-one. Let me add also that it has shown near half the species that were ever known in Great-Britain.[15][...]

FROM LETTER XLII
[*To Daines Barrington*]

Omnibus animalibus reliquis certus et unius modi,
et in suo cuique genere incessus est: aves solæ vario
meatu feruntur, et in terrâ, et in äere.
—Pliny. *Hist. Nat.* lib. x. cap. *88.*[16]

Selborne, Aug. 7, 1778.

Dear Sir,

A good ornithologist should be able to distinguish birds by their air as well as by their colours and shape; on the ground as well as on the wing, and in the bush as well as in the hand. For, though it must not be said that every species of birds has a manner peculiar to itself, yet there is somewhat in most genera at least, that at first sight discriminates them, and enables a ju-dicious observer to pronounce upon them with some certainty. Put a bird in motion

... Et vera incessu patuit ... [17]

Thus kites and buzzards sail round in circles with wings expanded and mo-tionless; and it is from their gliding manner that the former are still called

---

[15]Sweden 221, Great-Britain 252 species.

[16]"All the other animals' locomotion is definite, of one type, and particular to each spe-cies; only the birds move in a meandering course, both on land and in the air." Pliny, *Natural History* 10.11.4. [Ed.]

[17]"And her gate revealed her to be truly a goddess" is the complete passage. Virgil, *Aeneid* 1.405. [Ed.]

in the north of England gleads, from the Saxon verb *glidan,* to glide. The
kestrel, or wind-hover, has a peculiar mode of hanging in the air in one
place, his wings all the while being briskly agitated. Hen-harriers fly low
over heaths or fields of corn, and beat the ground regularly like a pointer
or setting-dog. Owls move in a buoyant manner, as if lighter than the
air; they seem to want ballast. There is a peculiarity belonging to ravens
that must draw the attention even of the most incurious—they spend all
their leisure time in striking and cuffing each other on the wing in a kind
of playful skirmish; and, when they move from one place to another, frequently turn on their backs with a loud croak, and seem to be falling to the
ground. When this odd gesture betides them, they are scratching themselves with one foot, and thus lose the center of gravity. Rooks sometimes
dive and tumble in a frolicksome manner; crows and daws swagger in their
walk; wood-peckers fly *volatu undoso,* opening and closing their wings at
every stroke, and so are always rising or falling in curves. All of this genus
use their tails, which incline downward, as a support while they run up
trees. Parrots, like all other hooked-clawed birds walk awkwardly, and
make use of their bill as a third foot, climbing and descending with ridiculous caution. All the *gallinae* parade and walk gracefully, and run nimbly;
but fly with difficulty, with an impetuous whirring, and in a straight line.
Magpies and jays flutter with powerless wings, and make no dispatch;
herons seem incumbered with too much sail for their light bodies; but
these vast hollow wings are necessary in carrying burdens, such as large
fishes, and the like; pigeons, and particularly the sort called smiters, have a
way of clashing their wings the one against the other over their backs with
a loud snap; another variety called tumblers turn themselves over in the
air. Some birds have movements peculiar to the season of love: thus ring-
doves, though strong and rapid at other times, yet in the spring hang about
on the wing in a toying and playful manner; thus the cocksnipe, while
breeding, forgetting his former flight, fans the air like the wind-hover; and
the greenfinch in particular exhibits such languishing and faultering ges-
tures as to appear like a wounded and dying bird; the king-fisher darts
along like an arrow; fern-owls, or goat-suckers, glance in the dusk over the
tops of trees like a meteor; starlings as it were swim along, while missel-
thrushes use a wild and desultory flight; swallows sweep over the surface of
the ground and water, and distinguish themselves by rapid turns and quick
evolutions; swifts dash round in circles; and the bank-martin moves with
frequent vacillations like a butterfly. Most of the small birds fly by jerks, rising and falling as they advance. Most small birds hop; but wagtails and
larks walk, moving their legs alternately. Skylarks rise and fall perpendicularly as they sing; woodlarks hang poised in the air; and titlarks rise and fall

in large curves, singing in their descent. The white-throat uses odd jerks and gesticulations over the tops of hedges and bushes. All the duck-kind waddle; divers and auks walk as if fettered, and stand erect on their tails: these are the *compedes* of Linnaeus. Geese and cranes, and most wild-fowls, move in figured flights, often changing their position. The secondary remiges of *Tringoe,* wild-ducks, and some others, are very long, and give their wings, when in motion, an hooked appearance. Dabchicks, moorhens, and coots, fly erect, with their legs hanging down, and hardly make any dispatch; the reason is plain, their wings are placed too forward out of the true center of gravity; as the legs of auks and divers are situated too backward.

FROM LETTER XLIII
[*To the Same*]

Selborne, Sept. 9, 1778.

Dear Sir,

From the motion of birds, the transition is natural enough to their notes and language, of which I shall say something. Not that I would pretend to understand their language like the vizier; who, by the recital of a conversation which passed between two owls, reclaimed a sultan, before delighting in conquest and devastation; but I would be thought only to mean that many of the winged tribes have various sounds and voices adapted to express their various passions, wants, and feelings; such as anger, fear, love, hatred, hunger, and the like. All species are not equally eloquent; some are copious and fluent as it were in their utterance, while others are confined to a few important sounds: no bird, like the fish kind, is quite mute, though some are rather silent. The language of birds is very ancient, and, like other ancient modes of speech, very elliptical; little is said, but much is meant and understood.

The notes of the eagle-kind are shrill and piercing; and about the season of nidification much diversified, as I have been often assured by the curious observer of Nature, who long resided at Gibraltar, where eagles abound. The notes of our hawks much resemble those of the king of birds. Owls have very expressive notes; they hoot in a fine vocal sound, much resembling the *vox humana,* and reducible by a pitch-pipe to a musical key. This note seems to express complacency and rivalry among the males: they use also a quick call and an horrible scream; and can snore and hiss when they mean to menace. Ravens, besides their loud croak, can exert a deep and solemn note that makes the woods to echo; the amorous sound of a crow is strange and ridiculous; rooks, in the breeding season, attempt sometimes in the gaiety of their hearts to sing, but with no great success; the parrot-kind have many modulations of voice, as appears by their aptitude to learn human sounds; doves coo in an amorous and mournful manner, and are emblems of despairing lovers; the woodpecker sets up a sort of loud and hearty laugh; the fern-owl, or goat-sucker, from the dusk till day-break, serenades his mate with the clattering of castanets. All the tuneful *passeres* express their complacency by sweet modulations, and a variety of melody. The swallow, as has been observed in a former letter, by a shrill alarm bespeaks the attention of the other *hirundines,* and bids them be aware that the hawk is at hand. Aquatic and gregarious birds, especially the nocturnal, that shift their quarters in the dark, are very noisy and loquacious; as cranes, wild-geese, wild-ducks, and the like: their perpetual clamour prevents them from dispersing and losing their companions.

In so extensive a subject, sketches and outlines are as much as can be expected; for it would be endless to instance in all the infinite variety of the feathered nation. We shall therefore confine the remainder of this letter to the few domestic fowls of our yards, which are most known, and therefore best understood. And first the peacock, with his gorgeous train, demands our attention; but, like most of the gaudy birds, his notes are grating and shocking to the ear: the yelling of cats, and the braying of an ass, are not more disgustful. The voice of the goose is trumpet-like, and clanking; and once saved the Capitol at Rome, as grave historians assert: the hiss also of the gander is formidable and full of menace, and "protective of his young."[...]

From Letter XLVI

Sounds do not always give us pleasure according to their sweetness and melody; nor do harsh sounds always displease. We are more apt to be captivated or disgusted with the associations which they promote, than with the notes themselves. Thus the shrilling of the field-cricket, though sharp and stridulous, yet marvellously delights some hearers, filling their minds with a train of summer ideas of every thing that is rural, verdurous, and joyous.

About the tenth of March the crickets appear at the mouths of their cells, which they then open and bore, and shape very elegantly. All that ever I have seen at that season were in their pupa state, and had only the rudiments of wings, lying under a skin or coat, which must be cast before the insect can arrive at its perfect state;[18] from whence I should suppose that the old ones of last year do not always survive the winter. In August their holes begin to be obliterated, and the insects are seen no more till spring.

Not many summers ago I endeavoured to transplant a colony to the terrace in my garden, by boring deep holes in the sloping turf. The new inhabitants stayed some time, and fed and sung; but wandered away by degrees, and were heard at a farther distance every morning; so that it appears that on this emergency they made use of their wings in attempting to return to the spot from which they were taken.

One of these crickets, when confined in a paper cage and set in the sun, and supplied with plants moistened with water, will feed and thrive, and become so merry and loud as to be irksome in the same room where a person is sitting: if the plants are not wetted it will die.

FROM LETTER XLVII

Far from all resort of mirth
Save the cricket on the hearth.
    —*Milton's* Il Penseroso.

Selborne.

Dear Sir,

While many other insects must be sought after in fields and woods, and waters, the *gryllus domesticus,* or house-cricket, resides altogether within our dwellings, intruding himself upon our notice whether we will or no. This species delights in new-built houses, being, like the spider, pleased with the moisture of the walls; and besides, the softness of the mortar enables them to burrow and mine between the joints of the bricks or stones, and to open communication from one room to another. They are particularly fond of kitchens and bakers' ovens, on account of their perpetual warmth.[. . .]

---

[18] We have observed that they cast these skins in April, which are then seen lying at the mouths of their holes.

From "Observations on Various Parts of Nature"

SWALLOWS, CONGREGATING AND DISAPPEARANCE OF

During the severe winds that often prevail late in the spring, it is easy to say how the hirundines[19] subsist: for they withdraw themselves, and are hardly ever seen, nor do any insects appear for their support. That they can retire to rest, and sleep away these uncomfortable periods, as bats do, is a matter rather to be suspected than proved: or do they not rather spend their time in deep and sheltered vales near waters, where insects are more likely to be found? Certain it is, that hardly any individuals of this genus have at such times been seen for several days together.

September 13, 1791.—The congregating flocks of hirundines on the church and tower are very beautiful and amusing! When they fly off together from the roof, on any alarm, they quite swarm in the air. But they soon settle in heaps, and preening their feathers, and lifting up their wings to admit the sun, seem highly to enjoy the warm situation. Thus they spend the heat of the day, preparing for their emigration, and, as it were, consulting when and where they are to go. The flight about the church seems to consist chiefly of house martins, about 400 in number: but there are other places of rendezvous about the village frequented at the same time.

It is remarkable, that though most of them sit on the battlements and roof, yet many hang or cling for some time by their claws against the surface of the walls, in a manner not practised by them at any other time of their remaining with us.

The swallows seem to delight more in holding their assemblies on trees.

November 3, 1789.—Two swallows were seen this morning at Newton vicarage-house, hovering and settling on the roofs and out-buildings. None have been observed at Selborne since October 11. It is very remarkable, that after the hirundines have disappeared for some weeks, a few are occasionally seen again: sometimes, in the first week in November and that only for one day. Do they not withdraw and slumber in some hiding place during the interval? For we cannot suppose they had migrated to warmer climes and so returned again for one day. Is it not more probable that they are awakened from sleep, and like the bats are come forth to collect a little food? Bats appear at all seasons through the autumn and spring months,

---

[19]Swallows. [Ed.]

when the thermometer is at 50, because then phalaenae and moths are stirring.

These swallows looked like young ones.[. . .]

Humming in the Air

There is a natural occurrence to be met with upon the highest part of our town in hot summer days, which always amuses me much, without giving me any satisfaction with respect to the cause of it; and that is a loud audible humming of bees in the air, though not one insect is to be seen. This sound is to be heard distinctly the whole common through, from the Money-dells, to Mr. White's avenue gate. Any person would suppose that a large swarm of bees was in motion, and playing about over his head. This noise was heard last week, on June 28th.

> Resounds the living surface of the ground,
> Nor undelightful is the ceaseless *hum*
> To him who muses . . . at noon.
> Thick in yon stream of light a thousand ways,
> 5 Upward and downward, thwarting and convolv'd,
> The quivering nations sport.[. . .]
> Thomson's *Seasons.*

Snakes Slough

> . . . There the snake throws her enamell'd skin.
> Shakespeare. *Midsummer Night's Dream.*

About the middle of this month (September) we found in a field near a hedge the slough of a large snake, which seemed to have been newly cast. From circumstances it appeared as if turned wrong side outward, and as drawn off backward, like a stocking or woman's glove. Not only the whole skin, but scales from the very eyes, are peeled off, and appear in the head of the slough like a pair of spectacles. The reptile, at the time of changing his coat, had entangled himself intricately in the grass and weeds, so that the friction of the stalks and blades might promote this curious shifting of his exuviae.

> . . . Lubrica serpens
> Exuit in spinis vestem. Lucretius.[20]

---

[20] "The slippery snake sloughs off its skin in the thorn bushes." *De Rerum Natura* 4.60–61. [Ed.]

It would be a most entertaining sight could a person be an eye-witness to such a feat, and see the snake in the act of changing his garment. As the convexity of the scales of the eyes in the slough is now inward, that circumstance alone is a proof that the skin has been turned: not to mention that now the present inside is much darker than the outer. If you look through the scales of the snake's eyes from the concave side, viz. as the reptile used them, they lessen objects much. Thus it appears from what has been said, that snakes crawl out of the mouth of their own sloughs, and quit the tail part last, just as eels are skinned by a cook maid. While the scales of the eyes are growing loose, and a new skin is forming, the creature, in appearance, must be blind, and feel itself in an awkward uneasy situation.[...]

FROZEN SLEET

January 20.—Mr. H.'s man says that he caught this day in a lane near Hackwood park, many rooks, which, attempting to fly, fell from the trees with their wings frozen together by the sleet, that froze as it fell. There were, he affirms, many dozen so disabled.

MIST, CALLED LONDON SMOKE

This is a blue mist which has somewhat the smell of coal smoke, and as it always comes to us with a N. E. wind, is supposed to come from London. It has a strong smell, and is supposed to occasion blights. When such mists appear they are usually followed by dry weather.

REFLECTION OF FOG

When people walk in a deep white fog by night with a lanthorn, if they will turn their backs to the light, they will see their shades impressed on the fog in rude gigantic proportions. This phenomenon seems not to have been attended to, but implies the great density of the meteor at that juncture.

HONEY DEW

June 4, 1783.—Vast honey dews this week. The reason of these seem to be, that in hot days the effluvia of flowers are drawn up by a brisk evaporation, and then in the night fall down with the dews with which they are entangled.

This clammy substance is very grateful to bees, who gather it with great assiduity, but it is injurious to the trees on which it happens to fall, by stopping the pores of the leaves. The greatest quantity falls in still close weather;

because winds disperse it, and copious dews dilute it, and prevent its ill effects. It falls mostly in hazy warm weather.

Morning Clouds

After a bright night and vast dew, the sky usually becomes cloudy by eleven or twelve o'clock in the forenoon, and clear again towards the decline of the day. The reason seems to be, that the dew, drawn up by evaporation, occasions the clouds; which, towards evening, being no longer rendered buoyant by the warmth of the sun, melt away, and fall down again in dews. If clouds are watched in a still warm evening, they will be seen to melt away, and disappear.

The Invitation to Selborne

See Selborne spreads her boldest beauties round
The varied valley, and the mountain ground,
Wildly majestic! what is all the pride
Of flats, with loads of ornament supply'd?
5 Unpleasing, tasteless, impotent expense,
Compar'd with nature's rude magnificence.
     Arise, my stranger, to these wild scenes haste;
The unfinish'd farm awaits your forming taste:
Plan the pavilion, airy, light and true;
10 Thro' the high arch call in the length'ning view;
Expand the forest sloping up the hill;
Swell to a lake the scant, penurious rill;
Extend the vista, raise the castle mound
In antique taste, with turrets ivy-crown'd;
15 O'er the gay lawn the flow'ry shrub dispread,
Or with the blending garden mix the mead;
Bid China's pale, fantastic fence, delight,
Or with the mimic statue trap the sight.
     Oft on some evening, sunny, soft and still,
20 The Muse shall lead thee to the beech-grown hill,

The Natural History of Selborne, to which are added *The Naturalist's Calendar, Miscellaneous Observations, and Poems.* London: Longman, 1813.

To spend in tea the cool, refreshing hour,
Where nods in air the pensile, nest-like bower;
Or where the Hermit hangs the straw-clad cell,
Emerging gently from the leafy dell;
25 By fancy plann'd; as once th' inventive maid
Met the hoar sage amid the secret shade;
Romantic spot! from whence in prospect lies
Whate'er of landscape charms our feasting eyes;
The pointed spire, the hall, the pasture-plain,
30 The russet fallow, or the golden grain,
The breezy lake that sheds a gleaming light,
Till all the fading picture fail the sight.

　　　Each to his task; all different ways retire,
Cull the dry stick; call forth the seeds of fire;
35 Deep fix the kettle's props, a forky row,
Or give with fanning hat the breeze to blow.

　　　Whence is this taste, the furnish'd hall forgot,
To feast in gardens, or th' unhandy grot?
Or novelty with some new charms surprizes,
40 Or from our very shifts some joy arises.
Hark, while below the village-bells ring round,
Echo, sweet nymph, returns the soften'd sound;
But if gusts rise, the rushing forests roar,
Like the tide tumbling on the pebbly shore.
45 　　Adown the vale, in lone, sequester'd nook,
Where skirting woods imbrown the dimpling brook,
The ruin'd Convent lies; here wont to dwell
The lazy canon midst his cloister'd cell;
While papal darkness brooded o'er the land,
50 Ere reformation made her glorious stand:
Still oft at eve belated shepherd-swains
See the cowl'd spectre skim the folded plains.

　　　To the high temple would my stranger go,
The mountain-brow commands the woods below;
55 In Jewry first this order found a name,
When madding Croisades set the world in flame;
When western climes, urg'd on by Pope and priest,
Pour'd forth their millions o'er the deluged east;
Luxurious knights, ill suited to defy
60 To mortal fight Turcéstan chivalry.

　　　Nor be the Parsonage by the muse forgot;
The partial bard admires his native spot;

Smit with its beauties, loved, as yet a child,
(Unconscious why) its scapes grotesque, and wild.
65 High on a mound th' exalted gardens stand,
Beneath, deep vallies scoop'd by nature's hand.
A Cobham here, exulting in his art,
Might blend the General's with the Gardener's part;
Might fortify with all the martial trade
70 Of rampart, bastion, fosse,[21] and palisade;
Might plant the mortar with wide threat'ning bore,
Or bid the mimic cannon seem to roar.
    Now climb the steep, drop now your eye below,
Where round the blooming village orchards grow;
75 There, like a picture, lies my lowly seat,
A rural, shelter'd, unobserv'd retreat.
    Me far above the rest Selbornian scenes,
The pendent forests, and the mountain-greens
Strike with delight; there spreads the distant view,
80 That gradual fades till sunk in misty blue:
Here nature hangs her slopy woods to sight,
Rills purl between and dart a quivering light.

On The Rainbow

Look upon the Rainbow, and praise him that made
it: very beautiful is it in the brightness thereof.

                        —Eccles, xliii. 11.

On morning or on evening cloud impress'd,
Bent in vast curve, the wat'ry meteor shines
Delightfully, to th' levell'd sun oppos'd:
Lovely refraction! while the vivid brede
5 In listed colours glows, th' unconscious swain
With vacant eye gazes on the divine
Phænomenon, gleaming o'er th' illumin'd fields,
Or runs to catch the treasure which it sheds.
10   Not so the sage, inspir'd with pious awe;

---

[21] A trench or sunken fence. [Ed.]

He hails the federal arch; and looking up
Adores that God, whose fingers form'd this bow
Magnificent, compassing heav'n about
With a resplendent verge. "Thou mad'st the cloud,
15 Maker omnipotent, and thou the bow;
And by that covenant graciously hast sworn
Never to drown the world again: henceforth,
Till time shall be no more, in ceaseless round,
Season shall follow season; day to night,
20 Summer to winter, harvest to seed time,
Heat shall to cold in regular array
Succeed." Heav'n taught, so sang the Hebrew bard.[22]

---

[22] Moses.

John Aikin (1747–1822)

John Aikin, younger brother of Anna Aikin (later Barbauld), was a physician and author who counted among his associates Joseph Priestley, Erasmus Darwin, Robert Southey, and the naturalist Thomas Pennant. He was also the editor of *Monthly Magazine* (1796–1806), a periodical that included influential essays and reviews of literature, politics, economics, divinity, experimental science, and theology. Coleridge was a contributor, and the magazine was widely read in radical and dissenting circles. Aikin also edited *The Athenaeum*. He supported and encouraged Anna Barbauld's writing throughout her literary career. Her first published poems appeared in his *Essays on Song Writing* (1771), and the two collaborated on numerous other volumes including a volume for children, *Evenings at Home* (1793).

In 1777, Aikin published *An Essay on the Application of Natural History to Poetry,* a work that directed poets toward the plants, animals, and natural phenomena around them. Anna Barbauld responded enthusiastically to her brother's essay in a letter: "I hope your Essay will bring down our poets from the garrets, to wander about the fields and hunt squirrels. I am clearly of your opinion, that the only chance we have of novelty is by a more accurate observation of the works of nature [. . . .] I have seen some rich descriptions of West Indies flowers and plants, but unpleasing merely because their names were uncouth, and forms not known generally enough to be put into verse" (Letter to John Aiken in Barbauld selections). Her comments clearly suggest that poets need more experience of the nonhuman world in order to do justice to their visions of nature.

What follows is the first section of John Aikin's essay, in which he cites a lack of accurate appreciation for the natural world as one of the main weaknesses in ancient poetry and in the poetry of the second half of the eighteenth century. Aikin anticipates Wordsworth,

Coleridge, and others in his complaint about the "insipidity of Modern Poetry." He dedicates this work to Thomas Pennant, at the time one of the most widely read natural historians in Britain. Aikin argues that poets should concentrate on their immediate observation and emotional appreciation of natural objects, and he praises those poets, past and present, who have developed the skills of the naturalist: Theocritus, Shakespeare, Milton, Thomson, Collins, Young, and Gray. Also included here is a selection from Aikin's *Calendar of Nature* (1798), edited and enlarged by his son Arthur Aikin, who went on to become an influential chemist and botanist.

From An Essay on the Application of Natural History to Poetry

to
THOMAS PENNANT, ESQ.
F.R.S.
of
DOWNING, FLINTSHIRE.

Sir,

INDEPENDENTLY of the desire I might have of publickly expressing my grateful sense of the friendship with which you honour me, justice would seem to require that a piece, the original idea of which was solely derived from an acquaintance with your works, and which to them is indebted for its most valuable materials, should be inscribed to you.

Its pupose is such as I flatter myself will obtain your approbation. It is to add incitements to the study of natural history, by placing in a stronger light than has yet been done, the advantages that may result from it to the most exalted and delightful of all arts, that of poetry. That this study is not

---

John Aikin. *An Essay on the Application of Natural History to Poetry*. Warrington: W. Eyres for J. Johnson, 1777.

only a source of agreeable and innocent amusement, but conduces to humanize and enlarge the mind, and in various ways to promote the happiness of mankind, has been sufficiently proved by the observations of many ingenious writers. But its application to the improvement of poetry, has not, I believe, been the subject of particular discussion. By considering it in this view, I therefore thought that something new in its favour might be suggested; and if what I have done shall be the means of acquiring you a single fellow-labourer in your interesting researches into British Zoology, I shall not be dissatisfied with my success.

I am,

SIR,

With the sincerest respect and esteem,

Your most obedient,

and obliged Servant,

WARRINGTON,   *JOHN AIKIN.*
Feb. 1, 1777.

No literary complaint is more frequent and general than that of the insipidity of Modern Poetry. While the votary of science is continually gratified with new objects opening to his view, the lover of poetry is wearied and disgusted with a perpetual repetition of the same images, clad in almost the same language. This is usually attributed to a real deficiency of poetical genius in the present age; and such causes are assigned for it as would leave us little room to hope for any favourable change. But this solution, as it is invidious in its application, and discouraging in its effects, is surely also contradictory to that just relish for the beauties of poetry, that taste for sound and manly criticism, and that improvement in the other elegant arts, which must be allowed to characterize our own times. The state in which poetry has been transmitted to us will probably afford a truer, as well as a more favourable explanation of the fact. It comes to us, worn down, enfeebled, and fettered.

The *Epopoea,*[1] circumscribed as it perhaps necessarily is within very narrow limits, scarcely offers to the most fertile invention a subject at the same time original and proper. Tragedy, exhausted by the infinite number of its productions, is nearly reduced to the same condition. The artificial

---

[1] Epic style. [Ed.]

construction of the Ode almost inevitably throws its composer into un-meaning imitation. Elegy, conversant with a confined, and almost uniform train of emotions, cannot but frequently become languid and feeble. Satire, indeed, is still sufficiently vigorous and prolific; but its offspring is little suited to please a mind sensible to the charms of genuine poetry. It would seem, then, that novelty was the present requisite, more, perhaps, than genius: it is therefore of importance to enquire what source is capable of affording it.

That novelty should have been the least sought for in that very walk which might be expected to yield it in the greatest abundance, will, doubt-less, appear extraordinary. Yet, if it be admitted that the grand and beauti-ful objects which nature every where profusely throws around us, are the most obvious store of new materials to the poet, it must also be confessed that it is the store which of all others he has the most sparingly touched. An ingenious critic, Mr. Warton, has remarked that "every painter of rural beauty since the time of Theocritus (except Thomson) has copied his im-ages from him, without ever looking abroad into the face of nature them-selves."[2] If this be not strictly just, it is at least certain that supineness and servile imitation have prevailed to a greater degree in the description of na-ture, than in any other part of poetry. The effect of this has been, that de-scriptive poetry has degenerated into a kind of phraseology, consisting of combinations of words which have been so long coupled together, that, like the hero and his epithet in Homer, they are become inseparable compan-ions. It is amusing, under some of the most common heads of description, in a poetical dictionary, to observe the wonderful sameness of thoughts and expressions in passages culled from a dozen different authors. An or-dinary versifier seems no more able to conceive of the Morn without rosy fingers and dewy locks, or Spring without flowers and showers, loves and groves, than of any of the heathen deities without their usual attributes. Even in poets of a higher order, the hand of a copyist may be traced much oftener than the strokes of an observer. Has a picturesque circumstance been imagined by some one original genius? Every succeeding composer introduces it on a similar occasion. He, perhaps, improves, amplifies, and in some respect varies the idea; and in so doing may exhibit considerable taste and ingenuity; but still he contents himself with an inferior degree of merit, while the materials are all before him for attaining the highest; and fails of gratifying that natural thirst after *novelty* which may be supposed peculiarly to incite the reader of poetry.

---

[2] Dedication of Warton and Pitt's Virgil.

The following example of this propensity to imitation, taken from writers of distinguished character, will aptly illustrate what has been advanced. Shakespeare, in *Macbeth*, thus paints the approach of night.

> —— to black Hecat's summons
> The shard-born beetle with his drowsy hums
> Hath rung night's yawning peal.

The same circumstance is represented in these lines of Milton's *Lycidas.*

> —— both together heard
> What time the gray-fly[3] winds her sultry horn,
> Battening our flocks with the fresh dews of night.

Gray's *Elegy in a country church-yard* next offers the beautiful line

> Save where the beetle wheels his droning flight.

Lastly, Collins, in his *Ode to Evening,* exhibits the same object more minutely.

> Or where the beetle winds
> His small, but sullen horn,
> As oft he rises midst the twilight path,
> Against the pilgrim borne in heedless hum.

Several other instances might be adduced of the introduction of the same circumstance into an evening landskip; but as they are chiefly to be met with in pieces of inferior reputation, it would be superfluous to particularize them. In all the preceding quotations the image is employed with propriety, and represented with elegance; but its successive adoption by so many different writers sufficiently evinces what I meant to deduce from it, a real want of variety in poetical imagery, proceeding from a scarcity of original observations of nature.

The want of variety and novelty is not, however, the only defect of those poets who have occasionally introduced the description of natural objects. It is no less common to find their descriptions faint, obscure, and ill characterized; the properties of things mistaken, and incongruous parts employed in the composition of the same picture. This is owing to a too

---

[3] The cockchaffer; the insect meant in all the four passages.

cursory and general survey of objects, without exploring their minuter distinctions and mutual relations; and is only to be rectified by accurate and attentive observation, conducted upon somewhat of a scientific plan. As the artist who has not studied the body with anatomical precision, and examined the proportions of every limb, both with respect to its own several parts, and the whole system, cannot produce a just and harmonious representation of the human frame; so the descriptive poet, who does not habituate himself to view the several objects of nature minutely, and in comparison with each other, must ever fail in giving his pictures the congruity and animation of real life.

As these defects constantly attend every writer of inferior rank, nothing would be easier than to multiply instances of them. I shall, however, confine myself to a few, which, that they may carry more weight, shall be drawn from respectable sources.

The genius of the eastern poets, bold, ardent, and precipitate, was peculiarly averse to precision and accuracy. Hurried away by the warm emotions arising from an idea forcibly impressed upon their minds, they often seem entirely to lose sight of the train of thought which the proposed subject would seem naturally to suggest. Hence their descriptions, however animated and striking in certain points, are seldom full and distinct enough to form accurate representations. I will venture to cite those highly celebrated zoological paintings in the book of Job in confirmation of this remark. In all of these it is found, that some one property of the animal, which it indeed possesses in an eminent degree, but not exclusively, gives the leading tone to the description, and occupies the whole attention of the poet, to the neglect of every minuter, though perhaps more discriminating circumstance. Thus, the sole quality of the horse which is dwelt upon, is his courage in war. This, indeed, is pictured with great force and sublimity; but by images, many of which are equally applicable to any other warlike creature. Even the noble expression of "his neck being cloathed with thunder," is not so finely descriptive, because it is less appropriated, than the "luxuriat toris animosum pectus" of Virgil;[4] and, for the same reason, I can scarcely agree with Mr. Warton in preferring the passage "He swalloweth the ground with fierceness and rage, neither believeth he that it is the sound of the trumpet," to the lines.

Stare loco nescit; micat auribus, & tremit artus;
Collectumque premens volvit sub naribus ignem.[5]

---

[4] "His [a war horse's] spirited chest swells with muscles." *Georgics* 3.81. [Ed.]

[5] "He cannot remain in place, his ears prick up and his limbs tremble, and through his nostrils he releases fiery vapor, collected under pressure." *Georgics* 3.84–85. [Ed.]

The indistinctness of most of the other descriptions in this book may be inferred from the very different opinions entertained by critics concerning the animals which the writer intended. Thus, the *behemoth* is by some supposed to be the elephant, by others the hippopotamus. The *reem,* absurdly in our version rendered the unicorn, is variously interpreted the rhinoceros, urus,[6] oryx,[7] and bison. What is more extraordinary, the *leviathan,* to which a whole chapter is appropriated, has, with almost equal plausibility, been maintained to be the whale and the crocodile—a fish, and an amphibious quadruped. It may indeed, be alledged, that the design of the poet in this place, which was to inculcate sublime ideas of the Divine Power and Majesty from considerations of the grandeur of his works, and sentiments of humiliation from the comparison of human strength and courage to those of other creatures, did not require, or even admit of minuteness in zoological description. Still, however, such want of precision in the great outlines of his figures, must be imputed to the prevalence of a characteristic manner, rather than to the decision of the judgment.

This fault, if we may venture to call it so, to which the oriental writers, from the peculiar cast of their genius, and an exuberance of that fire which constitutes the very essence of poetry, were liable, is not, however, that against which it is necessary to caution a modern poet. Want of knowledge, attention, or discernment, have occasioned those failures which the following instances are meant to exemplify.

Lucan, a poet much more conversant with the schools of rhetoricians than with the works of nature, has contrived to shew great ignorance in a close and servile copy from Virgil. That writer, in a passage hereafter to be quoted, describes with admirable truth and nature those presages of an impending storm which appear in the actions of certain animals. Among the rest, he mentions that of the heron's leaving its accustomed haunts in the marshes, and soaring to a great height in the air. This circumstance is thus varied in the representation by Lucan,

—————————————— ausa volare
Ardea sublimis, pennæ confisa natanti.

"The heron dares to fly on high, trusting to its swimming feather."

He seems to have concluded that the heron, as a fowl conversant with water, must be a swimmer; whereas every one in the least acquainted with the history of this bird knows that it takes its prey only by wading, for

---

[6] Wild ox. [Ed.]

[7] African antelope. [Ed.]

which its long legs are admirably adapted. Some of his commentators, indeed, have attempted to free him from the imputation of ignorance, by supposing that the epithet "*swimming* feather" was intended to denote that easy motion of a bird through the air which has often been resembled to sailing or swimming. But from the whole turn of the passage, it appears evident to me, that Lucan meant to improve upon his original by one of those antithetical points which on all occasions he so much delights to introduce: the images of *flying* and *swimming* are therefore set in opposition to each other; and unless the latter be employed in its simple signification, the words "daring" and "trusting" are not at all applicable. Were even the other explanation admitted, the smooth swimming motion would very ill apply to a bird which is remarkable for its heavy and laborious flight.

His variation of another circumstance in the same passage is equally erroneous. To the crow, which Virgil describes as stalking solitary over the dry sands, he also attributes the action which that poet rightly appropriates to water-fowl, of dashing the water over its body before stormy weather.

—— caput spargens undis, velut occupet imbrem,
Instabili gressu metitur litora cornix.[8]

Mr. Warton's translation of Virgil, though in general extremely chaste and correct, affords one instance of similar error in deviating from the original.

Behold for thee the neighb' ring naiad crops
The violet pale, and poppy's fragrant tops. *Ecl.* II.

The epithet *fragrant* is the translator's addition; and an improper one; since that plant has only a faint disagreeable odour.

A mistake, different in kind, since it relates to time rather than to quality, yet resembling in subject, appears in Pope's first pastoral. The rose is represented as blowing along with the crocus and violet; though, in reality, some months intervene betwixt their flowering.

Here the bright crocus and blue vi'let glow,
Here western winds on breathing roses blow.

Manilius, in a short description of Africa, has improperly introduced the peaceful and innoxious elephant into an enumeration of the fierce and venomous animals which infest that torrid region.

---

[8] "Sprinkling its head with the waves, as if trying to seize the water, the crow traverses the shore with a tottering step." Lucan, *Bellum Civile* 5.555–56. [Ed.]

Huic varias pestes, diversaque membra ferarum,
Concessit bellis natura infesta futuris;
Horrendos angues, habitataque membra venemo,
Et mortis partus, viventia crimina terræ;
5 Et vastos elephantes habet, sævosque leones,
In poenas sæcunda suas, parit horrida tellus.
ASTRONOM. lib. iv.

Mr. Creech, in his translation of this passage, has aggravated this impropriety almost to ridicule, by coupling the lion and elephant in one action, entirely unsuitable to the latter.

Here nature, angry with mankind, prepares
Strange monsters, instruments of future wars;
Here snakes, those cells of poison, take their birth,
Those living crimes and grievance of the earth;
5 Fruitful in its own plagues, the desert shore
Hears elephants and frightful lions *roar.*

Shakespeare, in *The Two Gentlemen of Verona,* gives the following beautiful lines to the banished Valentine.

Here can I sit alone, unseen of any,
And to the nightingale's complaining notes
Tune my distresses, and record my woes.

The plaintive character of the nightingale renders its introduction pleasing and proper; but Congreve, in a passage apparently imitated from this, has spoiled the image by transferring it to the lark, whose character is always cheerful and sprightly.

The morning lark to mine accords his note,
And tunes to my distress his warbling throat.

It has been already observed that the leviathan of Job is variously understood by critics for the whale and the crocodile. Both these animals are remarkable for the smallness of their eyes in proportion to the bulk of their bodies. Those of the crocodile are indeed said to be extremely piercing out of the water, in which sense, therefore, the poet's expression that "its eyes are like the eyelids of the morning" can only be applicable. Dr. Young, however, in his paraphrase on this part of Job, describing the crocodile as the animal intended in the original, has given the image an erroneous reference to the magnitude, rather than the brightness of its eye.

Large is his front; and when his burnish'd eyes
Lift their *broad* lids, the morning seems to rise.[9]

These instances might be infinitely multiplied, were we to include those false representations of nature which ancient error or fable first introduced, but which, having been made the foundation of ingenious figures and pleasing allusions, the poets of every age have adopted. Such are, the song of the dying swan; the halcyon's nest; the crocodile's tears; the pelican's feeding her young with her blood; and the whole existence of the phœnix. When we recollect the multitude of beautiful images and descriptions formed upon these fictions, and that the very language of poetry is in many instances derived from them, we shall be apt to regard them not only with indulgence, but veneration. Yet, on the other hand, if we adhere to this unquestionable principle, that nothing can be really beautiful which has not truth for its basis; if we attend to the boundless variety of genuine beauties, applicable to every purpose of ornament, which nature liberally scatters around us; if we reflect on the danger of suffering falsehood and error habitually to intrude even in matters of the slightest importance; we shall scarcely give our assent to a licence, as unnecessary as it is hazardous. A modern writer can lose nothing by this rigour; for since both true and false wit have so long been employed upon these topics, every thing brilliant or ingenious which they can suggest, must have long since been exhausted; and the revival of them at present is as much a proof of barren invention as of false taste.

Where the professed intention of the poet is the description of natural objects, it cannot be doubted that every fabulous idea should be religiously avoided. Thus, it has been remarked by Mr. Pennant, in his *British Zoology*, that Virgil, who, in speaking figuratively of the swan as the poet's bird, ascribes to it its usual musical attributes, when he mentions it under its proper character of a water-fowl, gives it the harsh note really belonging to that order of birds.

Dant sonitum *rauci* per stagna loquacia cygni.
                                        AEN. IX. 458.
The hoarse swans scream along the sounding marsh.

On the other hand, Lucretius has adopted the fabulous notion of the swan, even in the exemplification of a philosophical proposition. Speaking of the different nature of sounds, he says,

---

[9] Herodotus, speaking of the crocodile, says, that it has the eyes of a hog.

Nec simili penetrant aureis primordia forma,
Quom tuba depresso graviter sub murmure mugit,
Aut roboant raucum retrocita cornua bombum,
Valibus et cycni gelidis orti ex Heliconis
5 Cum liquidam tollunt lugubri voce querelam.

LIB. IV.

Nor are the figures of the seeds alike,
Which from the grave and murm'ring trumpet strike,
To those of dying swans, whose latest breath
In mournful strains laments approaching death.

CREECH.

And in another passage he blends this fiction with reality in a manner equally injudicious.

Parvus ut est cycni melior canor, ille gruum quam
Clamor, in aetheriis dispersus nubibus Austri.

IBID.

As the low warbling of the swan excels
The crane's loud clangor, scatter'd thro' the clouds.[10]

This latter passage, as well as the line above quoted from Virgil, is part of a simile; whence I take occasion to remark, that, as it is the business of every figure of comparison either to illustrate or to enforce the simple idea, it is certainly requisite that they should be founded upon circumstances to which the mind of the reader can assent; otherwise they can produce little effect. The writer of *Scriblerus* gives ludicrous example of a simile built upon fiction.

Thus have I seen in Araby the blest
A phœnix couch'd upon her funeral nest;

a sight which neither the author, nor any one else, ever did see. Obvious as the absurdity here is, the following passage in Milton, though written quite in the spirit of that divine poet, stands upon the very same ground of censure.

As when a gryffon thro' the wilderness
With winged course, o'er hill or moory dale
Pursues the Arimaspian, who by stealth

---

[10] Creech's translation of these lines is so very inadequate as to give no idea of the original.

Has from his wakeful custody purloin'd
5   The guarded gold.

PARAD. LOST.

Perhaps, in a modern writer we should require an adherence to truth, even in the representation of those higher and less obvious parts of the economy of nature which come under the survey of philosophy. The Copernican theory of the solar system has been now long enough established to take place of the Ptolemaic even in poetical allusion; and the sun, tranquilly seated in the center of its vast dependencies, cheering, invigorating, and animating the whole, may, on every occasion of sublime imagery, supercede the chariot of Phœbus, for every painfully dragged round the petty globe we inhabit. How inexcusable is the reasoning, the philosophical Dr. Young in adopting an absurd notion entertained by some of the fathers, that the final conflagration of the world will begin at midnight; as if it were possible for night at any one instant to be universal on the globe, or an equal portion of the earth were not always illuminated by the sun!

At midnight, when mankind is wrapt in peace,
And worldly fancy feeds on golden dreams,
To give more dread to man's most dreadful hour,
At midnight, 'tis presum'd, this pomp will burst
5   From tenfold darkness.

NIGHT THOUGHTS.

Even in the more confined parts of knowledge, with which it is not requisite for a person of liberal education to be intimately acquainted, exploded errors should be avoided, whenever it is thought proper to introduce such subjects. Allusions to chemistry were extremely fashionable in the poetry of the last century; but so many false opinions were then received into that science, that the same images would give disgust rather than pleasure to one acquainted with it in its present state of improvement. The fancied revivification of a flower from its ashes, which furnished a topic for the wit of Cowley and D'avenant, could scarcely be employed to advantage by a modern writer.

On the whole, although fictions of some kind have been justly accounted the very soul of poetry, and cannot be rejected without depriving it of its choicest ornaments, yet false representations of natural things, the real properties of which are commonly known, and are equally capable of poetical use, cannot stand the test of sound criticism. And especially, the trite and hackneyed fables of ancient poets, when copied by modern writers, must appear as frigid and uninteresting as they are extravagant and unnatural.

Hitherto it has been chiefly attempted to shew that the accurate and scientific study of nature would obviate many of the defects usually discoverable in poetical compositions. The more pleasing task succeeds, of exhibiting to view the beauties which the poet may derive from this source. And here, I shall first remark, that every part of natural history does not seem equally capable of affording poetical imagery. The vegetable creation, delightful as it is to the senses, and extensive in utility, yields comparatively few materials to the poet, whose art is principally defective in representing those qualities in which it chiefly excels; colour, scent, and taste. The mineral kingdom is still more steril, and uncommodated to description. The animal race, who, in common with their human lord and head, have, almost universally, somewhat of moral and intellectual character; whose motions, habitations, and pursuits, are so infinitely and curiously varied; and whose connection with man arises to a sort of companionship and mutual attachment; seem on these accounts peculiarly adapted to the purposes of poetry. Separately considered, they afford matter for pleasing and even sublime speculation; in the rural landskip they give animation to the objects around them; and viewed in comparison with human kind, they suggest amusing and instructive lessons. That part of natural history termed zoology has therefore almost solely furnished the subjects of the ensuing pages.

To shew, by examples drawn from those poets who have eminently succeeded in descriptions of animal nature, that this source has actually been productive of beauties of the most striking kind; and to point out from the writers in natural history some new objects which might have improved the poetry of past, or may adorn that of future composers, will be the attempt of the remaining part of this Essay. . . .

From The Natural History of the Year

May

Born in yon blaze of orient sky,
    Sweet May! thy radiant form unfold;
Unclose thy blue voluptuous eye,
    And wave thy shadowy locks of gold.

John Aikin, *The Natural History of the Year.* Ed. Arthur Aikin. London: J. Johnson, 1798.

5 For thee the fragrant zephyrs blow,
    For thee descends the sunny shower;
The rills in softer murmurs flow,
    And brighter blossoms gem the bower.

Light Graces dress'd in flowery wreaths,
10   And tiptoe joys their hands combine;
And Love his sweet contagion breaths,
    And laughing dances round thy shrine.

Warm with new life, the glittering throngs,
    On quivering fin and rustling wing,
15 Delighted join their votive songs,
    And hail thee goddess of the spring.
                [ERASMUS] DARWIN.

May has ever been the favourite month in the year for poetical description, but the praises originally lavished upon it were uttered in climates more southern than our own. In such it really unites all the soft beauties of spring with the radiance of summer, and possesses warmth enough to cheer and invigorate, without overpowering. With us, especially since we have reckoned by the new style, great part of the month is yet too chill for a perfect enjoyment of the charms of nature, and frequent injury is sustained by the flowers and young fruits during its course, from blights and blasting winds. May-day, though still observed as a rural festival, has often little pleasure to bestow except that arising from the name, while the scanty garlands composed in honour of the day, rather display the immature infancy than the luxuriant youth of the year. In a very elegant poem, entitled, *The Tears of Old May Day*, this newer rival is thus described,

Nor wonder, man, that Nature's bashful face,
    And opening charms her rude embraces fear:
Is she not sprung of April's wayward race,
    The sickly daughter of th' unripen'd year?
5 With show'rs and sunshine in her fickle eyes,
    With hollow smiles proclaiming treach'rous peace;
With blushes, harb'ring in their thin disguise,
    The blast that riots on the Spring's increase.[11]

The latter part of the month, however, on the whole, is even in this country sufficiently profuse of beauties. The earth is covered with the freshest green of the grass and young corn, and adorned with numerous

---

[11] By Edward Lovibond (1724–75). [Ed.]

flowers opening on every side. The trees put on all their verdure; the hedges are rich in fragrance from the snowy blossoms of the hawthorn; and the orchards display their highest beauty in the delicate bloom of the apple blossoms.

> One boundless blush, one white-empurpled shower
> Of mingled blossoms.
>
> THOMSON.

All these promising signs of future plenty are, however, liable to be cut off by the blights which peculiarly occur in this month, and frequently commit most dreadful ravages. The history and cause of blights is by no means exactly ascertained, and it is a subject which, from its actual importance, well deserves a minute investigation. There appear to be three kinds of blights: the first occurs in the early spring, about the time of the blossoming of the peach, and is nothing more than a dry frosty wind usually from the north or north-east, and principally affects the blossoms, causing them to fall off prematurely, and consequently to become unproductive. The two other kinds of blights occur in this month, affecting principally the apple and pear-trees, and sometimes the corn. One of these consists in the appearance of an immense multitude of aphides, a kind of small insect of a brown, or black, or green colour, attacking the leaves of plants, and entirely encrusting the young stems. These pests are, I believe, always found to make their appearance after a north-east wind; and it has been supposed by many that they are actually conveyed hither by the wind.

> For off, engend'red by the hazy north,
> Myriads on myriads, insect armies warp
> Keen in the poison'd breeze; and wasteful eat
> Thro' buds and bark, into the blackn'd core
> 5 Their eager way.
>
> THOMSON.

Many circumstances indeed favour this opinion, as the suddenness with which they appear, being generally in the course of a single night; and those trees that are sheltered from the wind being uninfected: indeed it frequently happens that a single branch that chances to be screened, will escape unhurt, while the rest of the tree is quite covered with these minute destroyers. A third reason may be derived from the inactivity of these insects: they generally remain almost immoveable on the branch or leaf where they are first seen, and are for the most part unprovided with wings; yet the places where they are commonly found are those parts of a tree which are furthest from the ground, and most exposed to the wind. The last kind of blight is preceded by a south or south-west wind, unaccompanied by insects; the effects of which are visible in the burnt appearance of all leaves and shoots that are exposed to that quarter; it attacks all vegetables indiscriminately, but those suffer most from it which are the loftiest, and whose leaves are the youngest; the oak therefore is peculiarly injured.

A cold and windy May is, however, accounted favourable to the corn; which, if brought forward by early warm weather, is apt to run into stalk, while its ears remain thin and light.

The leafing of trees is commonly completed in this month. It begins with the aquatic kinds, such as the willow, poplar, and alder, proceeds to the lime, sycamore, and horsechestnut, and concludes with the oak, beech, ash, walnut, and mulberry; these last, however, are seldom in full leaf till June.

> No tree in all the grove but has its charms,
> Tho' each its hue peculiar; paler some
> And of a wannish grey; the willow such
> And poplar, that with silver lines his leaf,
> 5 And ash, far stretching his umbrageous arm.
> Of deeper green the elm; and deeper still
> Lord of the woods, the long surviving oak.
> Some glossy-leav'd and shining in the sun,
> The maple, and the beech of oily nuts
> 10 Prolific, and the lime at dewy eve
> Diffusing odours: nor unnoted pass
> The sycamore, capricious in attire,
> Now green, now tawny, and ere autumn yet
> Have chang'd the woods, in scarlet honours bright.
>   COWPER'S TASK.

Among the numerous wild-flowers, none attracts more notice than the cowslip,

> Whose bashful flowers
> Declining, hide their beauty from the sun,
> Nor give their spotted bosoms to the gaze
> Of hasty passenger.

On hedge-banks the wild germander of a fine azure blue is conspicuous, and the whole surface of meadows is often covered by the yellow crowfoot. These flowers, also called buttercups, are erroneously supposed to communicate to the butter at this season its rich yellow tinge, as the cows will not touch it on account of its acrid biting quality; this is strikingly visible in pastures, where, though all the grass is cropt to the very roots, the numerous tufts of this weed spring up, flower, and shed their seeds in perfect security and the most absolute freedom from molestation by the cattle; they are indeed cut down and made into hay together with the rest of that rubbish that usually occupies a large proportion of every meadow; and in this state are eaten by cattle, partly because they are incapable of separating them, and partly because by drying their acrimony is considerably subdued; but there can be no doubt of their place being much better supplied by any sort of real grass. In the present age of agricultural improvement the subject of grass lands among others has been a good deal attended to, but much yet remains to be done, and the tracts of the ingenious Stillingfleet, and of Mr. Curtis on this important division of rural economy, are well deserving the notice of every liberal farmer. The excellence of a meadow consists in its producing as much herbage as possible, and that this herbage should be agreeable and nutritious to the animals which are fed with its crop. Every plant of crowfoot therefore ought, if practicable, to be extirpated, for, so far from being grateful and nourishing to any kind of cattle, it is notorious, that in its fresh state nothing will touch it. The same may be said of the hemlock, kex, and other umbelliferous plants[12] which are common in most fields, and which have entirely overrun others; for, these when fresh, are not only noxious to the animals that are fed upon hay, but from their rank and straggling manner of growth, occupy a very large proportion of the ground. Many other plants that are commonly found in meadows may upon the same principles be objected to, and though the present generation of farmers has done much, yet still more remains for their successors to perform.

The gardens now yield an agreeable though immature product in the young gooseberries and currants, which are highly acceptable to our tables, now almost exhausted of their store of preserved fruits.

Early in the month the latest species of the summer birds of passage arrive, generally in the following order: fern-owl or goat-sucker, fly-catcher, and sedge-bird.

This is also the principal time in which birds hatch and rear their young. The assiduity and patience of the female during the task of sitting is admirable, as well as the conjugal affection of the male, who sings to his mate, and often supplies her place; and nothing can exceed the parental tenderness of both when the young are brought to light.

Several species of insects are this month added to those which have already been enumerated; the chief of which are the great white cabbage

---

[12] Plants with flower stalks spreading from a common center. [Ed.]

butterfly (papilio brassicae), the may-chaffer, the favourite food of the fern-owl; the horse fly, or forest fly, so great a plague to horses and cattle, and several kinds of moths and butterflies.

Towards the end of May the beehives send forth their earlier swarms. These colonies consist of the young progeny and some old ones, now grown too numerous to remain in their present habitation, and sufficiently strong and vigorous to provide for themselves. One queen bee is necessary to form each colony; and wherever she flies they follow. Nature directs them to march in a body in quest of a new settlement, which, if left to their choice, would generally be some hollow trunk of a tree. But man, who converts the labours and instincts of so many animals to his own use, provides them with a dwelling and repays himself with their honey. The early swarms are generally the most valuable, as they have time enough to lay in a plentiful store of honey for their subsistence through the winter.

About the same time the glow-worm shines. Of this species of insects the females are without wings and luminous, the males are furnished with wings, but are not luminous; it is probable therefore that this light may serve to direct the male to the haunts of the female, as Hero of Sestos is said to have displayed a torch from the top of a high tower to guide her venturous lover Leander in his dangerous passage across the Hellespont.

> You (i.e. the Sylphs)
> Warm on her mossy couch the radiant worm,
> Guard from cold dews her love illumined form,
> From leaf to leaf conduct the virgin light,
> 5   Star of the earth, and diamond of the night.
>   [ERASMUS] DARWIN.

These little animals are found to extinguish their lamps between eleven and twelve at night.

Old May-day is the usual time for turning out cattle into the pastures, though frequently then very bare of grass. The milk soon becomes more copious, and of finer quality, from the juices of the young grass; and it is in this month that the making of cheese is usually begun in the dairies. Cheshire, Wiltshire, and the low parts of Gloucestershire, are the tracts in England most celebrated for the best cheese.

Many trees and shrubs flower in May, such as the oak, beech, maple, sycamore, barberry, laburnum, horse-chestnut, lilac, mountain ash, and Guelder rose; of the more humble plants the most remarkable are the lily of the valley, and woodrose in woods, the male orchis in meadows, and the lychnis, or cuckoo flower, on hedge-banks.

This month is not a very busy season for the farmer. Some sowing remains to be done in late years; and in forward ones, the weeds, which spring up abundantly in fields and gardens, require to be kept under. The husbandman now looks forwards with anxious hope to the reward of his industry.

> Be gracious, Heaven! for now laborious man
> Has done his part. Ye fostering breezes, blow!
> Ye softening dews, ye tender showers, descend!
> And temper all, thou world-reviving sun,
> 5 Into the perfect year!
>
> THOMSON.

AUGUST

> Fair Plenty now begins her golden reign,
> The yellow fields thick-wave with ripened grain;
> Joyous the swains renew their sultry toils,
> And bear in triumph home the harvest's wealthy spoils.

The commencement of this month is still hot, and usually calm and fair; and those vegetable productions that yet require the powerful influence of the sun are daily advancing to maturity. The farmer beholds the chief object of his culture, and the principal source of his riches, waiting only for the hand of the gatherer. Of the various kinds of grain, rye and oats are usually the first ripened; this, however, varies with the time of sowing, and some of every species may be seen at once fit for cutting.

Every fair day is now of great importance, since, when the corn is once ripe, it is liable to continual damage while standing, either from the shedding of the seeds, the depredations of birds, or sudden storms. The utmost diligence is therefore used by the careful husbandman to get it safely housed, and labourers are hired from all quarters to hasten the work.

> Pour'd from the villages, a numerous train
> Now spreads o'er all the field. In form'd array
> The reapers move, nor shrink for heat or toil,
> By emulation urg'd. Others dispers'd
> 5 Or bind in sheaves, or load or guide the wain
> That tinkles as it passes. Far behind,
> Old age and infancy with careful hand
> Pick up each straggling ear.

This interesting scene is beheld in full perfection only in the open-field countries, where the sight can at once take in an uninterrupted extent of land waving with corn, and a multitude of people engaged in the various parts of the labour. There is no prospect more generally pleasing than this, and which affords a more striking example of the effect of associated sentiments, in converting into a most delightful view that which, in itself considered, is certainly far inferior in variety and beauty to what is daily passed by with indifference or even disgust.

The gathering in of the harvest is a scene that addresses itself not so much to the eye as the heart, and the emotions that it gives birth to are not so much those of delight and surprise, as the satisfactory termination of anxiety, and, in consequence, benevolence to man and gratitude to the Being who fills our stores with plenty, and our minds with gladness.

> Be not too narrow, husbandmen! But fling
> From the full sheaf, with charitable stealth,
> The liberal handful. Think, oh! grateful, think,
> How good the God of harvest is to you,
> 5   Who pours abundance o'er your flowing fields.
>   THOMSON.

In a late season, or where favourable opportunities of getting in the harvest have been neglected, the corn often suffers greatly from heavy storms of wind and rain. It is beaten down to the ground, the seeds are shed or rotted by moisture; or if the weather continues warm, the corn grows, that is, the seeds begin to germinate and put out shoots. Grain in this state is sweet and moist; it soon spoils on keeping; and bread made from it is clammy and unwholesome.

Harvest concludes with the field-peas and beans, which are suffered to become quite dry and hard before they are cut down. The blackness of the bean-pods and stalks is disagreeable to the eye, though the crop is valuable to the farmer. In England they are used as food for cattle only, as the nourishment they afford, though strong, is gross and heavy; but in most of the other European countries they contribute largely to the sustenance of the lower classes.

The rural festival of harvest-home is an extremely natural one, and has been observed in almost all ages and countries. What can more gladden the heart than to see the long-expected products of the year, which have been the cause of so much anxiety, now safely housed and beyond the reach of injury?

> Inwardly smiling, the proud farmer views
> The rising pyramids that grace his yard,
> And counts his large increase; his barns are stor'd
> And groaning staddles bend beneath their load.
>   SOMERVILLE.

The poor labourer, too, who has toiled in securing another's wealth, justly expects to partake of the happiness. The jovial harvest-supper cheers his heart, and induces him to begin, without murmuring, the preparations for a future harvest.

Hops, which are much cultivated in some parts of England, afford their valuable produce generally in this month. The hop is a climbing plant, sometimes growing wild in hedges, and cultivated on account of its use in the making of malt liquors. Having large long roots, they flourish best in a deep and rich soil; and are set in small hills at regular distances from each other, about five plants, and three long poles for them to run upon, being placed in each hill. They appear above ground early in the spring, and as they grow fast, have generally by the latter end of June, or the beginning of July, reached the top of the poles, which are from sixteen to twenty feet long, after which they push out many lateral shoots and begin to flower. At this time the hop gardens make a most beautiful appearance, the poles being entirely covered with verdure, and the flowers depending from them in clusters and light festoons. The hops, which are the scaly seed-vessels of the female plants, are picked as soon as the seed is formed; for which purpose the poles are taken up with the plants clinging to them, and the hops picked off by women and children, after which they are dried over a charcoal fire, and exposed a few days to the air in order to take off the crispness produced by the heat; they are then closely packed in sacks and sent to market, where they are purchased by the brewers, who employ them in giving the fine bitter flavour to their beer, which both improves its taste and makes it keep longer than it otherwise would do. This crop is perhaps the most precarious and uncertain of any, on which account hops are a commodity that is more the object of commercial speculation than any other. The plants are infested by grubs that harbour in their roots, and greatly delay, and sometimes entirely prevent, their shooting; and these grubs changing into flies, swarm upon and destroy the leaves and shoots of such as escaped them in their grub state: this pest is called the fen. Blights, too, of various sorts, both with and without insects, often frustrate the hopes of the cultivator, and in a few days desolate the most promising plantations. No effectual remedy has yet been found for these evils; it is probable, however, that some benefit might be produced by planting a small number of male hops in each garden (for the hop is of that order of vegetables which bear the male and female flowers on different plants). The advantage of this practice is experimentally proved with regard to the ash and elm, which are of the same order; for it is remarked, that the plantations in which there is a mixture of male and female trees, are far more vigorous, and less liable to blights, than those which consist solely of females or males.

The number of plants in flower is now very sensibly diminished. Those of the former months are running fast to seed, and few new ones supply their places. The uncultivated heaths and commons are now, however, in their chief beauty from the flowers of the different kinds of heath or ling, with which they are covered, so as to spread a rich purple hue over the whole ground. Low moist lands, too, are adorned with the gentiana amarella, and the beautiful purple blossoms of the colchicum autumnale, or meadow saffron.

Several species of the numerous tribe of ferns begin now to flower. These plants, together with mosses, lichens, and the various kinds of seaweed, are arranged by botanists in the class *Cryptogamia*, the individuals of which have small inconspicuous and generally colourless flowers, or rather seed vessels, for they have no petals. The tallest species in these kindred families are the ferns, some of which, that are natives of America, greatly resemble, and equal in height, the lower of the kinds of palm trees. They may be distinguished by their pinnated or finely divided winged leaves, and their rust coloured seeds, which are produced in small circular dots, or lines, or patches, on the back of the leaves. One of the commonest species in this country is the fern, or brakes; another not unfrequent sort is the polypody, or harts-tongue, with long undivided leaves of a bright green, adorning with their tufts the base of moist shady rocks: but the most beautiful kind that this island produces is the female, or wood-polypody, with large deep green tufted leaves, very finely divided, frequently found in considerable plenty in rocky woods; when placed in a green-house it acquires a brighter colour, and a more luxuriant growth; it becomes an evergreen and extremely ornamental plant. The uses in the economy of nature of this numerous family are many and important: growing in places where few other vegetables will flourish, as heaths, commons, marshes, and woods, they afford by their broad spreading leaves a very acceptable shelter to various birds, and small quadrupeds, as well as to the more lowly and tender plants; the sweet mucilage with which their roots abound, gives nourishment to many insects, and contributes to the sustenance of the human species in the northern and most barren parts of the globe: in this country, the common brakes are made use of for littering cattle, and thatching, and when green, are burnt in great quantity for the alkali that they contain.

Some of the choicest wall fruits are now coming into season.

> The sunny wall
> Presents the downy peach, the shining plum,
> The ruddy fragrant nectarine, and dark
> Beneath his ample leaf, the luscious fig.

Some time about the middle of the month, the viper brings forth her young: they couple in March or April, and from twelve to twenty-five eggs are formed in the ovary of the female, and hatched there; from which soon after issue the young, nearly of the size of earth-worms.

The insects that make their appearance during this month, are the apis manicata, one of the species of solitary bees; the papilio machaon, semele, phlæas, and paphia, some of the latest butterflies; the phalena pacta, a white moth; and the ptinus pectinicornis, which in its larva state is well known by the holes that it bores in wooden furniture. Flies also abound in windows at this period. Bulls begin their shrill autumnal bellowing.

About the 12th of August the largest of the swallow tribe, the swift, or long-wings, disappears. As the weather is still warm, they cannot be supposed to retire to holes and caverns, and become torpid during the winter; and being so admirably formed for flight, it can scarcely be doubted that they now migrate to some of the southern regions. Nearly at the same time rooks no longer pass the night from home, but roost in their nest trees. Young broods of goldfinches are still seen; lapwings and linnets begin to congregate; and the redbreast, one of our finest, though commonest songsters, renews his music about the end of the month.

Anna (Aikin) Barbauld (1743–1825)

Anna Aikin, later Barbauld, was a popular writer of poetry and occasional prose. Joseph Priestley claimed that it was the reading of his early poetry that persuaded her to try her own hand at verse writing. He also called her "one of the best poets" in England. Her first volume, *Poems,* appeared in 1773 with the encouragement of her brother, John Aikin. The volume was an immediate success and went through four editions in its first year. The following year she published *Miscellaneous Pieces in Prose,* which she coauthored with her brother. Barbauld's poetry includes numerous verses based on careful observation of the natural world: "A Summer Evening's Meditation," "Ode to Spring," "Autumn," "The Caterpillar," "The Lark." "The Mouse's Petition," which follows, describes a captive mouse in Priestley's laboratory in anthropomorphic terms, but the poem also manages to maintain an unsentimental concern for the welfare of nonhuman creatures. Barbauld's letters likewise include numerous indications of her keen abilities as an appreciative observer of natural phenomena. She praised her brother's *Essay on the Application of Natural History to Poetry* as a work that might "bring down our poets from their garrets to wander about the fields."

She married the dissenting minister Rochemont Barbauld in 1774, and the two ran a school in Palgrave, Suffolk. The Barbaulds later moved to Hampstead to be closer to John Aikin. By the 1790s, Anna was writing and publishing a series of radical essays, including "An Appeal to the Opposers of the Repeal of the Corporation and Test Acts" and "Sins of the Government, Sins of the Nation." She spoke out against the slave trade and Britain's war with France and in favor of dissenters and popular education. She collaborated with her brother to publish a collection of children's fables entitled *Evenings at Home* (1793) and contributed to the *Monthly Magazine,* which John edited. Her husband's deteriorating mental condition led her to separate from him in 1808 after he physically attacked her. Rochemont Barbauld committed suicide later that same year.

Wordsworth greatly admired Mrs. Barbauld's writings, praising her especially for her poem "Life." She exchanged works and letters with Hannah More and Madame D'Arblay (Fanny Burney). Her literary associates included Sir Walter Scott, Charles Lamb, Maria Edgeworth, and Elizabeth and Henry Crabb Robinson. She wrote a poem, included here, praising Samuel Taylor Coleridge for his talent and genius. Even late in her life, Barbauld's writings continued to reflect her deep love for nature and her sympathetic identification with living creatures. In a letter written in January of 1814, Anna described her own old age in terms that a naturalist might appreciate: "There are animals that sleep all the winter; I am, I believe, become one of them: they creep into holes during the same season [. . .] If, indeed, a warm sunshiny day occurs, they sometimes creep out of their holes." She remained active as a poet until the 1820s.

From Poems

The Mouse's Petition,[1]
Found in the Trap where he had been confined all Night.

Parcere subjectis, & debellare superbos.
—VIRGIL.[2]

OH! hear a pensive prisoner's prayer,
For liberty that sighs;

Anna Laetitia Barbauld. *Poems.* 4th ed. London: Joseph Johnson, 1774.

[1] To Doctor Priestley. The Author is concerned to find, that what was intended as the petition of mercy against justice, has been construed as the plea of humanity against cruelty. She is certain that cruelty could never be apprehended from the Gentleman to whom this is addressed; and the poor animal would have suffered more as the victim of domestic economy, than of philosophical curiosity.

[2] "To spare the conquered and war down the proud." This is Rome's imperial mission as stated by Virgil, *Aeneid* 6.853. [Ed.]

And never let thine heart be shut
Against the wretch's cries.

5 For here forlorn and sad I sit,
Within the wiry grate;
And tremble at th' approaching morn,
Which brings impending fate.

If e'er thy breast with freedom glow'd,
10 And spurn'd a tyrant's chain,
Let not thy strong oppressive force
A free-born mouse detain.

Oh! do not stain with guiltless blood
Thy hospitable hearth;
15 Nor triumph that thy wiles betray'd
A prize so little worth.

The scatter'd gleanings, of a feast
My frugal meals supply;
But if thine unrelenting heart
20 That slender boon deny,

The cheerful light, the vital air,
Are blessings widely given;
Let nature's commoners enjoy
The common gifts of heaven.

25 The well-taught philosophic mind
To all compassion gives;
Casts round the world an equal eye,
And feels for all that lives.

If mind, as antient sages taught,
30 A never dying flame,
Still shifts thro' matter's varying forms,
In every form the same,

Beware, lest in the worm you crush
A brother's soul you find;
35 And tremble lest thy luckless hand
Dislodge a kindred mind.

Or, if this transient gleam of day
Be *all* of life we share,
Let pity plead within thy breast
40 That little *all* to spare.

So may thy hospitable board
With health and peace be crown'd;
And every charm of heartfelt ease
Beneath thy roof be found.

45 So, when destruction lurks unseen,
Which men like mice may share,
May some kind angel clear thy path,
And break the hidden snare.

To Mrs. P[riestley,]
With some Drawings of Birds and Insects.

The kindred arts to please thee shall conspire,
One dip the pencil, and one string the lyre.

—POPE.

Amanda bids; at her command again
I seize the pencil, or resume the pen;
No other call my willing hand requires,
And friendship, better than a Muse inspires.

5   Painting and poetry are near allied;
The kindred arts two sister Muses guide;
This charms the eye, that steals upon the ear;
There sounds are tun'd; and colours blended here.
This, with a silent touch inchants our eyes,
10 And bids a gayer, brighter world arise:
That, less allied to sense, with deeper art
Can pierce the close recesses of the heart;
By well set syllables, and potent sound,
Can rouse, can chill the breast, can sooth, can wound;
15 To life adds motion, and to beauty soul,
And breathes a spirit through the finish'd whole:
Each perfects each, in friendly union join'd;
This gives Amanda's form, and that her mind.

      But humbler themes my artless hand requires,
20 Nor higher than the feather'd tribe aspires.
Yet who the various nations can declare

That plough with busy wing the peopled air?
These cleave the crumbling bark for insect food;
Those dip their crooked beak in kindred blood;
25 Some haunt the rushy moor, the lonely woods;
Some bathe their silver plumage in the floods;
Some fly to man, his houshold gods implore,
And gather round his hospitable door;
Wait the known call, and find protection there
30 From all the lesser tyrants of the air.

    The tawny Eagle seats his callow brood
High on the cliff, and feasts his young with blood.
On Snowden's rocks, or Orkney's wide domain,
Whose beetling cliffs o'erhang the western main,
35 The royal bird his lonely kingdom forms
Amidst the gathering clouds, and sullen storms:
Thro' the wide waste of air he darts his sight
And holds his sounding pinions pois'd for flight;
With cruel eye premeditates the war,
40 And marks his destin'd victim from afar:
Descending in a whirlwind to the ground,
His pinions like the rush of waters sound;
The fairest of the fold he bears away,
And to his nest compels the struggling prey.
45 He scorns the game by meaner hunters tore,
And dips his talons in no vulgar gore.

    With lovelier pomp along the grassy plain
The silver Pheasant draws his shining train.
Once on the painted banks of Ganges' stream,
50 He spread his plumage to the sunny gleam;
But now the wiry net his flight confines,
He lowers his purple crest, and inly pines.
To claim the verse, unnumber'd tribes appear
That swell the music of the vernal year:
55 Seiz'd with the spirit of the kindly spring
They tune the voice, and sleek the glossy wing:
With emulative strife the notes prolong
And poor out all their little souls in song.
When winter bites upon the naked plain,
60 Nor food nor shelter in the groves remain;
By instinct led, a firm united band,
As marshal'd by some skilful general's hand,

The congregated nations wing their way
In dusky columns o'er the trackless sea;
65 In clouds unnumber'd annual hover o'er
The craggy Bass, or Kilda's utmost shore;[3]
Thence spread their sails to meet the southern wind,
And leave the gathering tempest far behind;
Pursue the circling sun's indulgent ray,
70 Course the swift seasons, and o'ertake the day.

   Not so the insect race, ordain'd to keep
The lazy sabbath of a half-year's sleep:
Entomb'd, beneath the filmy web they lie,
And wait the influence of a kinder sky.
75 When vernal sun-beams pierce their dark retreat
The heaving tomb distends with vital heat;
The full-form'd brood impatient of their cell
Start from their trance, and burst their silken shell;
Trembling awhile they stand, and scarcely dare
80 To launch at once upon the untried air:
At length assur'd, they catch the favouring gale,
And leave their sordid spoils, and high in Ether sail.
So when Rinaldo struck the conscious rind
He found a nymph in every trunk confin'd;[4]
85 The forest labours with convulsive throes,
The bursting trees the lovely births disclose,
And a gay troop of damsels round him stood,
Where late was rugged bark and lifeless wood.
Lo! the bright train their radiant wings unfold,
90 With silver fring'd and freckl'd o'er with gold:
On the gay bosom of some fragrant flower
They idly fluttering live their little hour;
Their life all pleasure, and their task all play,
All spring their age, and sunshine all their day.
95 Not so the child of sorrow, wretched man,
His course with toil concludes, with pain began;
That his high destiny he might discern,
And in misfortune's school this lesson learn,
Pleasure's the portion of th' inferior kind;
100 But glory, virtue, Heaven for Man design'd.

---

[3] Bass Rock and St. Kilda, isolated Scottish islands known for their seabird colonies. [Ed.]
[4] Story from Tasso's *Jerusalem Delivered*. [Ed.]

What atom-forms of insect life appear!
And who can follow nature's pencil here?
Their wings with azure, green, and purple gloss'd
Studded with colour'd eyes, with gems emboss'd,
105 Inlaid with pearl, and mark'd with various stains
Of lively crimson thro' their dusky veins.
Some shoot like living stars, athwart the night,
And scatter from their wings a vivid light,
To guide the Indian to his tawny loves,
105 As thro' the woods with cautious step he moves.
See the proud giant of the beetle race;
What shining arms his polish'd limbs enchase!
Like some stern warrior formidably bright
His steely sides reflect a gleaming light:
110 On his large forehead spreading horns he wears,
And high in air the branching antlers bears:
O'er many an inch extends his wide domain,
And his rich treasury swells with hoarded grain.

Thy friend thus strives to cheat the lonely hour,
115 With song, or paint, an insect, or a flower:
Yet, if Amanda praise the flowing line,
And bend delighted o'er the gay design,
I envy not, nor emulate the fame
Or of the painter's, or the poet's name:
120 Could I to both with equal claim pretend,
Yet far, far dearer were the name of FRIEND.

Letter to John Aikin

Palgrave, 1777.

You have given us too much pleasure lately not to deserve an earlier ac-
knowledgement. I hope you will believe we were not so dilatory in reading
your book[5] as we have been in thanking you for it. It is indeed a most ele-

---

The Works of Anna Laetitia Barbauld. With a Memoir by Lucy Aikin. Vol. 2.
London: Longman, 1825.

[5] *An Essay on the Application of Natural History to Poetry.*

gant performance; your thought is very just, and has never, I believe, been pursued before. Both the defects and beauties which you have noticed are very striking, and the result of the whole work, besides the truths it conveys, is a most pleasing impression left upon the mind from the various and picturesque images brought into view. I hope your Essay will bring down our poets from their garrets to wander about the fields and hunt squirrels. I am clearly of your opinion, that the only chance we have for novelty is by a more accurate observation of the works of Nature, though I think I should not have confined the track quite so much as you have done to the animal creation, because sooner exhausted than the vegetable; and some of the lines you have quoted from Thomson show, with how much advantage the latter may be made the subject of rich description. I think too, since you put me on criticizing, it would not have been amiss if you had drawn the line between the poet and natural historian; and shown how far, and in what cases, the one may avail himself of the knowledge of the other, at what nice period that knowledge becomes so generally spread as to authorise the poetical describer to use it without shocking the ear by the introduction of names and properties not sufficiently familiar, and when at the same time it retains novelty enough to strike. I have seen some rich descriptions of West Indian flowers and plants, just, I dare say, but unpleasing merely because their names were uncouth, and forms not known generally enough to be put into verse. It is not, I own, much to the credit of poets, but it is true, that we do not seem disposed to take their word for any thing, and never willingly receive *information* from them.

We are wondrous busy in preparing our play, *The Tempest;* and four or five of our little ones are to come in as fairies; and I am piecing scraps from the *Midsummer Night's Dream,* &c., to make a little scene instead of the mask of Ceres and Juno. We have read Gibbon lately, who is certainly a very elegant and learned writer, and a very artful one. No other new books have we yet seen, they come slow to Norfolk, but the Diaboliad,[6] the author of which has a pretty sharp pen-knife, and cuts up very handsomely. Many are the literary matters I want to talk over with you when we meet, which I now look forward to as not a far-distant pleasure.

We will come and endeavour to steal away Charles's heart before we run away with his person. Adieu! Heaven bless you and yours.

---

[6] Satirical poem by William Combe (1776). [Ed.]

From Evenings at Home

Animals, and Their Countries

O'er Afric's sand the tawny Lion stalks:
On Phasis' banks the graceful Pheasant walks:
The lonely Eagle builds on Kilda's shore:
Germania's forests feed the tusky Boar:
5 From Alp to Alp the sprightly Ibex bounds:
With peaceful lowings Britain's isle resounds:
The Lapland peasant o'er the frozen meer
Is drawn in sledges by his swift Rein-Deer:
The River-Horse[7] and scaly Crocodile
10 Infest the reedy banks of fruitful Nile:
Dire Dipsas'[8] hiss o'er Mauritania's plain:
And Seals and spouting Whales sport in the Northern Main.

From Monthly Magazine

To Mr. C[olerid]ge

Midway the hill of science, after steep
And rugged paths that tire the unpractised feet,
A grove extends, in tangled mazes wrought,
And filled with strange enchantment: dubious shapes
5 Flit through dim glades, and lure the eager foot
Of youthful ardour to eternal chase.
Dreams hang on every leaf; unearthly forms
Glide through the gloom, and mystic visions swim
Before the cheated sense. Athwart the mists,
10 Far into vacant space, huge shadows stretch
And seem realities; while things of life,
Obvious to sight and touch, all glowing round

London: J.Johnson, 1794.
Monthly Magazine 7 (April 1799): 231–32.
[7]Hippopotamus. [Ed.]
[8]Venomous serpent.[Ed.]

Fade to the hue of shadows. *Scruples* here
With filmy net, most like the autumnal webs
15 Of floating gossamer, arrest the foot
Of generous enterprise; and palsy hope
And fair ambition, with the chilling touch
Of sickly hesitation and blank fear.
Nor seldom *Indolence,* these lawns among
20 Fixes her turf-built seat, and wears the garb
Of deep philosophy, and museful sits,
In dreamy twilight of the vacant mind,
Soothed by the whispering shade; for soothing soft
The shades; and vistas lengthening into air,
25 With moon beam rainbows tinted. Here each mind
Of finer mould, acute and delicate,
In its high progress to eternal truth
Rests for a space, in fairy bowers entranced;
And loves the softened light and tender gloom;
30 And, pampered with most unsubstantial food,
Looks down indignant on the grosser world,
And matter's cumbrous shapings. Youth beloved
Of science—of the Muse beloved, not here,
Not in the maze of metaphysic lore
35 Build thou thy place of resting! lightly tread
The dangerous ground, on noble aims intent;
And be this Circe of the studious cell
Enjoyed, but still subservient. Active scenes
Shall soon with healthful spirit brace thy mind:
40 And fair exertion, for bright fame sustained.
For friends, for country, chase each spleen-fed fog
That blots the wide creation—
Now heaven conduct thee with a parent's love!

Joseph Priestley (1733–1804)

Priestley was a scientist whose interests reached far beyond the laboratory. He was one of the most wide ranging thinkers in an era known for its polymaths. Priestley produced important work in theology, history, politics, education, and English grammar, as well as groundbreaking experimental science. Here he comments on his own early poetic interests and influences: "I was myself far from having any pretension to the character of a poet; but in the early part of my life I was a great versifier, and this [. . .] contributed to the ease with which I always wrote prose. Mrs. Barbauld has told me that it was the perusal of some verses of mine that first induced her to write any thing in verse, so that this country is in some measure indebted to me for one of the best poets it can boast of. Several of her first poems were written at my house, on occasions that occurred while she was there" (*Memoirs* 1: 49). Priestley's scientific contributions are too numerous to list in a brief summary. He is credited with the discovery of oxygen, which he called dephlogisticated air. He was clearly the first experimenter to realize the importance of the colorless and odorless gas that caused a candle flame to burn with particular intensity. In addition to discovering ammonia, sulfur dioxide, nitrogen, and carbon monoxide, Priestley described the significance of sunlight to plant growth, and he explained the production of oxygen during photosynthesis.

Perhaps Priestley's most significant contribution beyond the laboratory was to the theological thinking of his time. He remained a dissenting minister throughout his decades as a scientist, and he published books, sermons, and tracts, including the *History of the Corruptions of Christianity,* in which he rejected the Trinity and any form of predestination. He pointed out numerous historical errors in the Bible, a text which he claimed could not have been divinely inspired. He moved through various stages of dissent, from the Calvinism of his childhood, through Arianism (which denied the divinity of Christ), toward Unitarianism of a kind that was echoed in the sentiments of many Romantic thinkers and writers. He also contributed to the understanding of the English language with *The Rudiments of English Grammar* (1761), perhaps the first grammar text to reply on spoken and written usage rather than on classical models.

Priestley spoke out forcefully in favor of civil and religious liberties. In recognition of his interdisciplinary accomplishments in language, religious history, and applied science, Edinburgh University awarded him an honorary degree. He was a member of the Lunar Society in Birmingham, where he engaged in discussions about links between science and the practical arts (industry and craft) with Erasmus Darwin, Josiah Wedgwood, and James Watt. Samuel Taylor Coleridge described him, in "Religious Musings" (1796), as "Patriot, and Saint, and Sage." Priestley's house, along with his library and laboratory, was destroyed by an antirevolutionary mob during riots in Birmingham on the second anniversary (1791) of the fall of the Bastille. He subsequently emigrated to the banks of the Susquehanna River in Northumberland, Pennsylvania, where he died. Priestley's life in America contributed to the unrealized plan by the poets Coleridge and Robert Southey to found a "pantisocratic" utopia in Pennsylvania.

Included here are selections from *The History and Present State of Electricity,* including disturbing descriptions of experiments on animals, which suggest just how far scientists of the time were willing to go in search of new knowledge. Unlike Mary Shelley's fictional Victor Frankenstein, however, Priestley admits that "it is paying dear for philosophical discoveries, to purchase them at the expence of humanity." The second extract comes from Priestley's debate with Erasmus Darwin on the subject of "spontaneous generation," a topic which neither scientists nor poets seemed able to ignore during this revolutionary era.

———

From The History and Present State of Electricity

FROM THE PREFACE

Natural history exhibits a boundless variety of scenes, and yet infinitely analogous to one another. A naturalist has, consequently, all the pleasure which the contemplation of uniformity and variety can give the mind; and this is one of the most copious sources of our intellectual pleasures. He is likewise entertained with a prospect of gradual improvement, while he sees every object in nature rising by due degrees to its maturity and perfection. And while new plants, new animals, and new fossils are perpetually pouring in upon him, the most pleasing views of the unbounded power, wisdom, and goodness of God are constantly present to his mind. But he has no direct view of human sentiments and human actions; which, by means of their endless associations, greatly heighten and improve all the pleasures of taste.

The history of philosophy enjoys, in some measure, the advantages both of civil and natural history, whereby it is relieved from what is most tedious and disgusting in both. Philosophy exhibits the powers of nature, discovered and directed by human art. It has, therefore, in some measure, the boundless variety with the amazing uniformity of the one, and likewise every thing that is pleasing and interesting in the other. And the idea of continual rise and improvement is conspicuous in the whole study, whether we be attentive to the part which nature, or that which men are acting in the great scene.

It is here that we see the human understanding to its greatest advantage, grasping at the noblest objects, and increasing its own powers, by acquiring to itself the powers of nature, and directing them to the accomplishment of its own views: whereby the security, and happiness of mankind are daily improved. Human abilities are chiefly conspicuous in adapting means to ends, and in deducing one thing from another by the method of analogy; and where shall we find instances of greater sagacity, than in philosophers diversifying the situations of things, in order to give them an opportunity of showing their mutual relations, affections, and influences; deducing one truth and one discovery from another, and applying them all to the useful purposes of human life.

Joseph Priestley. *The History and Present State of Electricity with Original Experiments,* 3rd ed. London: Bathurst, Lowndes, J. Johnson, 1775.

Joseph Priestley's laboratory equipment. Notice mouse in foreground bell jar and plant growing in jar to the far right. A number of Priestley's experiments were designed to reveal the effect of oxygen or its absence on living creatures.

If the exertion of human abilities, which cannot but form a delightful spectacle for the human imagination, give us pleasure, we enjoy it here in a higher degree than while we are contemplating the schemes of warriors, and the stratagems of their bloody art. Besides, the object of philosophical pursuits throws a pleasing idea upon the scenes they exhibit; whereas a reflection upon the real objects and views of most statesmen and conquerors cannot but take from the pleasure, which the idea of their sagacity, foresight, and comprehension would otherwise give to the virtuous and benevolent mind. Lastly, the investigation of the powers of nature, like the study of Natural History, is perpetually suggesting to us views of the divine perfections and providence, which are both pleasing to the imagination, and improving to the heart.

But though other kinds of history may, in some respects, vie with that of philosophy, nothing that comes under the denomination of history can exhibit instances of so fine a rise and improvement in things, as we see in the progress of the human mind, in philosophical investigations. [. . .]

EXPERIMENTS ON ANIMALS.

As I have constructed an electrical battery of considerably greater force than any other that I have yet heard of, and as I have sometimes exposed animals to the shock of it, and have particularly attended to several circumstances, which have been overlooked, or misapprehended by others; it may not be improper to relate a few of the cases, in which the facts were, in any respect, new, or worth notice.

June the 4th.—I killed a rat with the discharge of two jars, each containing three square feet of coated glass. The animal died immediately, after being universally convulsed, at the instant of the stroke. After some time, it was carefully dissected; but there was no internal injury perceived, particularly no extravasation,[1] either in the abdomen, thorax, or brain.

June the 19th.—I killed a pretty large kitten with the discharge of a battery of thirty-three square feet; but no other effect was observed, except that a red spot was found on the pericranium, where the fire entered. I endeavoured to bring it to life, by distending the lungs, blowing with a quill into the trachea, but to no purpose. The heart beat a short time after the stroke, but respiration ceased immediately.

June the 21st.—I killed a small field-mouse with the discharge of a battery of thirty-six square feet, but no other effect was perceived, except that the hair of the forehead was singed, and in part torn off. There was no extravasation any where, though the animal was so small, and the force with which it was killed so great. This fact, and many others of a similar nature, make me suspect some mistake, in cases where larger animals are said to have had all their blood vessels burst by a much inferior force.

In all the accounts that I have met with of animals killed by the electric shock, the victims were either small quadrupeds, or fowls; and they are all represented as killed so suddenly, that it could not be seen how they were affected previous to their expiration. In some of my experiments, the great force of my battery has afforded me a pretty fair opportunity of observing in what manner the animal system is affected by the electric shock, the animals which I have exposed to it being pretty large; so that a better judgment may be formed of their sensations, and consequently of the immediate cause of their death, by external signs. I do not pretend to draw any conclusion myself from the following facts. I have only noted them as carefully as I could for the use of physicians and anatomists.

June the 26th.—I discharged a battery of thirty-eight square feet of coated glass, through the head, and out at the tail of a full grown cat, three

---

[1] Leaking of fluids. [Ed.]

or four years old. At that instant, she was violently convulsed all over. After a short respite, there came on smaller convulsions, in various muscles, particularly on the sides; which terminated in a violent convulsive respiration, attended with a rattling in the throat. This continued five minutes, without any motion that could be called breathing, but was succeeded by an exceedingly quick respiration, which continued near half an hour. Towards the end of this time, she was able to move her head, and fore feet, so as to push herself backwards on the floor; but she was not able to move her hind feet in the least, notwithstanding the shock had not passed through them. While she continued in this condition, I gave her a second stroke, which was attended, as before, with the violent convulsion, the short respite, and the convulsive respiration; in which, after continuing about a minute, she died.

Being willing to try, for once, the effect of a much greater shock than that which killed the cat upon a large animal, I gave an explosion of sixty-two square feet of coated glass to a dog of the size of a common cur. The moment he was struck, which was on the head (but, not having a very good light, I could not tell exactly where) all his limbs were extended, he fell backwards, and lay without any motion, or sign of life for about a minute. Then followed convulsions, but not very violent, in all his limbs; and after that a convulsive respiration, attended with a small rattling in the throat. In about four minutes from the time that he was struck, he was able to move, though he did not offer to walk till about half an hour after; in all which time, he kept discharging a great quantity of saliva; and there was also a great flux of rheum from his eyes, on which he kept putting his feet; though in other respects he lay perfectly listless. He never opened his eyes all the evening in which he was struck, and the next morning he appeared to be quite blind, though seemingly well in every other respect.

Having dispatched the dog, by shooting him through the hinder part of his head, I examined one of his eyes (both of which had an uniform blueish cast, like a film over the pupil) and found all the three humours perfectly transparent, and, as far as could be judged, in their right state; but the cornea was throughout white and opaque, like a bit of gristle, and remarkably thick.

Before this experiment, I had imagined, that animals struck blind by lightning had probably a *gutta serena*,[2] on account of the concussion which is seemingly given to the nervous system by the electric shock; whereas this case was evidently an inflammation, occasioned by the explosion being

---

[2] Form of blindness in which the pupil remains clear. [Ed.]

made so near the eyes, terminating in a species of the *albugo;*[3] but which I suppose would have been incurable. One of the eyes of this dog was affected a little more than the other; owing, probably, to the stroke being made a little nearer to one eye than the other. I intended to give the stroke about an inch above the eyes.

In order to ascertain the effects of electricity on an animal body, I, after this, began a course of experiments on the conducting power of its constituent parts; and for some time imagined that a piece of spinal marrow of an ox conducted sensibly worse than the muscular flesh; but after a great number of trials with pieces of spinal marrow from various animals, and pieces of muscular flesh, of the same size and form, and in various states of moisture and dryness, I gave up that opinion as fallacious; but I cannot help wishing the experiments were resumed with some more accurate measure of conducting power than hath yet been contrived.

Being willing to observe, if possible, the immediate effect of the electric shock on the heart and lungs of animals, I gave, June the 5th, a shock from six square feet to a frog, in which the thorax had been previously laid open, so that the pulsation of the heart might be seen. Upon receiving the stroke, the lungs were instantly inflated: and, together with the other contents of the thorax, thrown quite out of the body. The heart, however, continued to beat, though very languidly, and there was no other sign of life for about ten minutes. After that, a motion was first perceived under its jaws; which was propagated, by degrees, to the muscles of the sides; and at last the creature seemed as if it would have come to life, if it had not been so much mangled. The stroke entered the head, and went out at the hind feet.

June the 6th.—I discharged a battery of thirty-three square feet through the head and whole extended body of another frog. Immediately upon receiving the stroke, there was, as it were, a momentary distention of all the muscles of the body, and it remained shrivelled up in a most surprising manner. For about five minutes there appeared no sign of life, and the pulsation of the heart could not be felt with the finger. But afterwards, there first appeared a motion under the jaws, then all along the sides, attended with convulsive motions of the other parts, and in about an hour it became, to all appearance, as well as ever.

The same day, I gave the same stroke to two other frogs. They were affected in the same manner, and perfectly recovered in less than three hours.

These facts surprised me very much. I attribute the recovery of the frogs partly to the moisture, which always seems to cover their body, and which might transmit a good part of the shock; and partly to that provision in

---

[3] White spots on the Cornea. [Ed.]

their constitution, whereby they can subsist a long time without breathing. To ascertain this, I would have given the shock to toads, serpents, fishes, &c. and various other exanguious animals, but I had not an opportunity. Besides, it is paying dear for philosophical discoveries, to purchase them at the expence of humanity. . . .

Observations and Experiments Relating to Equivocal, or Spontaneous, Generation

Read, Nov. 18th, 1803.

There is nothing in modern philosophy that appears to me so extraordinary, as the revival of what has long been considered as the exploded doctrine of *equivocal,* or, as Dr. Darwin calls it, *spontaneous generation;*[4] by which is meant the production of organized bodies from substances that have no organization, as plants and animals from no pre-existing germs of the same kinds, plants without seeds, and animals without sexual intercourse.

The germ of an organized body, the seed of a plant, or the embrio of an animal, in its first discoverable state, is now found to be the future plant or animal in miniature, containing every thing essential to it when full grown, only requiring to have the several organs enlarged, and the interstices filled with extraneous nutritious matter. When the external form undergoes the greatest change, as from an aquatic insect to a flying gnat, a caterpillar to a crysalis, a crysalis to a butterfly, or a tadpole to a frog, there is nothing new

---

Transactions of the American Philosophical Society. 6.1. Philadelphia: Conrad; London: Mawman, 1804.

[4]Thus the tall oak, the giant of the wood,
Which bears Britannia's thunders on the flood;
The whale, unmeasured monster of the main,
The lordly lion, monarch of the plain,
The eagle soaring in the realms of air,
Whose eye undazzled drinks the solar glare,
Imperious man, who rules the bestial crowd,
Of language, reason, and reflection proud,
With brow erect who scorns this earthly sod,
And styles himself the image of his God;
Arose from rudiments of form and sense,
An embrion point, or microscopic ens!!!
                                    Temple of Nature.

(Priestley's note from Erasmus Darwin. [Ed.])

in the organization; all the parts of the gnat, the butterfly, and the frog, having really existed, though not appearing to the common observer in the forms in which they are first seen. In like manner, every thing essential to the oak is found in the acorn.

It is now, however, maintained that bodies as exquisitely organized as any that we are acquainted with (for this is true of the smallest insect, as well as of the largest animal) arise, without the interposition of a creative power, from substances that have no organization at all, from mere brute matter—earth, water, or mucilage, in a certain degree of heat. Sometimes the term *organic particles* is made use of, as the origin of the plants and animals that are said to be produced this way; but as it is without meaning, the germs of those specific plants and animals which are said to come from them, and a great variety of these organized bodies are said to arise from the same organic particles, the case is not materially different. Still, completely organized bodies, of specific kinds, are maintained to be produced from substances that could not have any natural connexion with them, or particular relation to them. And this I assert is nothing less than the production of an effect without any adequate cause. If the organic particle, from which an oak is produced be not precisely an acorn, the production of it from any thing else is as much a miracle, and out of the course of nature, as if it had come from a bean, or a pea, or absolutely from nothing at all; and if miracles be denied, (as they are, I believe, by all the advocates for this doctrine of equivocal generation,) these plants and animals, completely organized as they are found to be, as well adopted to their destined places and uses in the general system as the largest plants and animals, have no intelligent cause whatever, which is unquestionably atheism. For if one part of the system of nature does not require an intelligent cause, neither does any other part, or the whole.

As Dr. Darwin presses my observations on the green matter, on which I formerly made some experiments, as producing dephlogisticated air by the influence of light, into the service of his hypothesis; I have this last summer given some attention to them, and have diversified them with that view; and from these it will appear that they are far from serving his purpose; since none of this green matter, which he does not doubt to be a vegetable, though of the smallest kind, is produced in any water, though ever so proper for it, unless its surface has been more or less exposed to the atmosphere, from which, consequently, the invisible seeds of this vegetable may come.

He says (*Temple of Nature, notes p. 4.*) "not only microscopic animals appear to be produced by a spontaneous vital process, and these quickly improve by solitary generation, like the buds of trees, or like the polypus and aphis, but there is one vegetable body which appears to be produced by a spontaneous vital process, and is believed to be propagated and enlarged in so short a time by solitary generation, as to become visible to the naked eye. I mean the green vegetable matter first attended to by Dr. Priestley, and called by him *conserva fontinalis*. The proofs that this material is a vegetable are from its giving up so much oxygen when exposed to the sun shine, as it grows in water, and from its green colour."

"D. Ingenhouz asserts that by filling a bottle with well-water, and inverting it immediately into a bason of well-water, this green vegetable is formed in great quantity; and he believes that the water itself, or some substance contained in the water, is converted into this kind of vegetation which then quickly propagates itself."

"Mr. Girtanner asserts that this green vegetable matter is not produced by water and heat alone, but requires the sun's light for this purpose, as he observed by many experiments, and thinks it arises from decomposing water deprived of a part of its oxygen; and he laughs at Dr. Priestley for believing that the seeds of this conserva, and the parents of microscopic animals, exist universally in the atmosphere, and penetrate the sides of glass jars." *Philosophical Magazine for May* 1800.

He further says, p. 9, "The green vegetable matter of Dr. Priestley, which is universally produced in stagnant water, and the mucor, or mouldiness, which is seen on the surface of all putrid vegetable and animal matter, have probably no parents, but a spontaneous origin from the congress of the decomposing organic articles, and afterwards propagate themselves."

Let us now compare this language with that of nature in my experiments. On the first of July I placed in the open air several vessels containing pump-water, two of them covered with olive oil, one in a phial with a ground glass stopper, one with a loose tin cover, and the rest with the surface of the water exposed to the atmosphere; and having found (as may be seen in the account of my former experiments on this green matter) that it was produced with the greatest facility, and in the greatest abundance, when a small quantity of vegetable matter, especially thin slices of raw potatoes, was put into the water, I put equal quantities, viz. twenty grains of potatoe, into each of the larger vessels and ten into each of the smaller. Into two very large decanters, the mouths of which were narrow, I put fifty grains of the same, one of them having oil on its surface, and the other none. At the same time having filled a large phial with the same water, I inverted it in a vessel of mercury.

In about a week the wide mouthed open vessel began to have green matter, and the large decanter with the narrow mouth had the same appearance in three weeks. On the first of August the vessel which had a loose tin cover, coming about half an inch below its edge, had a slight tinge of green, and on the first of September the phial with the ground glass stopper (but which, appeared by some of the water escaping, not to fit exactly) began to have green matter. But none of the vessels that were covered with oil, or that which had its mouth inverted in mercury, had any green matter at all on the 12th of September; when, having waited as I thought long enough, I put an end to the experiment.

Here we see that the wider was the mouth of the vessel, the sooner did the green matter appear in it; but that in time the germ (or whatever it may be called that produced it) found its way through the smallest apertures, and were ascended into the vessel with the tin cover before it could descend into it; but that when all access to the water was precluded by a covering of oil, or a quantity of mercury, no green matter was produced. These experiments, therefore, are far from favouring the doctrine of spontaneous generation, but are perfectly agreeable to the supposition that the seeds of this small vegetable float in the air, and insinuate themselves into water of a kind proper for their growth, through the smallest apertures.

Among the experimental facts, as Dr. Darwin calls them, in the support of his hypothesis, he says, p. 3. "that one or more of four persons, whom he names, put some boiling veal broth into a phial previously heated in the fire, and sealing it up hermetically, or with wax, observed it to be replete with animalcules in three or four days." But he should have said which of these four persons made the experiment, and have referred to the passage in their writings in which it is mentioned. Otherwise no judgment can be formed of its accuracy. And why did not the Doctor repeat the experiment himself, since it is so easily done? Besides, we know that even the heat of boiling water will not destroy some kinds of insects, and probably much less the eggs, or embryo's, of them.

He adds that "to suppose the eggs of former microscopic animals to float in the atmosphere, and pass through the sealed glass phial, is so contrary to apparent nature, as to be totally incredible." But who does, or would suppose this. That various animalcules, as well as the seeds of various plants, invisible to us, do float in the atmosphere, is unquestionable; but that they pass through glass I never heard before, though in a preceeding paragraph it is ascribed to myself. He adds, "as the latter are viviparous, it is equally absurd to suppose that their parents float universally in the atmosphere, to lay their young in paste or vinegar." To me, however, this does not appear to be at all impossible; and it is observation of facts, and not conjecture, that must determine the question of probability.

"Some other fungi" he says p. 9. "as those growing in close wine vaults, or others which arise from decaying trees, or rotten timber, may perhaps be owing to a similar spontaneous production, and not previously exist as perfect organic beings in the juices of the wood, as some have supposed. In the same manner it would seem that the common esculent mushroom is produced from horse dung at any time, and in any place, as is the common practice of many gardeners." This requires no particular answer. Decaying trees &c. may afford a proper *nidus*[5] for the seeds of vegetables that are invisible to us; and that any of them previously exist in the juices of the tree, was I believe, never supposed. The horse dung also may afford a proper nidus for the seeds of the mushroom. Besides these are only random observations, and the facts have never been investigated in an accurate philosophical manner.

It is said by many, that the different kinds of worms which are found in animal bodies have their origin there, and from no worms of the same kinds, but from the unorganized matter of which our food consists. But according to later observations, most of these very worms have been found out of the body, and therefore there is nothing improbable in the supposition of the seminal matter from which they came having been conveyed into the body in the food, &c. and if some of them have been found out of the body, the rest may in time be found out of it also. It is, besides, unworthy of philosophers to draw important conclusions from mere ignorance.

Having recited these facts, and supposed facts, I shall consider distinctly all that Dr. Darwin has advanced by way of argument in defence of the system that he has espoused.

He supposes, what no person will deny, that "dead organic matter, or that which had contributed to the growth of vegetable and animal bodies, may by chemical attractions, in the organs of plants and animals, contribute to the nourishment of other plants and animals." But he adds, p. 6. "the same particles of organic matter may form spontaneous microscopic animals, or microscopic vegetables, by chemical dissolutions, and new combinations of organic matter, in watery fluids, with sufficient moisture."

But these microscopic vegetables and animals, there is every reason to think, have as complete and exquisite an organic structure as the larger plants and animals, and have as evident marks of design in their organization, and therefore could not have been formed by any decomposition or composition of such dead matter, whether called organic or not, without the interposition of an intelligent author. Besides, these microscopic vegetables and animals are infinitely various, and therefore could never arise from the same dead materials, in the same circumstances, by the mere application of warmth and moisture. Each of these vegetables and animals must, according to the analogy of nature, have proceeded from an organized germ, containing all the necessary parts of the future plant or animal, as well as the largest trees and animals, though their minuteness elude our

---

[5]Nest or place to deposit seeds. [Ed.]

search, and though the manner in which their seeds or germs are conveyed from place to place be unknown to us. But the attention that is given to this subject by ingenious naturalists is continually discovering a greater analogy between these microscopic vegetables, and animals and those of the largest kinds. This argument from the production of minute plants and animals has no force but from our ignorance.

"It is as difficult," he says, p.7. "to understand the attraction of the parts of coutchouk,[6] and other kinds of attraction, as the spontaneous production of a fibre from decomposing animal or vegetable substances, which contracts in a similar manner, and this constitutes the primordia of life." But admitting that the power by which a fibre contracts to be not more difficult to comprehend than other contractions, and that fibres are the primordia of life, whence comes the regular arrangement of these fibres, and the various system of vessels formed by them, for the purposes of nutrition, the propagation of the species, &c. in the complex structure of these minute animals. There is nothing like that in the coutchouk, or any other substance that is not an animal.

Microscopic vegetables and animals remaining without any visible sign of life months and years is no proof that they were capable of deriving their origin from dead unorganized matter. While their organization is not destroyed, the motions which indicate life may be restored by proper degrees of heat and moisture; but this is not materially different from the case of frogs and other animals, which discover no sign of life, a great part of the winter, and revive with the warmth of spring.

That any thing composing an animal or vegetable should, after affording nutriment to other animals, attain some kind of organization, or even vitality, may be admitted; because the digestive powers of animals may not be able to destroy their organization, or vitality. But if it remain uninjured, and be afterwards revived, it cannot be any thing besides the very same organization that it had before. So birds feed upon seeds, which yet retain so much of their organization, and life, as to be able to produce the plants from which they came, but never any of a different kind. Beyond this no analogy in nature can carry us.

"These microscopic organic bodies," he says, p. 8. "are multiplied and enlarged by solitary re-production, without sexual intercourse, till they acquire greater perfection, or new properties. Liewenhook observed in rain water which had stood a few days, the smallest scarcely visible animalcules and in a few days more he observed others eight times as large." But this proves nothing more than an increase in bulk, and no change of a small an-

---

[6]India rubber plant. [Ed.]

imal into a larger of a different kind, which the argument requires. If it was the same animal that assumed a new form, in a more advanced state, it is no more than the case of a tadpole and a frog, or a caterpillar and butterfly. That several insects are multiplied without sexual intercourse is no proof of spontaneous generation. Plants are several ways produced without seeds; and according to Dr. Darwin's observations, this mode of animal re-production has its limits. For that after a certain number of such generations the last discover the properties of sex, and then produce others by sexual intercourse, so that it is probable, that if at that time they could be kept from sexual intercourse the re-production would cease.

Dr. Darwin, and all other advocates for spontaneous generation, speaks of some animals as simple and others as complete, some as imperfect and others as perfect; whereas, as far as we can discover, all animals, even the most minute that have been examined, appear to be as perfect, and to have a structure as wonderfully complicated, as the largest, though on account of their minuteness, we cannot dissect them to so much advantage. Their organs are equally adapted to their situations and occasions; and what is more, they have as great a degree of intelligence (which they discover by the methods of seeking their food, avoiding, or contending with their enemies) as the largest animals: besides, it is never pretended that any large species of animals, though called imperfect, as crabs and oysters, are ever produced by spontaneous generation.

The larger kinds of the more perfect animals Dr. Darwin does not pretend to have ever been "produced immediately in this mode of spontaneous generation;" but he supposes, what is even more improbable, viz. that "vegetables and animals improve by re-production; so that spontaneous vitality (p. 1.) is only to be looked for in the simplest organic beings, as in the smallest microscopic animalcules, which perpetually perhaps however enlarge themselves by re-production; and that the larger and more complicated animals have acquired their present perfection by successive generations, during an uncounted series of ages."

By this he must have meant to insinuate, for it is not clearly expressed (perhaps to avoid the ridicule of it) that lions, horses, and others, which he considers as more complicated animals, though they are not more so than flies and other insects, may have arisen from animals of different kinds, in the lowest state of organization, in fact, that they were once nothing more than microscopic animalcules.

But this is far from being analogous to any thing that we observe in the course of nature. We see no plants or animals, though ever so simple, growing to more than a certain size, and producing their like, and never any others organized in a different manner. Is it at all probable that lions, horses or elephants, were ever any other than they now are? Were they originally microscopic? And if they come to be what they now are by successive generations, why does not the change and improvement go on? Do we ever see any small animal become a larger of a different kind? Do any mice become rats, rats become dogs, or wolves, wasps become hornets, and yet this is precisely the analogy that the hypothesis requires.

In order to obviate the prejudice against this doctrine of spontaneous production, as favouring atheism, Dr. Darwin says of the objectors, p. 1. "They do not recollect that God created all things which exist, and that these have been from the beginning in a perpetual state of improvement, which appears from the globe itself, as well as from the animals and vegetables which possess it. And lastly, that there is more dignity in our idea of the Supreme Author of all things, when we conceive Him to be the cause of causes, than the cause simply of the events which we see, if there can be any difference in infinity of power."

The Supreme Being is, no doubt, the cause of all causes; but these causes have a regular connexion, which we are able to trace; and if any thing be produced in any different manner, we say it is not according to the course of nature, but a miracle. The world is, no doubt, in a state of improvement; but notwithstanding this, we see no change in the vegetable or animal systems, nor does the history of the most remote times favour the hypothesis. The plants and animals described in the book of Job are the same that they are now, and so are the dogs, asses, and lions of Homer.

Vegetables and animals do not by any improvement, natural or artificial, change into one another, or into vegetables and animals of other species. It is, therefore, contrary to analogy, or the established course of nature, that they should do so. If miracles; which imply an omnipotent and designing power (and which to the generality of mankind are the most striking proofs of the existence of such a power, and a power distinct from the visible parts of nature, the laws of which it counteracts) be denied, all changes that take place contrary to the observed analogy of nature must be events without a cause; and if one such event can take place, any others might, and consequently the whole system might have had no superior designing cause; and if there be any such thing as atheism, this is certainly it.

Dr. Darwin speaks of his organic particles as possessed of certain appetencies, or powers of attraction. But whence came these powers, or any others, such as those of electricity, magnetism? These powers discover as much wisdom, by their adaptation to each other, and their use in the general system, as the organic bodies which he supposes them to form; so that the supposition of these powers, which must have been imparted *ab extra,* only removes the difficulty he wishes to get quit of one step farther, and there it is left in as much force as ever. There are still marks of design, and therefore the necessity of a designing cause.

Oliver Goldsmith (1728–1774)

Oliver Goldsmith's *History of the Earth and Animated Nature* has been described as everything from "hackwork" to his "most substantial literary legacy" (Wardle 1957). The first edition (in eight volumes) appeared posthumously in London in 1774. The work sought to draw together all that was known about the planet Earth, its plants and animals, and even its human inhabitants described from a biological perspective. Goldsmith derived almost all of his information from the work of other naturalists, and he set out with a very Romantic goal in mind. He had first planned to translate Pliny's *Natural History,* but then, after reading Buffon, he decided that "the best imitation of the ancients was to write from our own feelings, and to imitate nature." This linking of emotion to observation of the natural world echoed precisely the claim that many poets would be making during the next century. Goldsmith's *Animated Nature* went through more than twenty editions in England and America. Although it can be criticized on technical grounds, the work became the source of what countless individuals in the English-speaking world knew about the natural world around them. Like much of Goldsmith's popular writing, *Animated Nature* drew on research and speculation by other authors and translators, but these ideas were made more concise and lively by Goldsmith's engaging and lucid prose style. Editions of Goldsmith's popular natural history remained on thousands of family and school bookshelves well into the Victorian era.

Goldsmith wrote with clarity and technical precision, even though he did not represent himself as a scientist. He describes, for example, one of the most common confusions in the natural history of the period in his discussion of the border between plants and animals:

> It frequently puzzles the naturalist to tell exactly where animal life begins, and vegetable terminates; nor, indeed, is it easy to resolve,

whether some objects offered to view be of the lowest of the animal, or the highest of the vegetable races. The sensitive plant, that moves at the touch, seems to have as much perception as the fresh water polypus, that is possessed of a still slower share of motion. Besides, the sensitive plant will not reproduce upon cutting in pieces, which the polypus is known to do; so that the vegetable production seems to have the superiority. ("History of Animals" 3)

He weighed in on the side of those who believed that all human races derived from a single type, admitting that great changes seemed able to occur in members of a species, including our own. His discussion of human beings takes place, significantly, in a section of his work entitled "A History of Animals." Goldsmith's collection of work from Linnaeus, Buffon, and Ray, among others, reproduced errors of fact and of emphasis, and his text included long sections of direct translation, but his *Animated Nature* came to have an influence far in excess of its value as science. Dr. Samuel Johnson wrote an epitaph in Westminster Abbey that affirms the importance of natural history in Goldsmith's career: "To the Memory of Oliver Goldsmith: poet, naturalist and historian."

From An History of the Earth and Animated Nature

FROM THE PREFACE

[*Defining Natural History*]

Some practice therefore, much instruction and diligent reading, are requisite to make a ready and expert naturalist, who shall be able, even by the help of a system, to find out the name of every object he meets with. But when this tedious, though requisite part of study is attained, nothing but delight and variety attend the rest of his journey. Wherever he travels, like a man in a country where he has many friends, he meets with nothing but

Oliver Goldsmith, *An History of the Earth and Animated Nature*. 8 vols. Dublin: James Williams, 1782.

acquaintances and allurements in all the stages of his way. The meer un-
informed spectator passes on in gloomy solitude; but the naturalist, in
every insect, and every pebble, finds something to entertain his curiosity,
and excite his speculation.

From hence it appears, that a system may be considered as a dictionary
in the study of nature. The ancients, however, who have all written most
delightfully on this subject, seem entirely to have rejected those humble
and mechanical helps to science. They contented themselves with seizing
upon the great outlines of history, and passing over what was common, as
not worth detail; they only dwelt upon what was new, great, and surprizing, and sometimes even warmed the imagination at the expence of truth.
Such of the moderns as revived this science in Europe undertook the task
more methodically, though not in a manner so pleasing. Aldrovandus,
Gesner, and Johnson, seemed desirous of uniting the entertaining and rich
descriptions of the ancients with the dry and systematic arrangement, of
which they were the first projectors. This attempt, however, was extremely
imperfect, as the great variety of nature was, as yet, but very inadequately
known. Nevertheless, by attempting to carry on both objects at once; first,
of directing us to the name of the thing; and then giving the detail of its
history, they drew out their works into a tedious and unreasonable length;
and thus mixing incompatible aims they have left their labours, rather to
be occasionally consulted than read with delight by posterity.

The later moderns, with that good sense which they have carried into
every other part of science, have taken a different method in cultivating
natural History. They have been content to give, not only the brevity, but
also the dry and disgusting air of a dictionary to their systems. Ray, Klin,
Brisson, and Linnæus, have had only one aim, that of pointing out the
object in nature, of discovering its name, and where it was to be found in
those authors that treated of it in a more prolix and satisfactory manner.
Thus natural history at present is carried on, in two distinct and separate
channels, the one serving to lead us to the thing, the other conveying the
history of the thing, as supposing it already known.

The following Natural History is written, with only such an attention to
system as serves to remove the reader's embarrassments, and allure him to
proceed. It can make no pretensions in directing him to the name of every
object he meets with; that belongs to works of a very different kind, and
written with very different aims. It will fully answer my design, if the
reader, being already possest of the name of any animal, shall find here a
short, though satisfactory history of its habitudes, its subsistence, its
manners, its friendships [...] I was therefore left to my own reading alone,
to make out the history of birds, fishes and insects, of which the arrangement was so difficult, and the necessary information so widely diffused and

so obscurely related when found, that it proved by much the most laborious part of the undertaking. Thus having made use of Mr. Buffon's lights in the first part of the work, I may, with some share of confidence, recommend it to the public. But what shall I say to that part, where I have been entirely left without his assistance? As I would affect neither modesty nor confidence, it will be sufficient to say, that my reading upon this part of the subject has been very extensive: and that I have taxed my scanty circumstances in procuring books which are on this subject, of all others, the most expensive. In consequence of this industry, I here offer a work to the public, of a kind, which has never been attempted in ours, or any other modern language, that I know of. The ancients, indeed, and Pliny in particular, have anticipated me, in the present manner of treating natural history. Like those historians who describe the events of a campaign, they have not condescended to give the private particulars of every individual that formed the army; they were content with characterizing the generals, and describing their operations, while they left it to meaner hands to carry the muster-roll. I have followed their manner, rejecting the numerous fables which they adopted, and adding the improvements of the moderns, which are so numerous, that they actually make up the bulk of natural history.

The delight which I found in reading Pliny, first inspired me with the idea of a work of this nature. Having a taste rather classical than scientific, and having but little employed myself in turning over the dry labours of modern systemmakers, my earliest intention was to translate this agreable writer, and by the help of a commentary to make my work as amusing as I could. Let us dignify natural history ever so much with the grave appellation of a useful science, yet still we must confess that it is the occupation of the idle and the speculative, more than of the busy and the ambitious part of mankind. My intention therefore was to treat what I then conceived to be an idle subject, in an idle manner; and not to hedge round plain and simple narratives with hard words, accumulated distinctions, ostentatious learning, and disquisitions that produced no conviction. Upon the appearance however of Mr. Buffon's work, I dropped my former plan, and adopted the present, being convinced by his manner, that the best imitation of the ancients was to write from our own feelings, and to imitate nature.

It will be my chief pride therefore, if this work may be found an innocent amusement for those who have nothing else to employ them, or who require a relaxation from labour. Professed naturalists will, no doubt, find it superficial: and yet I should hope that even these will discover hints, and remarks, gleaned from various reading, not wholly trite or elementary. I would wish for their approbation. But my chief ambition is to drag up the obscure and gloomy learning of the cell to open inspection; to strip it from its garb of austerity, and to shew the beauties of that form, which only the industrious and the inquisitive have been hitherto permitted to approach. . . .

A Comparison of Animals with the Inferior Ranks of Creation.

Having given an account of the earth in general, and the advantages and inconveniencies with which it abounds, we now come to consider it more minutely. Having described the habitation, we are naturally led to enquire after the inhabitants. Amidst the infinitely different productions which the earth offers, and with which it is every where covered, animals hold the first rank; as well because of the finer formation of their parts as of their superior power. The vegetable, which is fixed to one spot, and obliged to wait for its accidental supplies of nourishment, may be considered as the prisoner of nature. Unable to correct the disadvantages of its situation, or to shield itself from the dangers that surround it, every object that has motion may be its destroyer.

But, animals are endowed with powers, of motion and defence. The greatest part are capable, by changing place, of commanding Nature; and of thus obliging her to furnish that nourishment which is most agreeable to their state. Those few that are fixed to one spot, even in this seemingly helpless situation, are, nevertheless, protected from external injury, by an hard shelly covering; which they often can close at pleasure, and thus defend themselves from every assault. And here, I think, we may draw the line between the animal and vegetable kingdoms. Every animal, by some means or other, finds protection from injury; either from its force, or courage, its swiftness, or cunning. Some are protected by hiding in convenient places; and others by taking refuge in an hard resisting shell. But, vegetables are totally unprotected; they are exposed to every attack. In a word, an animal is an organized being that is in some measure provided for its own security; a vegetable is destitute of every protection.

But though it is very easy, without the help of definitions, to distinguish a plant from an animal, yet both possess many properties so much alike, that the two kingdoms, as they are called, seem mixed with each other. Hence it frequently puzzles the naturalist to tell exactly where animal life begins, and vegetative terminates; nor, indeed, is it easy to resolve, whether some objects offered to view be of the lowest of the animal, or the highest of the vegetable races. The sensitive plant,[1] that moves at the touch, seems

---

[1] Mimosa. [Ed.]

to have as much perception as the fresh water polypus, that is possessed of a still slower share of motion. Besides, the sensitive plant will not reproduce upon cutting in pieces, which the polypus is known to do; so that the vegetable production seems to have the superiority. But, notwithstanding this, the polypus hunts for its food, as most other animals do. It changes its situation; and, therefore possesses a power of chusing its food, or retreating from danger. Still, therefore, the animal kingdom is far removed above the vegetable, and its lowest denizen is possessed of very great privileges, when compared with the plants with which it is often surrounded.

However, both classes have many resemblances, by which they are raised above the un-organized and inert masses of nature. Minerals are mere inactive, insensible bodies, entirely motionless of themselves, and waiting some external force to alter their forms, or their properties. But it is otherwise with animals and vegetables; these are endued with life and vigour; they have their state of improvement and decay; they are capable of reproducing their kinds; they grow from seeds, in some, and from cuttings in others; they seem all possessed of sensation, in a greater or less degree; they both have their enmities and affections; and as some animals are, by nature, impelled to violence, so some plants are found to exterminate all others, and make a wilderness of the places round them. As the lion makes a desert of the forest where it resides, thus no other plant will grow under the shade of the machinel-tree.[2] Thus, also, that plant, in the West-Indies, called caraguata, clings round whatever tree it happens to approach: there it quickly gains the ascendant; and, loading the same with a verdure not its own, keeps away that nourishment designed to feed the trunk; and, at last, entirely destroys its supporter.

As all animals are ultimately supported upon vegetables, so vegetables are greatly propagated, by being made a part of animal food. Birds distribute the seeds wherever they fly, and quadrupeds prune them into greater luxuriance. By these means the quantity of food, in a state of nature, is kept equal to the number of the consumers; and, lest some of the weaker ranks of animals should find nothing for their support, but all the provisions be devoured by the strong, different vegetables are appropriated to different appetites. If transgressing this rule, the stronger ranks should invade the rights of the weak, and, breaking through all regard to appetite, should make an indiscriminate use of every vegetable, nature then punishes the transgression, and poison marks the crime as capital.

If again we compare vegetables and animals, with respect to the places where they are found, we shall find them bearing a still stronger similitude.

---

[2] The poison tree [Ed.]

The vegetables that grow in a dry and sunny soil, are strong and vigorous, though not luxuriant; so, also, are the animals of such a climate. Those, on the contrary, that are the joint product of heat and moisture, are luxuriant and tender: and the animals assimilating to the vegetable food, on which they ultimately subsist, are much larger in such places than in others. Thus, in the internal parts of South-America, and Africa, where the sun usually scorches all above, while inundations cover all below, the insects, reptiles, and other animals, grow to a prodigious size: the earth-worm of America is often a yard in length, and as thick as a walking cane; the boiguacu,[3] which is the largest of the serpent kind, is sometimes forty feet in length; the bats, in those countries, are as big as a rabbit; the toads are bigger than a duck, and their spiders are as large as a sparrow. On the contrary, in the cold frozen regions of the north, where vegetable nature is stinted of its growth, the few animals in those climates partake of the diminution; all the wild animals, except the bear, are much smaller than in milder countries; and such of the domestic kinds as are carried thither, quickly degenerate, and grow less. Their very insects are of the minute kinds, their bees and spiders being not half so large as those in the temperate zone.

The similitude between vegetables and animals is no where more obvious than in those that belong to the ocean, where the nature of one is admirably adapted to the necessities of the other. This element it is well known has its vegetables, and its insects that feed upon them in great abundance. Over many tracts of the sea, a weed is seen floating, which covers the surface, and gives the resemblance of a green and extensive meadow. On the under side of these unstable plants, millions of little animals are found, adapted to their situation. For as their ground, if I may so express it, lies over their heads, their feet are placed upon their backs, and as land animals have their legs below their bodies, these have them above. At land also, most animals are furnished with eyes to see their food, but at sea, almost all the reptile kinds are without eyes, which might only give them prospects of danger, at a time when unprovided with the means of escaping it.

Thus, in all places, we perceive an obvious similitude between the animals and the vegetables of every region. In general, however, the most perfect races have the least similitude to the vegetable productions on which they are ultimately fed; while, on the contrary, the meaner the animal, the more local it is found to be, and the more it is influenced by the varieties of the soil where it resides. Many of the more humble reptile kinds are not only confined to one country, but also to a plant; nay even to a leaf. Upon that they subsist; encreaste with its vegetation, and seem to decay as it

---

[3] Boa constrictor. [Ed.]

declines. They are merely the circumscribed inhabitants of a single vegetable; take them from that and they instantly die; being entirely assimilated
to the plant they feed on, assuming its colour, and even its medicinal properties. For this reason there are infinite numbers of the meaner animals
that we have never an opportunity of seeing in this part of the world; they
are incapable of living separate from their kindred vegetables, which grow
only in a certain climate.

Such animals as are formed more perfect, lead a life of less dependance;
and, some kinds are found to subsist in many parts of the world at the same
time. But, of all the races of animated nature, man is the least affected by
the soil where he resides, and least influenced by the variations of vegetable
sustenance: equally unaffected by the luxuriance of the warm climates, or
the sterility of the poles, he has spread his habitations over the whole earth;
and finds subsistence as well amidst the ice of the north as the burning
desarts under the line. All creatures of an inferior nature, as has been said,
have peculiar propensities to peculiar climates; they are circumscribed to
zones, and confined to territories where their proper food is found in
greatest abundance; but, man may be called the animal of every climate,
and suffers but very gradual alterations from the nature of any situation.

As to animals of a meaner rank, whom man compels to attend him in
his migrations, these being obliged to live in a state of constraint, and upon
vegetable food, often different from that of their native soil, they very soon
alter their natures with the nature of their nourishment, assimilate to the
vegetables upon which they are fed, and thus assume very different habits
as well as appearances. Thus, man, unaffected himself, alters and directs
the nature of other animals at his pleasure; encreases their strength for his
delight, or their patience for his necessities. . . .

THE TIGER

The ancients had a saying, *That as the peacock is the most beautiful
among birds, so is the tiger among quadrupedes.* In fact, no quadrupede can
be more beautiful than this animal; the glossy smoothness of his hair,
which lies much smoother, and shines with greater brightness than even
that of the leopard; the extreme blackness of the streaks with which he is
marked, and the bright yellow colour of the ground which they diversify,
at once strike the beholder. To this beauty of colouring is added an
extremely elegant form, much larger indeed than that of the leopard, but
more slender, more delicate, and bespeaking the most extreme swiftness
and agility. Unhappily, however, this animal's disposition is as mischievous
as its form is admirable, as if Providence was willing to shew the small value
of beauty, by bestowing it on the most noxious of quadrupedes. We have,

Plate XV

Vol.II *Page 135*

135

Tiger

Tyger, tyger. A tiger plate from Oliver Goldsmith's *An History of the Earth and Animated Nature*. This engraving was by Scot and Allardice, 1795. Archives and Special Collections, Dickinson College, Carlisle, PA.

at present, one of these animals in the Tower, which to the view appears the most good natured and harmless creature in the world: its physiognomy is far from fierce or angry; it has not the commanding stern countenance of the lion, but a gentle placid air; yet for all this it is fierce and savage beyond measure; neither correction can terrify, nor indulgence can tame it.

The chief and most observable distinction in the tiger, and in which it differs from all others of the mottled kind, is in the shape of its colours, which run in streaks or bands in the same direction as his ribs from the back down to the belly. The leopard, the panther, and the ounce, are all partly covered like this animal, but with this difference, that their colours are broken in spots all over the body; whereas in the tiger they stretch lengthwise, and there is scarce a round spot to be found on his skin. Besides this there are other observable distinctions: the tiger is much larger, and often found bigger even than the lion himself: it is much slenderer also in proportion to its size; its legs shorter, and its neck and body longer. In short, of all other animals, it most resembles the cat in shape; and, if we conceive the latter magnified to a very great degree, we shall have a tolerable idea of the former.

In classing carnivorous animals, we may place the lion foremost[4]; and immediately after him follows the tiger, which seems to partake of all the

---

[4]The remainder of this description is taken from Mr Buffon, except where marked with inverted commas.

noxious qualities of the lion without sharing any of his good ones. To pride, courage, and strength, the lion joins greatness, clemency, and generosity; but the tiger is fierce without provocation, and cruel without necessity. The lion seldom ravages except when excited by hunger; the tiger, on the contrary, though glutted with slaughter, is not satisfied, still continues the carnage, and seems to have its courage only enflamed by not finding resistance. In falling in among a flock or a herd, it gives no quarter, but levels all with indiscriminate cruelty, and scarce finds time to appease its appetite while intent upon satisfying the malignity of its nature. It thus becomes the scourge of the country where it is found; it fears neither the threats nor the opposition of mankind; the beasts both wild and tame fall equally a sacrifice to its insatiable fury; the young elephant and the rhinoceros become equally its prey; and it not unfrequent ventures to attack the lion himself.

Happily for the rest of nature, this animal is not common, and the species is chiefly confined to the warmest provinces of the east. The tiger is found in Malabar, in Siam, in Bengal, and in all the same countries which are inhabited by the elephant or the rhinoceros. Some even pretend that it has a friendship for, and often accompanies the latter, in order to devour its excrements, which serve it as a purge. Be this as it will, there is no doubt but that they are often seen together at the sides of lakes and rivers; where they are probably both compelled to go by the thirst which in that torrid climate they must very often endure. It is likely enough also that they seldom make war upon each other, the rhinoceros being a peaceable animal, and the tiger knowing its strength too well to venture the engagement. It is still more likely that the tiger finds this a very convenient situation, since it can there surprize a greater number of animals which are compelled thither from the same motives. In fact, it is generally known to lurk near such places where it has an opportunity of chusing its prey, or rather of multiplying its massacres. When it has killed one it often goes to destroy others, swallowing their blood at large draughts, and seeming rather glutted than satiated with its abundance.

However, when it has killed a large animal, such as an horse, or a buffalo, it immediately begins to devour it on the spot, fearing to be disturbed. In order to feast at its ease, it carries off its prey to the forest, dragging it along with such ease, that the swiftness of its motion seems scarce retarded by the enormous load it sustains. From this alone we may judge of its strength; but, to have a more just idea of this particular, let us stop a moment to consider the dimensions of this most formidable creature. Some travellers have compared it for size to an horse, and others to a buffalo, while others have contented themselves with saying that it was much larger than a lion. We have recent accounts of this animal's magnitude that deserve the most confidence. Mr. Buffon has been assured by one of his friends that he saw a tiger, in the East Indies, of fifteen feet long. "Supposing that he means including the tail, this animal allowing four feet for that, must have been eleven feet from the tip of the nose to the insertion of the tail. Indeed that which is now in the Tower is not so large, being as well as I could measure six feet from the tip to the insertion, and the tail was three feet more. Like all the rest of its kind, its motions are irregular and desultory; it bounds rather than runs; and like them rather chuses to take its prey by surprize than to be at the trouble of hunting it down." How large a leap it can take at once we may easily judge, by comparing what it might do to what we see so small an animal as a cat actually perform. The cat can leap several feet at a bound; and the tiger, who is ten times as long, can no doubt spring proportionably.

"The tiger is the only animal whose spirit seems untameable. Neither force nor constraint, neither violence nor flattery, can prevail in the least on its stubborn nature. The caresses of the keeper have no influence on their heart of iron; and time, instead of mollifying its disposition, only serves to encrease its fierceness and malignity. The tiger snaps at the hand that feeds it as well as that by which it is chastised: every object seems considered only as its proper prey, which it devours with a look; and although confined by bars and chains, still makes fruitless efforts, as if to shew its malignity when incapable of exerting its force."

To give a still more complete idea of the strength of this terrible creature, we shall quote a passage from Father Tachard, who was an eye-witness of a combat between a tiger and three elephants at Siam. For this purpose, the king ordered a lofty palisade to be built of bambou cane, about an hundred feet square; and in the midst of this were three elephants appointed for combating the tiger. Their heads and a part of their trunk was covered with a kind of armour, like a mask, which defended that part from the assaults of the fierce animal with which they were to engage. As soon, says this author, as we were arrived at the place, a tiger was brought forth from his den, of a size much larger than we had ever seen before. It was not first let loose, but held with chords so that one of the elephants approaching, gave it three or four terrible blows, with its trunk, on the back, with such force, that the tiger was for some time, stunned, and lay, without motion, as if it had been dead. However, as soon as it was let loose, and at full liberty, although the first blows had greatly abated its fury, it made at the elephant with a loud shriek, and aimed at seizing his trunk. But the elephant, wrinkling it up with great dexterity, received the tiger on his great teeth, and tossed it up into the air. This so discouraged the furious animal, that it no more ventured to approach the elephant, but made several circuits round the palisade, often attempting to fly at the spectators.

Shortly after, three elephants were sent against it, and they continued to strike it so terribly with their trunks, that it once more lay for dead; and they would certainly have killed it, had not there been a stop put to the combat.

From this account, we may readily judge of the strength of this animal, which, though reduced to captivity, and held by chords, though first disabled, and set alone against three, yet ventured to continue the engagement, and even that against animals covered and protected from its fury.

"Captain Hamilton informs us, that in the Sundah Rajha's dominions there are three sorts of tigers in the woods, and that the smallest are the fiercest. This is not above two feet high, appears to be extremely cunning, and delights in human flesh. The second kind is about three feet high, and hunts deer and wild hogs, besides the little animal which has been already described, under the name of the Chevrotain, or Guinea deer. The tiger of the largest sort, is above three feet and an half high; but, although endowed with greater powers, is, by no means, so rapacious as either of the former. This formidable animal, which is called the Royal Tiger (one of which we have at present in the Tower) does not seem so ravenous nor so dangerous, and is even more cowardly. A peasant in that country, as this traveller informs us, had a buffalo fallen into a quagmire, and, while he went for assistance, there came a large tiger, that, with its single strength, drew forth the animal, which the united force of many men could not effect. When the people returned to the place, the first object they beheld was the tiger, who had thrown the buffalo over its shoulder, as a fox does a goose, and was carrying it away, with the feet upward, towards its den; however, as soon as it saw the men, it let fall its prey, and instantly fled to the woods: but it had previously killed the buffalo, and sucked its blood; and, no doubt, the people were very well satisfied with its retreat. It may be observed, that some East-Indian buffaloes weigh above a thousand pounds, which is twice as heavy as the ordinary run of our black cattle; so that from hence we may form a conception of the enormous strength of this rapacious animal, that could thus run off with a weight at least twice as great as that of itself.

"Were this animal as common as the panther, or even as the lion himself, thus furnished as it is with the power to destroy, and the appetite for slaughter, the country would be uninhabitable where it resides. But luckily the species is extremely scarce; and has been so since the earliest accounts we have had of the tiger. About the times of Augustus, we are assured by Pliny, that when panthers were brought to Rome by hundreds, a single tiger was considered as an extraordinary sight; and he tells us, that the emperor Claudius was able to procure four only; which shews how difficultly they were procured. The incredible fierceness of this animal may be, in some measure, the cause of the scarcity which was then at Rome, since it was the opinion of Varro, that the tiger was never taken alive; but its being a native only of the east-Indies, and that particularly of the warmer regions, it is not to be wondered that the species should be so few."

We may, therefore, consider the species of the true streaked tiger, as one of the scarcest of animals, and much less diffused than that of the lion. As to the number of its young, we have no certain accounts; however, it is said, that it brings forth four or five at a time. Although furious at all times, the female, upon this occasion, exceeds her usual rapacity; and, if her young are taken from her, she pursues the spoiler with incredible rage; he, to save a part, is contented to lose a part, and drops one of her cubs, with which she immediately returns to her den, and again pursues him; he then drops another, and by the time she has returned with that, he generally escapes with the remainder. If she loses her young entirely, she then becomes desperate, boldly approaches even the towns themselves, and commits incredible slaughter. The tiger expresses its resentment in the same manner with the lion: it moves the muscles and skin of its face, shews its teeth, and shrieks in the most frightful manner. [. . .]

THE CAMELOPARD [5]

Were we to be told of an animal so tall, that a man on horseback could with ease ride under its belly, without stooping, we should hardly give credit to the relation; yet, of this extraordinary size is the camelopard, an animal that inhabits the Desarts of Africa, and the accounts of which are so well ascertained, that we cannot deny our assent to their authority. It is no easy matter to form an adequate idea of this creature's size, and the oddity of its formation. It exhibits somewhat the slender shape of the deer, or the camel, but destitute of their symmetry, or their easy power of motion. The head somewhat resembles that of the deer, with two round horns, near a foot long, and which it is probable, it sheds as deers are found to do; its neck resembles that of a horse; its legs and feet, those of the deer, but with this extraordinary difference, that the fore legs are near twice as long as the hinder. As these creatures have been found eighteen feet high, and ten from the ground to the top of the shoulders, so allowing three feet for the depth of the body, seven feet remain, which is high enough to admit a man mounted upon middle-sized horse. The hinder part, however, is much lower, so that when the animal appears standing, and at rest, it has somewhat the appearance of a dog sitting, and this formation of its legs,

---

[5] Giraffe. [Ed.]

gives it an awkward and laborious motion; which, though swift, must yet be tiresome. For this reason, the camelopard is an animal very rarely found, and only finds refuge in the most internal desert regions of Africa. The dimensions of a young one, as they were accurately taken by a person, who examined its skin, that was brought from the Cape of Good Hope, were found to be as follow: the length of the head, was one foot eight inches; the height of the fore leg, from the ground to the top of the shoulder, was ten feet; from the shoulder, to the top of the head, was seven; the height of the hind leg, was eight feet five inches; and from the top of the shoulder, to the insertion of the tail, was just seven feet long.

No animal, either from its disposition, or its formation, seems less fitted for a state of natural hostility; its horns are blunt, and even knobbed at the ends; its teeth, are made entirely for vegetable pasture; its skin is beautifully speckled with white spots, upon a brownish ground; it is timorous and harmless, and notwithstanding its great size, rather flies from, than resists the slightest enemy; it partakes very much of the nature of the camel, which it so nearly resembles: it lives entirely upon vegetables, and when grazing, is obliged to spread its fore legs very wide, in order to reach its pasture; its motion is a kind of pace, two legs on each side moving at the same time, whereas in other animals they move transversely. It often lies down with its belly to the earth, and like the camel, has a callous substance upon its breast, which, when reposed, defends it from injury. This animal was known to the ancients, but has been very rarely seen in Europe. One of them was sent from the East to the Emperor of Germany, in the year 1559, but they have often been seen tame at Grand Cairo, in Egypt; and I am told, there are two there at present. When ancient Rome was in its splendor, Pompey exhibited, at one time, no less than ten, upon the theatre. It was the barbarous pleasure of the people, at that time, to see the most terrible, and the most extraordinary animals produced in combat against each other. The lion, the lynx, the tiger, the elephant, the hippopotamos, were all let loose promiscuously, and were seen to inflict indiscriminate destruction. [. . .]

Erasmus Darwin (1731–1802)

Erasmus Darwin, grandfather of Charles Darwin, was educated at Cambridge and Edinburgh and settled near Lichfield and later at Derby. A remarkable polymath, he became a best-selling poet during the years that he worked as a country doctor, naturalist, medical botanist, and inventor. Darwin expounded an early theory of evolution ("all vegetables and animals now living were originally derived from the smallest microscopic ones"), and he described the importance of sexual selection in producing change within species ("the final cause of this contest among males seems to be, that the strongest and most active animal should propagate the species, which should thence become improved"). His two most important technical works were *Zoonomia* (1794), a medical textbook punctuated by reflections on philosophy, natural history, and human life, and *Phytologia* (1800), a scientific discussion of agriculture and gardening. His book-length poems, *The Botanic Garden* (1789–91) and *The Temple of Nature* (1803), were widely read and even more widely discussed.

Darwin's friends and associates included leading lights of the era: Joseph Priestley, Josiah Wedgwood, James Watt, Dr. Samuel Johnson, the poet Anna Seward (who also wrote *Memoirs of the Life of Dr. Darwin*), and R. L. Edgeworth, father of Maria. Darwin was a founder of the Lunar Society, second only to the Royal Society in its importance as a gathering place for scientists, inventors, and natural philosophers during the second half of the eighteenth century. He emphasized the role of sexuality in animal reproduction and attributed the possibility of emotion to plants. He expressed great interest in the work of Conte Alessandro Volta and Luigi Galvani on muscular contraction, arguing as early as 1791 that electricity was the basis of all nerve impulses. He recorded accurate observations on subjects ranging from photosynthesis to neurology, from meteorology and geology to psychology.

Lines from Darwin's *The Temple of Nature* anticipated the outlines of his grandson's theory by half a century:

> Organic Life beneath the shoreless waves
> Was born and nurs'd in Ocean's pearly caves;
> First forms minute, unseen by spheric glass,
> Move on the mud, or pierce the watery mass;
> 5 These, as successive generations bloom,
> New powers acquire, and larger limbs assume;
> Whence countless groups of vegetation spring,
> And breathing realms of fin, and feet, and wing. (I. v. 295–302)

Darwin exerted a powerful influence on Wordsworth, Coleridge, Percy Shelley, and Mary Shelley among other literary figures. Wordsworth cited him as a source for "Goody Blake and Harry Gill" in *Lyrical Ballads* (1800). Coleridge claimed that Darwin possessed "perhaps, a greater range of knowledge than any other man in Europe." Coleridge, however, also coined the term *darwinizing*, meaning to speculate wildly. In addition, Wordsworth and Coleridge were clearly referring to Darwin, among others, when they attacked the "gaudiness" of eighteenth-century poetic diction. Darwin was also in the minds of the Shelley Circle (Mary, Percy, Lord Byron, and John Polidori) during the Frankenstein summer of 1816. John Keats, who studied medicine before turning to poetry, was affected by Darwin's ideas about an organic unity that linked plants, animals, and human beings. While the Romantics criticized Darwin for his eighteenth-century poetic diction, his materialism, and the speculative aspects of his thinking, they were influenced by his carefully elaborated view of the natural world and his belief in powerful connections between human and nonhuman life.

From The Botanic Garden

FROM "THE ECONOMY OF VEGETATION"

IV. "Effulgent Maids! You round deciduous day,
Tressed with soft beams, your glittering bands array;
On Earth's cold bosom, as the Sun retires,   175
Confine with folds of air[1] the lingering fires;
5 O'er Eve's pale forms diffuse phosphoric light,[2]
And deck with lambent flames the shrine of Night.
So, warm'd and kindled by meridian skies,

The Botanic Garden; A Poem, in Two Parts. London: J. Johnson, 1791–94.

[1] *Confine with folds of air.* l. 174. The air, like all other bad conductors of electricity, is known to be a bad conductor of heat; and thence prevents the heat acquired from the sun's rays by the earth's surface from being so soon dissipated, in the same manner as a blanket, which may be considered as a sponge filled with air, prevents the escape of heat from the person wrapped in it. This seems to be one cause of the great degree of cold on the tops of mountains, where the rarity of the air is greater, and it therefore becomes a better conductor both of heat and electricity.

There is however another cause to which the great coldness of mountains and of the higher regions of the atmosphere is more immediately to be ascribed, explained by Dr. Darwin in the Philos. Trans. Vol. LXXVIII. who has there proved by experiments with the air-gun and air-pump, that when any portion of the atmosphere becomes mechanically expanded, it absorbs heat from the bodies in its vicinity. And as the air which creeps along the plains, expands itself by a part of the pressure being taken off when it ascends the sides of mountains; it at the same time attracts heat from the summits of those mountains, or other bodies which happen to be immersed in it, and thus produces cold. Hence he concludes that the hot air at the bottom of the Andes becomes temperate by its own rarefaction when it ascends to the city of Quito; and by its further rarefaction becomes cooled to the freezing point when it ascends to the snowy regions on the summits of those mountains. To this also he attributes the great degree of cold experienced by the aeronauts in their balloons; and which produces hail in summer at the height of only two or three miles in the atmosphere.

[2] *Diffuse phosphoric light.* l. 177. I have often been induced to believe from observation, that the twilight of the evenings is lighter than that of the mornings at the same distance from noon. Some may ascribe this to the greater height of the atmosphere in the evenings having been rarefied by the sun during the day; but as its density must at the same time be diminished, its power of refraction would continue the same. I should rather suppose that it may be owing to the phosphorescent quality (as it is called) of almost all bodies; that is, when they have been exposed to the sun they continue to emit light for a considerable time afterwards. This is generally believed to arise either from such bodies giving out the light which they had previously absorbed; or to the continuance of a slow combustion which the light they had been previously exposed to had excited. See the next note.

And view'd in darkness with dilated eyes,   180
Bologna's chalks with faint ignition blaze,
10   Beccari's shells[3] emit prismatic rays.
So to the sacred Sun in Memnon's fane,
Spontaneous concords quired the matin strain;
— Touch'd by his orient beam, responsive rings   185
The living lyre, and vibrates all its strings;
15   Accordant ailes the tender tones prolong,
And holy echoes swell the adoring song.

        "You with light Gas the lamps nocturnal[4] feed,
Which dance and glimmer o'er the marshy mead;   190

---

[3] *Beccari's shells.* l. 182. Beccari made made many curious experiments on the phosphoric light, as it is called, which becomes visible on bodies brought into a dark room, after having been previously exposed to the sunshine. It appears from these experiments, that almost all inflammable bodies possess this quality in a greater or less degree; white paper or linen thus examined after having been exposed to the sunshine, is luminous to an extraordinary degree; and if a person shut up in a dark room, puts one of his hands out into the sun's light for a short time and then retracts it, he will be able to see that hand distinctly, and not the other. These experiments seem to countenance the idea of light being absorbed and again emitted from bodies when they are removed into darkness. But Beccari further pretended, that some calcareous compositions when exposed to red, yellow, or blue light, through coloured glasses, would on their being brought into a dark room emit coloured lights. This mistaken fact of Beccari's, Mr. Wilson decidedly refutes; and among many other curious experiments discovered, that if oyster-shells were thrown into a common fire and calcined for about half an hour, and then brought to a person who had previously been some minutes in a dark room, that many of them would exhibit beautiful irises of prismatic colours, from whence probably arose Beccari's mistake. Mr. Wilson from hence contends, that these kinds of phosphori do not emit the light they had previously received, but that they are set on fire by the sun's rays, and continue for some time a slow combustion after they are withdrawn from the light. Wilson's Experiments on Phosphori. Dodsley, 1775.

The Bolognian stone is a selenite, or gypsum, and has been long celebrated for its phosphorescent quality after having been burnt in a sulphurous fire; and exposed when cold to the sun's light. It may be thus well imitated: Calcine oyster-shells half an hour, pulverize them when cold, and add one third part of flowers of sulphur, press them close into a small crucible, and calcine them for an hour or longer, and keep the powder in a phial close stopped. A part of this powder is to be exposed for a minute or two to the sunbeams, and then brought into a dark room. The calcined Bolognian stone becomes a calcareous hepar of sulphur; but the calcined shells, as they contain the animal acid, may also contain some of the phosphorus of Kunkel.

[4] *The lamps nocturnal.* l. 189. The ignis fatuus or Jack a lantern, so frequently alluded to by poets, is supposed to originate from the inflammable air, or Hydrogene, given up from morasses; which being of a heavier kind from its impurity than that obtained from iron and water, hovers near the surface of the earth, and uniting with common air gives out light by its slow ignition. Perhaps such lights have no existence, and the reflection of a star on watery ground may have deceived the travellers, who have been said to be

Shine round Calendula[5] at twilight hours,
20 And tip with silver all her saffron flowers;
Warm on her mossy couch the radiant Worm,
Guard from cold dews her love-illumin'd form,
From leaf to leaf conduct the virgin light,   195
Star of the earth, and diamond of the night.
25 You bid in air the tropic Beetle burn,
And fill with golden flame his winged urn;
Or gild the surge with insect-sparks, that swarm
Round the bright oar, the kindling prow alarm;   200
Or arm in waves, electric in his ire,
30 The dread Gymnotus[6] with ethereal fire.
Onward his course with waving tail he helms,
And mimic lightenings scare the watery realms,

---

bewildered by them? If the fact was established it would much contribute to explain the phenomena of northern lights. I have travelled much in the night, in all seasons of the year, and over all kinds of soil, but never saw one of these Will o'wisps.

[5]*The marigold.* [Ed.]

[6] *The dread Gymnotus.* l. 202. The Gymnotus electricus is a native of the river of Surinam in South America; those which were brought over to England about eight years ago were about three or four feet long, and gave an electric shock (as I experienced) by putting one finger on the back near its head, and another of the opposite hand into the water near its tail. In their native country they are said to exceed twenty feet in length, and kill any man who approaches them in an hostile manner. It is not only to escape its enemies that this surprizing power of the fish is used, but also to take its prey; which it does by benumbing them and then devouring them before they have time to recover, or by perfectly killing them; for the quantity of the power seemed to be determined by the will or anger of the animal; as it sometimes struck a fish twice before it was sufficiently benumbed to be easily swallowed.

The organs productive of this wonderful accumulation of electric matter have been accurately dissected and described by Mr. J. Hunter. Philos. Trans. Vol. LXV. And are so divided by membranes as to compose a very extensive surface, and are supplied with many pairs of nerves larger than any other nerves of the body; but how so large a quantity is so quickly accumulated as to produce such amazing effects in a fluid ill adapted for the purpose is not yet satisfactorily explained. The Torpedo possesses a similar power in a less degree, as was shewn by Mr. Walch, and another fish lately described by Mr. Paterson. Philo. Trans. Vol. LXXVI.

In the construction of the Leyden-Phial, (as it is called) which is coated on both sides, it is known, that above one hundred times the quantity of positive electricity can be condensed on every square inch of the coating on one side, than could have been accumulated on the same surface if there had been no opposite coating communicating with the earth; because the negative electricity, or that part of it which caused its expansion, is now drawn off through the glass. It is also well known, that the thinner the glass is (which is thus coated on both sides so as to make a Leyden-phial, or plate) the more electricity can be condensed on one of its surfaces, till it becomes so thin as to break, and thence discharge itself.

So, when with bristling plumes the Bird of Jove[7]   205
Vindictive leaves the argent fields above,
35 Borne on broad wings the guilty world he awes,
And grasps the lightening in his shining claws.[8][. . .]

    IX. The Goddess paused, admired with conscious pride
The effulgent legions marshal'd by her side,
Forms sphered in fire with trembling light array'd,
40 Ens[9] without weight, and substance without shade;
And, while tumultuous joy her bosom warms,   425
Waves her white hand, and calls her hosts to arms,

    "Unite, illustrious Nymphs! your radiant powers,
Call from their long repose the Vernal Hours.
45 Wake with soft touch, with rosy hands unbind
The struggling pinions of the western Wind;[10]   430
Chafe his wan cheeks, his ruffled plumes repair,
And wring the rain-drops from his tangled hair.
Blaze round each frosted rill, or stagnant wave,
50 And charm the Naiad from her silent cave;
Where, shrined in ice, like Niobe she mourns,   435

Now it is possible, that the quantity of electricity condensible on one side of a coated phial may increase in some high ratio in respect to the thinness of the glass, since the power of attraction is known to decrease as the squares of the distances, to which this circumstance of electricity seems to bear some analogy. Hence if an animal membrane, as thin as the silk-worm spins its silk, could be so situated as to be charged like the Leyden bottle, without bursting (as such thin glass would be liable to do), it would be difficult to calculate the immense quantity of electric fluid, which might be accumulated on its surface. No land animals are yet discovered which possess this power, though the air would have been a much better medium for producing its effects; perhaps the size of the necessary apparatus would have been inconvenient to land animals.

[7] The eagle. [Ed.]

[8] *In his shining claws.* l. 208. Alluding to an antique gem in the collection of the Grand Duke of Florence.

[9] An entity, something which has existence. [Ed.]

[10] *Of the Western Wind.* l. 430. The principal frosts of this country are accompanied or produced by a N.E. wind, and the thaws by a S.W. wind; the reason of which is that the N.E. winds consist of regions of air brought from the north, which appear to acquire an easterly direction as they advance; and the S.W. winds consist of regions of air brought from the south, which appear to acquire a westerly direction as they advance. The surface of the earth nearer the pole moves slower than it does in our latitude; whence the regions of air brought from thence, move slower, when they arrive hither, than the earth's surface with which they now become in contact; that is they acquire an apparent easterly direction, as the earth moves from west to east faster than this new part of its atmosphere. The S.W. winds on the contrary consist of regions of air brought from the

And clasps with hoary arms her empty urns.
Call your bright myriads, trooping from afar,
With beamy helms, and glittering shafts of war;
55 In phalanx firm the Fiend of Frost[11] assail,   440
Break his white towers, and pierce his crystal mail;
To Zembla's[12] moon-bright coasts the Tyrant bear,
And chain him howling to the Northern Bear.

"So when enormous Grampus,[13] issuing forth
60 From the pale regions of the icy North;
Waves his broad tail, and opes his ribbed mouth,   445
And seeks on winnowing fin the breezy South;
From towns deserted rush the breathless hosts,

---

south, where the surface of the earth moves faster than in our latitude; and have therefore a westerly direction when they arrive hither by their moving faster than the surface of the earth, with which they are in contact; and in general the nearer to the west and the greater the velocity of these winds the warmer they should be in respect to the season of the year, since they have been brought more expeditiously from the south, than those winds which have less westerly direction, and have thence been less cooled in their passage.

Sometimes I have observed the thaw to commence immediately on the change of the wind, even within an hour, if I am not mistaken, or sooner. At other times the S.W. wind has continued a day, or even two, before the thaw has commenced; during which time some of the frosty air, which had gone southwards, is driven back over us; and in consequence has taken a westerly direction, as well as a southern one. At other times I have observed a frost with a N.E. wind every morning, and a thaw with a S.W. wind every noon for several days together.

[11] *The Fiend of Frost.* l. 439. The principal injury done to vegetation by frost is from the expansion of the water contained in the vessels of plants. Water converted into ice occupies a greater space than it did before, as appears by the bursting of bottles filled with water at the time of their freezing. Hence frost destroys those plants of our island first, which are most succulent; and the most succulent parts first of other plants; as their leaves and last year's shoots; the vessels of which are distended and burst by the expansion of their freezing fluids, while the drier or more resinous plants, as pines, yews, laurels, and other ever-greens, are less liable to injury from cold. The trees in vallies are on this account more injured by the vernal frosts than those on eminencies, because their early succulent shoots come out sooner. Hence fruit trees covered by a six-inch coping of a wall are less injured by the vernal frosts because their being shielded from showers and the descending night-dews has prevented them from being moist at the time of their being frozen: which circumstance has given occasion to a vulgar error amongst gardeners, who suppose frost to descend.

As the common heat of the earth in this climate is 48 degrees, those tender trees which will bear bending down, are easily secured from the frost by spreading them upon the ground, and covering them with straw or fern. This particularly suits fig-trees, as they easily bear bending to the ground, and are furnished with an acrid juice, which secures them from the depredations of insects; but are nevertheless liable to be eaten by mice.

[12] The Russian arctic. [Ed.]

[13] An arctic whale, from "great fish." [Ed.]

Swarm round the hills, and darken all the coasts;
65 Boats follow boats along the shouting tides,
And spears and javelins pierce his blubbery sides;   450
Now the bold Sailor, raised on pointed toe,
Whirls the wing'd harpoon on the slimy foe;
Quick sinks the monster in his oozy bed,
70 The blood-stain'd surges circling o'er his head,
Steers to the frozen pole his wonted track,   455
And bears the iron tempest on his back. [. . .]

II. "When Morn, escorted by the dancing Hours,
O'er the bright plains her dewy lustre showers;   26
75 Till from her sable chariot Eve serene
Drops the dark curtain o'er the brilliant scene;
You form with chemic hands the airy surge,
Mix with broad vans, with shadowy tridents urge.   30
Sylphs! from each sun-bright leaf, that twinkling shakes
80 O'er Earth's green lap, or shoots amid her lakes,
Your playful bands with simpering lips invite,
And wed the enamour'd Oxygene[14] to Light.
Round their white necks with fingers interwove,   35
Cling the fond Pair with unabating love;
85 Hand link'd in hand on buoyant step they rise,
And soar and glisten in unclouded skies.

---

[14] *The enamour'd oxygene.* l. 34. The common air of the atmosphere appears by the analysis of Dr. Priestley and other philosophers to consist of about three parts of an elastic fluid unfit for respiration or combustion, called azote by the French school, and about one fourth of pure vital air fit for the support of animal life and of combustion, called oxygene. The principal source of the azote is probably from the decomposition of all vegetable and animal matters by putrefaction and combustion; the principal source of vital air or oxygene is perhaps from the decomposition of water in the organs of vegetables by means of sun's light. The difficulty of injecting vegetable vessels seems to shew that their perspirative pores are much less than those of animals, and that the water which constitutes their perspiration is so divided at the time of its exclusion that by means of the sun's light it becomes decomposed, the inflammable air or hydrogene, which is one of its constituent parts, being retained to form the oil, resin, wax, honey, &c. of the vegetable economy; and the other part, which united with light or heat becomes vital air or oxygene gas, rises into the atmosphere and replenishes it with the food of life.

Dr. Priestley has evinced by very ingenious experiments that the blood gives out phlogiston, and receives vital air, or oxygene-gas by the lungs. And Dr. Crawford has shewn that the blood acquires heat from the vital air in respiration. There is however still a something more subtil than heat, which must be obtained in respiration from the vital air, a something which life can not exist a few minutes without, which seems necessary to the vegetable as well as to the animal world, and which as no organized vessels can confine it, requires perpetually to be renewed.

Whence in bright floods the Vital Air expands,
And with concentric spheres involves the lands;   40
Pervades the swarming seas, and heaving earths,
90 Where teeming Nature broods her myriad births;
Fills the fine lungs of all that *breathe* or *bud*,
Warms the new heart, and dyes the gushing blood;
With Life's first spark inspires the organic frame,   45
And, as it wastes, renews the subtile flame. [. . .]

95   XIV. I. "Sylphs! if with morn destructive Eurus[15] springs,
O, clasp the Harebel with your velvet wings;
Screen with thick leaves the Jasmine as it blows,   525
And shake the white rime from the shuddering Rose;
Whilst Amaryllis turns with graceful ease
100 Her blushing beauties, and eludes the breeze.
Sylphs! if at noon the Fritillary droops,
With drops nectarous hang her nodding cups;   530
Thin clouds of Gossamer in air display,
And hide the vale's chaste Lily from the ray;
105 Whilst Erythrina[16] o'er her tender flower
Bends all her leaves, and braves the sultry hour;
Shield, when cold Hesper[17] sheds his dewy light,   535
Mimosa's soft sensations from the night;
Fold her thin foilage, close her timid flowers,
110 And with ambrosial slumbers[18] guard her bowers;
O'er each warm wall while Cerea flings her arms,
And wastes on night's dull eye a blaze of charms. [. . .]   540

---

[15] The god of the east wind. [Ed.]

[16] The breadfruit tree. [Ed.]

[17] The evening star. [Ed.]

[18] *With ambrosial slumbers.* l. 538. Many vegetables during the night do not seem to respire, but to sleep like the dormant animals and insects in winter. This appears from the mimosa and many other plants closing the upper sides of their leaves together in their sleep, and thus precluding that side of them from both light and air. And from many flowers closing up the polished or interior side of their petals, which we have also endeavoured to shew to be a respiratory organ.

The irritability of plants is abundantly evinced by the absorption and pulmonary circulation of their juices; their sensibility is shewn by the approaches of the males to the females, and of the females to the males in numerous instances; and, as the essential circumstance of sleep consists in the temporary abolition of voluntary power alone, the sleep of plants evinces that they possess voluntary power; which also indisputably appears in many of them by closing their petals or their leaves during cold, or rain, or darkness, or from mechanic violence.

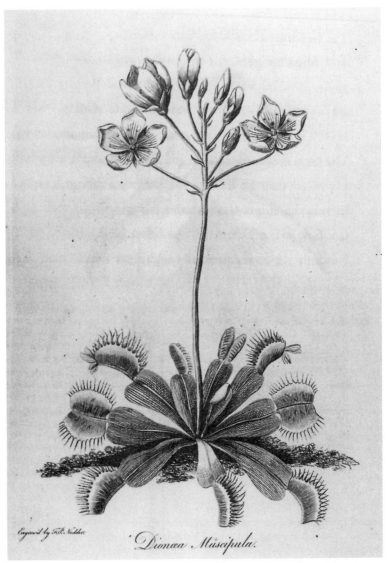

Engraved by T.E. Noddes.

Dionæa Muscipula.

The Venus fly-trap steps out of the Great Chain of Being. This plate depicting *Dionaea muscipula* is taken from Erasmus Darwin's *The Botanic Garden.* Darwin says, "In the Dionaea muscipula there is a still more wonderful contrivance to prevent the depredations of insects; the leaves are armed with long teeth, like the antennae of insects, and lie spread upon the ground round the stem; and are so irritable, that when an insect creeps upon them, they fold up, and crush or pierce it to death" (*Botanic Garden,* "Loves of the Plants," London: Joseph Johnson, 1791: I, 19).

From "The Loves of the Plants"

The fell Silene[19] and her sisters fair,
Skill'd in destruction, spread the viscous snare.   140
The harlot-band *ten* lofty bravoes screen,
And frowning guard the magic nets unseen.
5 Haste, glittering nations, tenants of the air,
Oh, steer from hence your viewless course afar!
If with soft words, sweet blushes, nods, and smiles,   145
The *three* dread Syrens lure you to their toils,
Limed by their art in vain you point your stings,
10 In vain the efforts of your whirring wings!
Go, seek your gilded mates and infant hives,
Nor taste the honey purchas'd with your lives!   150

When heaven's high vault condensing clouds deform,
Fair Amaryllis[20] flies the incumbent storm,

---

[19] *Silene.* l. 139. Catchfly. Three females and ten males inhabit each flower; the viscous material, which surrounds the stalks under the flowers of this plant, and of the Cucubulus Otites, is a curious contrivance to prevent various insects from plundering the honey, or devouring the seed. In the Dionaea Muscipula there is a still more wonderful contrivance to prevent the depredations of insects: The leaves are armed with long teeth, like the antennae of insects, and lie spread upon the ground round the stem; and are so irritable, that when an insect creeps upon them, they fold up, and crush or pierce it to death. The last professor Linneus, in his Supplementum Plantarum, gives the following account of the Arum Muscivorum. The flower has the smell of carrion; by which the flies are invited to lay their eggs in the chamber of the flower, but in vain endeavour to escape, being prevented by the hairs pointing inwards; and thus perish in the flower, whence its name of fly-eater. P. 411. In the Dypsacus is another contrivance for this purpose, a bason of water is placed round each joint of the stem. In the Drosera is another kind of fly-trap. See Dypsacus and Drosera; the flowers of Siléne and Cucúbalus are closed all day, but are open and give an agreeable odour in the night.

[20] *Amaryllis.* l. 152. Formosissima. Most beautiful Amaryllis. Six males, one female. Some of the bell-flowers close their apertures at night, or in rainy or cold weather, as the convolvulus, and thus protect their included stamens and pistils. Other bell-flowers hang their apertures downwards, as many of the lilies; in those the pistil, when at maturity, is longer than the stamens; and by this pendant attitude of the bell, when the anthers burst, their dust falls on the stigma: and these are at the same time sheltered as with an umbrella from rain and dews. But, as a free exposure to the air is necessary for their fecundation, the style and filaments in many of these flowers continue to grow longer after the bell is open, and hang down below its rim. In others, as in the martagon, the bell is deeply divided, and the divisions are reflected upwards, that they may not prevent the access of air, and at the same time afford some shelter from perpendicular rain or dew. Other bell-flowers, as the hemerocallis and amaryllis, have their bells nodding only,

15 Seeks with unsteady step the shelter'd vale,
  And turns her blushing beauties from the gale.
  Six rival youths, with soft concern impress'd,   155
  Calm all her fears, and charm her cares to rest.
  So shines at eve the sun-illumin'd fane,
20 Lifts its bright cross, and waves its golden vane;
  From every breeze the polish'd axle turns,
  And high in air the dancing meteor burns. [. . .]   160

        Queen of the marsh, imperial Drosera[21] treads
  Rush-fringed banks, and moss-embroider'd beds;
25 Redundant folds of glossy silk surround
  Her slender waist, and trail upon the ground;
  Five sister-nymphs collect with graceful ease,   235
  Or spread the floating purple to the breeze;
  And *five* fair youths with duteous love comply
30 With each soft mandate of her moving eye.
  As with sweet grace her snowy neck she bows,
  A zone of diamonds trembles round her brows;   240
  Bright shines the silver halo, as she turns;
  And, as she steps, the living lustre burns. [. . .]

35   Weak with nice sense, the chaste Mimosa[22] stands,
  From each rude touch withdraws her timid hands;

---

as it were, or hanging obliquely toward the horizon; which, as their stems are slender, turn like a weathercock from the wind; and thus very effectually preserve their inclosed stamens and anthers from the rain and cold. Many of these flowers, both before and after their season of fecundation, erect their heads perpendicular to the horizon, like the Meadia, which cannot be explained from mere mechanism.

[21] *Drosera.* l. 231. Sun-dew. Five males, five females. The leaves of this marsh-plant are purple, and have a fringe very unlike other vegetable productions. And, which is curious, at the point of every thread of this erect fringe stands a pellucid drop of mucilage, resembling a ducal coronet. This mucus is a secretion from certain glands, and like the viscous material round the flower-stalks of Silene (catchfly) prevents small insects from infesting the leaves. As the ear wax in animals seems to be in part designed to prevent fleas and other insects from getting into their ears. See Silene. Mr. Wheatly, an eminent surgeon in Cateaton-street, London, observed these leaves to bend upwards, when an insect settled on them, like the leaves of the muscipula veneris, and pointing all their globules of mucus to the centre, that they compleatly intangled and destroyed it.

[22] *Mimosa.* l. 321. The sensitive plant. Of the class Polygamy, one house. Naturalists have not explained the immediate cause of the collapsing of the sensitive plant; the leaves meet and close in the night during the sleep of the plant, or when exposed to much cold in the day-time, in the same manner as when they are affected by external violence, folding their upper surfaces together, and in part over each other like scales or tiles; so as to

Oft as light clouds o'er-pass the Summer-glade,
Alarm'd she trembles at the moving shade;
And feels, alive through all her tender form,   305
40 The whisper'd murmurs of the gathering storm;
Shuts her sweet eye-lids to approaching night;
And hails with freshen'd charms the rising light.
Veil'd, with gay decency and modest pride,
Slow to the mosque she moves, an eastern bride;   310
45 There her soft vows unceasing love record,
Queen of the bright seraglio of her Lord.
So sinks or rises with the changeful hour
The liquid silver in its glassy tower.
So turns the needle to the pole it loves,   315
50 With fine librations quivering as it moves.

All wan and shivering in the leafless glade
The sad Anemone[23] reclined her head;
Grief on her cheeks had paled the roseate hue,
And her sweet eye-lids dropp'd with pearly dew.   320
55 "See, from bright regions, borne on odorous gales
The Swallow,[24] herald of the summer, sails;

---

expose as little of the upper surface as may be to the air; but do not indeed collapse quite so far, since I have found, when touched in the night during their sleep, they fall still further; especially when touched on the foot-stalks between the stems and leaflets, which seems to be their most sensitive or irritable part. Now as their situation after being exposed to external violence resembles their sleep, but with a greater degree of collapse, may it not be owing to a numbness or paralysis consequent to too violent irritation, like the faintings of animals from pain or fatigue? I kept a sensitive plant in a dark room till some hours after day-break: its leaves and leaf-stalks were collapsed as in its most profound sleep, and on exposing it to the light, above twenty minutes passed before the plant was thoroughly awake and had quite expanded itself. During the night the upper or smoother surfaces of the leaves are appressed together; this would seem to shew that the office of this surface of the leaf was to expose the fluids of the plant to the light as well as to the air. Many flowers close up their petals during the night.

[23] *Anemone.* l. 318. Many males, many females. Pliny says this flower never opens its petals but when the wind blows; whence its name: it has properly no calix, but two or three sets of petals, three in each set, which are folded over the stamens and pistil in a singular and beautiful manner, and differs also from ranunculus in not having a melliferous pore on the claw of each petal.

[24] *The Swallow.* l. 322. There is a wonderful conformity between the vegetation of some plants, and the arrival of certain birds of passage. Linneus observes that the wood anemone blows in Sweden on the arrival of the swallow; and the marsh mary-gold, Caltha, when the cuckoo sings. Near the same coincidence was observed in England by Stillingfleet. The word Coccux in Greek signifies both a young fig and a cuckoo, which

Breathe, gentle Air! from cherub-lips impart
Thy balmy influence to my anguish'd heart; 324
Thou, whose soft voice calls forth the tender blooms,
60 Whose pencil paints them, and whose breath perfumes;
O chase the Fiend of Frost, with leaden mace
Who seals in death-like sleep my hapless race;
Melt his hard heart, release his iron hand,
And give my ivory petals to expand. 330
65 So may each bud, that decks the brow of spring,
Shed all its incense on thy wafting wing!"[...]

Where seas of glass with gay reflections smile
Round the green coasts of Java's palmy isle; 220
A spacious plain extends its upland scene,
70 Rocks rise on rocks, and fountains gush between;
Soft zephyrs blow, eternal summers reign,
And showers prolific bless the soil, in vain!
No spicy nutmeg scents the vernal gales, 225
Nor towering plaintain shades the mid-day vales;
75 No grassy mantle hides the sable hills,
No flowery chaplet crowns the trickling rills;
Nor tufted moss, nor leathery lichen creeps
In russet tapestry o'er the crumbling steeps. 230
80 No step retreating, on the sand impress'd,
Invites the visit of a second guest;
No refluent fin the unpeopled stream divides,
No revolant pinion cleaves the airy tides;
Nor handed moles, nor beaked worms return, 235

---

is supposed to have arisen from the coincidence of their appearance in Greece. Perhaps a similar coincidence of appearance in some parts of Asia gave occasion to the story of the loves of the rose and nightingale, so much celebrated by the eastern poets. See Dianthus. The times however of the appearance of vegetables in the spring seem occasionally to be influenced by their acquired habits, as well as by their sensibility to heat: for the roots of potatoes, onions, &c. will germinate with much less heat in the spring than in the autumn; as is easily observable where these roots are stored for use; and hence malt is best made in the spring. 2d. The grains and roots brought from more southern latitudes germinate here sooner than those which are brought from more northern ones, owing to their acquired habits. Fordyce on Agriculture. 3d. It was observed by one of the scholars of Linneus, that the apple-trees sent from hence to New England blossomed for a few years too early for that climate, and bore no fruit; but afterwards learnt to accommodate themselves to their new situation. (Kalm's Travels.)

85 That mining pass the irremeable[25] bourn.
  Fierce in dread silence on the blasted heath
  Fell Upas[26] sits, the Hydra-Tree of death.
  Lo! from one root, the envenom'd soil below,
  A thousand vegetative serpents grow;   240
90 In shining rays the scaly monster spreads
  O'er ten square leagues his far diverging heads;
  Or in one trunk entwists his tangled form,
  Looks o'er the clouds, and hisses in the storm.
  Steep'd in fell poison, as his sharp teeth part,   245
95 A thousand tongues in quick vibration dart;
  Snatch the proud Eagle towering o'er the heath,
  Or pounce the Lion, as he stalks beneath;
  Or strew, as marshall'd hosts contend in vain,
  With human skeletons the whiten'd plain.   250
100 Chain'd at his root two scion-demons dwell,
  Breathe the faint hiss, or try the shriller yell;
  Rise, fluttering in the air on callow wings,
  And aim at insect-prey their little stings.
  So Time's strong arms with sweeping scythe erase   255
105 Art's cumberous works, and empires, from their base;
  While each young Hour its sickle fine employs,
  And crops the sweet buds of domestic joys! [. . .]

---

[25] Without the possibility of returning. [Ed.]

[26] *Upas.* l. 238. There is a poison-tree in the island of Java, which is said by its effluvia to have depopulated the country for 12 or 14 miles round the place of its growth. It is called, in the Malayan language, Bohon-Upas; with the juice of it the most poisonous arrows are prepared; and, to gain this, the condemned criminals are sent to the tree with proper direction both to get the juice and to secure themselves from the malignant exhalations of the tree; and are pardoned if they bring back a certain quantity of the poison. But by the registers there kept, not one in four are said to return. Not only animals of all kinds, both quadrupeds, fish, and birds, but all kinds of vegetables also are destroyed by the effluvia of the noxious tree; so that, in a district of 12 or 14 miles round it, the face of the earth is quite barren and rocky, intermixed only with the skeletons of men and animals; affording a scene of melancholy beyond what poets have described or painters delineated. Two younger trees of its own species are said to grow near it. See London Magazine for 1784, or 1783. Translated from a description of the poison-tree of the island of Java, written in Dutch by N. P. Foersch.

FRONTISPIECE.

THE TEMPLE OF NATURE.

Unveiling the secrets of nature. This image depicts the goddess of poetry pulling aside a curtain to reveal the many-breasted Artemis of Ephesus, goddess of wild nature. One tradition claims that the goddess said, "I am the Mother without spouse, the Original Mother; all are my children, and therefore none has ever dared to approach me" (J. G. Frazer, *The Golden Bough*). The original for this engraving was drawn by Henry Fuseli. Frontispiece to Erasmus Darwin's *The Temple of Nature* (London: Joseph Johnson 1803).

From The Temple of Nature

Hence without parent by spontaneous birth
Rise the first specks of animated earth;
From Nature's womb the plant or insect swims,
And buds or breathes, with microscopic limbs.   250

5   "In earth, sea, air, around, below, above,
Life's subtle woof in Nature's loom is wove;
Points glued to points a living line extends,
Touch'd by some goad approach the bending ends;
Rings join to rings, and irritated tubes
10 Clasp with young lips the nutrient globes or cubes;
And urged by appetencies new select,
Imbibe, retain, digest, secrete, eject.
In branching cones[27] the living web expands,
Lymphatic ducts, and convoluted glands;   260
15 Aortal tubes propel the nascent blood,
And lengthening veins absorb the refluent flood;[28]
Leaves, lungs, and gills, the vital ether breathe
On earth's green surface, or the waves beneath.
So Life's first powers arrest the winds and floods,
20 To bones convert them, or to shells, or woods;
Stretch the vast beds of argil, lime, and sand,
And from diminish'd oceans[29] form the land!

The Temple of Nature. London: J. Johnson, 1803.

[27] *In branching cones,* l. 259. The whole branch of an artery or vein may be considered as a cone, though each distinct division of it is a cylinder. It is probable that the amount of the areas of all the small branches from one trunk may equal that of the trunk, otherwise the velocity of the blood would be greater in some parts than in others, which probably only exists when a part is compressed or inflamed.

[28] *Absorb the refluent flood,* l. 262. The force of the arterial impulse appears to cease, after having propelled the blood through the capillary vessels; whence the venous circulation is owing to the extremities of the veins absorbing the blood, as those of the lymphatics absorb the fluids. The great force of absorption is well elucidated by Dr. Hales's experiment on the rise of the sap-juice in a vine-stump.

[29] *And from diminish'd oceans,* l. 268. The increase of the solid parts of the globe by the recrements of organic bodies, as limestone rocks from shells and bones, and the beds of clay, marl, coals, from decomposed woods, is now well known to those who have attended to modern geology; and Dr. Halley, and others, have endeavoured to show, with great probability, that the ocean has decreased in quantity during the short time which human history has existed. Whence it appears, that the exertions of vegetable and

"Next the long nerves unite their silver train,
And young Sensation[30] permeates the brain;   270
25 Through each new sense the keen emotions dart,
Flush the young cheek, and swell the throbbing heart.
From pain and pleasure quick Volitions rise,
Lift the strong arm, or point the inquiring eyes;
With Reason's light bewilder'd Man direct,
30 And right and wrong with balance nice detect.
Last in thick swarms Associations spring,
Thoughts join to thoughts, to motions motions cling;
Whence in long trains of catenation[31] flow
Imagined joy, and voluntary woe.   280

35   "So, view'd through crystal spheres in drops saline,
Quick-shooting salts in chemic forms combine;
Or Mucor-stems,[32] a vegetative tribe,
Spread their fine roots, the tremulous wave imbibe.
Next to our wondering eyes the focus brings
40 Self-moving lines, and animated rings;
First Monas moves, an unconnected point,
Plays round the drop without a limb or joint;
Then Vibrio waves, with capillary eels,
And Vorticella whirls her living wheels;   290
45 While insect Proteus sports with changeful form
Through the bright tide, a globe, a cube, a worm.
Last o'er the field the Mite enormous swims,
Swells his red heart, and writhes his giant limbs.

---

animal life convert the fluid parts of the globe into solid ones; which is probably effected by combining the matter of heat with the other elements, instead of suffering it to remain simply diffused amongst them, which is a curious conjecture, and deserves further investigation.

[30] *And young Sensation*, l. 270. Both sensation and volition consist in an affection of the central part of the sensorium, or of the whole of it; and hence cannot exist till the nerves are united in the brain. The motions of a limb of any animal cut from the body, are therefore owing to irritation, not to sensation or to volition.

[31] Like the links in a chain. [Ed.]

[32] *Or Mucor-stems*, l. 283. Mucor or mould in its early state is properly a microscopic vegetable, and is spontaneously produced on the scum of all decomposing organic matter. The Monas is a moving speck, the Vibrio an undulating wire, the Proteus perpetually changes its shape, and the Vorticella has wheels about its mouth, with which it makes an eddy, and is supposed thus to draw into its throat invisible animalcules. These names are from Linneus and Muller.

V. "Organic Life beneath the shoreless waves[33]
50 Was born and nurs'd in Ocean's pearly caves;
First forms minute, unseen by spheric glass,
Move on the mud, or pierce the watery mass;
These, as successive generations bloom,
New powers acquire, and larger limbs assume;   300
55 Whence countless groups of vegetation spring,
And breathing realms of fin, and feet, and wing.

"Thus the tall Oak, the giant of the wood,
Which bears Britannia's thunders on the flood;
The Whale, unmeasured monster of the main,
60 The lordly Lion, monarch of the plain,
The Eagle soaring in the realms of air,
Whose eye undazzled drinks the solar glare,
Imperious man, who rules the bestial crowd,
Of language, reason, and reflection proud,   310
55 With brow erect who scorns this earthy sod,
And styles himself the image of his God;
Arose from rudiments of form and sense,
An embryon point,[34] or microscopic ens![35]

---

[33] *Beneath the shoreless waves,* l. 295. The earth was originally covered with water, as appears from some of its highest mountains, consisting of shells cemented together by a solution of part of them, as the limestone rocks of the Alps; Ferber's *Travels.* It must be therefore concluded, that animal life began beneath the sea.

Nor is this unanalogous to what still occurs, as all quadrupeds and mankind in their embryon state are aquatic animals; and thus may be said to resemble gnats and frogs. The fetus in the uterus has an organ called the placenta, the fine extremities of the vessels of which permeate the arteries of the uterus, and the blood of the fetus becomes thus oxygenated from the passing stream of the maternal arterial blood; exactly as is done by the gills of fish from the stream of water, which they occasion to pass through them.

But the chicken in the egg possesses a kind of aerial respiration, since the extremities of its placental vessels terminate on a membranous bag, which contains air, at the broad end of the egg; and in this the chick in the egg differs from the fetus in the womb, as there is in the egg no circulating maternal blood for the insertion of the extremities of its respiratory vessels, and in this also I suspect that the eggs of birds differ from the spawn of fish; which latter is immersed in water, and which has probably the extremities of its respiratory organ inserted into the soft membrane which covers it, and is in contact with the water.

[34] *An embryon point,* l. 314. The arguments showing that all vegetables and animals arose from such a small beginning, as a living point or living fibre, are detailed in Zoonomia, Sect. XXXIX. 4. 8. on Generation.

[35] See footnote 9. [Ed.]

"Now in vast shoals beneath the brineless tide,[36]
60 On earth's firm crust testaceous tribes reside;
Age after age expands the peopled plain,
The tenants perish, but their cells remain;
Whence coral walls and sparry hills ascend
From pole to pole, and round the line extend.   320

65   "Next when imprison'd fires in central caves
Burst the firm earth, and drank the headlong waves;
And, as new airs with dread explosion swell,
Form'd lava-isles, and continents of shell;
Pil'd rocks on rocks, on mountains mountains raised,
70 And high in heaven the first volcanoes blazed;
In countless swarms an insect-myriad moves[37]
From sea-fan gardens, and from coral groves;
Leaves the cold caverns of the deep, and creeps
On shelving shores, or climbs on rocky steeps.   330
75 As in dry air the sea-born stranger roves,
Each muscle quickens, and each sense improves;

---

[36] *Brineless tide*, l. 315. As the salt of the sea has been gradually accumulating, being washed down into it from the recrements of animal and vegetable bodies, the sea must originally have been as fresh as river water; and as it is not saturated with salt, must become annually saline. The sea-water about our island contains at this time from about one twenty-eighth to one thirtieth part of sea salt, and about one eightieth of magnesian salt; Brownrigg on Salt.

[37] *An insect-myriad moves*, l. 327. After islands or continents were raised above the primeval ocean, great numbers of the most simple animals would attempt to seek food at the edges or shores of the new land, and might thence gradually become amphibious; as is now seen in the frog, who changes from an aquatic animal to an amphibious one; and in the gnat, which changes from a natant to a volant state.

At the same time new microscopic animalcules would immediately commence wherever there was warmth and moisture, and some organic matter, that might induce putridity. Those situated on dry land, and immersed in dry air, may gradually acquire new powers to preserve their existence; and by innumerable successive reproductions for some thousands, or perhaps millions of ages, may at length have produced many of the vegetable and animal inhabitants which now people the earth.

As innumerable shell-fish must have existed a long time beneath the ocean, before the calcareous mountains were produced and elevated; it is also probable, that many of the insect tribes, or less complicate animals, existed long before the quadrupeds or more complicate ones, which in some measure accords with the theory of Linneus in respect to the vegetable world; who thinks, that all the plants now extant arose from the conjunction and reproduction of about sixty different vegetables, from which he constitutes his natural orders.

As the blood of animals in the air becomes more oxygenated in their lungs, than that

Cold gills aquatic form respiring lungs,
And sounds aerial flow from slimy tongues.

 "So Trapa rooted[38] in pellucid tides,
80 In countless threads her breathing leaves divides,
Waves her bright tresses in the watery mass,
And drinks with gelid gills the vital gas;
Then broader leaves in shadowy files advance,
Spread o'er the crystal flood their green expanse;   340
85 And, as in air the adherent dew exhales,
Court the warm sun, and breathe ethereal gales.

 "So still the Tadpole[39] cleaves the watery vale
With balanc'd fins, and undulating tail;

---

of animals in water by their gills; it becomes of a more scarlet colour, and from its greater stimulus the sensorium seems to produce quicker motions and finer sensations; and as water is a much better vehicle for vibrations or sounds than air, the fish, even when dying in pain, are mute in the atmosphere, though it is probable that in the water they may utter sounds to be heard at a considerable distance.

[38] *So Trapa rooted,* l. 335. The lower leaves of this plant grow under water, and are divided into minute capillary ramifications; while the upper leaves are broad and round, and have air bladders in their footstalks to support them above the surface of the water. As the aerial leaves of vegetables do the office of lungs, by exposing a large surface of vessels with their contained fluids to the influence of the air; so these aquatic leaves answer a similar purpose like the gills of fish, and perhaps gain from water a similar material. As the material thus necessary to life seems to be more easily acquired from air than from water, the subaquatic leaves of this plant and of sisymbrium, oenanthe, ranunculus aquatilis, water crow-foot, and some others, are cut into fine divisions to increase the surface, whilst those above water are undivided.

Few of the water plants of this country are used for economical purposes, but the ranunculus fluviatilis may be worth cultivation; as on the borders of the river Avon, near Ringwood, the cottagers cut this plant every morning in boats, almost all the year round, to feed their cows, which appear in good condition, and give a due quantity of milk.

[39] *So still the Tadpole,* l. 343. The transformation of the tadpole from an aquatic animal into an aerial one is abundantly curious, when first it is hatched from the spawn by the warmth of the season, it resembles a fish; it afterwards puts forth legs, and resembles a lizard; and finally losing its tail, and acquiring lungs instead of gills, becomes an aerial quadruped.

The rana temporaria of Linneus lives in the water in spring, and on the land in summer, and catches flies. Of the rana paradoxa the larva or tadpole is as large as the frog, and dwells in Surinam, whence the mistake of Merian and of Seba, who call it a frog fish. The esculent frog is green, with three yellow lines from the mouth to the anus; the back transversely gibbous, the hinder feet palmated; its more frequent croaking in the evenings is said to foretell rain.

Linneus asserts in his introduction to the class Amphibia, that frogs are so nearly allied to lizards, lizards to serpents, and serpents to fish, that the boundaries of these orders can scarcely be ascertained.

New lungs and limbs proclaim his second birth,
90 Breathe the dry air, and bound upon the earth.
So from deep lakes the dread Musquito springs,
Drinks the soft breeze, and dries his tender wings,
In twinkling squadrons cuts his airy way,
Dips his red trunk in blood, and man his prey.   350

95   "So still the Diodons,[40] amphibious tribe,
With two-fold lungs the sea or air imbibe;
Allied to fish, the lizard cleaves the flood
With one-cell'd heart, and dark frigescent blood;
Half-reasoning Beavers long-unbreathing dart
100 Through Erie's waves with perforated heart;
With gills and lungs respiring Lampreys steer,
Kiss the rude rocks, and suck till they adhere;
The lazy Remora's inhaling lips,
Hung on the keel, retard the struggling ships;   360
105 With gills pulmonic breathes the enormous Whale,
And spouts aquatic columns to the gale;
Sports on the shining wave at noontide hours,[41]
And shifting rainbows crest the rising showers.

       "So erst, ere rose the science to record
110 In letter'd syllables the volant word;
Whence chemic arts, disclosed in pictured lines,
Liv'd to mankind by hieroglyphic signs;
And clustering stars, pourtray'd on mimic spheres,
Assumed the forms of lions, bulls, and bears;   370
115 So erst, as Egypt's rude designs explain,
Rose young Dione[42] from the shoreless main;

---

[40] Balloon fish or puffer fish. [Ed.]

[41] *At noontide hours,* l. 363. The rainbows in our latitude are only seen in the mornings or evenings, when the sun is not much more than forty-two degrees high. In the more northern latitudes, where the meridian sun is not more than forty-two degrees high, they are also visible at noon.

[42] *Rose young Dione,* l. 372. The hieroglyphic figure of Venus rising from the sea supported on a shell by two tritons, as well as that of Hercules armed with a club, appear to be remains of the most remote antiquity. As the former is devoid of grace, and of the pictorial art of design, as one half of the group exactly resembles the other; and as that of Hercules is armed with a club, which was the first weapon.

   The Venus seems to have represented the beauty of organic Nature rising from the sea, and afterwards became simply an emblem of ideal beauty; while the figure of Adonis was probably designed to represent the more abstracted idea of life or animation. Some of these hieroglyphic designs seem to evince the profound investigations in science of

Type of organic Nature! source of bliss!
Emerging Beauty from the vast abyss!
Sublime on Chaos borne, the Goddess stood,
120 And smiled enchantment on the troubled flood;
The warring elements to peace restored,
And young Reflection wondered and adored."

Now paused the Nymph, The Muse responsive cries,
Sweet admiration sparkling in her eyes,   380
125 "Drawn by your pencil, by your hand unfurl'd,
Bright shines the tablet of the dawning world;
Amazed the Sea's prolific depths I view,
And Venus rising from the waves in You!

"Still Nature's births enclosed in egg or seed
130 From the tall forest to the lowly weed,
Her beaux and beauties, butterflies and worms,
Rise from aquatic to aerial forms.
Thus in the womb the nascent infant laves
Its natant form in the circumfluent waves;   390
135 With perforated heart unbreathing swims,
Awakes and stretches[43] all its recent limbs;
With gills placental[44] seeks the arterial flood,
And drinks pure ether from its Mother's blood.
Erewhile the landed Stranger bursts his way,
140 From the warm wave emerging into day;
Feels the chill blast, and piercing light, and tries
His tender lungs, and rolls his dazzled eyes;[45]

---

the Egyptian philosophers, and to have outlived all written language; and still constitute the symbols, by which painters and poets give form and animation to abstracted ideas, as to those of strength and beauty in the above instances.

[43] *Awakes and stretches,* l. 392. During the first six months of gestation, the embryon probably sleeps, as it seems to have no use for voluntary power; it then seems to awake, and to stretch its limbs, and change its posture in some degree, which is termed quickening.

[44] *With gills placental,* l. 393. The placenta adheres to any side of the uterus in natural gestation, or of any other cavity in extra-uterine gestation; the extremities of its arteries and veins probably permeate the arteries of the mother, and absorb from thence through their fine coats the oxygen of the mother's blood; hence when the placenta is withdrawn, the side of the uterus, where it adhered, bleeds; but not the extremities of its own vessels.

[45] *His dazzled eyes,* l. 398. Though the membrana pupillaris described by modern anatomists guards the tender retina from too much light; the young infant nevertheless seems to feel the presence of it by its frequently moving its eyes, before it can distinguish common objects.

Gives to the passing gale his curling hair,
And steps a dry inhabitant of air.   400

145   "Creative Nile, as taught in ancient song,
So charm'd to life his animated throng;
O'er his wide realms the slow-subsiding flood
Left the rich treasures of organic mud;
While with quick growth young Vegetation yields
150 Her blushing orchards, and her waving fields;
Pomona's hand replenish'd Plenty's horn,
And Ceres laugh'd amid her seas of corn.
Bird, beast, and reptile, spring from sudden birth,
Raise their new forms, half-animal, half-earth;   410
155 The roaring lion shakes his tawny mane,
His struggling limbs still rooted in the plain;
With flapping wings assurgent eagles toil
To rend their talons from the adhesive soil;
The impatient serpent lifts his crested head,
160 And drags his train unfinish'd from the bed.
As Warmth and Moisture[46] blend their magic spells,
And brood with mingling wings the slimy dells;
Contractile earths in sentient forms arrange,
And Life triumphant stays their chemic change." [. . .]   420

-----

[46] *As warmth and moisture,* l. 417.

          In eodem corpore sæpe
Altera pars vivit; rudis est pars altera tellus.
Quippe ubi temperiem sumpsêre humorque calorque,
Concipiunt; & ab his oriuntur cuncta duobus.
                              Ovid. Met. 1. 1. 430.[47]

This story from Ovid of the production of animals from the mud of the Nile seems to be of Egyptian origin, and is probably a poetical account of the opinions of the magi or priests of that country; showing that the simplest animations were spontaneously produced like chemical combinations, but were distinguished from the latter by their perpetual improvement by the power of reproduction, first by solitary, and then by sexual generation; whereas the products of natural chemistry are only enlarged by accretion, or purified by filtration.

[47] "Often (they find that) in the same body one part is alive, while another part is raw clay. For when moisture and heat combine in mixture, they become fecund. And from these two forces all things arise." *Metamorphoses* 1. 428 – 431. [Ed.]

Thomas Bewick (1753–1828)

Thomas Bewick is the best-known British illustrator of natural history subjects. From early childhood he combined a fascination for drawing with his own detailed observations of the natural world. Bewick claimed that his desire to produce works of natural history originated in the 1780s with dissatisfaction over the books to which he had access as a young boy. He set out to reform not only the style of natural illustration but also the methods of print production. His technical innovations included the rediscovery of various aspects of woodblock engraving. His carved images produced a wide range of textures and visual effects, primarily because he cut parallel lines in his blocks as opposed to the more usual crosshatching. He also relied on the technique of white-line printing, in which the ink is placed on the raised edge of the carved relief instead of in the grooves between the edges. He achieved new effects in dimensional depth and atmospherics by lowering the background areas of his print block images, thus producing shades of gray around the central objects being depicted.

Ralph Beilby, to whom Bewick had initially been apprenticed, became Bewick's partner in 1777, a partnership that lasted for two decades. Thomas Pennant's *General History of Quadrupeds* had first appeared in 1781, and Gilbert White's *Natural History of Selborne* followed in 1789. In 1790, Bewick and Beilby published the first edition of their own *General History of Quadrupeds*. By 1824 the work had appeared in eight editions. Since Bewick did not have access to most of the larger animals he was depicting, he based many of these illustrations on Buffon's *Histoire Naturelle* (1749–1804), which was translated into English by W. Smellie (1781–85). Bewick and Beilby both contributed to the text of their natural history volumes, although a disagreement over the extent of Beilby's role (he wanted to claim authorship of the volumes) led to the eventual dissolution of the partnership.

Bewick's wood engravings were notable for their accuracy, delicate attention to detail, and lifelike poses. An avid naturalist himself, Bewick based many of his designs for British creatures and scenes (to which he did have access) on personal observations of birds and animals in their natural settings, or from specimens and skins sent to him by other naturalists. *The History of British Birds,* Bewick's most widely known work, began with *Land Birds* in 1797, followed by *Water Birds* in 1804. For these volumes, Bewick stated his desire to "stick to nature." He issued revised editions in 1809 and 1816. Eight editions of *Land Birds* and six of *Water Birds* were in print by 1826. Bewick apprenticed first his brother and later his son in his studio. He died in 1828, a year after having been visited by John James Audubon.

Bewick's visual work often captures a mood that is reflected in the poetry of James Thomson, Robert Burns, and John Clare, among others. "O that the genius of Bewick were mine," Wordsworth says in *Lyrical Ballads.* Charlotte Brontë wrote a poem to Bewick when she was only 16, and Brontë's most famous character is reading Bewick's *History of British Birds* at the opening of *Jane Eyre.* In fact, Jane Eyre quotes from Bewick, who is himself quoting James Thomson:

Where the Northern Ocean, in vast whirls
Boils around the naked, melancholy isles
Of farthest Thule; and the Atlantic surge
Pours among the stormy Hebrides.

The passage is from Thomson's *Seasons.* Jane Eyre says that she can never merely pass over those passages "which treat of the haunts of seafowl; of 'the solitary rocks and promontories' by them only inhabited" (20–21).

From A General History of Quadrupeds

The Tiger is the most rapacious and destructive of all carnivorous animals. Fierce without provocation, and cruel without necessity, its thirst for blood is insatiable: Though glutted with slaughter, it continues its carnage, nor ever gives up so long as a single object remains in its fight. Flocks and herds fall indiscriminate victims to its fury: It fears neither the sight nor the opposition of man, whom it frequently makes its prey; and it is even said to prefer human flesh to that of any other animal.

The Tiger is peculiar to Asia; and is found as far North as China and Chinese Tartary: It inhabits Mount Ararat, and Hyrcania of old, famous for its wild beasts. The greatest numbers are met with in India, and its islands: They are the scourge of the country: They lurk among the bushes, by the sides of rivers, and almost depopulate many places. They seldom pursue their prey; but bound upon it from the place of their ambush, with an elasticity, and from a distance, scarcely credible. It is highly probable, that, from this circumstance, the Tiger may derive its name, which, in the Armenian language, signifies an arrow; to the flight of which this creature may very properly be compared, in the quickness and agility of its bounds.

The strength of this animal is so great, that, when it has killed an animal, whether it be a Horse, a Buffalo, or a Deer, it carries it off with such ease, that it seems no impediment to its flight. If it be undisturbed, it plunges its head into the body of the animal up to its very eyes, as if to satiate itself with blood.

The Tiger is perhaps the only animal whose ferocity can never be subdued: Neither gentleness nor constraint has any effect in softening its temper. It does not seem sensible of the attention of its keeper; and would equally tear the hand that feeds, with that by which it is chastised.

Notwithstanding the cruelty of this creature's disposition, a sudden check has sometimes had a good effect in preventing its meditated attack. Some ladies and gentlemen being on a party of pleasure, under a shade of trees, on the banks of a river in Bengal, were suddenly surprized at seeing a Tiger ready to make its fatal spring: One of the ladies, with amazing presence of mind, laid hold of an umbrella, and unfurling it directly in the animal's face, it instantly retired. Another party had not the same good fortune. A Tiger darted among them whilst they were at dinner, seized on a gentleman, and carried him off in the sight of his disconsolate companions.

Thomas Bewick, *A General History of Quadrupeds*. Newcastle: S. Hodgson, Beilby, and Bewick, 1790.

They attack all kinds of animals, even the Lion; and furious combats have frequently been maintained between them, in which both have perished. Father Tachard gives an account of a battle between a Tiger and two Elephants, at Siam, of which he was an eye-witness. The heads, and part of the trunks of the Elephants, were defended from the claws of the Tiger by a covering made for the purpose. They were placed in the midst of a large inclosure. One of them was suffered to approach the Tiger, which was confined by cords, and received two or three heavy blows from the trunk of the Elephant upon its back, which beat it to the ground, where it lay for some time as if it were dead: But, though this attack had a good deal abated its fury, it was no sooner untied, than, with a horrible roar, it made a spring at the Elephant's trunk, which that animal dexterously avoided by drawing it up; and, receiving the Tiger on its tusks, threw it up into the air. The two Elephants were then allowed to come up; and, after giving it several heavy blows, would undoubtedly have killed it, if an end had not been put to the combat. Under such restraints and disadvantages, we cannot wonder that the issue was unfavourable to the Tiger. We may, however, judge of its exceedingly great strength and fierceness, that, after being disabled by the first attack of the Elephant, whilst it was held by its cords, it would venture to continue such an unequal engagement.

We are happy in being able to present our curious readers with an engraving of this rare animal, drawn from the life, from a Tiger that was exhibited at Newcastle, in 1787; and was generally allowed to be one of the finest creatures of its kind ever seen in England. The beautiful bars of black with which every part of its body was streaked, are accurately copied: The colour of the ground was yellow, deeper on the back, and softening by degrees towards the belly, where it was white; as were also the throat and insides of the legs: A white space, spotted with black, surrounded each eye; and on each cheek, a stripe of the same colour extended from the ears to the throat. It was nearly the same height as the Lion; and was of the largest species of the Tiger, which is called the *Royal Tiger*. The smallest of them is not above two feet high, said to be extremely cunning, and delights in human flesh. The second kind is about three feet high, and is fond of Deer, wild Hogs, &c. which it frequently takes by the sides of rivers, as they come down to quench their thirst.

The skin of this animal is much esteemed all over the East, particularly in China. The Mandarins cover their seats of justice with it; and, during the winter, use it for cushions and pillows. [. . .]

From A History of British Birds

PREFACE

To those who attentively consider the subject of Natural History, as displayed in the animal creation, it will appear, that though much has been done to explore the intricate paths of Nature, and follow her through all her various windings, much yet remains to be done before the great œconomy is completely developed. Notwithstanding the laborious and not unsuccessful inquiries of ingenious men in all ages, the subject is far from being exhausted. Systems have been formed and exploded, and new ones have appeared in their stead; but, like skeletons injudiciously put together, they give but an imperfect idea of that order and symmetry to which they are intended to be subservient: they have, however, their use, but it is chiefly the skilful practitioner who is enabled to profit by them; to the less informed they appear obscure and perplexing, and too frequently deter him from the great object of his pursuit.

To investigate, with any tolerable degree of success, the more retired and distant parts of the animal œconomy, is a task of no small difficulty. An enquiry so desirable and so eminently useful would require the united efforts of many to give it the desired success. Men of leisure, of all descriptions, residing in the country, could scarcely find a more delightful employment than in attempting to elucidate, from their own observations, the various branches of Natural History, and in communicating them to others. Something like a society in each county, for the purpose of collecting a variety of these observations, as well as for general correspondence, would be extremely useful. Much might be expected from a combination of this kind, extending through every part of the kingdom; a general mode of communication might be thereby established, in order to ascertain the changes which are continually taking place, particularly among the feathered tribes; the times of their appearing and disappearing would be carefully noted; the differences of age, sex, food, &c. would claim a particular degree of attention, and would be the means of correcting the errors which have crept into the works of some of the most eminent ornithologists, from an over-anxious desire of increasing the number of species: but it is reserved, perhaps, for times of greater tranquillity, when the human mind,undisturbed by public calamities, shall find leisure to employ itself, without interruption, in the pursuit of those objects which enlarge its powers and give dignity to its exertions, to carry into the fullest effect a plan for investigations of this sort.

Thomas Bewick, *A History of British Birds*. London: Longman, 1816.

As a naturalist no author has been more successful than the celebrated Count de Buffon: despising the restraints which methodical arrangements generally impose, he ranges at large through the various walks of Nature, and describes her with a brilliancy of colouring which only the most lively imagination could suggest. It must, however, be allowed, that in many instances this ingenious philosopher has overstepped the bounds of Nature, and, in giving the reins to his own luxuriant fancy, has been too frequently hurried into the wild paths of conjecture and romance. The late Mr White, of Selborne, has added much to the general stock of knowledge on this delightful subject, by attentively and faithfully recording whatever fell under his own observation, and by liberal communications to others.

As far as we could, consistently with the plan laid down in the following work, we have consulted, and we trust with some advantage, the works of these and other naturalists. In the arrangement of the various classes, as well as in the descriptive part, we have taken as a guide, our ingenious countryman Mr Pennant, to whose elegant and useful labours the world is indebted for a fund of the most rational entertainment, and who will be remembered by every lover of Nature as long as her works have power to charm. The communications with which we have been favoured by those gentlemen who were so good as to notice our growing work, have been generally acknowledged, each in its proper place; it remains only that we be permitted to insert this testimony of our grateful sense of them.

In a few instances we have ventured to depart from the usual method of classification: by placing the hard-billed birds, or those which live chiefly on seeds, next to those of the Pie kind, there seems to be a more regular gradation downwards, since only a few anomalous birds, such as the Cuckoo, Hoopoe, Nuthatch, &c. intervene. The soft-billed birds, or those which subsist chiefly on worms, insects, and such like, are by this mode placed all together, beginning with those of the Lark kind. To this we must observe, that, by dividing the various families of birds into two grand divisions, viz. Land and Water, a number of tribes have thereby been included among the latter, which can no otherwise be denominated Water Birds than as they occasionally seek their food in moist places, by small streamlets, or on the sea-shore; such as the Curlew, Woodcock, Snipe, Sandpiper, and many others. These, with such as do not commit themselves wholly to the waters, are thrown into a separate division, under the denomination of Waders. To this class we have ventured to remove the Kingfisher, and the Water Ouzel: the former lives entirely on fish, is constantly found on the margins of still waters, and may with greater propriety be denominated a Water Bird than many which come under that description; the latter seems to have no connection with those birds among which it is usually classed;

it is generally found among rapid running streams, in which it chiefly delights, and from which it derives its support.

It may be proper to observe, that while one of the editors of this work was engaged in preparing the cuts, which are faithfully drawn from Nature, and engraved upon wood, the compilation of the descriptions (*of the Land Birds*) was undertaken by the other, subject, however, to the corrections of his friend, whose habits had led him to a more intimate acquaintance with this branch of Natural History: the compiler, therefore, is answerable for the defects which may be found in this part of the undertaking, concerning which he has little to say, but that it was the production of those hours which could be spared from a laborious employment, and on that account he hopes the severity of criticism will be spared, and that it will be received with that indulgence which has been already experienced on a former occasion.

Newcastle upon Tyne, September, 1797.

OF THE LARK

Among the various kinds of singing birds with which this country abounds, there is none more eminently conspicuous than those of the Lark kind. Instead of retiring to woods and deep recesses, or lurking in thickets, where it may be heard without being seen, the Lark is seen abroad in the fields; it is the only bird which chaunts on the wing, and while it soars beyond the reach of our sight, pours forth the most melodious strains, which may be distinctly heard at an amazing distance. The great poet of nature thus beautifully describes it as the leader of the general chorus:

> . . . . Up springs the Lark,
> Shrill-voic'd and loud, the messenger of morn;
> Ere yet the shadows fly, he, mounted, sings
> Amid the dawning clouds, and from their haunts
> 5 Calls up the tuneful nations.

From the peculiar construction of the hinder claws, which are very long and straight, Larks generally rest upon the ground; those which frequent trees perch only on the larger branches. They all build their nests upon the ground, which exposes them to the depredations of the smaller kinds of voracious animals, such as the weasel, stoat, &c. which destroy great numbers of them. The Cuckoo likewise, which makes no nest of its own, frequently substitutes its eggs in the place of theirs. The general characters of this species are thus described: The bill is straight and slender, bending a little towards the end, which is sharp-pointed; the nostrils are covered with feathers and bristles; the tongue is cloven at the end; tail somewhat forked; the toes divided to the origin; claw of the hinder toe very long, and almost straight; the fore claws very short, and slightly curved.

THE SKYLARK

Lavrock

(*ALAUDA ARVENSIS*, LIN. — *L' ALOUETTE*, BUFF.)

Length nearly seven inches. Bill dusky, under mandible somewhat yellow; eyes hazel; over each eye there is a pale streak, which extends to the bill, and round the eye on the under side; on the upper parts of the body the feathers are of a reddish brown colour, dark in the middle, with pale edges; the fore part of the neck is of a reddish white, dashed with brown; breast, belly, and thighs white; the quills brown, with pale edges; tail the same, and somewhat forked, the two middle feathers darkest, the outermost white on the outer edge; the legs dusky. In some of our specimens the feathers on the top of the head were long, and formed a sort of crest behind. The Lesser Crested Lark of Pennant and Latham is perhaps only a variety of this, the difference being trifling. It is said to be found in Yorkshire.

The Lark begins its song very early in the spring, and is heard chiefly in the morning; it rises in the air almost perpendicularly and by successive springs, and hovers at a vast height; its descent, on the contrary, is in an oblique direction, unless it is threatened by birds of prey, or attracted by its mate, and on these occasions it drops like a stone. Its makes it nest on the ground, between two clods of earth, and lines it with dried grass and roots: the female lays four or five eggs, of a greyish brown colour, marked with darker spots: she generally has two broods in the year, and sits only about fifteen days. As soon as the young have escaped from the shell, the attachment of the parent bird seems to increase; she flutters over their heads, directs all their motions, and is ever ready to screen them from danger.

The Lark is diffused almost universally throughout Europe; it is every where extremely prolific, and in some places the prodigious numbers that are frequently caught are truly astonishing. In Germany there is an excise upon them, which has produced, according to Keysler, the sum of 6000 dollars in one year to the city of Leipsic alone. Mr Pennant says, the neighbourhood of Dunstable is famous for the great numbers of these birds found there, and that 4000 dozen have been taken between September and February, for the London markets. Yet, notwithstanding the great havoc made among these birds, they are extremely numerous. The winter is the best season for taking them, as they are then very fat, being almost constantly on the ground, feeding in great flocks; whereas in summer they are very lean; they then always go in pairs, eat sparingly, and sing incessantly while on the wing. [...]

THE NIGHTINGALE

(*MOTACILLA LUSCINIA*, LIN. — *LE ROSSIGNOL*, BUFF.)
This bird, so deservedly esteemed for the excellence of its song, is not remarkable for the variety or richness of its colours. It is somewhat more than six inches in length. Its bill is brown, yellow on the edges at the base; eyes hazel; the whole upper part of the body is of a rusty brown, tinged with olive; the under parts pale ash colour, almost white at the throat and vent;

236   BRITISH BIRDS.

THE NIGHTINGALE.

Thomas Bewick's 1797 engraving of the nightingale (*Luscinia megarhynchos*). Perhaps the quintessential poetic bird, even before the time of the Romantics. In addition to Keats's often-quoted lyric, Wordsworth, Coleridge, and Charlotte Smith, among others, all produced poems in praise of the nightingale's melodious song. This engraving from *A History of British Birds* (Newcastle, 1832). Archives and Special Collections, Dickinson College, Carlisle, PA.

the quills are brown, with reddish margins: legs pale brown. The male and female are very similar.

Although the Nightingale is common in this country, it never visits the northern parts of our island, and is but seldom seen in the western counties of Devonshire and Cornwall: it leaves us some time in the month of August, and makes its regular return in the beginning of April; it is supposed, during that interval, to visit the distant regions of Asia; this is probable, as these birds do not winter in any part of France, Germany, Italy, Greece, &c. neither does it appear that they stay in Africa, but are seen at all times in India, Persia, China, and Japan; in the latter country they are much esteemed for their song, and sell at great prices. They are spread generally throughout Europe, even as far north as Siberia and Sweden, where they are said to sing delightfully; they, however, are partial to particular places, and avoid others which seem as likely to afford them the necessary means of support. It is not improbable, however, that, by planting a colony in a well-chosen situation, these delightful songsters might be induced to haunt places where they are not at present seen; the experiment might be easily tried, and should it succeed, the reward would be great in the rich and varied song of this unrivalled bird. The following animated description of it is taken from the ingenious author of the *Histoire des Oiseaux:* "The leader of the vernal chorus begins with a low and timid voice, and he prepares for the hymn to nature by assaying his powers and attuning his organs; by degrees the sound opens and swells, it bursts with loud and vivid flashes, it flows with smooth volubility, it faints and murmurs, it shakes with rapid and violent articulations; the soft breathings of love and joy are poured from his inmost soul, and every heart beats in unison, and melts with delicious languor. But this continued richness might satiate the ear. The strains are at times relieved by pauses, which bestow dignity and elevation. The mild silence of evening heightens the general effect, and not a rival interrupts the solemn scene."

Nightingales begin to build about the end of April or the beginning of May; they make their nest in the lower part of a thick bush or hedge; the female lays four or five eggs, of a greenish brown colour. The nest is composed of dry grass and leaves, intermixed with small fibres, and lined with hair, down, and other soft and warm substances. The business of incubation is entirely performed by the female, whilst the cock, at no great distance, entertains her with his delightful melody: as soon, however, as the young are hatched, he leaves off singing, and joins her in the care of providing for the young brood. These birds make a second hatch, and sometimes a third; and in hot countries they are said to have four.

The Nightingale is a solitary bird, and never unites in flocks like many of the smaller birds, but hides itself in the thickest parts of the bushes, and sings generally in the night: its food consists principally of insects, small worms, eggs of ants, and sometimes berries of various kinds. Nightingales, though timorous and shy, are easily caught; snares of all sorts are laid for them, and generally succeed; they are likewise caught on lime twigs. Young ones are sometimes brought up from the nest, and fed with great care till they are able to sing. It is with great difficulty that old birds are induced to sing after being taken; for a considerable time they refuse to eat, but by great attention to their treatment, and avoiding every thing that might agitate them, they at length resume their song, and continue it during the greater part of the year. [. . .]

The Throstle

Thrush, Grey Bird, or Mavis

(*Turdus Musicus*, Lin.—*La Grive*, Buff.)
This is larger than the Redwing, but much less than the Missel, to which it bears a strong resemblance both in form and colours. A small notch is observable at the end of the bill, which belongs to this and every bird of the Thrush kind: the throat is white, and the spots on the breast more regularly formed than those of the Missel Thrush, being of a conical shape; the inside of the wings and the mouth are yellow, as are also the legs; the claws are strong and black.

The Throstle is distinguished among our singing birds by the clearness and fullness of its note; it charms us not only with the sweetness, but variety of its song, which it begins early in the spring, and continues during part of the summer. This bold and pleasing songster, from his high station, seems to command the concert of the grove, whilst in the beautiful language of the poet,

The Jay, the Rook, the Daw,
And each harsh pipe (discordant heard alone)
Aid the full concert, while the Stock-Dove breathes
A melancholy murmur through the whole.

The female builds her nest generally in bushes; it is composed of dried grass, with a little earth or clay intermixed, and lined with rotten wood; she lays five or six eggs, of a pale blue colour, marked with dusky spots.

Although this species is not considered with us as migratory, it has, nevertheless, been observed in some places in great numbers during the spring and summer, where not one was to be seen in the winter, which has induced an opinion that they either shift their quarters entirely, or take shelter in the more retired parts of the woods. The Throstle is migratory in France: M. de Buffon says that it appears in Burgundy about the end of September, before the Redwing and Fieldfare, and that it feeds upon the ripe grapes, and sometimes does much damage to the vineyard. The females of all the Thrush kind are very similar to the males, and differ chiefly in a less degree of brilliancy in the colours. [. . .]

OF THE SWALLOW

Of all the various families of birds, which resort to this island for food and shelter, there is none which has occasioned so many conjectures respecting its appearance and departure as the Swallow tribe: of this we have already hazarded our opinion in the introductory part of the work, to which we refer the reader. The habits and modes of living of this tribe are perhaps more conspicuous than those of any other. From the time of their arrival to that of their departure they seem continually before our eyes. The Swallow lives habitually in the air, and performs its various functions in that element; and whether it pursues its fluttering prey, and follows the devious windings of the insects on which it feeds, or endeavours to escape the birds of prey by the quickness of its motion, it describes lines so mutable, so varied, so interwoven, and so confused, that they hardly can be pictured by words. "The Swallow tribe is of all others the most inoffensive, harmless, entertaining and social; all, except one species, attach themselves to our houses, amuse us with their migrations, songs, and marvellous agility, and clear the air of gnats and other troublesome insects, which would otherwise much annoy and incommode us. Whoever contemplates the myriads of insects that sport in the sun-beams of a summer evening in this country, will soon be convinced to what degree our atmosphere would be choaked with them, were it not for the friendly interposition of the Swallow tribe."[1]

Not many attempts have been made to preserve Swallows alive during the winter, and of these, few have succeeded. The following experiments, by Mr James Pearson, of London, communicated to us by Sir John Trevelyan, Bart. are highly interesting, and throw great light upon the natural history of the Swallow; we shall give them nearly in Mr Pearson's own words.

Five or six of these birds were taken about the latter end of August, 1784, in a bat fowling-net, at night; they were put separately into small cages, and fed with Nightingale's food: in about a week or ten days they took food of

---

[1] White's Selborne.

themselves; they were then put altogether into a deep cage, four feet long, with gravel at the bottom; a broad shallow pan with water was placed in it, in which they sometimes washed themselves, and seemed much strengthened by it. One day Mr Pearson observed that they went into the water with unusual eagerness, hurrying in and out again repeatedly, with such swiftness as if they had been suddenly seized with a frenzy. Being anxious to see the result, he left them to themselves about half an hour, and on going to the cage again, found them all huddled together in a corner, apparently dead; the cage was then placed at a proper distance from the fire, when only two of them recovered, and were as healthy as before—the rest died. The two remaining ones were allowed to wash themselves occasionally for a short time only; but their feet soon after became swelled and inflamed, which Mr. P. attributed to their perching, and they died about Christmas: thus the first year's experiment was in some measure lost. Not discouraged by the failure of this, Mr P. determined to make a second trial the succeeding year, from a strong desire of being convinced of the truth respecting their going into a state of torpidity. Accordingly, the next season, having taken some more birds, he put them into the cage, and in every respect pursued the same methods as with the last; but to guard their feet from the bad effects of the damp and cold, he covered the perches with flannel, and had the pleasure to observe that the birds throve extremely well; they sung their song through the winter, and soon after Christmas began to moult, which they got through without any difficulty, and lived three or four years, regularly moulting every year at the usual time. On the renewal of their feathers it appeared that their tails were forked exactly the same as in those birds which return hither in the spring, and in every respect their appearance was the same. These birds, says Mr Pearson, were exhibited to the society for promoting Natural History, on the 14th day of February, 1786, at the time they were in a deep moult, during a severe frost, when the snow was on the ground. Minutes of this circumstance were entered in the books of the society. These birds died at last from neglect, during a long illness which Mr Pearson had: they died in the summer. Mr P. concludes his very interesting account in these words: "January 20, 1797, 1481 have now in my house, No. 21, Great Newport-street, Long-Acre, four Swallows in moult, in as perfect health as any birds ever appeared to be when moulting."

The result of these experiments pretty clearly proves, that Swallows do not in any material instance differ from other birds in their nature and propensities; but that they leave us, like many other birds, when this country can no longer furnish them with a supply of their proper and natural food, and that consequently they seek it in other places, where they meet with that support which enables them to throw off their feathers.

Swallows are found in every country of the known world, but seldom remain the whole year in the same climate; the times of their appearance and departure in this country are well known: they are the constant harbingers of spring, and on their arrival all nature assumes a more cheerful aspect. The bill of this genus is short, very broad on the base, and a little bent; the head is flat, and the neck scarcely visible; the tongue is short, broad, and cloven; tail mostly forked; wings long; legs short. [. . .]

William Blake (1757–1827)

W illiam Blake is a particularly complex figure in terms of a Romantic natural history. On the one hand, Blake was hostile to "vegetable" nature in all its forms. He saw the natural world as a sign of our fallen condition, and his antimaterialism disdained all forms of embodied spirit, a category that included, for him, at least humans and perhaps other aspects of animate nature as well. At the same time, Blake makes powerful use of natural imagery throughout his poems and artistic productions. For Blake, to be in nature is to be always removed from the idealized world of visionary imagination, but that does not prevent him from suggesting an interconnectedness that links all living things. As a result, his illustrated caterpillars and butterflies often have human faces, while his human figures sometimes sprout roots and branches. His birds' tails and wings echo flower stalks and vines, while his mythic figures often connect the "human form divine" with the botanic or the bestial. In Blake's visual and verbal representation of nature, we find a strange combination of distrust and reverence, skepticism and worship.

Blake may have distrusted nature in visionary terms, but he celebrated its physical beauty, its sensuous details, and its crucial role in our awareness of our human place in the cosmos. In "Auguries of Innocence," for example, he reveals the cost of human ignorance of those connections that unite all aspects of creation: "The wanton Boy that kills the Fly / Shall feel the Spider's enmity," or, "He who shall hurt the little Wren / Shall never be belov'd by Men." In many of his songs and short lyrics, Blake suggests that it is only human beings who upset the balances that exist throughout the rest of the natural world. "The Book of Thel" presents a cloud, a lily, a clod of clay, and a worm that all accept their roles in a cycle of organic life and death in a way that the humanized Thel cannot. *The Four Zoas* imagines an idealized future state in which the fallen aspects of human psychic integrity are reunited with themselves and with the rest of animate creation. "The Sick Rose," by contrast, suggests that nature employs destructive processes that are at odds with all human hopes and optimism: "And his dark secret love / Does thy life destroy." At his most cryptic, of course, Blake understands that "nature" is a category created by us, even as we are creatures bound up in its material reality: "Where man is not, nature is barren" ("The Marriage of Heaven and Hell").

From Songs of Innocence

The Lamb

Little Lamb who made thee
Dost thou know who made thee,
Gave thee life and bid thee feed,
By the stream and o'er the mead;
5 Gave thee clothing of delight,
Softest clothing wooly bright;
Gave thee such a tender voice,
Making all the vales rejoice;
Little Lamb who made thee
10 Dost thou know who made thee?

Little Lamb I'll tell thee,
Little Lamb I'll tell thee;
He is called by thy name,
For he calls himself a Lamb;
15 He is meek and he is mild,
He became a little child:
I a child and thou a lamb.
We are called by his name.
Little Lamb God bless thee
20 Little Lamb God bless thee.

William Blake, *Songs of Innocence*. London, 1789.

The Blossom

Merry Merry Sparrow
Under leaves so green
A happy Blossom
Sees you swift as arrow
5 Seek your cradle narrow
Near my Bosom.

Pretty Pretty Robin
Under leaves so green
A happy Blossom
10 Hears you sobbing sobbing
Pretty Pretty Robin
Near my Bosom.

From **Songs of Experience**

The Sick Rose

O Rose, thou art sick,
The invisible worm
That flies in the night
In the howling storm:
5 Has found out thy bed
Of crimson joy:
And his dark secret love
Does thy life destroy.

The Fly

Little Fly
Thy summers play
My thoughtless hand
Has brush'd away.

William Blake, *Songs of Experience.* London, 1794.

5 Am not I
    A fly like thee?
    Or art not thou
    A man like me?

    For I dance
10 And drink and sing:
    Till some blind hand
    Shall brush my wing.

    If thought is life
    And strength and breath,
15 And the want of thought is death;

    Then am I
    A happy fly,
    If I live,
    Or if I die.

A Poison Tree

    I was angry with my friend;
    I told my wrath, my wrath did end.
    I was angry with my foe;
    I told it not, my wrath did grow.

5 And I water'd it in fears,
    Night and morning with my tears;
    And I sunned it with smiles,
    And with soft deceitful wiles.

    And it grew both day and night,
10 Till it bore an apple bright.
    And my foe beheld it shine,
    And he knew that it was mine.

    And into my garden stole,
    When the night had veil'd the pole:
15 In the morning glad I see
    My foe outstretch'd beneath the tree.

The Tyger.

Tyger Tyger, burning bright,
In the forests of the night;
What immortal hand or eye,
Could frame thy fearful symmetry?

In what distant deeps or skies.
Burnt the fire of thine eyes?
On what wings dare he aspire?
What the hand, dare sieze the fire?

And what shoulder, & what art,
Could twist the sinews of thy heart?
And when thy heart began to beat,
What dread hand? & what dread feet?

What the hammer? what the chain,
In what furnace was thy brain?
What the anvil? what dread grasp,
Dare its deadly terrors clasp!

When the stars threw down their spears
And water'd heaven with their tears;
Did he smile his work to see?
Did he who made the Lamb make thee?

Tyger Tyger burning bright,
In the forests of the night;
What immortal hand or eye,
Dare frame thy fearful symmetry?

"Tyger, Tyger, burning bright." Blake's tiger from *Songs of Experience* seems somewhat gentler than Goldsmith's comparable drawing, but the pose of Blake's creature has surely been drawn from natural history illustrations of the period. Copy Z, Plate 42. Illustration copyright *The Blake Archive / Library of Congress*.

The Tyger

Tyger Tyger, burning bright,
In the forests of the night;
What immortal hand or eye,
Could frame thy fearful symmetry?

5 In what distant deeps or skies,
Burnt the fire of thine eyes?
On what wings dare he aspire?
What the hand, dare seize the fire?

And what shoulder, and what art,
10 Could twist the sinews of thy heart?
And when thy heart began to beat,
What dread hand? And what dread feet?

What the hammer? What the chain,
In what furnace was thy brain?
15 What the anvil? What dread grasp,
Dare its deadly terrors clasp?

When the stars threw down their spears
And water'd heaven with their tears;
Did he smile his work to see?
20 Did he who made the Lamb make thee?

Tyger Tyger burning bright,
In the forests of the night;
What immortal hand or eye,
Dare frame thy fearful symmetry?

Ah! Sun-flower

Ah Sun-flower! weary of time,
Who countest the steps of the Sun;
Seeking after that sweet golden clime
Where the travellers journey is done.

5 Where the Youth pined away with desire,
And the pale Virgin shrouded in snow,
Arise from their graves and aspire
Where my Sun-flower wishes to go.

The Lilly

The modest Rose puts forth a thorn:
The humble Sheep, a threat'ning horn;
While the Lilly white shall in love delight,
Nor a thorn nor a threat stain her beauty bright.

From "Auguries of Innocence"

To see a World in a Grain of Sand
And a Heaven in a Wild Flower,
Hold Infinity in the palm of your hand
And Eternity in an hour.

5 A Robin Red breast in a Cage
Puts all Heaven in a Rage.
A dove house fill'd with doves & Pigeons
Shudders Hell thro' all its regions.
A dog starv'd at his Master's Gate
10 Predicts the ruin of the State.
A Horse misus'd upon the Road
Calls to Heaven for Human blood.
Each outcry of the hunted Hare
A fibre from the Brain does tear.
15 A Skylark wounded in the wing,
A Cherubim does cease to sing.
The Game Cock clipp'd and arm'd for fight
Does the Rising Sun affright.
Every Wolf's & Lion's howl
20 Raises from Hell a Human Soul.
The wild deer, wand'ring here & there,
Keeps the Human Soul from Care.
The Lamb misus'd breeds public strife
And yet forgives the Butcher's Knife.

Dante Gabriel Rossetti edition, in Alexander Gilchrist, *Life of William Blake, Pictor Ignotus*. London: Macmillan, 1863.

"The catterpillar on the Leaf / Repeats to thee thy Mother's grief."
Blake produces a plate clearly inspired by natural history
illustration as the frontispiece to *For the Sexes: The Gates of
Paradise*. The caption to the curious image is less cryptic: "What
is Man? The Sun's Light when he unfolds it / Depends on the
Organ that beholds it." Plate 1. image copyright: The Blake
Archive / Pierpont Morgan Library.

25 The Bat that flits at close of Eve
   Has left the Brain that won't believe.
   The Owl that calls upon the Night
   Speaks the Unbeliever's fright.
   He who shall hurt the little Wren
30 Shall never be belov'd by Men.
   He who the Ox to wrath has mov'd
   Shall never be by Woman lov'd.
   The wanton Boy that kills the Fly
   Shall feel the Spider's enmity.
35 He who torments the Chafer's sprite
   Weaves a Bower in endless Night.
   The Catterpillar on the Leaf
   Repeats to thee thy Mother's grief.
   Kill not the Moth nor Butterfly,
40 For the Last Judgement draweth nigh.

William Wordsworth (1770–1850)

William Wordsworth is probably the Romantic poet most often described as a nature writer. What the word *nature* meant to Wordsworth, however, is a complicated issue. On the one hand, Wordsworth was the quintessential poet as naturalist, always paying close attention to details of the physical environment around him: plants, animals, geography, and weather. It is this first category of nature poetry that is emphasized in the selections that follow. At the same time, Wordsworth was a self-conscious literary artist who described the "mind of man" as the "main haunt and region of [his] song." This tension between objective describer of the natural scene and subjective shaper of sensory experience is partly the result of Wordsworth's view of the mind as "creator and receiver both." Wordsworth consistently describes his own mind as the recipient of external sensations, which are then rendered into its own mental creations. Shelley makes a related claim in "Mont Blanc" when he says that his mind "passively / Now renders and receives fast influencings, / Holding an unremitting interchange / With the clear universe of things around" (ll. 37–40).

Such an alliance between the inner life and the outer world is at the heart of Wordsworth's descriptions of nature. Wordsworth's ideas about memory, the importance of childhood experiences, and the power of the mind to bestow an "auxiliar" light on the objects it beholds all depend on his ability to record experiences carefully at the moment of observation but then to shape those same experiences in the mind over time. This often autobiographical poet made widespread use of many other texts in the production of his own Wordsworthian sublime (which Keats called "egotistical"): poems by Coleridge, his sister Dorothy's journals, and the works of Milton, Shakespeare, Thomson, and others. Wordsworthian "nature" emerges as much the product of his widespread reading as of his wanderings amid the affecting landscapes of the Lake District.

Wordsworth's poems often present an instant when nature speaks to the poet, and the poet then responds by suddenly speaking for nature. The "language" of nature in such instances is, like the language Wordsworth uses to record these events, frequently cryptic and enigmatic. Wordsworth longs for a version of nature that will redeem him from the vagaries of passing moments, but he usually emphasizes those natural phenomena that record only the passing of time and the cyclical transience of natural process. *The Prelude* wants to keep us in touch with a childhood and subsequent adult identity realized within the natural world. At the same time, Wordsworth's autobiographical epic leaves most adult readers feeling a long way from the "spots of time" of childhood. Nothing in Wordsworth is ever simple or singular. His perceptions of nonhuman nature are particularly open-ended. Wordsworth's view of the natural world does, however, point away from the closed neoclassical world of theocentric symbol making toward the unstable world of postmodern meanings. At the same time, his poems help to consolidate a naturalistic tradition that reaches from James Thomson and William Cowper to Derek Walcott and Seamus Heaney.

The selections that follow include many of the poems that make Wordsworth seem most like a natural historian, paying close attention to the physical details of his surroundings. These selections also includes an extract from *The Excursion* (1814), a poem disliked by many of its readers then and now, but also the first published poem in which Wordsworth clearly articulates the full effect that the natural world might have on the mind of a sensitive observer.

From Lyrical Ballads

Lines

Written at a small distance from my house,

and sent by my little boy to the person to whom

they are addressed

It is the first mild day of March:
Each minute sweeter than before,
The red-breast sings from the tall larch
That stands beside our door.

5 There is a blessing in the air,
Which seems a sense of joy to yield
To the bare trees, and mountains bare,
And grass in the green field.

My Sister! ('tis a wish of mine)
10 Now that our morning meal is done,
Make haste, your morning task resign;
Come forth and feel the sun.

Edward will come with you, and pray,
Put on with speed your woodland dress,
15 And bring no book, for this one day
We'll give to idleness.

No joyless forms shall regulate
Our living Calendar:
We from to-day, my friend, will date
20 The opening of the year.

Love, now an universal birth,
From heart to heart is stealing,
From earth to man, from man to earth,
It is the hour of feeling.

25 One moment now may give us more
Than fifty years of reason;
Our minds shall drink at every pore
The spirit of the season.

Lyrical Ballads. London: J. and A. Arch, 1798.

Some silent laws our hearts may make,
30 Which they shall long obey;
We for the year to come may take
Our temper from to-day.

And from the blessed power that rolls
About, below, above;
35 We'll frame the measure of our souls,
They shall be tuned to love.

Then come, my sister! come, I pray,
With speed put on your woodland dress,
And bring no book; for this one day
40 We'll give to idleness.

Lines

Written in early spring

I heard a thousand blended notes,
While in a grove I sate reclined,
In that sweet mood when pleasant thoughts
Bring sad thoughts to the mind.

5 To her fair works did nature link
The human soul that through me ran;
And much it griev'd my heart to think
What man has made of man.

Through primrose-tufts, in that sweet bower,
10 The periwinkle trail'd its wreathes;
And 'tis my faith that every flower
Enjoys the air it breathes.

The birds around me hopp'd and play'd:
Their thoughts I cannot measure,
15 But the least motion which they made,
It seem'd a thrill of pleasure.

The budding twigs spread out their fan,
To catch the breezy air;
And I must think, do all I can,
20 That there was pleasure there.

If I these thoughts may not prevent,
If such be of my creed the plan,
Have I not reason to lament
What man has made of man?

Expostulation and Reply

"Why William, on that old grey stone,
Thus for the length of half a day,
Why William, sit you thus alone,
And dream your time away?

5 Where are your books? that light bequeath'd
To beings else forlorn and blind!
Up! Up! and drink the spirit breath'd
From dead men to their kind.

You look round on your mother earth,
10 As if she for no purpose bore you;
As if you were her first-born birth,
And none had lived before you!"

One morning thus, by Esthwaite lake,
When life was sweet I knew not why,
15 To me my good friend Matthew spake,
And thus I made reply.

"The eye it cannot chuse but see,
We cannot bid the ear be still;
Our bodies feel, where'er they be,
20 Against, or with our will.

Nor less I deem that there are powers,
Which of themselves our minds impress,
That we can feed this mind of ours,
In a wise passiveness.

25 Think you, mid all this mighty sum
Of things for ever speaking,
That nothing of itself will come,
But we must still be seeking?

Then ask not wherefore, here, alone,
30 Conversing as I may,
I sit upon this old grey stone,
And dream my time away."

The Tables Turned

An evening scene, on the same subject

Up! up! my friend, and clear your looks,
Why all this toil and trouble?
Up! up! my friend, and quit your books,
Or surely you'll grow double.

5   The sun above the mountain's head,
A freshening lustre mellow,
Through all the long green fields has spread,
His first sweet evening yellow.

Books! 'tis a dull and endless strife,
10 Come, hear the woodland linnet,
How sweet his music; on my life
There's more of wisdom in it.

And hark! how blithe the throstle sings!
And he is no mean preacher;
15 Come forth into the light of things,
Let Nature be your teacher.

She has a world of ready wealth,
Our minds and hearts to bless—
Spontaneous wisdom breathed by health,
20 Truth breathed by chearfulness.

One impulse from a vernal wood
May teach you more of man;
Of moral evil and of good,
Than all the sages can.

25 Sweet is the lore which nature brings;
Our meddling intellect
Mishapes the beauteous forms of things;
We murder to dissect.

Enough of science and of art;
30 Close up these barren leaves;
Come forth, and bring with you a heart
That watches and receives.

Lines

Written a few miles above

Tintern Abbey

ON REVISITING THE BANKS OF THE WYE DURING A TOUR, JULY 13, 1798.

Five years have passed; five summers, with the length
Of five long winters! and again I hear
These waters, rolling from their mountain-springs
With a sweet inland murmur.[1] Once again
5   Do I behold these steep and lofty cliffs,
Which on a wild secluded scene impress
Thoughts of more deep seclusion; and connect
The landscape with the quiet of the sky.
The day is come when I again repose
10 Here, under this dark sycamore, and view
These plots of cottage-ground, these orchard-tufts,
Which, at this season, with their unripe fruits,
Among the woods and copses lose themselves,
Nor, with their green and simple hue, disturb
15 The wild green landscape. Once again I see
These hedge-rows, hardly hedge-rows, little lines
Of sportive wood run wild; these pastoral farms
Green to the very door; and wreathes of smoke
Sent up, in silence, from among the trees,
20 With some uncertain notice, as might seem,
Of vagrant dwellers in the houseless woods,
Or of some hermit's cave, where by his fire
The hermit sits alone.

                  Though absent long,
25 These forms of beauty have not been to me,
As is a landscape to a blind man's eye:
But oft, in lonely rooms, and mid the din
Of towns and cities, I have owed to them,
In hours of weariness, sensations sweet,
30 Felt in the blood, and felt along the heart,
And passing even into my purer mind

---

[1] The river is not affected by the tides a few miles above Tintern.

With tranquil restoration: feelings too
Of unremembered pleasure; such, perhaps,
As may have had no trivial influence
35 On that best portion of a good man's life;
His little, nameless, unremembered acts
Of kindness and of love. Nor less, I trust,
To them I may have owed another gift,
Of aspect more sublime; that blessed mood,
40 In which the burthen of the mystery,
In which the heavy and the weary weight
Of all this unintelligible world
Is lighten'd: that serene and blessed mood,
In which the affections gently lead us on,
45 Until, the breath of this corporeal frame,
And even the motion of our human blood
Almost suspended, we are laid asleep
In body, and become a living soul:
While with an eye made quiet by the power
50 Of harmony, and the deep power of joy,
We see into the life of things.

                              If this
Be but a vain belief, yet, oh! how oft,
In darkness, and amid the many shapes
55 Of joyless day-light; when the fretful stir
Unprofitable, and the fever of the world,
Have hung upon the beatings of my heart,
How oft, in spirit, have I turned to thee
O sylvan Wye! Thou wanderer through the wood
60 How often has my spirit turned to thee!

And now, with gleams of half-extinguish'd thought,
With many recognitions dim and faint,
And somewhat of a sad perplexity,
The picture of the mind revives again:
65 While here I stand, not only with the sense
Of present pleasure, but with pleasing thoughts
That in this moment there is life and food
For future years. And so I dare to hope
Though changed, no doubt, from what I was, when first
70 I came among these hills; when like a roe
I bounded o'er the mountains, by the sides
Of the deep rivers, and the lonely streams,

Wherever nature led; more like a man
Flying from something that he dreads, than one
75 Who sought the thing he loved. For nature then
(The coarser pleasures of my boyish days,
And their glad animal movements all gone by,)
To me was all in all. I cannot paint
What then I was. The sounding cataract
80 Haunted me like a passion: the tall rock,
The mountain, and the deep and gloomy wood,
Their colours and their forms, were then to me
An appetite: a feeling and a love,
That had no need of a remoter charm,
85 By thought supplied, or any interest
Unborrowed from the eye. That time is past,
And all its aching joys are now no more,
And all its dizzy raptures. Not for this
Faint I, nor mourn nor murmur: other gifts
90 Have followed, for such loss, I would believe,
Abundant recompence. For I have learned
To look on nature, not as in the hour
Of thoughtless youth, but hearing oftentimes
The still, sad music of humanity,
95 Not harsh nor grating, though of ample power
To chasten and subdue. And I have felt
A presence that disturbs me with the joy
Of elevated thoughts; a sense sublime
Of something far more deeply interfused,
100 Whose dwelling is the light of setting suns,
And the round ocean, and the living air,
And the blue sky, and in the mind of man,
A motion and a spirit, that impels
All thinking things, all objects of all thought,
105 And rolls through all things. Therefore am I still
A lover of the meadows and the woods,
And mountains; and of all that we behold
From this green earth; of all the mighty world
Of eye and ear, both what they half-create,[2]

---

[2]This line has a close resemblance to an admirable line of Young, the exact expression of
which I cannot recollect.

110 And what perceive; well pleased to recognize
In nature and the language of the sense,
The anchor of my purest thoughts, the nurse,
The guide, the guardian of my heart, and soul
Of all my moral being.

115   Nor, perchance,
If I were not thus taught, should I the more
Suffer my genial spirits to decay:
For thou art with me, here, upon the banks
Of this fair river; thou, my dearest Friend,[3]
120 My dear, dear Friend, and in thy voice I catch
The language of my former heart, and read
My former pleasures in the shooting lights
Of thy wild eyes. Oh! yet a little while
May I behold in thee what I was once,
125 My dear, dear Sister! And this prayer I make,
Knowing that Nature never did betray
The heart that loved her; 'tis her privilege,
Through all the years of this our life, to lead
From joy to joy: for she can so inform
130 The mind that is within us, so impress
With quietness and beauty, and so feed
With lofty thoughts, that neither evil tongues,
Rash judgments, nor the sneers of selfish men,
Nor greetings where no kindness is, nor all
135 The dreary intercourse of daily life,
Shall e'er prevail against us, or disturb
Our chearful faith that all which we behold
Is full of blessings. Therefore let the moon
Shine on thee in thy solitary walk;
140 And let the misty mountain winds be free
To blow against thee: and in after years,
When these wild ecstasies shall be matured
Into a sober pleasure, when thy mind
Shall be a mansion for all lovely forms,
145 Thy memory be as a dwelling-place
For all sweet sounds and harmonies; Oh! then,
If solitude, or fear, or pain, or grief,

---

[3] Dorothy. [Ed.]

Should be thy portion, with what healing thoughts
Of tender joy wilt thou remember me,
150 And these my exhortations! Nor, perchance,
If I should be, where I no more can hear
Thy voice, nor catch from thy wild eyes these gleams
Of past existence, wilt thou then forget
That on the banks of this delightful stream
155 We stood together; and that I, so long
A worshipper of Nature, hither came,
Unwearied in that service: rather say
With warmer love, oh! with far deeper zeal
Of holier love. Nor wilt thou then forget,
160 That after many wanderings, many years
Of absence, these steep woods and lofty cliffs,
And this green pastoral landscape, were to me
More dear, both for themselves, and for thy sake.

From Poems in Two Volumes

The Redbreast and the Butterfly

Art thou the Bird whom Man loves best,
The pious Bird with the scarlet breast,
      Our little English Robin;
The Bird that comes about our doors
5   When Autumn winds are sobbing?
Art thou the Peter of Norway Boors?
      Their Thomas in Finland,
      And Russia far inland?
The Bird, whom by some name or other
10 All men who know thee call their Brother,
The Darling of Children and men?
Could Father Adam open his eyes,
And see this sight beneath the skies,
He'd wish to close them again.

Poems in Two Volumes. London: Longman, 1807.

15 If the Butterfly knew but his friend
Hither his flight he would bend,
And find his way to me
Under the branches of the tree:
In and out, he darts about;
20 His little heart is throbbing:
Can this be the Bird, to man so good,
    Our consecrated Robin!
That, after their bewildering,
Did cover with leaves the little children,
25   So painfully in the wood?

What ail'd thee Robin that thou could'st pursue
    A beautiful Creature,
That is gentle by nature?
Beneath the summer sky
30 From flower to flower let him fly;
'Tis all that he wishes to do.
The Chearer Thou of our in-door sadness,
He is the Friend of our summer gladness:
What hinders, then, that ye should be
35 Playmates in the sunny weather,
And fly about in the air together?
Like the hues of thy breast
His beautiful wings in crimson are drest,
A brother he seems of thine own:
40 If thou would'st be happy in thy nest,
O pious Bird! whom Man loves best,
Love him, or leave him alone!

To the Small Celandine[4]

Pansies, Lilies, Kingcups, Daisies,
Let them live upon their praises;
Long as there's a sun that sets
Primroses will have their glory;

---

[4]Common Pilewort.

5 Long as there are Violets,
They will have a place in story:
There's a flower that shall be mine,
'Tis the little Celandine.

Eyes of some men travel far
10 For the finding of a star;
Up and down the heavens they go,
Men that keep a mighty rout!
I'm as great as they, I trow,
Since the day I found thee out,
15 Little flower! I'll make a stir
Like a great Astronomer.

Modest, yet withal an Elf
Bold, and lavish of thyself,
Since we needs must first have met
20 I have seen thee, high and low,
Thirty years or more, and yet
'Twas a face I did not know;
Thou hast now, go where I may,
Fifty greetings in a day.

25 Ere a leaf is on a bush,
In the time before the Thrush
Has a thought about its nest,
Thou wilt come with half a call,
Spreading out thy glossy breast
30 Like a careless Prodigal;
Telling tales about the sun,
When we've little warmth, or none.

Poets, vain men in their mood!
Travel with the multitude;
35 Never heed them; I aver
That they all are wanton Wooers;
But the thrifty Cottager,
Who stirs little out of doors,
Joys to spy thee near her home,
40 Spring is coming, Thou art come.

Comfort have thou of thy merit,
Kindly, unassuming Spirit!
Careless of thy neighbourhood,
Thou dost shew thy pleasant face

45 On the moor, and in the wood,
In the lane—there's not a place,
Howsoever mean it be,
But 'tis good enough for thee.

Ill befal the yellow Flowers,
50 Children of the flaring hours!
Buttercups, that will be seen,
Whether we will see or no;
Others, too, of lofty mien;
They have done as worldlings do,
55 Taken praise that should be thine,
Little, humble Celandine!

Prophet of delight and mirth,
Scorn'd and slighted upon earth!
Herald of a mighty band,
60 Of a joyous train ensuing,
Singing at my heart's command,
In the lanes my thoughts pursuing,
I will sing, as doth behove,
Hymns in praise of what I love!

To the Same Flower

Pleasures newly found are sweet
When they lie about our feet:
February last my heart
First at sight of thee was glad;
5 All unheard of as thou art,
Thou must needs, I think, have had,
Celandine! and long ago,
Praise of which I nothing know.

I have not a doubt but he,
10 Whosoe'er the man might be,
Who the first with pointed rays,
(Workman worthy to be sainted)
Set the Sign-board in a blaze,
When the risen sun he painted,
15 Took the fancy from a glance
At thy glittering countenance.

Soon as gentle breezes bring
News of winter's vanishing,
And the children build their bowers,
20 Sticking 'kerchief-plots of mold
All about with full-blown flowers,
Thick as sheep in shepherd's fold
With the proudest Thou art there,
Mantling in the tiny square.

25 Often have I sigh'd to measure
By myself a lonely pleasure,
Sigh'd to think, I read a book
Only read perhaps by me;
Yet I long could overlook
30 Thy bright coronet and Thee,
And thy arch and wily ways,
And thy store of other praise.

Blithe of heart, from week to week
Thou dost play at hide-and-seek;
35 While the patient Primrose sits
Like a Beggar in the cold,
Thou, a Flower of wiser wits,
Slipp'st into thy shelter'd hold;
Bright as any of the train
40 When ye all are out again.

Thou art not beyond the moon,
But a thing "beneath our shoon;"
Let, as old Magellen did,
Others roam about the sea;
45 Build who will a pyramid;
Praise it is enough for me,
If there be but three or four
Who will love my little Flower.

Among All Lovely Things

Among all lovely things my Love had been;
Had noted well the stars, all flowers that grew
About her home; but she had never seen
A Glow-worm, never one, and this I knew.

5 While riding near her home one stormy night
    A single Glow-worm did I chance to espy;
    I gave a fervent welcome to the sight,
    And from my Horse I leapt; great joy had I.

    Upon a leaf the Glow-worm did I lay,
10 To bear it with me through the stormy night:
    And, as before, it shone without dismay;
    Albeit putting forth a fainter light.

    When to the Dwelling of my Love I came,
    I went into the Orchard quietly;
15 And left the Glow-worm, blessing it by name,
    Laid safely by itself, beneath a Tree.

    The whole next day, I hoped, and hoped with fear;
    At night the Glow-worm shone beneath the Tree:
    I led my Lucy to the spot, "Look here!"
20 Oh! joy it was for her, and joy for me!

To a Sky-lark

    Up with me! up with me into the clouds!
      For thy song, Lark, is strong;
    Up with me, up with me into the clouds!
      Singing, singing,
5 With all the heav'ns about thee ringing,
      Lift me, guide me, till I find
    That spot which seems so to thy mind!
    I have walk'd through wildernesses dreary,
      And today my heart is weary;
10   Had I now the soul of a Faery,
      Up to thee would I fly.
    There is madness about thee, and joy divine
      In that song of thine;
    Up with me, up with me, high and high,
15 To thy banqueting-place in the sky!
      Joyous as Morning,
      Thou art laughing and scorning;
    Thou hast a nest, for thy love and thy rest:
    And, though little troubled with sloth,
20 Drunken Lark! thou would'st be loth

To be such a Traveller as I.
   Happy, happy Liver!
With a soul as strong as a mountain River,
Pouring out praise to the Almighty Giver,
25 Joy and jollity be with us both!
  Hearing thee, or else some other,
   As merry a Brother,
I on the earth will go plodding on,
By myself, chearfully, till the day is done.

To a Butterfly

Stay near me—do not take thy flight!
A little longer stay in sight!
Much converse do I find in Thee,
Historian of my Infancy!
5 Float near me; do not yet depart!
Dead times revive in thee:
Thou bring'st, gay Creature as thou art!
A solemn image to my heart,
My Father's Family!
10 Oh! pleasant, pleasant were the days,
The time, when in our childish plays
My sister Emmeline and I
Together chaced the Butterfly!
A very hunter did I rush
15 Upon the prey: with leaps and springs
I follow'd on from brake to bush;
But She, God love her! feared to brush
The dust from off its wings.

The Sun Has Long Been Set

The Sun has long been set:
The Stars are out by twos and threes;
The little Birds are piping yet
Among the bushes and trees;
5 There's a Cuckoo, and one or two thrushes;
And a noise of wind that rushes,

With a noise of water that gushes;
And the Cuckoo's sovereign cry
Fills all the hollow of the sky!

10 Who would go "parading"
In London, and "masquerading,"
On such a night of June?
With that beautiful soft half-moon,
And all these innocent blisses,
15 On such a night as this is!

O Nightingale!

O Nightingale! thou surely art
A Creature of a fiery heart—
These notes of thine they pierce, and pierce;
Tumultuous harmony and fierce!
5 Thou sing'st as if the God of wine
Had help'd thee to a Valentine;
A song in mockery and despite
Of shades, and dews, and silent Night,
And steady bliss, and all the Loves
10 Now sleeping in these peaceful groves!
I heard a Stockdove sing or say
His homely tale, this very day.
His voice was buried among trees,
Yet to be come at by the breeze:
15 He did not cease; but coo'd—and coo'd;
And somewhat pensively he woo'd:
He sang of love with quiet blending,
Slow to begin, and never ending;
Of serious faith, and inward glee;
20 That was the Song, the Song for me!

My Heart Leaps Up

My heart leaps up when I behold
      A Rainbow in the sky:
So was it when my life began;

So is it now I am a Man;
5   So be it when I shall grow old,
        Or let me die!
The Child is Father of the Man;
And I could wish my days to be
Bound each to each by natural piety.

From The Excursion

[THE POWER OF NATURE]

[. . .] But he[5] had felt the power
Of Nature, and already was prepared,
By his intense conceptions, to receive
Deeply the lesson deep of love which he,
5   Whom Nature, by whatever means, has taught
To feel intensely, cannot but receive.

From early childhood, even, as hath been said,
From his sixth year, he had been sent abroad
In summer to tend herds: such was his task
10 Thenceforward 'till the later day of youth.
O then what soul was his, when, on the tops
Of the high mountains, he beheld the sun
Rise up, and bathe the world in light! He looked —
Ocean and earth, the solid frame of earth
15 And ocean's liquid mass, beneath him lay
In gladness and deep joy. The clouds were touch'd,
And in their silent faces did he read
Unutterable love. Sound needed none,
Nor any voice of joy; his spirit drank
20 The spectacle; sensation, soul, and form
All melted into him; they swallowed up
His animal being; in them did he live,
And by them did he live; they were his life.
In such access of mind, in such high hour

The Excursion. London: Longman, 1814.

[5]The Wanderer. [Ed.]

25 Of visitation from the living God,
   Thought was not; in enjoyment it expired.
   No thanks he breathed, he proffered no request;
   Rapt into still communion that transcends
   The imperfect offices of prayer and praise,
30 His mind was a thanksgiving to the power
   That made him; it was blessedness and love!

    A Herdsman on the lonely mountain tops,
   Such intercourse was his, and in this sort
   Was his existence oftentimes *possessed*.
35 Oh then how beautiful, how bright appeared
   The written Promise! He had early learned
   To reverence the Volume which displays
   The mystery, the life which cannot die:
   But in the mountains did he *feel* his faith;
40 There did he see the writing; all things there
   Breathed immortality, revolving life
   And greatness still revolving; infinite;
   There littleness was not; the least of things
   Seemed infinite; and there his spirit shaped
45 Her prospects, nor did he believe, he *saw*.
   What wonder if his being thus became
   Sublime and comprehensive! Low desires,
   Low thoughts had there no place; yet was his heart
   Lowly; for he was meek in gratitude,
50 Oft as he called those extacies to mind,
   And whence they flowed: and from them he acquired
   Wisdom, which works through patience; thence he learned
   In many a calmer hour of sober thought
   To look on Nature with a humble heart,
55 Self-questioned where it did not understand,
   And with a superstitious eye of love.

    So passed the time; yet to a neighbouring town
   He duly went with what small overplus
   His earnings might supply, and brought away
60 The Book which most had tempted his desires
   While at the Stall he read. Among the hills
   He gazed upon that mighty Orb of Song
   The divine Milton. Lore of different kind,
   The annual savings of a toilsome life,

65 His Step-father supplied; books that explain
The purer elements of truth involved
In lines and numbers, and, by charm severe,
(Especially perceived where nature droops
And feeling is suppressed,) preserve the mind
70 Busy in solitude and poverty.
These occupations oftentimes deceived
The listless hours, while in the hollow vale,
Hollow and green, he lay on the green turf
In pensive idleness. What could he do
75 With blind endeavours, in that lonesome life,
Thus thirsting daily? Yet still uppermost
Nature was at his heart as if he felt,
Though yet he knew not how, a wasting power
In all things which from her sweet influence
80 Might tend to wean him. Therefore with her hues,
Her forms, and with the spirit of her forms,
He clothed the nakedness of austere truth.
While yet he lingered in the rudiments
Of science, and among her simplest laws,
85 His triangles — they were the stars of heaven,
The silent stars! Oft did he take delight
To measure th' altitude of some tall crag
Which is the eagle's birth-place, or some peak
Familiar with forgotten years, that shews
90 Inscribed, as with the silence of the thought,
Upon its bleak and visionary sides,
The history of many a winter storm,
Or obscure records of the path of fire.

      And thus, before his eighteenth year was told,
95 Accumulated feelings pressed his heart
With an increasing weight; he was o'erpower'd
By Nature, by the turbulence subdued
Of his own mind; by mystery and hope,
And the first virgin passion of a soul
100 Communing with the glorious Universe.
Full often wished he that the winds might rage
When they were silent; far more fondly now
Than in his earlier season did he love
Tempestuous nights — the conflict and the sounds
105 That live in darkness: from his intellect

And from the stillness of abstracted thought
He asked repose; and I have heard him say
That often, failing at this time to gain
The peace required, he scanned the laws of light
110 Amid the roar of torrents, where they send
From hollow clefts up to the clearer air
A cloud of mist, which in the sunshine frames
A lasting tablet—for the observer's eye
Varying its rainbow hues. But vainly thus,
115 And vainly by all other means, he strove
To mitigate the fever of his heart. [. . .]

　　　"Happy is He who lives to understand
Not human Nature only, but explores
All Natures, to the end that he may find
120 The law that governs each; and where begins
The union, the partition where, that makes
Kind and degree, among all visible Beings;
The constitutions, powers, and faculties,
Which they inherit, cannot step beyond,
125 And cannot fall beneath; that do assign
To every Class its station and its office,
Through all the mighty Commonwealth of things;
Up from the creeping plant to sovereign Man.
Such Converse, if directed by a meek,
130 Sincere, and humble Spirit, teaches love;
For knowledge is delight; and such delight
Breeds love; yet, suited as it rather is
To thought and to the climbing intellect,
It teaches less to love, than to adore;
135 If that be not indeed the highest Love!"

　　　"Yet," said I, tempted here to interpose,
"The dignity of Life is not impaired
By aught that innocently satisfies
The humbler cravings of the heart; and He
140 Is a still happier Man, who, for those heights
Of speculation not unfit, descends;
And such benign affections cultivates
Among the inferior Kinds; not merely those
That he may call his own, and which depend,
145 As individual objects of regard,
Upon his care, from whom he also looks

For signs and tokens of a mutual bond,
But others, far beyond this narrow sphere,
Whom, for the very sake of love, he loves.
150 Nor is it a mean praise of rural life
And solitude, that they do favour most,
Most frequently call forth, and best sustain
These pure sensations; that can penetrate
The obstreperous City; on the barren Seas
155 Are not unfelt, and much might recommend,
How much they might inspirit and endear,
The loneliness of this sublime Retreat!"

      "Yes," said the Sage[6], resuming the discourse
Again directed to his downcast Friend,[7]
160 "If, with the froward will and groveling soul
Of Man offended, liberty is here,
And invitation every hour renewed,
To mark *their* placid state, who never heard
Of a command which they have power to break,
165 Or rule which they are tempted to transgress;
These, with a soothed or elevated heart,
May we behold, their knowledge register,
Observe their ways; and, free from envy, find
Complacence there: but wherefore this to You?
170 I guess that, welcome to your lonely hearth,
The Redbreast feeds in winter from your hand;
A box perchance is from your casement hung
For the small Wren to build in; not in vain,
The barriers disregarding that surround
175 This deep Abiding-place, before your sight
Mounts on the breeze the Butterfly—and soars,
Small Creature as she is, from earth's bright flowers
Into the dewy clouds. Ambition reigns
In the waste wilderness: the Soul ascends
180 Towards her native firmament of heaven,
When the fresh Eagle, in the month of May,
Upborne, at evening, on replenished wing,
This shady valley leaves, and leaves the dark

---

6 The Wanderer. [Ed.]
7 The Solitary. [Ed.]

Empurpled hills, conspicuously renewing
185 A proud communication with the sun
Low sunk beneath the horizon! List! I heard,
From yon huge breast of rock, a solemn bleat;
Sent forth as if it were the Mountain's voice,
As if the visible Mountain made the cry.
190 Again!" The effect upon the soul was such
As he expressed; for, from the mountain's heart
The solemn bleat appeared to come; there was
No other—and the region all around
Stood silent, empty of all shape of life.
195 It was a Lamb—left somewhere to itself,
The plaintive Spirit of the Solitude!
He paused, as if unwilling to proceed,
Through consciousness that silence in such place
Was best, the most affecting eloquence.
200 But soon his thoughts returned upon themselves,
And, in soft tone of speech, he thus resumed.

"Ah! if the heart, too confidently raised,
Perchance too lightly occupied, or lulled
Too easily, despise or overlook
205 The vassalage that binds her to the earth,
Her sad dependance upon time, and all
The trepidations of mortality,
What place so destitute and void—but there
The little Flower her vanity shall check;
210 The trailing Worm reprove her thoughtless pride?

These craggy regions, these chaotic wilds,
Does that benignity pervade, that warms
The Mole contended with her darksome walk
In the cold ground; and to the Emmet[8] gives
215 Her foresight; and the intelligence that makes
The tiny Creatures strong by social league;
Supports the generations, multiplies
Their tribes, till we behold a spacious plain
Or grassy bottom, all, with little hills—
220 Their labour—covered, as a Lake with waves;
Thousands of Cities, in the desart place

---

[8] Ant. [Ed.]

Built up of life, and food, and means of life!
Nor wanting here, to entertain the thought,
Creatures, that in communities exist,
225 Less, as might seem, for general guardianship
Or through dependance upon mutual aid,
Than by participation of delight
And a strict love of fellowship, combined.
What other spirit can it be, that prompts
230 The gilded summer Flies to mix and weave
Their sports together in the solar beam,
Or in the gloom of twilight hum their joy?
More obviously, the self-same influence rules
The feathered kinds; the Fieldfare's pensive flocks,
235 The cawing Rooks, and Sea-mews from afar,
Hovering above these inland Solitudes,
Unscattered by the wind, at whose loud call
Their voyage was begun: nor is its power
Unfelt among the sedentary Fowl
240 That seek yon Pool, and there prolong their stay
In silent congress; or together rouzed
Take flight; while with their clang the air resounds.
And, over all, in that etherial arch
Is the mute company of changeful clouds;
245 Bright apparition suddenly put forth
The Rainbow, smiling on the faded storm;
The mild assemblage of the starry heavens;
And the great Sun, earth's universal Lord!

How bountiful is Nature! he shall find
250 Who seeks not; and to him, who hath not asked,
Large measure shall be dealt. Three sabbath-days
Are scarcely told, since, on a service bent
Of mere humanity, You clomb those Heights;
And what a marvellous and heavenly Shew
255 Was to your sight revealed! the Swains moved on,
And heeded not; you lingered, and perceived.
There is a luxury in self-dispraise;
And inward self-disparagement affords
To meditative Spleen a grateful feast.
260 Trust me, pronouncing on your own desert,
You judge unthankfully; distempered nerves
Infect the thoughts; the languor of the Frame

Depresses the Soul's vigour. Quit your Couch—
Cleave not so fondly to your moody Cell;
265 Nor let the hallowed Powers, that shed from heaven
Stillness and rest, with disapproving eye
Look down upon your taper, through a watch
Of midnight hours, unseasonably twinkling
In this deep Hollow; like a sullen star
270 Dimly reflected in a lonely pool.
Take courage, and withdraw yourself from ways
That run not parallel to Nature's course.
Rise with the Lark! your Matins shall obtain
Grace, be their composition what it may,
275 If but with hers performed; climb once again,
Climb every day, those ramparts; meet the breeze
Upon their tops, adventurous as a Bee
That from your garden thither soars, to feed
On new-blown heath; let yon commanding rock
280 Be your frequented Watch-tower; roll the stone
In thunder down the mountains: with all your might
Chase the wild Goat; and, if the bold red Deer
Fly to these harbours, driven by hound and horn
Loud echoing, add your speed to the pursuit:
285 So, wearied to your Hut shall you return,
And sink at evening into sound repose." [. . .]

"To every Form of Being is assigned,"
Thus calmly spake the venerable Sage,[9]
"An *active* principle: howe'er removed
290 From sense and observation, it subsists
In all things, in all natures, in the stars
Of azure heaven, the unenduring clouds,
In flower and tree, in every pebbly stone
That paves the brooks, the stationary rocks,
295 The moving waters, and the invisible air.
Whate'er exists hath properties that spread
Beyond itself, communicating good,
A simple blessing, or with evil mixed;
Spirit that knows no insulated spot,

---

[9]The Wanderer [Ed.]

300 No chasm, no solitude; from link to link
It circulates, the Soul of all the Worlds.
This is the freedom of the Universe;
Unfolded still the more, more visible,
The more we know; and yet is reverenced least,
305 And least respected, in the human Mind,
Its most apparent home. [. . .]

William Bartram (1739–1823)

Illiam Bartram is the only American included in this anthology, but that is because he had perhaps as much impact on Romantic writers as any other eighteenth-century naturalist. His direct influence is evident in works by William Wordsworth, Dorothy Wordsworth, Samuel Coleridge, Percy Shelley, and many others. His *Travels through North and South Carolina, Georgia, East and West Florida* (1791) became throughout the nineteenth century a source for images ranging from alligators and waterfalls to magnolias and natural fountains. Coleridge virtually quotes him in "Kubla Khan," as does Wordsworth in "Ruth": "He spoke of plants that hourly change / Their blossoms, through a boundless range.[. . .] He told of the magnolia, spread / High as a cloud, high over head!"

A sample of Bartram's lavish prose suggests why he was so important to these poets:

> Near me, on the left, was a point or projection of an entire grove of the aromatic *Illisium Floridanum;* on my right and all around behind me, was a fruitful Orange grove, with Palms and Magnolias interspersed; in front, just under my feet was the inchanting and amazing chrystal fountain, which incessantly threw up, from dark, rocky caverns below, tons of water every minute, forming a bason, capacious enough for large shallops to ride in, and a creek of four or five feet depth of water, and near twenty yards over, which meanders six miles through green meadows. . . .

Ever since John Livingston Lowes chronicled every detail that might have fostered Coleridge's eidetic imagination, we have appreciated the way that Bartram's roaring alligators, unfolding tropical blossoms, and lush Floridian landscapes played on the minds of poets in the chilly mists of the Lake District. Dorothy Wordsworth's *Journals* can occasionally adopt a syntax or a cadence that echoes Bartram's diction directly. His detailed, flowing, and sometimes startled prose reminds us of the way that verbal pictures of the vastness, strangeness, and natural beauty of America have stimulated European imaginations over the past two centuries.

From Travels

But admirable are the properties of the extraordinary Dionea muscipula![1] A great extent on each side of that serpentine rivulet, is occupied by those sportive vegetables—let us advance to the spot in which nature has seated them. Astonishing production! see the incarnate lobes expanding, how gay and ludicrous they appear! ready on the spring to intrap incautious deluded insects, what artifice! there behold one of the leaves just closed upon a struggling fly, another has got a worm, its hold is sure, its prey can never escape—carnivorous vegetable! Can we after viewing this object, hesitate a moment to confess, that vegetable beings are endued with some sensible faculties or attributes, similar to those that dignify animal nature; they are organical, living and self-moving bodies, for we see here, in this plant, motion and volition.

What power or faculty is it, that directs the cirri of the Cucurbita, Momordica, Vitis and other climbers, towards the twigs of shrubs, trees and other friendly support? we see them invariably leaning, extending and like the fingers of the human hand, reaching to catch hold of what is nearest, just as if they had eyes to see with, and when their hold is fixed, to coil the tendril in a spiral form, by which artifice it becomes more elastic and effectual, than if it had remained in a direct line, for every revolution of the coil adds a portion of strength, and thus collected, they are enabled to dilate and contract as occasion or necessity require, and thus by yielding to, and humouring the motion of the limbs and twigs, or other support on which they depend, are not so liable to be torn off by sudden blasts of wind or other assaults; is it sense or instinct that influences their actions? it must be some impulse; or does the hand of the Almighty act and perform this work in our sight?

William Bartram, *Travels through North and South Carolina, Georgia, East and West Florida.* Philadelphia: James and Johnson, 1791.

[1] Venus's flytrap. [Ed.]

The vital principle or efficient cause of motion and action, in the animal and vegetable system, perhaps, may be more similar than we generally apprehend. Where is the essential difference between the seed of peas, peaches and other tribes of plants and trees, and that of oviparous animals? as the eggs of birds, snakes or butterflies, spawn of fish, &c. Let us begin at the source of terrestrial existence. Are not the seed of vegetables, and the eggs of oviparous animals fecundated, or influenced with the vivific principle of life, through the approximation and intimacy of the sexes, and immediately after the eggs and seeds are hatched, the young larva and infant plant, by heat and moisture, rises into existence, increases, and in due time arrives to a state of perfect maturity. The physiologists agree in opinion, that the work of generation in viviparous animals, is exactly similar, only more secret and inveloped. The mode of operation that nature pursues in the production of vegetables, and oviparous animals is infinitely more uniform and manifest, than that which is or can be discovered to take place in viviparous animals.

The most apparent difference between animals and vegetables are, that animals have the powers of sound, and are locomotive, whereas vegetables are not able to shift themselves from the places where nature has planted them: yet vegetables have the power of moving and exercising their members, and have the means of transplanting or colonising their tribes almost over the surface of the whole earth, some seeds, for instance, grapes, nuts, smilax, peas, and others whose pulp or kernel is food for animals, such seed will remain several days without injuring in stomachs of pigeons and other birds of passage; by this means such sorts are distributed from place to place, even across seas; indeed some seeds require this preparation, by the digestive heat of the stomach of animals, to dissolve and detach the oily, viscid pulp, and to soften the hard shells of others. Small seeds are sometimes furnished with rays of hair or down, and others with thin light membranes attached to them, which serve the purpose of wings, on which they mount upward, leaving the earth, float in the air, and are carried away by the swift winds to very remote regions before they settle on the earth; some are furnished with hooks, which catch hold of the wool and hair of animals passing by them, are by that means spread abroad; other seeds ripen in pericarpes, which open with elastic force, and shoot their feed to a very great distance round about; some other seeds, as of the Mosses and Fungi, are so very minute as to be invisible, light as atoms, and these mixing with the air, are wafted all over the world.

The animal creation also, excites our admiration, and equally manifests the almighty power, wisdom and beneficence of the Supreme Creator and Sovereign Lord of the universe; some in their vast size and strength, as the mamoth, the elephant, the whale, the lion and alligator; others in agility;

others in their beauty and elegance of colour, plumage and rapidity of flight, have the faculty of moving and living in the air; others for their immediate and indispensable use and convenience to man, in furnishing means for our clothing and sustenance, and administering to our help in the toils and labours through life; how wonderful is the mechanism of these finely formed, self-moving beings, how complicated their system, yet what unerring uniformity prevails through every tribe and particular species! the effect we see and contemplate, the cause is invisible, incomprehensible, how can it be otherwise? when we cannot see the end or origin of a nerve or vein, while the divisibility of mater or fluid, is infinite. We admire the mechanism of a watch, and the fabric of a piece of brocade, as being the production of art; these merit our admiration, and must excite our esteem for the ingenious artist or modifier, but nature is the work of God omnipotent: and an elephant, even this world is comparatively but a very minute part of his works. If then the visible, the mechanical part of the animal creation, the mere material part is so admirably beautiful, harmonious and incomprehensible, what must be the intellectual system? that inexpressibly more essential principle, which secretly operates within? that which animates the inimitable machines, which gives them motion, impowers them to act, speak and perform, this must be divine and immortal?

I am sensible that the general opinion of philosophers, has distinguished the moral system of the brute creature from that of mankind, by an epithet wich implies a mere mechanical impulse, which leads and impels them to necessary actions, without any premeditated design or contrivance, this we term instinct, which faculty we suppose to be inferior to reason in man.

The parental, and filial affections seem to be as ardent, their sensibility and attachment, as active and faithful, as those observed to be in human nature.

When travelling on the East coast of the isthmus of Florida, ascending the South Musquitoe river, in a canoe, we observed numbers of deer and bears, near the banks, and on the islands of the river, the bear were feeding on the fruit of the dwarf creeping Chamerops, (this fruit is of the form and size of dates, and are delicious and nourishing food) we saw eleven bears in the course of the day, they seemed no way surprized or affrighted at the sight of us; in the evening my hunter, who was an excellent marksman, said that he would shoot one of them, for the sake of the skin and oil, for we had plenty and variety of provisions in our bark. We accordingly, on sight of two of them, planned our approaches, as artfully as possible, by crossing over to the opposite shore, in order to get under cover of a small island, this we cautiously coasted round, to a point, which we apprehended would take us within shot of the bear, but here finding ourselves at too great a distance from them, and discovering that we must openly show ourselves, we had no other alternative to effect our purpose, but making oblique approaches; we gained gradually on our prey by this artifice, without their noticing us, finding ourselves near enough, the hunter fired, and laid the largest dead on the spot, where she stood, when presently the other, not seeming the least moved, at the report of our piece, approached the dead body, smelled, and pawed it, and appearing in agony, fell to weeping and looking upwards, then towards us, and cried out like a child. Whilst our boat approached very near, the hunter was loading his rifle in order to shoot the survivor, which was a young cub, and the slain supposed to be the dam; the continual cries of this afflicted child, bereft of its parent, affected me very sensibly, I was moved with compassion, and charging myself as if accessary to what now appeared to be a cruel murder, and endeavoured to prevail on the hunter to save its life, but to no effect! for by habit he had become insensible to compassion towards the brute creation, being now within a few yards of the harmless devoted victim, he fired, and laid it dead, upon the body of the dam.

If we bestow but a very little attention to the economy of the animal creation, we shall find manifest examples of premeditation, perseverance, resolution, and consumate artifice, in order to effect their purpose. The next morning, after the slaughter of the bears whilst my companions were striking our tent and preparing to re-embark, I resolved to make a little botanical excursion alone; crossing over a narrow isthmus of sand hills which separated the river from the ocean, I passed over a pretty high hill, its summit crested with a few Palm trees, surrounded with an Orange grove; this hill, whose base was washed on one side, by the floods of the Musquitoe river, and the other side by the billows of the ocean; was about one hundred yards diameter, and seemed to be an entire heap of sea hills. I continued along the beech, a quarter of a mile, and came up to a forest of the Agave vivipara (though composed of herbaceous plants, I term it a forest, because their scapes or flower-stems arose erect near 30 feet high) their tops regularly branching in the form of a pyramidal tree, and these plants growing near to each other, occupied a space of ground of several acres: when their seed is ripe they vegetate, and grow on the branches, until the scape dries when the young plants fall to the ground, take root, and fix themselves in the sand: the plant grows to a prodigious size before the scape shoots up from its centre. Having contemplated this admirable grove, I proceeded towards the shrubberies on the banks of the river, and though it was now late in December, the aromatic groves appeared in full bloom. The broad leaved sweet Myrtus, Erythrina corrallodendrum, Cactus cochenellifer, Cacalia suffruticosa, and particularly, Rhizophora conjugata, which stood close to, and in the salt water of the river, were in full bloom, with beautiful white sweet scented flowers, which attracted to them, two or three species of very beautiful butterflies, one of which was black, the upper pair of its wings very long and narrow, marked with transverse stripes of pale yellow, with some spots of a crimson colour near the body. Another species remarkable for splendor, was of a larger size, the wings were undulated and obtusely crenated round their ends, the nether pair terminating near the body, with a long narrow forked tail; the ground light yellow, striped oblique-transversely, with stripes of pale celestial blue, the ends of them adorned with little eyes encircled with the finest blue and crimson, which represented a very brilliant rosary. But those which were the most numerous were as white as snow, their wings large, their ends lightly crenated and ciliated, forming a fringed border, faintly marked with little black crescents, their points downward, with a cluster of little brilliant orbs of blue and crimson, on the nether wings near the body; the numbers were incredible, and there seemed to be scarcely a flower for each fly, multitudinous as they were, besides clouds of them hovering over the mellifluous groves. Besides these papiles, a variety of other insects come in for share, particularly several species of bees.

As I was gathering specimens of flowers from the shrubs, I was greatly surprised at the sudden appearance of a remarkable large spider, on a leaf, of the genus Araneus saliens, at sight of me he boldly faced about, and raised himself up as if ready to spring upon me; his body was about the size of a pigeons egg, of a buff colour, which with his legs were covered with short silky hair, on the top of the abdomen was a round red spot or ocelle encircled with black; after I had recovered from the surprise, and observing the wary hunter had retired under cover, I drew near again, and presently discovered that I had surprised him on predatory attempts against the insect tribes, I was therefore determined to watch his proceedings, I soon noticed that the object of his wishes was a large fat bomble bee (apis bombylicus) that was visiting the flowers, and piercing their nectariferous tubes; this cunning intripid hunter (conducted his subtil approaches, with the circumspection and perseverance of a Siminole, when hunting a deer) advancing with slow steps obliquely, or under cover of dense foliage, and behind the limbs, and when the bee was engaged in probing a flower he would leap nearer, and then instantly retire out of sight, under a leaf or behind a branch, at the same time keeping a sharp eye upon me; when he had now got within two feet of his prey, and the bee was intent on sipping the delicious nectar from a flower, with his back next the spider, he instantly sprang upon him, and grasped him over the back and shoulder, when for some moments they both disappeared, I expected the bee had carried off his enemy, but to my surprise they both together rebounded back again, suspended at the extremity of a strong elastic thread or web, which the spider had artfully let fall, or fixed on the twig, the instant he leaped from it; the rapidity of the bee's wings, endeavouring to extricate himself, made them both together appear as a moving vapor, until the bee became fatigued by whirling round, first one way and then back again; at length, in about a quarter of an hour, the bee quite exhausted by his struggles, and the repeated wounds of the butcher, became motionless, and quickly expired in the arms of the devouring spider, who, ascending the rope with his game, retired to feast on it under cover of leaves; and perhaps before night became himself, the delicious evening repast of a bird or lizard.[. . .]

The verges and islets of the lagoon were elegantly embellished with flowering plants and shrubs; the laughing coots with wings half spread were tripping over the little coves and hiding themselves in the tufts of grass; young broods of the painted summer teal, skimming the still surface of the waters, and following the watchful parent unconscious of danger, were frequently surprised by the voracious trout, and he in turn, as often by the subtle, greedy alligator. Behold him rushing forth from the flags and reeds. His enormous body swells. His plaited tail brandished high, floats upon the lake. The waters like a cataract descend from his opening jaws. Clouds of smoke issue from his dilated nostrils. The earth trembles with his thunders. When immediately from the opposite coast of the lagoon, emerges from the deep his rival champion. They suddenly dart upon each other. The boiling surface of the lake marks their rapid course, and a terrific conflict commences. They now sink to the bottom folded together in horrid wreaths. The water becomes thick and discoloured. Again they rise, their jaws clap together, re-echoing through the deep surrounding forests. Again they sink, when the contest ends at the muddy bottom of the lake, and the vanquished makes a hazardous escape, hiding himself in the muddy turbulent waters and sedge on a distant shore. The proud victor exulting returns to the place of action. The shores and forests resound his dreadful roar, together with the triumphing shouts of the plaited tribes around, witnesses of the horrid combat.

My apprehensions were highly alarmed after being a spectator of so dreadful a battle, it was obvious that every delay would but tend to encrease my dangers and difficulties, as the sun was near setting, and the alligators gathered around my harbour from all quarters; from these considerations I concluded to be expeditious in my trip to the lagoon, in order to take some fish. Not thinking it prudent to take my fusee with me, lest I might lose it overboard in case of a battle, which I had every reason to dread before my return, I therefore furnished myself with a club for my defence, went on board, and penetrating the first line of those which surrounded my harbour, they gave way; but being pursued by several very large ones, I kept strictly on the watch, and paddled with all my might towards the entrance of the lagoon, hoping to be sheltered there from the multitude of my assailants; but ere I had half-way reached the place, I was attacked on all sides, several endeavouring to overset the canoe. My situation now became precarious to the last degree: two very large ones attacked me closely, at the same instant, rushing up with their heads and part of their bodies above the water, roaring terribly and belching floods of water over me. They struck their jaws together so close to my ears, as almost to stun me, and I expected every moment to be dragged out of the boat and instantly devoured, but I applied my weapons so effectually about me, though at random, that I was so successful as to beat them off a little; when, finding that they designed to renew the battle, I made for the shore, as the only means left me for my preservation, for, by keeping close to it, I should have my enemies on one side of me only, whereas I was before surrounded by them, and there was a probability, if pushed to the last extremity, of saving myself, by jumping out of the canoe on shore, as it is easy to outwalk them on land, although comparatively as swift as lightning in the water. I found this last expedient alone could fully answer my expectations, for as soon as I gained the shore they drew off and kept aloof. This was a happy relief, as my confidence was, in some degree, recovered by it. On recollecting myself, I discovered that I had almost reached the entrance of the lagoon, and determined to venture in, if possible to take a few fish and then return to my harbour, while day-light continued; for I could now, with caution and resolution, make my way with safety along shore, and indeed there was no other way to regain my camp, without leaving my boat and making my retreat through the marshes and reeds, which, if I could even effect, would have been in a manner throwing myself away, for then there would have been no hopes of ever recovering my bark, and returning in safety to any settlements of men. I accordingly proceeded and made good my entrance into the lagoon, though not without opposition from the alligators, who formed a line across the entrance, but did not pursue me into it, nor was I molested by any there, though there were some very large ones in a cove at the upper end. I soon caught more trout than I had present occasion for, and the air was too hot and sultry to admit of their being kept for many hours, even though salted or barbecued. I now prepared for my return to camp, which I succeeded in with but little trouble, by keeping close to the shore, yet I was opposed upon re-entering the river out of the lagoon, and pursued near to my landing (though not closely attacked) particularly by an old daring one, about twelve feet in length, who kept close after me, and when I stepped on shore and turned about, in order to draw up my canoe, he rushed up near my feet and lay there for some time, looking me in the face, his head and shoulders out of water; I resolved he should pay for his temerity, and having a heavy load in my fusee, I ran to my camp, and returning with my piece, found him with his foot on the gunwale of the boat, in search of fish, on my coming up he withdrew sullenly and slowly into the water, but soon returned and placed himself in his former position, looking at me and seeming neither fearful or any way disturbed. I soon dispatched him by lodging the contents of my gun in his head, and then proceeded to cleanse and prepare my fish for supper, and accordingly took them out of the boat, laid them down on the sand close to the water, and began to scale them, when, raising my head, I saw before me, through the clear water, the head and shoulders of a very large alligator, moving slowly towards me; I instantly stepped back, when, with a sweep of his tail, he brushed off several of my fish. It was certainly most providential that I looked up at that instant, as the monster would probably, in less than a minute, have seized and dragged me into the river. This incredible boldness of the animal disturbed me greatly, supposing there could now be no reasonable safety for me during the night, but by keeping continually on the watch; I therefore, as soon as I had prepared the fish, proceeded to secure myself and effects in the best manner I could in the first place, I hauled my bark upon the shore, almost clear out of the water, to prevent their oversetting or sinking her, after this every moveable was taken out and carried to my camp, which was but a few yards off; then ranging some dry wood in such order as was the most convenient, cleared the ground round about it, that there might be no impediment in my way, in case of an attack in the night, either from the water or the land; for I discovered by this time, that this small isthmus, from its remote situation and fruitfulness, was resorted to by bears and wolves. Having prepared myself in the best manner I could, I charged my gun and proceeded to reconnoitre my camp and the adjacent grounds; when I discovered that the peninsula and grove, at the distance of about two hundred yards from my encampment, on the land side, were invested by a Cypress swamp, covered with water, which below was joined to the shore of the little lake, and above to the marshes surrounding the lagoon, so that I was confined to an islet exceedingly circumscribed, and I found there was no other retreat for me, in case of an attack, but by either ascending one of the large Oaks, or pushing off with my boat.

It was by this time dusk, and the alligators had nearly ceased their roar, when I was again alarmed by a tumultuous noise that seemed to be in my harbour, and therefore engaged my immediate attention. Returning to my camp I found it undisturbed, and then continued on to the extreme point of the promontory, where I saw a scene, new and surprising, which at first threw my senses into such a tumult, that it was some time before I could comprehend what was the matter; however, I soon accounted for the prodigious assemblage of crocodiles at this place, which exceeded every thing of the kind I had ever heard of.

How shall I express myself so as to convey an adequate idea of it to the reader, and at the same time avoid raising suspicions of my want of veracity. Should I say, that the river (in this place) from shore to shore, and perhaps near half a mile above and below me, appeared to be one solid bank of fish, of various kinds, pushing through this narrow pass of St. Juans into the little lake, on their return down the river, and that the alligators were in such incredible numbers, and so close together from shore to shore, that it would have been easy to have walked across on their heads, had the animals been harmless. What expressions can sufficiently declare the shocking scene that for some minutes continued, whilst this mighty army of fish were forcing the pass? During this attempt, thousands, I may say hundreds of thousands of them were caught and swallowed by the devouring alligators. I have seen an alligator take up out of the water several great fish at a time, and just squeeze them betwixt his jaws, while the tails of the great trout flapped about his eyes and lips, ere he had swallowed them. The horrid noise of their closing jaws, their plunging amidst the broken banks of fish, and rising with their prey some feet upright above the water, the floods of water and blood rushing out of their mouths, and the clouds of vapour issuing from their wide nostrils, were truly frightful. This scene continued at intervals during the night, as the fish came to the pass. After this sight, shocking and tremendous as it was, I found myself somewhat easier and more reconciled to my situation, being convinced that their extraordinary assemblage here, was owing to this annual feast of fish, and that they were so well employed in their own element, that I had little occasion to fear their paying me a visit.

It being now almost night, I returned to my camp, where I had left my fish broiling, and my kettle of rice stewing, and having with me, oil, pepper and salt, and excellent oranges hanging in abundance over my head (a valuable substitute for vinegar) I sat down and regaled myself chearfully, having finished my repast, I re-kindled my fire for light, and whilst I was revising the notes of my past day's journey, I was suddenly roused with a noise behind me toward the main land; I sprang up on my feet, and listning, I distinctly heard some creature wading in the water of the isthmus; I seized my gun and went cautiously from my camp, directing my steps towards the noise; when I had advanced about thirty yards, I halted behind a coppice of Orange trees, and soon perceived two very large bears, which had made their way through the water, and had landed in the grove, about one hundred yards distance from me, and were advancing towards me. I waited until they were within thirty yards of me, they there began to snuff and look towards my camp, I snapped my piece, but it flashed, on which they both turned about and galloped off, plunging through the water and swamp, never halting as I suppose, until they reached fast land, as I could hear them leaping and plunging a long time; they did not presume to return again, nor was I molested by any other creature, except being occasionally awakened by the whooping of owls, screaming of bitterns, or the wood-rats running amongst the leaves.[. . .]

I now directed my steps towards my encampment, in a different direction. I seated myself upon a swelling green knoll, at the head of the chrystal bason. Near me, on the left, was a point or projection of an entire grove of the aromatic Illisium Floridanum; on my right and all around behind me, was a fruitful Orange grove, with Palms and Magnolias interspersed; in front, just under my feet was the inchanting and amazing chrystal fountain, which incessantly threw up, from dark, rocky caverns below, tons of water every minute, forming a bason, capacious enough for large shallops to ride in, and a creek of four or five feet depth of water, and near twenty yards over, which meanders six miles through green meadows, pouring its limpid waters into the great Lake George, where they seem to remain pure and unmixed. About twenty yards from the upper edge of the bason, and directly opposite to the mouth or outlet to the creek, is a continual and amazing ebullition, where the waters are thrown up in such abundance and amazing force, as to jet and swell up two or three feet above the common surface: white sand and small particles of shells are thrown up with the waters, near to the top, when they diverge from the center, subside with the expanding flood, and gently sink again, forming a large rim or funnel round about the aperture or mouth of the fountain, which is a vast perforation through a bed of rocks, the ragged points of which are projected out on every side. Thus far I know to be matter of real fact, and I have related it as near as I could conceive or express myself. But there are yet remaining scenes inexpressibly admirable and pleasing.

Behold, for instance, a vast circular expanse before you, the waters of which are so extremely clear as to be absolutely diaphanous or transparent as the ether; the margin of the bason ornamented with a great variety of fruitful and floriferous trees, shrubs and plants, the pendant golden Orange dancing on the surface of the pellucid waters, the balmy air vibrates the melody of the merry birds, tenants of the encircling aromatic grove.

At the same instant innumerable bands of fish are seen, some cloathed in the most brilliant colours; the voracious crocodile stretched along at full length, as the great trunk of a tree in size, the devouring garfish, inimical trout, and all the varieties of gilded painted bream, the barbed catfish, dreaded sting-ray, skate and flounder, spotted bass, sheeps head and ominous drum; all in their seperate bands and communities, with free and unsuspicious intercourse performing their evolutions: there are no signs of enmity, no attempt to devour each other; the different bands seem peaceably and complaisantly to move a little aside, as it were to make room for others to pass by.

But behold yet something far more admirable, see whole armies descending into an abyss, into the mouth of the bubbling fountain, they disappear! are they gone forever? is it real? I raise my eyes with terror and astonishment, I look down again to the fountain with anxiety, when behold them as it were emerging from the blue ether of another world, apparently at a vast distance, at their first appearance, no bigger than flies or minnows, now gradually enlarging, their brilliant colours begin to paint the fluid.

Now they come forward rapidly, and instantly emerge, with the elastic expanding column of chrystaline waters, into the circular bason or funnel, see now how gently they rise, some upright, others obliquely, or seem to lay as it were on their sides, suffering themselves to be gently lifted or born up, by the expanding fluid towards the surface, sailing or floating like butterflies in the cerulean ether: then again they as gently descend, diverge and move off; when they rally, form again and rejoin their kindred tribes.

This amazing and delightful scene, though real, appears at first but as a piece of excellent painting; there seems no medium, you imagine the picture to be within a few inches of your eyes, and that you may without the least difficulty touch any one of the fish, or put your finger upon the crocodile's eye, when it really is twenty or thirty feet under water.

And although this paradise of fish, may seem to exhibit a just representation of the peaceable and happy state of nature which existed before the fall, yet in reality it is a mere representation; for the nature of the fish is the same as if they were in lake George or the river; but here the water or element in which they live and move, is so perfectly clear and transparent, it places them all on an equality with regard to their ability to injure or escape from one another; (as all river fish of prey, or such as feed upon each other, as well as the unwieldly crocodile, take their prey by surprise; secreting themselves under covert or in ambush, until an opportunity offers, when they rush suddenly upon them) but here is no covert, no ambush, here the trout freely passes by the very nose of the alligator and laughs in his face, and the bream by the trout.

But what is really surprising, that the consciousness of each others safety or some other latent cause, should so absolutely alter their conduct, for here is not the least attempt made to injure or disturb one another.

The sun passing below the horizon, and night approaching, I arose from my seat, and proceeding on arrived at my camp, kindled my fire, supped and reposed peaceably. And rising early, employed the fore part of the day in collecting specimens of growing roots and seeds.[. . .]

But let us again resume the subject of the rattlesnake; a wonderful creature, when we consider his form, nature and disposition, it is certain that he is capable by a puncture or scratch of one of his fangs, not only to kill the largest animal in America, and that in a few minutes time, but to turn the whole body into corruption; but such is the nature of this dreaded reptile, that he cannot run or creep faster than a man or child can walk, and he is never known to strike until he is first assaulted or fears himself in danger, and even then always gives the earliest warning by the rattles at the extremity of his tail. I have in the course of my travels in the Southern states (where they are the largest, most numerous and supposed to be the most venemous and vindictive) stept unknowingly so close as almost to touch one of them with my feet, and when I perceived him he was already drawn up in circular coils ready for a blow. But however incredible it may appear, the generous, I may say magnanimous creature lay as still and motionless as if inanimate, his head crouched in, his eyes almost shut, I precipitately withdrew, unless when I have been so shocked with surprise and horror as to be in a manner rivetted to the spot, for a short time not having strength to go away, when he often slowly extends himself and quietly moves off in a direct line, unless pursued when he erects his tail as far as the rattles extend, and gives the warning alarm by intervals, but if you pursue and overtake him with a shew of enmity, he instantly throws himself into the spiral coil, his tail by the rapidity of its motion appears like a vapour, making a quick tremulous sound, his whole body swells through rage, continually rising and falling as a bellows; his beautiful particoloured skin becomes speckled and rough by dilatation, his head and neck are flattened, his cheeks swollen and his lips constricted, discovering his mortal fangs; his eyes red as burning coals, and his brandishing forked tongue of the colour of the hottest flame, continually menaces death and destruction, yet never strikes unless sure of his mark.

The rattle snake is the largest serpent yet known to exist in North America, I have heard of their having been seen formerly, at the first settling of Georgia, seven, eight and even ten feet in length, and six or eight inches diameter, but there are none of that size now to be seen, yet I have seen them above six feet in length, and about six inches in thickness, or as large as a man's leg, but their general size is four, five and six feet in length. They are supposed to have the power of fascination in an eminent degree, so as to inthral their prey. It is generally believed that they charm birds, rabbits, squirrels and other animals, and by stedfastly looking at them possess them with infatuation; be the cause what it may, the miserable creatures undoubtedly strive by every possible means to escape, but alas! their endeavours are in vain, they at last lose the power of resistance, and flutter or move slowly, but reluctantly towards the yawning jaws of their devourers, and creep into their mouths or lay down and suffer themselves to be taken and swallowed.

Sir Humphry Davy (1778–1829)

If the term *poet-scientist* can be applied to any individual during this era, that person is Sir Humphry Davy. Davy's account of his upbringing reflected the emerging Romantic discourse of childhood. He describes a youthful version of himself wandering with fishing tackle and natural history specimens, rapt in scenic images of mountain and seaside. Davy originally wanted to be a poet, but his plans to write a volume of verse were cut short when he devoted himself seriously to the study of experimental science, which he called natural philosophy. Davy first served as assistant to Thomas Beddoes at the pneumatic institution in Bristol. He coined the term *phosoxygen* to describe a combination of light and oxygen, which he imagined condensing as a form of electricity at the ends of nerves in order to produce physical sensations. He became a close friend of Coleridge, and he visited Wordsworth and Sir Walter Scott in the Lake District. Wordsworth wrote to Davy in 1800, asking him to correct the punctuation of Wordsworth's own lyrics. Davy corresponded with Coleridge throughout his life.

Davy argued that plants, like the sensitive mimosa and the *Dionaea* (Venus's flytrap), manifested "an irritability so exquisite as to border on the sensibility of the animals." By 1815 he agreed with Erasmus Darwin about the fundamentals of an evolutionary principle, claiming that "probably there is an analogy in all existence: the divided tail of the fish is linked in a long succession of like objects with the biped man" and "beasts fight animated by the passion of love, and the strongest perpetuate the species" (Ritterbush 183). He established the foundations of electrochemistry through his use of bimetal batteries. In 1810, Davy demonstrated the first electric arc light, using a 2,000-plate voltaic battery that belonged to the Royal Society. He was well known for his experiments with nitrous oxide, or laughing gas, which would prove influential as an early anesthetic. He tested this psychoactive gas on Coleridge, Southey, and himself.

He also developed an effective miner's lamp that could be used without fear of underground explosions.

Davy was a scientist who expounded on the value of the imagination to scientific research. He argued for the importance of analogy in scientific progress, claiming that a scientist who used his imagination would be "more fitted to enjoy the blaze of light of Milton, to pass into the proteus-forms of humanity with Shakespeare, and to move through the heavens with Newton"; he also argued that "Imagination, as well as reason, is necessary to perfection in the philosophical mind. A rapidity of combination, a power of perceiving analogies, and of comparing them by facts, is the creative source of discovery" (Ritterbursh 185). Davy assisted in the founding of the Zoological Society and the development of the Regent's Park Zoo, which opened to the public in 1828. His late book *Salmonia: or Days of Fly Fishing* included engravings taken from Davy's own drawings.

The selections reproduced here include poems from Robert Southey's *Annual Anthology* (1799, 1800). These lyrics suggest the range of Davy's literary interests at the time, from the Augustan cadences of "The Sons of Genius" (in praise of natural scientists) to the Wordsworthian echoes in "Lines, Descriptive of feelings produced by a Visit to the place where the first nineteen years of my Life were spent, in a stormy day, after an absence of thirteen months." Also included are selections from *Elements of Chemical Philosophy,* which emphasize the importance of the history of science to the kind of analogical progress favored by Davy, as well as poetic fragments, extracts from his notebooks, and an engaging experiment on the torpedo fish, a species we now call the electric ray.

From The Annual Anthology
The Sons of Genius

Bright bursting thro' the awful veil of night
   The lunar beams upon the ocean play,
The watry billows shine with trembling light
   Where the swift breezes skim along the sea.

Robert Southey, ed., *The Annual Anthology.* London: Longman and Rees, 1799, 1800.

5   The glimmering stars in yon etherial plain
        Grow pale and fade before the lucid beams
    Save where fair Venus shining oe'r the main
        Conspicuous still with fainter radiance gleams.

    Clear is the azure firmament above,
10   Save where the white cloud floats upon the breeze,
    All tranquil is the bosom of the grove
        Save where the Zephyr warbles thro' the trees.

    Now the poor shepherd wandering to his home
        Surveys the darkening scene with fearful eye,
15 On every green sees little Elfins roam
        And haggard Sprites along the moon-beams fly.

    Whilst Superstition rules the vulgar soul,
        Forbids the energies of man to rise,
    Rais'd far above her low, her mean controul,
20   Aspiring Genius seeks her native skies.

    She loves the silent solitary hours,
        She loves the stillness of the starry night,
    When o'er the brightening view Selene pours
        The soft effulgence of her pensive light.

25 'Tis then disturb'd not by the glare of day
        To mild tranquillity alone resign'd,
    Reason extends her animating sway
        O'er the calm empire of the peaceful mind.

    Before her lucid all-enlightening ray,
30   The pallid Spectres of the night retire,
    She drives the gloomy terrors far away
        And fills the bosom with celestial fire.

    Inspired by her the sons of Genius rise
        Above all earthly thoughts, all vulgar care,
35 Wealth, power and grandeur, they alike despise,
        Enraptur'd by the good, the great, the fair.

    A thousand varying joys to them belong
        The charms of Nature and her changeful scenes,
    Theirs is the music of the vernal song —
40   And theirs the colors of the vernal plains.

    Theirs is the purple-tinged evening ray
        With all the radiance of the morning sky,

Theirs is the splendour of the risen day
    Enshrined in glory by the sun's bright eye.

45 For them the zephyr fans the odorous dale,
    For them the warbling streamlet softly flows,
    For them the Dryads shade the verdant vale,
       To them sweet Philomel[1] attunes her woes.

To them no wakeful moon-beam shines in vain
50   On the dark bosom of the trackless wood,
Sheds its mild radiance o'er the desart plain
    Or softly glides along the chrystal flood,

Yet not alone delight the soft and fair
    Alike the grander scenes of Nature move,
55 Yet not alone her beauties claim their care,
    The great, sublime and terrible, they love.

The sons of Nature they alike delight
    In the rough precipices broken steep,
In the black terrors of the stormy night,
60   And in the thunders of the threatening deep;

When the red ligtnings thro' the ether fly,
    And the white foaming billows lash the shores,
When to the rattling thunders of the sky
    The angry Daemon of the waters roars.

65 And when untouch'd by Nature's living fires
    No native rapture fills the drowsy soul,
Then former ages with their tuneful lyres
    Can bid the fury of the passions fall.

By the blue taper's melancholy light
70   Whilst all around the midnight torrents pour,
And awful glooms beset the face of night
    They wear the silent solitary hour.

Ah then, how sweet to pass the night away
    In silent converse with the Grecian page,
75 Whilst Homer tunes his ever-living lay,
    Or Reason listens to the Athenian sage.

To scan the laws of Nature, to explore
    The tranquil reign of mild Philosophy,

---

[1] The nightingale. [Ed.]

Or on Newtonian wings sublime to soar
80   Thro' the bright regions of the starry sky.

Ah! who can paint what raptures fill the soul
   When Attic Freedom rises to the war,
Bids the loud thunders of the battle roll
And drives the Tyrant trembling from her shore?

85 From these pursuits the Sons of Genius scan
   The end of their creation, hence they know
The fair, sublime, immortal hopes of man
   From whence alone undying pleasures flow.

By science calm'd, over the peaceful soul,
90   Bright with eternal wisdom's lucid ray,
Peace, meek of eye, extends her soft controul,
   And drives the fury passions far away.

Virtue, the daughter of the skies supreme,
   Directs their life, informs their glowing lays,
95 A steady friend, her animating beam
   Sheds its soft lustre o'er their latter days.

When Life's warm fountains feel the frost of time,
   When the cold dews of darkness close their eyes,
She shows the parting soul uprais'd sublime,
100   The brighter glories of her kindred skies.

Thus the pale moon whose pure celestial light
   Has chased the gloomy clouds of heaven away,
Rests her white cheek with silver radiance bright
   On the soft bosom of the western sea.

105 Lost in the glowing wave her radiance dies,
   Yet while she sinks she points her ling'ring ray
To the bright azure of the orient skies,
   To the fair dawning of the glorious day.

Like the tumultuous billows of the sea
110   Succeed the generations of mankind,
Some in oblivious silence pass away
   And leave no vestige of their lives behind.

Others, like those proud waves which beat the shore
   A loud and momentary murmur raise,
115 But soon their transient glories are no more,
   No future ages echo with their praise.

Like yon proud rocks amidst the sea of time
   Superior scorning all the billow's rage,
The living Sons of Genius stand sublime,
120   The immortal children of another age.

For those exist whose pure etherial minds
   Imbibing portions of celestial day,
Scorn all terrestrial cares, all mean designs,
   As bright-eyed Eagles scorn the lunar ray.

125 Theirs is the glory of a lasting name
   The meed of Genius and her living fires,
Theirs is the laurel of eternal fame,
   And theirs the sweetness of the Muses lyres.

Ode To St. Michael's Mount

In Cornwall

The sober eve with purple bright
Sheds o'er the hills her tranquil light
   In many a lingering ray;
The radiance trembles on the deep,
5   Where rises rough thy rugged steep,
   Old Michael, from the sea.

Around thy base in azure pride,
Flows the silver-crested tide,
   In gently winding waves;
10 The zephyr creeps thy cliffs around,
Thy cliffs, with whispering ivy crown'd,
   And murmurs in thy caves.

Majestic steep! Ah yet I love
With many a lingering step to rove
15   Thy ivied rocks among:
Thy ivied, wave-beat rocks recall
The former pleasures of my soul,
   When life was gay and young.

Enthusiasm, Nature's child,
20 Here sung to me her wood-songs wild,
   All warm with native fire;

I felt her soul-awakening flame,
It bade my bosom burn for fame,
   It bade me strike the lyre.

25 Soft as the morning sheds her light
Thro' the dark azure of the night
   Along the tranquil sea,
So soft the bright-eyed Fancy shed
Her rapturing dreams around my head,
30   And drove my cares away.

When the white moon with glory crown'd
The azure of the sky around,
   Her silver radiance shed;
When shone the waves with trembling light,
35 And slept the lustre palely-bright,
   Upon thy tower-clad head.

Then Beauty bade my pleasures flow,
Then Beauty bade my bosom glow
   With mild and gentle fire!
40 Then mirth, and cheerfulness, and love,
Around my soul were wont to move,
   And thrill'd upon my lyre.

But when the Daemon of the deep
Howl'd around thy rocky steep,
45   And bade the tempests rise,
Bade the white foaming billows roar,
And murmuring dash the rocky shore,
   And mingle with the skies;

Ah, then my soul was rais'd on high,
50 And felt the glow of ecstacy,
   With *great* emotions fill'd;
Thus joy and terror reign'd by turns,
And now with Love the bosom burns,
   And now by Fear is chilled.

55 Thus to the sweetest dreams resign'd,
The fairy Fancy ruled my mind,
   And shone upon my youth;
But now to awful reason given,
I leave her dear ideal heaven,
60   To hear the voice of Truth.

She claims my best, my loftiest song,
She leads a brighter maid along—
   Divine Philosophy,
Who bids the mounting soul assume
65 Immortal Wisdom's eagle plume,
   And penetrating eye.

Above delusion's dusky maze,
Above deceitful Fancy's ways,
   With roses clad to rise;
70 To view a gleam of purest light
Bursting thro' Nature's misty night,
   The radiance of the skies.

The Tempest

The Tempest has darken'd the face of the skies,
   The winds whistle wildly across the waste plain,
The Fiends of the whirlwind terrific arise,
   And mingle the clouds with the white-foaming main.

5 All dark is the night and all gloomy the shore,
   Save when the red lightnings the ether divide,
Then follows the thunder with loud sounding roar
   And echoes in concert the billowy tide.

But tho' now all is murky and shaded with gloom,
10   Hope the soother soft whispers the tempests shall cease;
Then Nature again in her beauty shall bloom,
   And enamoured embrace the fair sweet-smiling Peace.

For the bright-blushing morning all rosy with light
   Shall convey on her wings the Creator of Day,
15 He shall drive all the tempests and terrors of night,
   And Nature enlivened again shall be gay.

Then the warblers of Spring shall attune the soft lay,
   And again the bright flowret shall blush in the dale;
On the breast of the ocean the Zephyr shall play,
20   And the sun-beam shall sleep on the hill and the dale.

If the tempests of Nature so soon sink to rest,
   If her once faded beauties so soon glow again,

Shall Man be for ever by tempests oppress'd,
   By the tempests of passion, of sorrow, and pain?

25 Ah no! for his passions and sorrows shall cease
   When the troublesome fever of life shall be o'er;
In the night of the grave he shall slumber in peace,
   And passion and sorrow shall vex him no more.

And shall not this night and its long dismal gloom,
30   Like the night of the tempest again pass away;
Yes! the dust of the earth in bright beauty shall bloom,
   And rise to the morning of heavenly day!

Lines

Descriptive of feelings produced by a Visit to

the place where the first nineteen years of my Life

were spent, in a stormy day, after an absence

of thirteen months.

Thou Ocean dark and terrible in storms!
My eye is closed upon thee, and I view
The light of other days. The sunbeams dance
Upon thy waves, the purple clouds of morn
5 Hang o'er thy rocks resplendent. Scenes beloved!
Scenes of my youth! within my throbbing breast
Ye have awakened rapture. Round me crowd
Tumultuous passions, all the joys and cares
Of Infancy, the glittering dreams of youth
10 Ambitious and energic.
                 Here my eyes
First trembled with the lustre of the day,
And here the gently-soothing sounds of love
First lulled my feeble spirit to repose.
15 Here first a mother's care awoke my sense
To mild enjoyment. Here my opening mind
First in the mingled harmony of voice
And speaking countenance, astonished read
Another's living feelings and his thoughts.
20 Here first I woo'd thee Nature, in the forms

Of majesty and freedom, and thy charms
Soft mingling with the sports of infancy
Its rising social passions and its wants
Intense and craving, kindled into one
25 Supreme emotion.
                             Hence awoke to life
Sublimest thoughts, a living energy
That still has warm'd my beating heart, and still
Its objects varying, has impelled me on
30 To various action.
                             Here the novel sense
Of beauty thrilling through my new-tuned frame,
Called into being gentlest sympathies:
Then through the trembling moonshine of the grove
35 My earliest lays were wafted by the breeze.
Here first my serious spirit learnt to trace
The mystic laws, from whose high energy
The moving atoms in eternal change
Still rise to animation.
40   Many days
Are passed, O scene beloved! since last my eyes
Beheld the moon-beams gild thy foaming waves.
Ambitious then, confiding in her powers,
Spurning her prison, onward flew my soul
45 To mingle with her kindred. In the breeze
That wafts futurity upon its wings
To hear the sounds of praise.
                                      And not in vain
Have those high hopes existed. Not in vain
50 The dew of labor has oppressed my brow,
On which the rose of pleasure never glow'd;
For I have tasted of that sacred stream
Of Science, whose delicious waters flow
From Nature's bosom. I have felt the warm,
55 The gentle influence of congenial souls
Whose kindred hopes have cheered me. Who have taught
My irritable spirit how to bear
Injustice and oppression, nor to droop
In its high flight beneath the feeble rage
60 Of noisy tempests, whose kind hands have given
New plumes of rapture to my drooping wing
When ruffled by their wild and angry breath.
Beloved rocks! thou Ocean, white with mist

Once more ye live upon my humid eyes,
65 Again ye waken in my throbbing breast
The sympathies of Nature.
                    Now I go
Once more to visit my remembered home,
With heart-felt rapture, there to mingle tears
70 Of purest joy, to feel the extatic glow
Of warm affection, and again to view
The rosy light that shone upon my youth.

From Elements of Chemical Philosophy

Nothing tends so much to the advancement of knowledge as the application of a new instrument. The native intellectual powers of men in different times, are not so much the causes of the different success of their labours, as the peculiar nature of the means and artificial resources in their possession. Independent of vessels of glass, there could have been no accurate manipulations in common chemistry: the air pump was necessary for the investigation of the properties of gaseous matter; and without the Voltaic apparatus, there was no possibility of examining the relations of electrical polarities to chemical attractions.

By researches, the commencement of which is owing to Messrs. Nicholson and Carlisle, in 1800, which were continued by Cruickshank, Henry, Wollaston, Children, Pepys, Pfaff, Desormes, Biot, Thenard, Hissinger, and Berzelius, it appeared that various compound bodies were capable of decomposition by electricity; and experiments, which it was my good fortune to institute, proved that several substances which had never been separated into any other forms of matter in the common processes of experiment, were susceptible of analysis by electrical powers: in consequence of these circumstances, the fixed alkalies and several of the earths have been shewn to be metals combined with oxygene; various new agents have been furnished to chemistry, and many novel results obtained by their application, which at the same time that they have strengthened some of the doctrines of the school of Lavoisier, have overturned others, and have proved that the generalizations of the antiphlogistic philosophers were far from having anticipated the whole progress of discovery.

Sir Humphry Davy, *Elements of Chemical Philosophy*. Philadelphia: Bradford and Inskeep; London: J. Johnson, 1812.

Certain bodies which attract each other chemically, and combine when their particles have freedom of motion, when brought into contact, still preserving their aggregation, exhibit what may be called electrical polarities; and by certain combinations these polarities may be highly exalted; and in this case they become subservient to chemical decompositions; and by means of electrical arrangements the constituent parts of bodies are separated in a uniform order, and in definite proportions.

Bodies combine with a force, which in many cases is correspondent to their power of exhibiting electrical polarity by contact; and heat, or heat and light, are produced in proportion to the energy of their combination. Vivid inflammation occurs in a number of cases in which gaseous matter is not fixed; and this phaenomenon happens in various instances without the interference of free or combined oxygene.

Experiments made by Richter and Moryeau had shewn that, when there is an interchange of elements between two neutrals salts, there is never an excess of acid or basis; and the same law seems to apply generally to double decompositions. When one body combines with another in more than one proportion, the second proportion appears to be some multiple or divisor of the first; and this circumstance, observed and ingeniously illustrated by Mr. Dalton, led him to adopt the atomic hypothesis of chemical changes, which had been ably defended by Mr. Higgins in 1789, namely, that the chemical elements consist of certain indestructible particles which unite one and one, or one and two, or in some definite numbers.

Whether matter consists of indivisible corpuscles, or physical points endowed with attraction and repulsion, still the same conclusions may be formed concerning the powers by which they act, and the quantities in which they combine; and the powers seem capable of being measured by their electrical relations, and the quantities on which they act of being expressed by numbers.

In combination certain bodies form regular solids; and all the varieties of crystalline aggregates have been resolved by the genius of Haüy into a few primary forms. The laws of crystallization, of definite proportions, and of the electrical polarities of bodies, seem to be intimately related; and the complete illustration of their connection, probably will constitute the mature age of chemistry.

To dwell more minutely upon the particular merits of the chemical philosophers of the present age, will be a grateful labour for some future historian of chemistry; but for a contemporary writer, it would be indelicate to assume the right of arbitrator, even where praise only can be bestowed. The just fame of those who have enlightened the science by new and accurate experiments, cannot fail to be universally acknowledged; and concerning the publication of novel facts there can be but one judgment; for facts are independent of fashion, taste, and caprice, and are subject to no code of criticism; they are more useful perhaps even when they contradict, than when they support received doctrines, for our theories are only imperfect approximations to the real knowledge of things; and, in physical research, doubt is usually of excellent effect, for it is a principal motive for new labours, and tends continually to the development of truth.

The slight sketch that has been given of the progress of chemistry, has necessarily been limited to the philosophical details of discovery. To point out in historical order the manner in which the truths of the science have been applied to the arts of life, or the benefits derived by society from them, would occupy many volumes. From the first discovery of the production of metals from rude ores, to the knowledge of the bleaching liquor, chemistry has been continually subservient to cultivation and improvement. In the manufacture of porcelain and glass, in the arts of dyeing and tanning, it has added to the elegancies, refinement, and comforts of life; in its application to medicine it has removed the most formidable of diseases; and in leading to the discovery of gunpowder, it has changed the institutions of society, and rendered war more independent of brutal strength, less personal, and less barbarous.

It is indeed a double source of interest in this science, that whilst it is connected with the grand operations of nature, it is likewise subservient to the common processes as well as the most refined arts of life. New laws cannot be discovered in it, without increasing our admiration of the beauty and order of the system of the universe; and no new substances can be made known which are not sooner or later subservient to some purpose of utility.

When the great progress made in chemistry within the few last years is considered, and the number of able labourers who are at present actively employed in cultivating the science, it is impossible not to augur well concerning its rapid advancement and future applications. The most important truths belonging to it are capable of extremely simple numerical expressions, which may be acquired with facility by students; and the apparatus for pursuing original researches is daily improved, the use of it rendered more easy, and the acquisition less expensive.

Complexity almost always belongs to the early epochs of every science; and the grandest results are usually obtained by the most simple means. A great part of the phaenomena of chemistry may be already submitted to calculation; and there is great reason to believe, that at no very distant period the whole science will be capable of elucidation by mathematical principles. The relations of the common metals to the bases of the alkalies and earths, and the gradations of resemblance between the bases of the earths and acids, point out as probable a similarity in the constitution of all inflammable bodies; and there are not wanting experiments, which render their possible decomposition far from a chimerical idea. It is contrary to the usual order of things, that events so harmonious as those of the system of the earth, should depend on such diversified agents, as are supposed to exist in our artificial arrangements; and there is reason to anticipate a great reduction in the number of the undecompounded bodies, and to expect that the analogies of nature will be found conformable to the refined operations of art. The more the phaenomena of the universe are studied, the more distinct their connection appears, the more simple their causes, the more magnificent their design, and the more wonderful the wisdom and power of their Author.

From Memoirs

[Notes]

After reading a few books, I was seized with the desire to narrate, to gratify the passions of my youthful auditors. I gradually began to invent, and form stories of my own. Perhaps this passion has produced all my originality. I never loved to imitate, but always to invent: this has been the case in all the sciences I have studied.[. . .]

General terms—what some metaphysicians have called abstract ideas, arise from the association of analogy by a very simple operation—not, as Jean Jacques Rousseau supposed, by a very complicated one.

No metaphysical system, and, indeed, no system can be any thing more than a history, not in the order of impression, but in the order of arrangement by analogy.

Atheism the necessary consequence of materialism.[. . .]

We are accustomed to consider thought and language as almost synonymous. What an immensity of feelings, what an innumerable quantity of perception, must necessarily impress the mind of all men. Writing and speaking are arts, like music and painting, to express some of them only.[. . .]

Our actions are neither the result of feelings or opinions; they are modified by them both, but are produced by habits.

What is imagination? Almost always the recurrence of remembered visible imagery, under the influence of hope or fear.[. . .]

The sciences and the arts ought to be considered as related to man only so far as they are capable of promoting his happiness. Our knowledge of their capabilities must be founded upon an estimate of the powers and faculties of the human mind, and the sources of enjoyment which are within the reach of these faculties and powers.[. . .]

Sir Humphry Davy. *The Collected Works,* Ed. John Davy, London: Smith and Elder, 1839–40.

[Poetic Fragment] to the Fire-Flies

Baths of Lucca, 1819.

Ye moving stars that flit along the glade!
Ye animated lamps that 'midst the shade
Of ancient chesnuts, and the lofty hills
Of Lusignana, by the foaming rills
5   That clothe the Serchio in the evening play!
So bright your light, that in the unbroken ray
Of the meridian moon it lovely shines.
How gaily do ye pass beneath the vines
Which clothe the nearest slopes! how thro' the groves
10 Of Lucca do ye dance! The breeze that moves
Their silver leaves, a mountain zephyr's wing,
Has brought you here to cheer our tardy spring.
Oft had I seen ye 'midst thy orange bowers,
Parthenope! and where Velino pours
15 In thundering cataracts; but ne'er before
So high upon the mountains, where ye soar
E'en in mid air, leaving those halcyon plains
Where spring or summer everlasting reigns,
Where flowers and fruit mature together grow,
20 To visit our rude peaks, where still the snow
Glitters e'en in the genial month of flowers.
But brightly do ye move in fiery showers,
Seen like the falling meteor from afar,
Or like the kindred of the erring star.
25 May not the stars themselves in orbits whirl'd,
Be but a different animated world,
In which a high and lofty breath of life,
Of worlds and insects calms the wakening strife,
Commands the elements, and bids them move
30 In animation to the voice of Love!
                    * * *
Thou loveliest form of the celestial world,
When in the circle of thy brightness
Thou sheddest in the blue unclouded sky
All thy meridian lustre! in the north,
35 Above the heath-clad mountains have I seen
Thy clear and mellow light; and when the waves

Of the Atlantic raised their foaming surge
Against the eternal rocks, where fabled sleeps
The last of western Titans—then, when young
40 In mind, and light of heart, thy rays had power
To solemnize and tune to thoughts sublime
My vagrant spirit; *now*, in these fair climes,
Where in a purer and more balmy air,
And in a sky whose tints of ether seem
45 Giving a saint-like glory to thy rays,
Thy influence is e'en stronger in a heart
Wearied, but not yet broken or subdued.
Though many chequer'd years have passed away
Since first the sense of beauty thrill'd my nerves,
50 Yet still my heart is sensible to thee,
As when it first received the flood of life
In youth's full spring-tide; and to me it seems
As if thou wert a sister to my soul,
An animated being, carrying on
55 An intercourse of sweet and lofty thoughts,
Wakening the slumbering powers of inspiration
In their most sacred founts of feeling high.

* * *

The tempest gather'd on thy verdant hills,
O Lusignano! The azure southern sky
60 Was dimm'd by fleeting mists. Soon the dark cloud
Form'd more compact, and to the zenith rose;
The bright blue of the northern distance then,
And all the mountains show'd their shaggy crests
Of ancient chesnuts, dark and deep in shade.
65 To the feverish flush of the meridian sun
Succeeded quick a damp and sudden chill;
The lightning flash'd. At first, a feeble light,
Scarce seen, even in the darkest part of heaven,
Succeeded by low murmurings; brighter gleam'd
70 Each flash that follow'd, and now louder roar'd
The thunder distant, but it soon became
The loudest burst of heaven's artillery.

* * *

The whirlwind gone,
A calm, a soothing freshness soon succeed.
75 Thus in the mind springs new-born energy,

——————— Thoughts that were dead are roused,
And all the purer being wakes again.
The slime of foulness and impurity
Are borne into the ocean deep of reason,
80 And new creations dance upon its waves,
E'en as they purify—a thousand forms
Of beauty, and of goodness, and of grace.
The intellectual soul, freshen'd by dew
From heaven, enrich'd, is glad and green with life.

* * *

85 Again that lovely lamp from half its orb
Sends forth a mellow lustre, that pervades
The eastern sky, and meets the rosy light
Of the last sunbeams dying in the west.
The mountains all above are clear and bright,
90 Their giant forms distinctly visible,
Crested with shaggy chesnuts, or erect,
Bearing the helmed pine, or raising high
Their marble columns crown'd with grassy slopes.
From rock to rock the foaming Lima pours
95 Full from the thunder storm, rapid, and strong,
And turbid. Hush'd is the air in silence;
The smoke moves upwards, and its curling waves
Stand like a tree above. E'en in my heart,
By sickness weaken'd and by sorrow chill'd,
100 The balm of calmness seems to penetrate,
Mild, soothing, genial in its influence.
Again I feel a freshness, and a power,
As in my youthful days, and hopes and thoughts
Heroical and high! The wasted frame
105 Soon in corporeal strength recruits itself,
And wounds the deepest heal; so in the mind,
The dearth of objects and the loss of hope
Are in the end succeeded by some births
Of new creative faculties and powers,
110 Brought forth with pain, but, like a vigorous child,
Repaying by its beauty for the pang.

An Account of Some Experiments on the Torpedo[2]

Amidst the variety of researches which have been pursued respecting the different forms and modes of excitation and action of electricity, it is surprising to me that the electricity of living animals has not been more an object of attention, both on account of its physiological importance, and its general relation to the science of electro-chemistry.

In reading an account of the experiments of Walsh, it is impossible not to be struck by some peculiarities of the electricity of the organ of the Torpedo and Gymnotus; such as its want of power to pass through air, and the slight effects of ignition produced by the strongest shocks: and though Mr. Cavendish, with his usual sagacity, compared its action to that of a battery weakly charged, when the electricity was large in quantity but low in intensity, yet the peculiarities which I have just mentioned are not entirely in harmony with this view of the subject.

When Volta discovered his wonderful pile, he imagined he had made a perfect resemblance of the organ of the Gymnotus and Torpedo; and whoever has felt the shocks of the natural and artificial instruments, must have been convinced, as far as sensation is concerned, of their strict analogy. After the discovery of the chemical power of the voltaic instrument, I was desirous of ascertaining if this property of electricity was possessed by the electrical organs of living animals; and being in 1814 and 1815 on the coast of the Mediterranean, I made use of the opportunities which offered themselves of making experiments on this subject. Having obtained in the Bay of Naples, in May 1815, two small torpedos alive, I passed the shocks through the interrupted circuit made by silver wire, without being able to perceive the slightest decomposition of that fluid; and I repeated the same experiments at Mola di Gaeta, with an apparatus in which the smallest possible surface of silver was exposed, and in which good conductors, such as solutions of potassa and sulphuric acid, were made to connect the circuit; but with the same negative results.

Having obtained a larger Torpedo at Rimini, in June in the same year, I repeated the experiments, using all the precautions I could imagine, with the like results; and at the same time I passed the shock through a very small circuit, which was completed by a quarter of an inch of extremely fine silver wire, drawn by the late Mr. Cavendish for using in a micrometer, and which was less than 1/1,000th of an inch in diameter; but no ignition of the wire took place. It appeared to me after these experiments, that

---

[2]From Phil. Trans. for 1829. Read before the Royal Society, Nov. 20, 1828. (Electric ray. [Ed.])

the comparison of the organ of the Torpedo to an electrical battery weakly charged, and of which the charged surfaces were imperfect conductors, such as water, was more correct than that of the comparison to the pile: but on mentioning my researches to Signor Volta, with whom I passed some time at Milan that summer, he showed me another form of his instrument, which appeared to him to fulfil the conditions of the organs of the torpedo; a pile, of which the fluid substance was a very imperfect conductor, such as honey or a strong saccharine extract, which required a certain time to become charged, and which did not decompose water, though when charged it communicated weak shocks.

The discovery of Œrsted, of the effects of voltaic electricity on the magnetic needle, made me desirous to ascertain if the electricity of living animals possessed this power; and after several vain attempts to procure living torpedos sufficiently strong and vigorous to give powerful shocks, I succeeded in October of this year, through the kind assistance of George Deering, Esq., His Majesty's Consul at Trieste, in obtaining two lively and recently caught torpedos, one a foot long, the other smaller. I passed the shocks from the largest of these animals a number of times through the circuit of an extremely delicate magnetic electrometer, (of the same kind, but more sensible than that I have described in my last paper on the electro-chemical phenomena, which the Royal Society has honoured with a place in their Transactions for 1826,) but without perceiving the slightest deviation of an effect on the needle; and I convinced myself that the circuit was perfect, by making my body several times a part of it, holding the silver spoon, by which the shock was taken, in one hand, wetted in salt and water, and keeping the wire connected with the electrometer in the other wet hand; the shocks which passed through the reduplications of the electrometer were sufficiently powerful to be felt at both elbows, and once even in the shoulders.

The negative results may be explained by supposing that the motion of the electricity in the torpedinal organ is in no measurable time, and that a current of some continuance is necessary to produce the deviation of the magnetic needle; and I found that the magnetic electrometer was equally insensible to the weak discharge of a Leyden jar as to that of the torpedinal organ; though whenever there was a continuous current from the smallest surfaces in voltaic combinations of the weakest power, but in which some chemical action was going on, it was instantly and powerfully affected. Two series of zinc and silver, and paper moistened in salt and water, caused the permanent deviation of the needle several degrees, though the plates of zinc were only 1/6 of an inch in diameter.

It would be desirable to pursue these inquiries with the electricity of the Gymnotus, which is so much more powerful than that of the Torpedo: but if they are now to be reasoned upon, they seem to show a stronger analogy between common and animal electricity, than between voltaic and animal electricity: it is, however, I think, more probable that animal electricity will be found of a distinctive and peculiar kind.

Common electricity is excited upon non-conductors and readily carried off by conductors and imperfect conductors. Voltaic electricity is excited upon combinations of perfect and imperfect conductors, and is only transmitted by perfect conductors, or imperfect conductors of the best kind.

Magnetism, if it be a form of electricity, belongs only to perfect conductors; and, in its modifications, to a peculiar class of them.

The animal electricity resides only in the imperfect conductors forming the organs of living animals, and its object in the economy of nature is to act on living animals.

Distinctions might be established in pursuing the various modifications or properties of electricity in these different forms, but it is scarcely possible to avoid being struck by another relation of this subject. The torpedinal organ depends for its power upon the will of the animal. John Hunter has shown how copiously it is furnished with nerves. In examining the columnar structure of the organ of the Torpedo, I have never been able to discover arrangements of different conductors similar to those in galvanic combinations, and it seems not improbable that the shock depends upon some property developed by the action of the nerves.

To attempt to reason upon any phenomena of this kind as dependent upon a specific fluid, would be wholly vain.

Little as we know of the nature of electrical action, we are still more ignorant of the nature and of the functions of the nerves. There seems, however, a gleam of light worth pursuing in the peculiarities of animal electricity, its connection with so large a nervous system, its dependence upon the will of the animal, and the instantaneous nature of its transfer, which may lead, when pursued by adequate inquiriers, to results important for physiology.

The weak state of my health will, I fear, prevent me from following this subject with the attention it seems to desire; and I communicate these imperfect trials to the Royal Society, in the hope that they may lead to more extensive and profound researches.

October 24th, 1828,
Lubiana, Illyria.

SAMUEL TAYLOR COLERIDGE
(1772–1834)

Samuel Taylor Coleridge took his revolutionary ideals to an extreme when he spoke directly to a quadruped in "To a Young Ass," saying, "I hail thee BROTHER." Coleridge's poetry and prose writings, however, are pervaded by the sense that an understanding of the natural world is a key to human happiness and wisdom. At the same time, nature in Coleridge is sometimes terrifying but never quite as terrifying as the human mind. When asked why he attended so many public lectures on chemistry and physiology in London, he said, "To improve my stock of metaphors." Few poets could claim as detailed or as wide an understanding of the scientific tenor of their times as Coleridge. He corresponded regularly with Sir Humphry Davy, electrochemist, poet, and discoverer of nitrous oxide (laughing gas). Coleridge's polymathic writings also reveal familiarity with Newton's mechanics, Herschel's astronomy, Priestley's optics, William Bartram's natural history, and Erasmus Darwin's botany, among many other scientific advances of his day.

"Nature" for Coleridge, as for Wordsworth, was a complex and sometimes contradictory category. "The Rime of the Ancient Mariner" is perhaps the greatest Romantic statement about the consequences of psychic separation of the individual from the natural world. At the same time, a poem like "To Nature" suggests just how much of our idea of the nonhuman may be constructed within our own mind:

> It may indeed be phantasy, when I
> > Essay to draw from all created things
> > Deep, heartfelt, inward joy that closely clings;
> > And trace in leaves and flowers that round me lie
> 5 Lessons of love and earnest piety.

For Coleridge, poetry, the human mind, and the natural world are often linked as part of that "one Life within us and abroad," a force that can connect the apparently disparate aspects of reality into a unity perceived by the creative intellect. Of course, such a radical idea has as many consequences for the science of Coleridge's time as for poetry: "And what if all of animated nature / Be but organic harps diversely framed" ("The Eolian Harp").

Here is Coleridge, writing to Joseph Cottle about his plans to write an epic, a project that will require that he become as much a natural scientist as a poet: "I should not think of devoting less than 20 years to an Epic Poem. Ten to collect materials and warm my mind with universal science. I would be a tolerable Mathematician, I would thoroughly know Mechanics, Hydrostatics, Optics, and Astronomy, Botany, Metallurgy, Fossilism, Chemistry, Geology, Anatomy, Medicine—then the mind of man—then the minds of men—in all Travels, Voyages and Histories" (April 1797). Coleridge's poetry and prose writings are shot through with images drawn from just such widespread reading and study. At times he seems to doubt the unifying efficacy of the natural world when confronted with the human mind's imagining:

> I may not hope from outward forms to win
> The passion and the life, whose fountains are within.
> O Lady! we receive but what we give,
> And in our life alone does nature live. ("Dejection: An Ode")

But Coleridge is also a poet and thinker who provides an entire generation with new ways of thinking about the wonders and strangeness of the natural world.

From Poems on Various Subjects

To the Nightingale

Sister of love-lorn Poets, Philomel!
How many Bards in city garret pent,
While at their window they with downward eye
Mark the faint Lamp-beam on the kennell'd mud,
5   And listen to the drowsy cry of Watchmen,
(Those hoarse unfeather'd Nightingales of Time!)
How many wretched Bards address *thy* name,
And Her's, the full-orb'd Queen, that shines above.
But I *do* hear thee, and the high bough mark,

S. T. Coleridge, *Poems on Various Subjects.* London: Robinson and Cottle, 1796.

10 Within whose mild moon-mellow'd foliage hid
    Thou warblest sad thy pity-pleading strains.
    O! have I listen'd, till my working soul,
    Wak'd by those strains to thousand phantasies,
    Absorb'd hath ceas'd to listen! Therefore oft,
15 I hymn thy name: and with a proud delight
    Oft will I tell thee, Minstrel, of the Moon!
    "Most musical, most melancholy" Bird!
    That all thy soft diversities of tone,
    Tho' sweeter far than the delicious airs
20 That vibrate from a white-arm'd Lady's harp,
    What time the languishment of lonely love
    Melts in her eye, and heaves her breast of snow,
    Are not so sweet, as is the voice of her,
    My Sara—best belov'd of human Kind!
25 When breathing the pure soul of Tenderness
    She thrills me with the Husband's promis'd name!

From Sibylline Leaves

The Raven

A Christmas Tale, told by a School-boy

to his little Brothers and Sisters.

Underneath a huge oak tree
There was, of swine, a huge company,
That grunted as they crunch'd the mast:
For that was ripe, and fell full fast.
5 Then they trotted away, for the wind grew high:
One acorn they left, and no more might you spy.
Next came a raven, that liked not such folly:
He belonged, it was said, to the witch Melancholy!
Blacker was he than blackest jet,
10 Flew low in the rain, and his feathers not wet.
He pick'd up the acorn and buried it strait
By the side of a river both deep and great.
            Where then did the raven go?

S. T. Coleridge *Sibylline Leaves*. London: Rest Fenner, 1817.

He went high and low,
15 Over hill, over dale, did the black raven go.
    Many autumns, many springs
    Travell'd he with wandering wings.
    Many summers, many winters—
    I can't tell half his adventures.

20 At length he came back, and with him a she,
And the acorn was grown to a tall oak tree.
    They built them a nest in the topmost bough,
    And young ones they had, and were happy enow.
    But soon came a woodman, in leathern guise,
25   His brow, like a pent-house, hung over his eyes.
    He'd an ax in his hand, not a word he spoke,
    But with many a hem! and a sturdy stroke,
    At length be brought down the poor raven's own oak.
His young ones were kill'd: for they could not depart,
30 And their mother did die of a broken heart.

The boughs from the trunk the woodman did sever—
And they floated it down on the course of the river.
They saw'd it in planks, and its bark they did strip,
And with this tree and others they made a good ship.
35 The ship, it was launch'd; but in sight of the land
Such a storm there did rise as no ship could withstand.
It bulg'd on a rock, and the waves rush'd in fast:
The old raven flew round and round, and caw'd to the blast.

He heard the last shriek of the perishing souls—
40 See! see! o'er the topmast the mad water rolls!
    Right glad was the raven, and off he went fleet,
And Death riding home on a cloud he did meet,
    And he thank'd him again and again for this treat:
    They had taken his all, and revenge was sweet!
45 We must not think so; but forget and forgive,
And what Heaven gives life to, we'll still let it live?

Something Childish, But Very Natural

Written in Germany.

If I had but two little wings,
    And were a little feathery bird,
        To you I'd fly, my dear!

But thoughts like these are idle things,
5   And I stay here.

But in my sleep to you I fly:
    I'm always with you in my sleep;
      The world is all one's own.
But then one wakes, and where am I?
10   All, all alone.

Sleep stays not, though a monarch bids:
    So I love to wake ere break of day:
      For though my sleep be gone,
Yet, while 'tis dark, one shuts one's lids,
15   And still dreams on.

Answer to a Child's Question

Do you ask what the birds say? The Sparrow, the Dove,
The Linnet and Thrush say, "I love and I love!"
In the winter they're silent—the wind is so strong;
What it says, I don't know, but it sings a loud song.
5 But green leaves, and blossoms, and sunny warm weather,
And singing, and loving—all come back together.
But the Lark is so brimful of gladness and love,
The green fields below him, the blue sky above,
That he sings, and he sings; and for ever sings he—
10 "I love my Love, and my Love loves me!"

On Observing a Blossom

On the 1st of February, 1796.

Sweet Flower! that peeping from thy russet stem
Unfoldest timidly, (for in strange sort
This dark, freeze-coated, hoarse, teeth-chattering Month
Hath borrow'd Zephyr's voice, and gaz'd upon thee
5 With blue voluptuous eye) alas, poor Flower!
These are but flatteries of the faithless year.
Perchance, escaped its unknown polar cave,
Ev'n now the keen North-East is on its way.

Flower that must perish! shall I liken thee
10 To some sweet girl of too too rapid growth
Nipp'd by Consumption mid untimely charms?
Or to Bristowa's Bard,[1] the wonderous boy!
An Amaranth, which Earth scarce seem'd to own,
Blooming mid poverty's drear wintry waste,
15 Till Disappointment came, and pelting wrong
Beat it to Earth? or with indignant grief
Shall I compare thee to poor Poland's Hope,
Bright flower of Hope kill'd in the opening bud?
Farewell, sweet blossom! better fate be thine
20 And mock my boding! Dim similitudes
Weaving in moral strains, I've stolen one hour
From anxious Self, Life's cruel Task-Master!
And the warm wooings of this sunny day
Tremble along my frame and harmonize
25 Th' attemper'd organ, that even saddest thoughts
Mix with some sweet sensations, like harsh tunes
Play'd deftly on a soft-toned instrument.

The Eolian Harp

Composed at Clevedon, Somersetshire.

My pensive Sara! thy soft cheek reclined
Thus on mine arm, most soothing sweet it is
To sit beside our cot, our cot o'ergrown
With white-flower'd Jasmin, and the broad-leav'd Myrtle,
5 (Meet emblems they of Innocence and Love!)
And watch the clouds, that late were rich with light,
Slow sad'ning round, and mark the star of eve
Serenely brilliant (such should wisdom be)
Shine opposite! How exquisite the scents
10 Snatch'd from yon bean-field! and the world so hush'd!
The stilly murmur of the distant Sea
Tells us of Silence.
                            And that simplest Lute,
Placed length-ways in the clasping casement, hark!
15 How by the desultory breeze caress'd,

---

[1]Chatterton.

Like some coy maid half yielding to her lover,
It pours such sweet upbraidings, as must needs
Tempt to repeat the wrong! And now, its strings
Boldlier swept, the long sequacious notes
20 Over delicious surges sink and rise,
Such a soft floating witchery of sound
As twilight Elfins make, when they at eve
Voyage on gentle gales from Fairy-Land,
Where Melodies round honey-dropping flowers,
25 Footless and wild, like birds of Paradise,
Nor pause, nor perch, hovering on untamed wing!
Methinks, it should have been impossible
Not to love all things in a world like this,
Where even the breezes, and the common air,
30 Contain the power and spirit of Harmony.

   And thus, my love! as on the midway slope
Of yonder hill I stretch my limbs at noon,
Whilst thro' my half-closed eye-lids I behold
The sunbeams dance, like diamonds, on the main,
35 And tranquil muse upon tranquillity;
Full many a thought uncall'd and undetain'd,
And many idle flitting phantasies,
Traverse my indolent and passive brain,
As wild and various as the random gales
40 That swell and flutter on this subject lute!
   And what if all of animated nature
Be but organic harps diversly fram'd,
That tremble into thought, as o'er them sweeps
Plastic and vast, one intellectual breeze,
45 At once the Soul of each, and God of All?

   But thy more serious eye a mild reproof
Darts, O beloved woman! nor such thoughts
Dim and unhallow'd dost thou not reject,
And biddest me walk humbly with my God.
50 Meek daughter in the family of Christ!
Well hast thou said and holily disprais'd
These shapings of the unregenerate mind,
Bubbles that glitter as they rise and break
On vain Philosophy's aye-babbling spring.
55 For never guiltless may I speak of him,
Th' Incomprehensible! save when with awe

I praise him, and with Faith that inly feels;
Who with his saving mercies healed me,
A sinful and most miserable Man,
60 Wilder'd and dark, and gave me to possess
Peace, and this Cot, and Thee, heart-honor'd Maid!

This Lime-Tree Bower My Prison

Advertisement.

*In the June of 1797, some long-expected Friends paid a
visit to the Author's Cottage; and on the morning of
their arrival, he met with an accident, which disabled
him from walking during the whole time of their stay.
One Evening, when they had left him for a few hours,
he composed the following lines in the Garden-Bower.*

Well, they are gone, and here must I remain,
This Lime-Tree Bower my Prison! I have lost
Such beauties and such feelings, as had been
Most sweet to my remembrance, even when age
5 Had dimmed mine eyes to blindness! They, meanwhile,
My Friends, whom I may never meet again,
On springy heath, along the hill-top edge,
Wander in gladness, and wind down, perchance,
To that still roaring dell, of which I told;
10 The roaring dell, o'erwooded, narrow, deep,
And only speckled by the mid-day Sun;
Where its slim trunk the Ash from rock to rock
Flings arching like a Bridge; that branchless Ash,
Unsunn'd and damp, whose few poor yellow leaves
15 Ne'er tremble in the gale, yet tremble still,
Fann'd by the water-fall! and there my friends
Behold the dark green file of long lank Weeds,[2]
That all at once (a most fantastic sight!)

---

[2] *Of long lank Weeds.* The Asplenium Scolopendrium, called in some countries the
Adder's Tongue, in others the Hart's Tongue: but Withering gives the Adder's Tongue as
the trivial name of the Ophioglossum only.

Still nod and drip beneath the dripping edge
20 Of the blue clay-stone.

              Now, my Friends emerge
Beneath the wide wide Heaven—and view again
The many-steepled track magnificent
Of hilly fields and meadows, and the sea,
25 With some fair bark, perhaps, whose Sails light up
The slip of smooth clear blue betwixt two Isles
Of purple shadow! Yes! they wander on
In gladness all; but thou, methinks, most glad,
My gentle-hearted Charles! for thou hast pined
30 And hunger'd after Nature, many a year,
In the great City pent, winning thy way
With sad yet patient soul, through evil and pain
And strange calamity! Ah! slowly sink
Behind the western ridge, thou glorious Sun!
35 Shine in the slant beams of the sinking orb
Ye purple heath-flowers! richlier burn, ye clouds!
Live in the yellow light, ye distant groves!
And kindle, thou blue Ocean! So my Friend
Struck with deep joy may stand, as I have stood,
40 Silent with swimming sense; yea, gazing round
On the wild landscape, gaze till all doth seem
Less gross than bodily; a living thing
Which acts upon the mind—and with such hues
As cloath the Almighty Spirit, when he makes
45 Spirits perceive his presence.

              A delight
Comes sudden on my heart, and I am glad
As I myself were there! Nor in this bower,
This little lime-tree bower, have I not mark'd
50 Much that has sooth'd me. Pale beneath the blaze
Hung the transparent foliage; and I watch'd
Some broad and sunny leaf, and lov'd to see
The shadow of the leaf and stem above
Dappling its sunshine! And that Walnut-tree
55 Was richly ting'd, and a deep radiance lay
Full on the ancient Ivy, which usurps
Those fronting elms, and now, with blackest mass
Makes their dark branches gleam a lighter hue
Through the late twilight: and though now the Bat

60 Wheels silent by, and not a Swallow twitters,
   Yet still the solitary humble Bee
   Sings in the bean-flower! Henceforth I shall know
   That Nature ne'er deserts the wise and pure,
   No Plot so narrow, be but Nature there,
65 No waste so vacant, but may well employ
   Each faculty of sense, and keep the heart
   Awake to Love and Beauty! and sometimes
   'Tis well to be bereft of promised good,
   That we may lift the Soul, and contemplate
70 With lively joy the joys we cannot share.
   My gentle-hearted Charles! when the last Rook
   Beat its straight path along the dusky air
   Homewards, I blest it! deeming, its black wing
   (Now a dim speck, now vanishing in the light)
75 Had cross'd the mighty Orb's dilated glory,
   While thou stood'st gazing; or when all was still,
   Flew creeking[3] o'er thy head, and had a charm
   For thee, my gentle-hearted Charles, to whom
   No Sound is dissonant which tells of Life.

The Nightingale

A conversation poem. Written in April 1798.

   No cloud, no relique of the sunken day
   Distinguishes the West, no long thin slip
   Of sullen light, no obscure trembling hues.
   Come, we will rest on this old, mossy bridge!
5 You see the glimmer of the stream beneath,
   But hear no murmuring: it flows silently
   O'er its soft bed of verdure. All is still,
   A balmy night! and tho' the stars be dim,
   Yet let us think upon the vernal showers
10 That gladden the green earth, and we shall find

---

[3] *Flew creeking.* Some months after I had written this line, it gave me pleasure to observe that Bartram had observed the same circumstance of the Savanna Crane. "When these Birds move their wings in flight, their strokes are slow, moderate and regular; and even when at a considerable distance or high above us, we plainly hear the quill-feathers; their shafts and webs upon one another creek as the joints or working of a vessel in a tempestuous sea."

A pleasure in the dimness of the stars.
And hark! the Nightingale begins its song,
"Most musical, most melancholy" Bird![4]
A melancholy Bird? Oh! idle thought!
15 In nature there is nothing melancholy.
But some night-wandering man, whose heart was pierced
With the remembrance of a grievous wrong,
Or slow distemper, or neglected love,
(And so poor Wretch! fill'd all things with himself
20 And made all gentle sounds tell back the tale
Of his own sorrow) he, and such as he,
First named these notes a melancholy strain:
And many a poet echoes the conceit;
Poet who hath been building up the rhyme
25 When he had better far have stretch'd his limbs
Beside a brook in mossy forest-dell,
By Sun or Moon-light, to the influxes
Of shapes and sounds and shifting elements
Surrendering his whole spirit, of his song
30 And of his fame forgetful! so his fame
Should share in Nature's immortality,
A venerable thing! and so his song
Should make all Nature lovelier, and itself
Be lov'd like Nature! But 'twill not be so;
35 And youths and maidens most poetical,
Who lose the deep'ning twilights of the spring
In ball-rooms and hot theatres, they still
Full of meek sympathy must heave their sighs
O'er Philomela's pity-pleading strains.

40   My Friend, and thou, our Sister! we have learnt
A different lore: we may not thus profane
Nature's sweet voices, always full of love
And joyance! 'Tis the merry Nightingale
That crowds, and hurries, and precipitates
45 With fast thick warble his delicious notes,

---

[4]*"Most musical, most melancholy."* This passage in Milton possesses an excellence far
superior to that of mere description. It is spoken in the character of the melancholy man,
and has therefore a dramatic propriety. The author makes this remark, to rescue himself
from the charge of having alluded with levity, to a line in Milton: a charge than which
none could be more painful to him, except perhaps that of having ridiculed his Bible.

As he were fearful that an April night
Would be too short for him to utter forth
His love-chant, and disburthen his full soul
Of all its music!

50   And I know a grove
Of large extent, hard by a castle huge,
Which the great lord inhabits not; and so
This grove is wild with tangling underwood,
And the trim walks are broken up, and grass,
55 Thin grass and king-cups grow within the paths.
But never elsewhere in one place I knew
So many Nightingales; and far and near,
In wood and thicket, over the wide grove,
They answer and provoke each other's songs—
60 With skirmish and capricious passagings,
And murmurs musical and swift jug jug,
And one, low piping, sounds more sweet than all—
Stirring the air with such an harmony,
That should you close your eyes, you might almost
65 Forget it was not day! On moonlight bushes,
Whose dewy leafits are but half disclosed,
You may perchance behold them on the twigs,
Their bright, bright eyes, their eyes both bright and full,
Glistening, while many a glow-worm in the shade
70 Lights up her love-torch.

           A most gentle Maid,
Who dwelleth in her hospitable home
Hard by the castle, and at latest eve
(Even like a Lady vow'd and dedicate
75 To something more than Nature in the grove)
Glides thro' the pathways; she knows all their notes,
That gentle Maid! and oft a moment's space,
What time the Moon was lost behind a cloud,
Hath heard a pause of silence; till the Moon
80 Emerging, hath awaken'd earth and sky
With one sensation, and these wakeful Birds
Have all burst forth in Choral ministrelsy,
As if one quick and sudden Gale had swept
An hundred airy harps! And she hath watch'd
85 Many a Nightingale perch giddily
On blosmy twig still swinging from the breeze,

And to that motion tune his wanton song
Like tipsy joy that reels with tossing head.

    Farewell, O Warbler! till to-morrow eve,
90 And you, my friends! farewell, a short farewell!
We have been loitering long and pleasantly,
And now for our dear homes. That strain again?
Full fain it would delay me! My dear babe,
Who, capable of no articulate sound,
95 Mars all things with his imitative lisp,
How he would place his hand beside his ear,
His little hand, the small forefinger up,
And bid us listen! And I deem it wise
To make him Nature's Play-mate. He knows well
100 The evening-star; and once, when he awoke
In most distressful mood (some inward pain
Had made up that strange thing, an infant's dream)
I hurried with him to our orchard-plot,
And he beheld the Moon, and, hush'd at once,
105 Suspends his sobs, and laughs most silently,
While his fair eyes, that swam with undropt tears
Did glitter in the yellow moon-beam! Well!
It is a father's tale: But if that Heaven
Should give me life, his childhood shall grow up
110 Familiar with these songs, that with the night
He may associate joy! Once more farewell,
Sweet Nightingale! Once more, my friends! farewell.

Frost At Midnight

The frost performs its secret ministry,
Unhelp'd by any wind. The owlet's cry
Came loud—and hark, again! loud as before.
The inmates of my cottage, all at rest,
5 Have left me to that solitude, which suits
Abstruser musings: save that at my side
My cradled infant slumbers peacefully.
'Tis calm indeed! so calm, that it disturbs
And vexes meditation with its strange
10 And extreme silentness. Sea, hill, and wood,

This populous village! Sea, and hill, and wood,
With all the numberless goings on of life,
Inaudible as dreams! the thin blue flame
Lies on my low burnt fire, and quivers not;
15 Only that film, which flutter'd on the grate,
Still flutters there, the sole unquiet thing.
Methinks, its motion in this hush of nature
Gives it dim sympathies with me who live,
Making it a companionable form,
20 To which the living spirit in our frame,
That loves not to behold a lifeless thing,
Transfuses its own pleasures, its own will.

How oft, at school, with most believing mind,
Presageful, have I gaz'd upon the bars,
25 To watch that fluttering *stranger!* and as oft
With unclosed lids, already had I dreamt
Of my sweet birth-place, and the old church-tower,
Whose bells, the poor man's only music, rang
From morn to evening, all the hot fair day,
30 So sweetly, that they stirred and haunted me
With a sweet pleasure, falling on mine ear
Most like articulate sounds of things to come!
So gaz'd I, till the soothing things, I dreamt,
Lull'd me to sleep, and sleep prolong'd my dreams!
35 And so I brooded all the following morn,
Aw'd by the stern preceptor's face, mine eye
Fix'd with mock study on my swimming book:
Save if the door half open'd, and I snatch'd
A hasty glance, and still my heart leapt up,
40 For still I hop'd to see the *stranger's* face,
Townsman, or aunt, or sister more beloved,
My play-mate when we both were cloth'd alike!

Dear Babe, that sleepest cradled by my side,
Whose gentle breathings, heard in this dead calm,
45 Fill'd up the interspersed vacancies
And momentary pauses of the thought!
My Babe so beautiful! it fills my heart
With tender gladness, thus to look at thee,
And think that thou shalt learn far other lore
50 And in far other scenes! For I was rear'd
In the great city, pent 'mid cloisters dim,

And saw nought lovely but the sky and stars.
But *thou*, my babe! shalt wander like a breeze
By lakes and sandy shores, beneath the crags
55 Of ancient mountain, and beneath the clouds
Which image in their bulk both lakes and shores
And mountain crags: so shalt thou see and hear
The lovely shapes and sounds intelligible
Of that eternal language, which thy God
60 Utters, who from eternity doth teach
Himself in all, and all things in himself.
Great universal Teacher! he shall mould
Thy spirit, and by giving make it ask.

    Therefore all seasons shall be sweet to thee,
65 Whether the summer clothe the general earth
With greenness, or the redbreast sit and sing
Betwixt the tufts of snow on the bare branch
Of mossy apple-tree, while the nigh thatch
Smokes in the sun-thaw; whether the eve-drops fall,
70 Heard only in the traces of the blast,
Or if the secret ministry of frost
Shall hang them up in silent icicles,
Quietly shining to the quiet Moon.

From Anima Poetae

Human happiness, like the aloe, is a flower of slow growth.

. . . .

ON INFANCY:

   2. Asleep with the polyanthus held fast in its hand, its bells dropping over the rosy face.

   3. Stretching after the stars.

   4. Seen asleep by the light of glowworms.

. . . .

S. T. Coleridge, *Anima Poetae*. Ed. E. H. Coleridge. London: Heinemann, 1895.

The whale is followed by waves. I would glide down the rivulet of quiet life, a trout.

. . . .

Snails of intellect who see only by their feelers.

. . . .

I discovered unprovoked malice in his hard heart, like a huge toad in the centre of a marble rock.

. . . .

Men anxious for this world are like owls that wake all night to catch mice.

. . . .

The kingfisher . . . its slow, short flight permitting you to observe all its colours, almost as if it had been a flower.

. . . .

The nightingales in a cluster or little wood of blossomed trees, and a bat wheeling incessantly round and round! The noise of the frogs was not unpleasant, like the humming of spinning wheels in a large manufactory— now and then a distinct sound, sometimes like a duck, and, sometimes, like the shrill notes of sea-fowl. [May 20, 1799.]

. . . .

The beards of thistle and dandelions flying about the lonely mountains like life—and I saw them through the trees skimming the lake like swallows.

. . . .

I addressed a butterfly on a pea-blossom thus, "Beautiful Psyche, soul of a blossom, that art visiting and hovering over thy former friend whom thou hast left!" Had I forgot the caterpillar? Or did I dream like a mad metaphysician that the caterpillar's hunger for plants was self-love, recollection, and a lust that in its next state refined itself into love? [Dec. 12, 1804.]

. . . .

In Reimarus[5] on *The Instincts of Animals,* Tom Wedgwood's ground-principle of the influx of memory on perception is fully and beautifully detailed.

. . . .

---

[5] H. M. Reimarus (1694–1768), German philosopher and deist. [Ed.]

I have read with wonder and delight the passages in Reimarus in which he speaks of the immense multitude of plants, and the curious, regular choice of different herbivorous animals with respect to them, and the following pages in which he treats of the pairing of insects and the equally wonderful processes of egg-laying and so forth. All in motion! The sea-fish to the shores and rivers—the land crab to the seashore! I would fain describe all the creation thus agitated by the one or the other of the three instincts— self-preservation, childing, and child-preservation. Set this by [Erasmus] Darwin's theory of the maternal instinct—O mercy! The blindness of the man! And it is imagination, forsooth! that misled him—too much poetry in his philosophy!

. . . .

The hirschkafer (stag-beetle) in its worm state makes its bed-chamber, prior to its metamorphosis, half as long as itself. Why? There was a stiff horn turned under its belly, which in the fly state must project and harden, and this required exactly that length.

. . . .

The sea-snail creeps out of its house, which, thus hollowed, lifts him aloft, and is his boat and cork jacket; the Nautilus, additionally, spreads a thin skin as a sail.

. . . .

All creatures obey the great game-laws of Nature, and fish with nets of such meshes as permit many to escape, and preclude the taking of many.

. . . .

Wonderful, perplexing divisibility of life! It is related by D. Unzer, an authority wholly to be relied on, that an ohrwurm (earwig) cut in half ate its own hinder part! Will it be the reverse with Great Britain and America? The head of the rattlesnake severed from the body bit it and squirted out its poison, as is related by Beverley in his *History of Virginia.* Lyonnet in his *Insect. Theol.* tells us that he tore a wasp in half and, three days after, the fore-half bit whatever was presented to it of its former food, and the hind-half darted out its sting at being touched. Stranger still, a turtle has been known to live six months with his head off, and to wander about, yea, six hours after its heart and intestines (all but the lungs) were taken out! How shall we think of this compatibly with the monad soul? . . . Is not the reproduction of the lizard a complete generation? O it is easy to dream, and, surely, better of these things than of a 20,000 prize in the lottery, or of a place at Court. [Dec. 13, 1804.]

. . . .

The drollest explanation of instinct is that of Mylius, who attributes every act to pain, and all the wonderful webs and envelopes of spiders, caterpillars, etc., absolutely to fits of colic or paroxysms of dry belly-ache!

. . . .

O how the honey tells the tale of its birthplace to the sense of sight and odour! And to how many minute and uneyeable insects beside! So, I cannot but think, ought I be talking to Hartley [his infant son], and sometimes to detail all the insects that have arts resembling human – the sea-snails, with the nautilus at their head; the wheel-insect, the galvanic eel, etc.

. . . .

In looking at objects of Nature while I am thinking, as at yonder moon dim-glimmering through the dewy window-pane, I seem rather to be seeking, as it were asking for, a symbolical language for something within me that already and for ever exists, than observing anything new. [April 14, 1805.]

. . . .

I would not willingly kill even a flower. [April 17, 1805.]

. . . .

Yesterday I saw seven or eight water-wagtails following a feeding horse in the pasture, fluttering about and hopping close by his hoofs, under his belly, and even so as often to tickle his nostrils with their pert tails. The horse shortens the grass and they get the insects.

. . . .

O that sweet bird! Where is it? It is engaged somewhere out of sight; but from my bedroom at the Courier office, from the windows of which I look out on the walls of the Lyceum, I hear it at early dawn, often, alas! . . . It is in prison, all its instincts ungratified, yet it feels the influence of spring, and calls with unceasing melody to the Loves that dwell in field and greenwood bowers, unconscious, perhaps, that it calls in vain. O are they the songs of a happy, enduring day-dream? Has the bird hope? Or does it abandon itself to the joy of its frame, a living harp of Eolus?

. . . .

Sir G. Staunton asserts that, in the forest of Java, spiders' webs are found of so strong a texture as to require a sharp-cutting instrument to make way through them. Pity that he did not procure a specimen and bring it home with him. It would be a pleasure to see a sailing-boat rigged with them—

twisting the larger threads into ropes and weaving the smaller into a sort of silk canvas resembling the indestructible white cloth of the arindy or palma Christi silkworm.

. . . .

The merry little gnats (Tipulidae minimae) I have myself often watched in an April shower, evidently "dancing the hayes" in and out between the falling drops, unwetted, or, rather, un-down-dashed by rocks of water many times larger than their whole bodies.

. . . .

[Erasmus] Darwin possesses the epidermis of poetry but not the cutis; the cortex without the liber, alburnum, lignum, or medulla.

. . . .

The humming-moth with its glimmer-mist of the rapid unceasing motion before, the humble-bee within the flowing bells and cups—and the evil level with the clouds, himself a cloudy speck, surveys the vale from mount to mount.

. . . .

The child collecting shells and pebbles on the sea-shore or lake-side, and carrying each with a fresh shout of delight and admiration to the mother's apron, who smiles and assents to each "This is pretty!" "Is not that a nice one?" . . . such are our first discoveries both in science and philosophy. [Oct. 21, 1819.]

Charlotte Smith (1749–1806)

Like Cowper and Clare, Charlotte Smith elevated the ordinary details of the natural world into suitable subjects for poetry. She also helped to establish natural history, and poems about natural history, as suitable subjects for children [see, for example, Harriet Ventum, *Surveys of Nature* (1802); John Aikin, *The Calendar of Nature* (1816); and Mary Elliott, *The Rambles of a Butterfly* (1819) and *The Sunflower, or Poetical Truths for Young Minds* (1822)]. Smith's poems often had a theological function: the wonders of the deity's creation revealed the wonders of the creator. These poems, however, also set forth a strong sense of the interconnectedness of living things and of the poet's ability to apply human categories to the nonhuman world. Smith's poems remind us of a genre that was increasingly widespread by the time that William Blake was producing his own imitations (and perhaps parodies) of such lyrics: "The Lamb," "The Tyger," "The Fly," and "The Sick Rose." According to Stuart Curran, Smith "was the first poet in England whom in retrospect we would call Romantic" (*Poems* xix–xxix). In her own prolific literary output, Smith links eighteenth-century ideas about the beauty and sensibility of nature to a more purely Romantic sense of the power and strangeness of a nonhuman world that is, by turns, both comforting and alienating.

Smith's poems and prose works were praised by Godwin, Southey, Wordsworth, Leigh Hunt, and Jane Austen. Her novels included *Emmeline* (1788), *Desmond* (1792), and *The Old Manor House* (1793). Her fiction was celebrated by Sir Walter Scott and was notable for its Gothicism, as well as for its links to the works of Austen, the Brontë sisters, and Dickens. Smith's novels, like her poetry, are characterized by a powerful sense of the wonders and mystery of an aestheticized natural world. In *Marchmont* (1796), for example, Smith describes a rocky beach landscape in terms of its natural history: "to their rude surface, clams, limpets, and mussels adhered, among the seaweed that grew streaming among them. All was wild, solitary and gloomy; the low murmur of the water formed a sort of accompaniment to the cries of the sand-piper, the puffin-awk; while the screaming gull, and the hoarse and heavy cormorant were heard, at intervals, still louder" (2: 199). Smith is also an early example of a woman who sought to support herself by writing. She lived for seven months in debtors prison with her husband, Benjamin Smith, and their children. After subsequently leaving her husband in the 1790s, she was described by William Cowper: "Chain'd to her desk like a slave to his oar, with no other means of subsistence for herself and her numerous children" (To William Hayley, 29 January 1793). Among her later works she produced *Rural Walks* and *Rambles Farther* (both 1796), as well as the selection included here from *Conversations Introducing Poetry, Chiefly on the Subjects of Natural History, for the Use of Young Persons*, first published in 1804.

From Poetry, Chiefly on Subjects of Natural History

In the vast woods of America there are wild bees that make great quantities of honey in the hollows of trees, and the settlers and Indians are guided to these treasures by a bird, who knows where they are deposited. There are many other particulars, which at some future time we will collect. At present our business is with the honey-bee of our own country.

Invitation to the Bee

Child of patient industry,
Little active busy bee,
Thou art out at early morn,
Just as the opening flowers are born;
5 Among the green and grassy meads
Where the cowslips hang their heads;

Charlotte Smith, *Poetry, Chiefly on subjects of Natural History, for the Use of Young Persons*. London: Whittingham and Arliss, 1819.

Or by hedge-rows, while the dew
Glitters on the barebell blue.

Then on eager wing art flown,
10 To thymy hillocks on the down;
Or to revel on the broom;
Or suck the clover's crimson bloom;
Murmuring still thou busy bee
Thy little ode to industry;
15 Go while summer suns are bright,
Take at large thy wandering flight;
Go and load thy tiny feet
With every rich and various sweet,
Cling around the flow'ring thorn,
20 Dive in the woodbine's honied horn,
Seek the wild rose that shades the dell,
Explore the foxglove's freckled bell,
Or in the heath flower's fairy cup
Drink the fragrant spirit up.

25 But when the meadows shall be mown,
And summer's garlands overblown;
Then come, thou little busy bee,
And let thy homestead be with me,
There, shelter'd by thy straw-built hive,
30 In my garden thou shalt live,
And that garden shall supply
Thy delicious alchemy;
There for thee, in autumn, blows
The Indian pink and latest rose,
35 The mignionette perfumes the air,
And stocks, unfading flowers, are there.

Yet fear not when the tempests come,
And drive thee to thy waxen home,
That I shall then most treacherously
40 For thy honey murder thee.

Ah, no! throughout the winter drear
I'll feed thee, that another year
Thou may'st renew thy industry
Among the flowers, thou little busy bee.

The Hedge-Hog Seen in a Frequented Path

Wherefore should man or thoughtless boy
Thy quiet, harmless life destroy,
Innoxious urchin? for thy food
Is but the beetle and the fly,
5   And all thy harmless luxury
The swarming insects of the wood.

Should man, to whom his God has given
Reason, the brightest ray of heaven,
Delight to hurt, in senseless mirth,
10 Inferior animals? and dare
To use his power in waging war
Against his brethren of the earth?

Poor creature! to the woods resort,
Lest lingering here, inhuman sport
15 Should render vain thy thorny case;
And whelming water, deep and cold,
Make thee thy spiny ball unfold,
And shew thy simple negro face!

Fly from the cruel! know than they
20 Less fierce are ravenous beasts of prey,
And should perchance these last come near thee;
And fox or martin cat assail,
Thou, safe within thy coat of mail,
May cry—Ah! noli me tangere.[1]

The Mimosa

Softly blow the western breezes,
Sweetly shines the evening sun;
But you, mimosa! nothing pleases,
You, what delights your comrades teizes,
5 What they enjoy you try to shun.

Alike annoy'd by heat or cold,
Ever too little or too much,

---

[1] "Do not touch me." Words spoken by Jesus to Mary Magdalen. [Ed.]

a. Mimosa Spuria de Pernambuco, insempfindlich Kraut.
b. Mimosa Zeylanica major non spinosa flore luteo, Kräusch Kraut.

Sensitive plant. *Mimosa spuria,* Erasmus Darwin notes that
"Naturalists have not explained the immediate cause of the
collapsing of the sensitive plant" (*Botanic Garden,* "Loves of the
Plants," note 1:29). And also "Of Vegetable Animation": "The fibres
of the vegetable world, as well as those of the animal, are excitable
into a variety of motions by irritations of external objects. This
appears particularly in the mimosa or sensitive plant, whose leaves
contract on the slightest injury" (*Zoonomia* 1:73). Engraved by
J. W. Weinna, c. 1740.

As if by heaviest winds controùl'd,
Your leaves before a zephyr fold,
10 And tremble at the slightest touch.

Flutt'ring around, in playful rings,
A gilded fly your beauty greeted;
But, from his light and filmy wings,
As if he had lanced a thousand stings,
15 Your shuddering folioles[2] retreated!

Those feathery leaves are like the plume,
Pluck'd from the bird of Indian skies;
But should you therefore thus presume,
While others boast a fairer bloom,
20 All that surrounds you to despise?

The rose, whose blushing blossoms blow,
Pride of the vegetal creation,
The air and light disdains not so,
And the fastidious pride you show,
25 Is not reserve, but affectation.

The Dormouse Just Taken

Sleep on, sleep on, poor captive mouse,
Oh, sleep! unconscious of the fate
That ruthless spoil'd thy cosey[3] house,
And tore thee from thy mate.

5 What barbarous hand could thus molest
A little innocent like thee,
And drag thee from thy mossy nest
To sad captivity?

Ah! when suspended life again
10 Thy torpid senses shall recall,
Poor guiltless prisoner! what pain
Thy bosom shall appal.

---

[2] Division of a compound leaf. [Ed.]
[3] Cosey, a Scottish expression for snug.

When starting up in wild affright,
Thy bright round eyes shall vainly seek
15 Thy tiny spouse, with breast so white,
Thy whisker'd brethren sleek;

Thy snug warm nest with feathers lin'd,
Thy winter store of roots and corn;
Nor nuts nor beech-mast shalt thou find,
20 The toil of many a morn.

Thy soft white feet around thy cage
Will cling; while thou in hopeless pain
Wilt waste thy little life in rage,
To find thy struggles vain!

25 Yet since thou'rt fall'n in gentle hands,
Oh! captive mouse, allay thy grief,
For light shall be thy silken bands,
And time afford relief.

Warm is the lodging, soft the bed,
30 Thy little mistress will prepare;
By her kind hands thou shalt be fed,
And dainties be thy fare.

But neither men nor mice forget
Their native home, where'er they be,
35 And fondly thou wilt still regret
Thy wild woods, loves, and liberty!

The Grasshopper

Happy insect, what can be
In happiness compar'd to thee,
Fed with nourishment divine,
The dewy morning's chrystal wine;
5 For Nature waits upon thee still,
And thy verdant cup doth fill.
All the fields which thou dost see,
All the plants belong to thee;
All that Summer suns produce
10 Are, blest insect! for thy use.
While thy feast doth not destroy

The verdure thou dost thus enjoy;
But the blythe shepherd, haileth thee,
Singing as musical as he;
15 And peasants love thy voice to hear,
Prophet of the ripening year.
To thee of all things upon earth,
Life is no longer than thy mirth.
Insect truly blest! for thou
20 Dost neither age nor winter know;
But, when thou hast danc'd and sung
Thy fill, the flowers and leaves among,
Sated with thy Summer feast
Thou retir'st to endless rest.

The Glow-Worm

Bright insect! that on humid leaves and grass
Lights up thy fairy lamp; as if to guide
The steps of labouring swains that homeward pass,
Well pleas'd to see thee cheer the pathway side,
5 Betokening cloudless skies and pleasant days;
While he whom evening's sober charms invite
In shady woodlanes, often stops to gaze,
And moralizing hails thy emerald light!
On the fair tresses of the roseate morn,
10 Translucent dews, as precious gems appear,
Not less dost thou the night's dark hour adorn,
"Like a rich jewel in an Ethiop's ear." [4]
Though the rude bramble, or the fan-like ferns,
Around thee their o'ershadowing branches spread,
15 Steady and clear thy phosphor brilliance burns,
And thy soft rays illuminate the shade.
Thus the calm brightness of superior minds
Makes them amid misfortune's shadow blest,
And thus the radiant spark of Genius shines,
20 Though screen'd by Envy, or by Pride oppress'd.

---

[4] William Shakespeare, *Romeo and Juliet,* Act I, scene 5, 1.46. [Ed.]

The Captive Fly

Seduced by idle change and luxury,
See in vain struggle the expiring fly,
He perishes! for lo, in evil hour,
He rushed to taste of yonder garish flower.
5 Which in young beauty's loveliest colours drest,
Conceals destruction in her treacherous breast,
While round the roseate chalice odours breathe,
And lure the wanderer to voluptuous death.

Ill-fated vagrant! did no instinct cry,
10 Shun the sweet mischief? No experienc'd fly
Bid thee of this fair smiling fiend beware,
And say, the false Apocynum[5] is there?
Ah wherefore quit for this Circean draught
The Bean's ambrosial flower, with incense fraught,
15 Or where with promise rich, Fragaria spreads
Her spangling blossoms on her leafy beds;
Could thy wild flight no softer blooms detain?
And tower'd the Lilac's purple groups in vain?
Or waving showers of golden blossoms, where
20 Laburnum's pensile tassels float in air,
When thou within those topaz keels might creep
Secure, and rock'd by lulling winds to sleep.

But now no more for thee shall June unclose
Her spicy Clove-pink, and her damask Rose;
25 Not for thy food shall swell the downy Peach,
Nor Raspberries blush beneath the embowering Beech.
In efforts vain thy fragile wings are torn,
Sharp with distress resounds thy small shrill horn,
While thy gay happy comrades hear thy cry,
30 Yet heed thee not, and careless frolic by,
Till thou, sad victim, every struggle o'er,
Despairing sink, and feel thy fate no more.

An insect lost should thus the muse bewail?
Ah no! but 'tis the *moral* points the *tale*
35 From the mild friend, who seeks with candid truth

---

[5] Medicinal plant; also called bitter root. [Ed.]

To show its errors to presumptuous Youth;
From the fond caution of parental care,
Whose watchful love detects the hidden snare,
How do the Young reject, with proud disdain,
40 Wisdom's firm voice, and Reason's prudent rein,
And urge, on pleasure bent, the impetuous way,
Heedless of all but of the present day,
Then while false meteor-lights their steps entice,
They taste, they drink, the empoisoned cup of vice;
45 Till misery follows; and too late they mourn,
Lost in the fatal gulph, from whence there's no return.

The Cricket

Little inmate full of mirth,
Chirping on my humble hearth,
Wheresoe'er be thine abode,
Always harbinger of good,
5 Pay me for thy warm retreat
With a song most soft and sweet,
In return thou shalt receive
Such a song as I can give.

Though in voice and shape they be
10 Form'd as if akin to thee,
Thou surpassest, happier far,
Happiest Grasshoppers that are;
Theirs is but a Summer song,
Thine endures the Winter long,
15 Unimpair'd, and shrill and clear,
Melody throughout the year.

Neither night nor dawn of day
Puts a period to thy lay.
Then Insect! let thy simple song
20 Chear the winter evening long,
While secure from every storm,
In my cottage snug and warm,
Thou shalt my merry minstrel be,
And I delight to shelter thee.

The Wheat-Ear[6]

From that deep shelter'd solitude,
Where in some quarry wild and rude,
Your feather'd mother reared her brood,
      Why, pilgrim, did you brave,
5 The upland winds so bleak and keen,
To seek these hills? whose slopes between
Wide stretch'd in grey expanse is seen,
      The Ocean's toiling wave?

Did instinct bid you linger here,
10 That broad and restless Ocean near,
And wait, till with the waning year
      Those northern gales arise,
Which, from the tall cliff's rugged side
Shall give your soft light plumes to glide,
15 Across the channel's refluent tide,
      To seek more favoring skies?

Alas! and has not instinct said
That luxury's toils for you are laid,
And that by groundless fears betray'd
20   You ne'er perhaps may know
Those regions, where the embowering vine
Loves round the luscious fig to twine,
And mild the Suns of Winter shine,
      And flowers perennial blow.

25 To take you, shepherd boys prepare
The hollow turf, the wiry snare,
Of those weak terrors well aware,
      That bid you vainly dread
The shadows floating o'er the downs,
30 Or murmuring gale, that round the stones
Of some old beacon, as it moans,
      Scarce moves the thistle's head.

And if a cloud obscure the Sun
With faint and fluttering heart you run,

---

[6] Songbird of the genus *Oenanthe*. [Ed.]

35 And to the pitfall you should shun
              Resort in trembling haste;
    While, on that dewy cloud so high,
    The lark, sweet minstrel of the sky,
    Sings in the morning's beamy eye,
40   And bathes his spotted breast.

    Ah! simple bird, resembling you
    Are those, that with distorted view
    Thro' life some selfish end pursue,
              With low inglorious aim;
45 *They* sink in blank oblivious night,
    While minds superior dare the light,
    And high on honor's glorious height
              Aspire to endless fame.

The Cankered Rose

    As Spring to Summer hours gave way,
    And June approach'd, beneath whose sway
    My lovely Fanny saw the day,
              I mark'd each blossom'd bower,
5   And bade each plant its charms display,
              To crown the favour'd hour.

    The favour'd hour to me so bright,
    When Fanny first beheld the light,
    And I should many a bloom unite,
10   A votive wreath to twine,
    And with the lily's virgin white,
              More glowing hues combine.

    A wreath that, while I hail'd the day,
    All the fond things I meant, might say
15 (As Indian maids their thoughts array,
              By artful quipo's[7] wove;)
    And fragrant symbols thus convey
              My tenderness and love.

---

[7] Incan recording device, colored strings along which knots were tied. [Ed.]

For this I sought where long had grown,
20 A rosarie I call'd my own,
Whose rich unrivall'd flowers were known
        The earliest to unclose,
And where I hoped would soon be blown,
        The first and fairest Rose.

25 An infant bud there cradled lay,
Mid new born leaves; and seem'd to stay
Till June should call, with warmer ray,
        Its embryo beauty forth;
Reserv'd for that propitious day
30   That gave my Fanny birth.

At early morning's dewy hour,
I watch'd it in its leafy bower,
And heard with dread the sleety shower,
        When eastern tempests blew,
35 But still unhurt my favourite flower
        With fairer promise grew.

From rains and breezes sharp and bleak,
Secur'd, I saw its calyx break,
And soon a lovely blushing streak
40   The latent bloom betray'd;
(Such colours on my Fanny's cheek,
        Has cunning Nature laid.)

Illusive hope! The day arriv'd,
I saw my cherish'd rose—It lived,
45 But of its early charms depriv'd,
        No odours could impart;
And scarce with sullied leaves, surviv'd
        The canker at its heart.

There unsuspected, long had fed
50 A noxions worm, and mining spread,
The dark pollution o'er its head,
        That drooping seem'd to mourn
Its fragrance pure, and petals red,
        Destroy'd e'er fully born.

55 Unfinished now, and incomplete,
My garland lay at Fanny's feet,
She smil'd; ah could I then repeat

What youth so little knows,
How the too trusting heart must beat
60 With pain, when treachery and deceit
In some insidious form, defeat
Its fairest hopes; as cankers eat
The yet unfolded rose.

Giovanni Aldini (1762–1834)

Giovanni Aldini was a nephew of Luigi Galvani and a defender of his uncle's often controversial ideas. Galvani, a physician and anatomist at the University of Bologna, had noticed that dead frogs' legs began to twitch when stimulated by various metals and electric charges. His experiments led to the discovery of what he called "animal electricity." Galvani published these findings in 1791. The word *galvanized* and the galvanometer (which measures current in a conductor) derive from his work. Galvani and Alessandro Volta subsequently engaged in a heated controversy: Galvani claimed that this biological electricity was the vital "fluid" (or perhaps life itself), and Volta claimed that external electric charges merely triggered dead muscles into motion. Volta's continuing researches led to the development of the voltaic pile and the storage battery. Galvanism and the galvanic controversy occasioned widespread public discussion throughout Europe in the early years of the nineteenth century.

Aldini was a professor of physics at Bologna who became widely known for the theatricality of his scientific performances. He traveled throughout Europe defending the idea of a uniquely biological form of electricity against the attacks of Volta and his followers. Aldini's experiments included "reanimations" of animal and human corpses during public displays that were as spectacular as they were terrifying. At the same time, Aldini offered a number of insights that proved accurate and almost prophetic. He treated mental patients with an early form of shock therapy, electric currents applied directly to the head, and he reported electric cures of what we would now call emotional illnesses. Percy Shelley, Lord Byron, and John Polidori no doubt included Aldini's work in their 1816 discussions of "galvanism" with Mary Shelley that led to *Frankenstein*. Anne Mellor conveys a sense of Aldini's likely contribution to the Frankenstein myth:

Galvani's theories made the British headlines in December 1802, when in the presence of their Royal Highnesses the Prince of Wales, the Duke of York, the Duke of Clarence, and the Duke of Cumberland, Galvani's nephew, disciple and ardent defender, Professor Giovanni Aldini of Bologna University, applied a Voltaic pile connected by metallic wires to the ear and nostrils of a recently killed ox-head.[. . .] But Professor Aldini's most notorious demonstration of galvanic electricity took place on January 17, 1803. On that day he applied galvanic electricity to the corpse of the murderer Thomas Forster. The body of the recently hanged criminal was collected from Newgate where it had lain in the prison yard at a temperature of 30 degrees Fahrenheit for one hour by the President of the College of Surgeons, Mr. Keate, and brought immediately to Mr. Wilson's Anatomical Theatre where the following experiments were performed. When wires attached to a pile composed of 120 plates of zinc and 120 plates of copper were connected to the ear and mouth of the dead criminal, Aldini later reported, "the jaw began to quiver, the adjoining muscles were horribly contorted, and the left eye actually opened." (105)

The selections included here come from Aldini's 1803 account of the experiments described by Mellor. Aldini also published *General Views on the Application of Galvanism to Medical Purposes; principally in cases of suspended animation* (1819), in which he argued that electricity might restore the life of patients who had been drowned or asphyxiated.

From An Account
of the Late
Improvements in Galvanism

A just tribute of applause has been bestowed on the celebrated Professor Volta for his late discovery; and I have no desire to deprive him of any part of that honour to which he is so justly entitled; but I am far from entertaining an idea that we ought, on this account, to neglect the first labours

Giovanni Aldini, *An Account of the Late Improvements in Galvanism*. London: Cuthell and Martin, 1803.

of Galvani. Though these two philosophers pursued different routes, they concurred to throw considerable light on the same points of science; and the question now is, to determine which of them deduced the most just consequences from the facts he observed; and then to ascertain whether the facts established by Galvani lead to the theory of Volta, or whether those discovered by Volta are connected with the theory of Galvani. For my part, I am of opinion that these two theories may serve in an eminent degree to illustrate each other.

Last year Professor Volta announced to the public the action of the metallic pile. I here propose to exhibit, according to the principles of Professor Galvani, the action of the animal pile.

Such is the plan I have conceived in order to reconcile the systems of these two illustrious philosophers: it forms the object of the present work, which is divided into three parts. In the first I shall exhibit the action of Galvanism independently of metals, and explain some of its general properties. The second will contain experiments on the power of Galvanism to excite the vital forces. In the third I shall propose some useful applications of it to medicine, and explain the principles on which the new medical administration of Galvanism is founded. To render the work as methodical as possible, I have endeavoured to arrange the experiments in such a manner that they may serve as proofs to a series of general propositions, which, it is hoped, will be of use to physiology and to the doctrine of the animal economy.

Part the First.
Of the Nature and General Properties of Galvanism.

Proposition I.

Muscular contractions are excited by the development
of a fluid in the animal machine, which is conducted
from the nerves to the muscles without the
concurrence or action of metals.

EXPERIMENT I.

Having provided the head of an ox, recently killed, I thrust a finger of one of my hands, moistened with salt water, into one of the ears, at the same time that I held a prepared frog in the other hand, in such a manner that

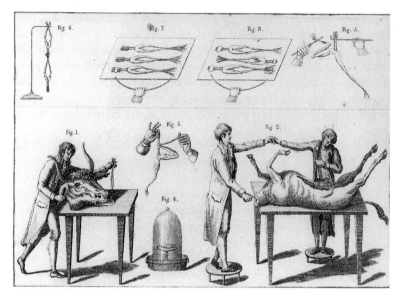

Galvani's frog legs and Aldini's ox tongues. This plate reveals several of the experiments demonstrated by Giovanni Aldini, nephew of Luigi Galvani, during his 1803 "performances" in London. His use of electricity produced dramatic results: severed frog legs twitched, a decapitated bull's tongue protruded, and the eye of a convict (hanged at Newgate earlier that day) "actually opened." From *An Account of the Late Improvements in Galvanism* (London: Cuthell and Martin, 1803).

its spinal marrow touched the upper part of the tongue. When this arrangement was made, strong convulsions were observed in the frog; but on separating the arc all the contractions ceased.

This experiment will succeed still better if the arc be conveyed from the tongue of the ox to the spinal marrow of the frog. This method was found to be exceedingly convenient for trying the effect of Galvanism on several calves.

EXPERIMENT II.

Having provided the trunk of a calf, I conveyed the arc from the muscles of the abdomen to the spinal marrow of a frog, prepared and arranged in the usual manner. The frog seemed much affected, and the contractions were exceedingly violent when the arc was composed of a chain of different persons, united together by the hands moistened with salt water.

EXPERIMENT III.

I connected, by means of one chain of moisture, the heads of two or three calves, and observed that by this combination the force of the Galvanism was exerted with more energy: a frog, which was not affected by touching one head, experienced violent contractions when applied to a series of several heads connected together.

EXPERIMENT IV.

I think it proper here to mention a very curious observation which I made lately at Paris, in company with professor Huzzard, and in the presence of the Commissioners of the National Institute. On applying the spinal marrow of a prepared frog to the cervical muscles of a horse's head, separated from the body, no muscular convulsions took place; but if, at the same time, another person touched with his hand, moistened by a solution of muriate of soda, the spinal marrow of the horse, convulsions were always produced in the frog, though there was no communication between the persons, except that formed by a floor on which they stood.

Proposition II.

The Galvanism excited, in the preceding experiments,
is not owing to the communication nor to the
transfusion of the general electricity, but to an
electricity peculiar to animals, which acts a very
distinguished part in the animal economy.

EXPERIMENT I.

Having placed the trunk of a calf on an insulated table, I made a longitudinal incision in the breast, in order to obtain a long series of muscles uncovered. I then arranged two insulated persons in such a manner that the one with a finger, moistened by salt water, touched the spinal marrow of the calf, while the other applied the spinal marrow of a frog to the muscles of the trunk. Every time this arc was formed, muscular contractions were produced in the frog. When the two persons let go each other's hands, the contractions ceased. I repeated this experiment, with the same success, on the insulated head of an ox, conveying the arc from the spinal marrow of the frog to the tongue. Frogs were as violently affected when the experiment was made with the insulated trunks of different kinds of birds.

This experiment, in my opinion, affords a decisive proof that the Galvanic fluid is peculiar to the animal machine, independently of the influence of metals, or of any other foreign cause. In these experiments, indeed, we have some animal machines, so combined that the result is

strong contractions in the frog. All the bodies were insulated; and, therefore, it cannot be supposed that the contractions were occasioned by the
direct influence of that general principle, which pervades every body in
nature. Hence it is evident, whether it be ascribed to the action of the animal chain, formed by the arms of the persons, or to the animal pile, formed
by the trunk of the calf, that we shall still be obliged to acknowledge the
action of a principle which belongs to the organization of the animal
machine, without having any dependence on metals.

To prove in the animal body the existence of a principle which philosophers can by certain means excite and direct at pleasure in their experiments, is a matter of the greatest importance; though the manner in which
it is put in action by nature, however wonderful, is unknown to us. Here
then we have developed a very energetic fluid, capable of transmission, and
deriving its origin from the action of the animal forces; since the parts of
bodies separated from the common reservoir of general electricity have still
of themselves the faculty of reproducing it, and of causing it to circulate in
a manner proper for exciting muscular contractions.

Proposition III.

Galvanism develops itself in a powerful manner,
independently of metals, by means of the human
animal machine.

EXPERIMENT I.

If you hold in your hand, moistened with salt water, the muscles of a prepared frog, and apply the crural nerves to the tip of your tongue, you will
immediately see violent contractions produced in the frog. All suspicion of
any stimulant exerting an action in this case, may be removed by repeating
the experiment with the frog held in the dry hand: the muscular contractions will then cease, unless the action of Galvanism in the frog, or in the
animal machine, be uncommonly powerful; in which case contractions
may be produced without establishing an arc from the nerves to the
muscles.

EXPERIMENT II.

I held the muscles of a prepared frog in one of my hands, moistened by salt
water, and brought a finger of the other hand, well moistened, near to the
crural nerves. When the frog possessed a great deal of vitality the crural
nerves gradually approached my hand, and strong contractions took place
at the point of contact. This experiment proves the existence of a very

remarkable kind of attraction, observed not only by myself, but also by those whom I requested to repeat the experiment.

EXPERIMENT III.

The above experiment requires great precision in the preparation, and a considerable degree of vital power in the frog. I have been informed by Professor Fontana,[1] in a letter lately received from him, that this phæ-nomenon depends on very delicate circumstances, which he proposes to explain. He assures me, at the same time, that he has twice seen the nerve attracted, in this manner, by the muscle. Being desirous to render this phænomenon more evident, I formed the arc, by applying one of my hands to the spinal marrow of a warm-blooded animal, while I held a frog in the other, in such a manner that the crural nerves were brought very near to the abdominal muscles. By this arrangement the attraction of the nerves of the frog became very sensible. I performed this experi-ment for the first time, at Oxford, before Sir Christopher Pegge and Dr. Bancroft, and repeated it in the anatomical theatres of St. Thomas's and Guy's hospitals.

EXPERIMENT IV.

I made the same observations on the body of a man as I had before made on the head and trunk of an ox. Having obtained the body of an executed criminal, I formed an arc from the spinal marrow to the muscles, a pre-pared frog being placed between, and always obtained strong contractions without the aid of the pile, and without the least influence from metals. I obtained the same result, in a certain degree, from the bodies of men who had died a natural death.

EXPERIMENT V.

Let four or more persons hold each other by the hands, moistened by a solution of muriate of soda, so as to form a long animal chain. If the first hold in his hand the muscles of a prepared frog; and if the last, at the other end of the chain, touch the spinal marrow or the crural nerves, contrac-tions will be produced: if the animal chain be broken, the contractions will immediately cease. I performed this experiment, making the animal chain to consist of two persons, before the Galvanic Society at Paris, and in Mr. Wilson's anatomical theatre, Windmill-street.

---

[1] Felix Fontana, director of the Museum of Physics and Natural History in Florence. [Ed.]

Proposition IV.

Muscular contractions can be excited, under
certain conditions, without establishing a
continued arc from the nerves to the muscles.

EXPERIMENT.

Having obtained the body of an executed criminal, I caused the biceps
muscle to be laid bare, and brought near to it the spinal marrow of a prepared frog. By these means contractions were produced in it much
stronger than I had ever obtained in warm-blooded animals. I repeated the
experiment, being myself insulated, and observed no signs of contraction.
The same phænomena were exhibited with the head of an ox, which possessed an extraordinary degree of vitality.

Proposition V.

The effects of Galvanism, in the preceding
experiments, do not depend on the action of any
stimulant, which occurs in performing the
experiments, and ought not to be confounded with
the effects of that action.

EXPERIMENT I.

In the experiment of the frog applied to the uncovered biceps muscle of the
body of the malefactor, if any other body be made to touch the frog it will
remain motionless. This proves that the contractions produced in the frog
do not arise from the impulse of the mere contact of the spinal marrow
with the muscle of the human animal machine.

EXPERIMENT II.

To remove still further all suspicion of the action of stimulants, in the preceding experiments, I prepared two frogs, and connected the extremities of
one with the spinal marrow of the other. I then held in my hand the
extremities of one of the frogs, and applied the spinal marrow of the other
to the uncovered muscles of the head of an ox, which possessed a great
degree of vitality. By these means contractions were produced in both the
frogs. It is evident, in this experiment, that the force of the stimulant, if
there were any, might act on the second frog, but not on the first.[. . .]

EXPERIMENT VIII.

Having obtained the bodies of some executed criminals, I exposed to the action of an insulated plenum the nervous and muscular fibres, and the substance of the brain. The elevations of the water were remarkable, in consequence of the different substances subjected to experiment, which, according to their different characters, exercised a different action on the oxygen. This fact ought to induce physiologists to undertake experiments of a similar kind with other gases, to enable them to determine the strength of the affinity exerted by animal substances to combine with oxygen.

EXPERIMENT IX.

As fishes, and in particular the torpedo,[2] furnish a large quantity of animal or Galvanic electricity, I was inclined to think they would exhibit the before-mentioned effects in a very striking manner in an insulated plenum. I mentioned to Professor Mojon of Genoa the experiment I proposed to make; and, in a letter which I lately received from him, he informed me of the result, as follows:

> I took a strong torpedo, and, as soon as it was dead, armed its nerves with the usual armature. Having then placed it on an insulating stool, a little elevated above water, I covered it with a bell-glass the content of which was equal to 432 cubic inches. At the end of some hours I observed, with great surprise, that the water under the insulated plenum began to rise progressively during about ten hours; and at the end of forty-eight I found that it had risen an inch; so that it occupied a ninth part of the capacity of the bell, that is to say, forty-eight cubic inches. I analyzed the remaining air, and found that the bell contained no more than 80 cubic inches of oxygen gas, and 324 of azotic gas; and that, during the above period, more than two-fifths of the oxygen gas contained in the bell had been absorbed.

I propose going to the sea-coast, in order that I may repeat the experiment on the torpedo without any armature; and I shall embrace that opportunity of making various researches in regard to the new theory of Galvanism. I think it necessary, in general, to submit to new experiments the different animal parts immersed in the different aëriform fluids, fixing their various combinations according to the degrees of Galvanic force which they may possess.[. . .]

---

[2] The electric ray. [Ed.]

Proposition XVII.

The hypothesis of an animal pile, analogous to
that formed artificially, seems well calculated to
explain the sensations and contractions in the
animal machine.

It seems to be proved by the observations of Mr. Davy,[3] Professor in the Royal Institution of Great Britain, and those of M. Gautherot at Paris, that a pile may be composed without any metallic substances whatever. We are therefore naturally led to suppose, that one may be composed also of animal substances alone. Though this has never yet been obtained by art, we behold it with admiration constructed by nature in various animals. If we examine, indeed, the structure of the regular bodies which succeed each other in the torpedo, the electrical eel of Surinam, and in the silurus, we shall find them to be real animal piles, differently arranged: and if an animal pile, exceedingly strong, be capable of communicating a shock, why should not one of a more moderate nature excite that activity which is necessary to produce muscular convulsions? I have already proved, that the system of the nerves and that of the muscles possess different Galvanic powers, or, as it were, different kinds of electricity, to which the animal moisture serves as a conductor. In this point of view, the discovery of the pile of the celebrated Volta, instead of destroying the principle of Galvanism, tends rather in a powerful manner to support it. The object of Galvani's system is to prove the existence of an animal electricity, and then to explain how its action operates in producing muscular sensations and contractions. The first part of his system rests upon facts, the truth of which neither time, nor the different experiments made by philosophers, have been able to weaken. The second presents an hypothesis which, perhaps, may be further illustrated when the physiology of the human body is better known. Galvani, to explain the activity of animal electricity, supposes the nerves and muscles to be like the Leyden jar;[4] and this idea I confidently adopted. But by the expression "Leyden flask" he meant nothing else than that in the animal machine there are two opposite kinds of electricity, resulting from the nervous and the muscular systems, to which animal moisture continually serves as a vehicle. It was in this sense that he announced his theory of the Leyden flask, in his public lectures, and in his last works. No better comparison was then known, in the language of philosophy, to express this action. It however

---

[3] Humphry Davy. [Ed.]

[4] A device for storing static electricity. [Ed.]

affords me great pleasure, that I can now substitute for it the pile discovered by Volta, which is perfectly consistent with the system of Galvani; and since I am ready to allow that the invention of the metallic pile gives Volta a title to the discovery of metallic electricity, I hope the discovery of animal electricity, properly so called, will be allowed to Galvani, as similar phænomena are exhibited by the nervous and muscular systems, independently of common electricity.[...]

APPENDIX.

No. I.

An Account of the Experiments performed by
J. Aldini on the Body of a Malefactor executed at
Newgate Jan. 17th 1803.

INTRODUCTION.

The unenlightened part of mankind are apt to entertain a prejudice against those, however laudable their motives, who attempt to perform experiments on dead subjects; and the vulgar in general even attach a sort of odium to the common practice of anatomical dissection. It is, however, an incontrovertible fact, that such researches in modern times have proved a source of the most valuable information, in regard to points highly interesting to the knowledge of the human frame, and have contributed in an eminent degree to the improvement of physiology and anatomy. Enlightened legislators have been sensible of this truth; and therefore it has been wisely ordained by the British laws, which are founded on the basis of humanity aud public benefit, that the bodies of those who during life violated one of the most sacred rights of mankind, should after execution be devoted to a purpose which might make some atonement for their crime, by rendering their remains beneficial to that society which they offended.

In consequence of this regulation, I lately had an opportunity of performing some new experiments, the principal object of which was to ascertain what opinion ought to be formed of Galvanism as a mean of excitement in cases of asphyxia and suspended animation. The power which exists in the muscular fibre of animal bodies some time after all other signs of vitality have disappeared, had before been examined according to the illustrious Haller's doctrine of irritability; but it appeared to me that muscular action might be excited in a much more efficacious manner by the power of the Galvanic apparatus.

In performing these experiments, I had another object in view. Being favoured with the assistance and support of gentlemen eminently well skilled in the art of dissection, I proposed, when the body should be opened, to perform some new experiments which I never before attempted, and to confirm others which I had made above a year ago on the bodies of two robbers decapitated at Bologna.

To enlarge on the utility of such researches, or to point out the advantages which may result from them, is not my object at present. I shall here only observe, that as the bodies of valuable members of society are often found under similar circumstances, and with the same symptoms as those observed on executed criminals; by subjecting the latter to proper experiments, some speedier and more efficacious means than any hitherto known, of giving relief in such cases, may, perhaps, be discovered. In a commercial and maritime country like Britain, where so many persons, in consequence of their occupations at sea, on canals, rivers, and in mines, are exposed to drowning, suffocation, and other accidents, this object is of the utmost importance in a public view, and is entitled to every encouragement.

Forster, on whose body these experiments were performed, was twenty-six years of age, seemed to have been of a strong, vigorous constitution, and was executed at Newgate on the 17th of January 1803. The body was exposed for a whole hour in a temperature two degrees below the freezing point of Fahrenheit's thermometer; at the end of which long interval it was conveyed to a house not far distant, and, in pursuance of the sentence, was delivered to the College of Surgeons. Mr. Keate, master of that respectable society, having been so kind as to place it under my direction, I readily embraced that opportunity of subjecting it to the Galvanic stimulus, which had never before been tried on persons put to death in a similar manner: and the result of my experiments I now take the liberty of submitting to the public.

Before I conclude this short introduction, I consider it as my duty to acknowledge my obligations to Mr. Carpue, lecturer on anatomy, and Mr. Hutchins, a medical pupil, for the assistance they afforded me in the dissection. I was also much indebted to Mr. Cuthbertson, an eminent mathematical instrument maker, who directed and arranged the Galvanic apparatus. Encouraged by the aid of these gentlemen, and the polite attention of Mr. Keate, I attempted a series of experiments, of which the following is a brief account.

EXPERIMENT I.
One arc being applied to the mouth, and another to the ear, wetted with a solution of muriate of soda (common salt), Galvanism was communicated by means of three troughs combined together, each of which contained forty plates of zinc, and as many of copper. On the first application of the arcs the jaw began to quiver, the adjoining muscles were horribly contorted, and the left eye actually opened.

EXPERIMENT II.

On applying the arc to both ears, a motion of the head was manifested, and a convulsive action of all the muscles of the face: the lips and eyelids were also evidently affected; but the action seemed much increased by making one extremity of the arc to communicate with the nostrils, the other continuing in one ear.

EXPERIMENT III.

The conductors being applied to the ear, and to the rectum, excited in the muscles contractions much stronger than in the preceding experiments. The action even of those muscles furthest distant from the points of contact with the arc was so much increased as almost to give an appearance of re-animation.

EXPERIMENT IV.

In this state, wishing to try the power of ordinary stimulants, I applied volatile alkali to the nostrils and to the mouth, but without the least sensible action: on applying Galvanism great action was constantly produced. I then administered the Galvanic stimulus and volatile alkali together; the convulsions appeared to be much increased by this combination, and extended from the muscles of the head, face, and neck, as far as the deltoid. The effect in this case surpassed our most sanguine expectations, and vitality might, perhaps, have been restored, if many circumstances had not rendered it impossible.

EXPERIMENT V.

I next extended the arc from one ear to the biceps flexor cubiti, the fibres of which had been laid bare by dissection. This produced violent convulsions in all the muscles of the arm, and especially in the biceps and the coraco brachialis even without the intervention of salt water.

EXPERIMENT VI.

An incision having been made in the wrist, among the small filaments of the nerves and cellular membrane, on bringing the arc into contact with this part, a very strong action of the muscles of the fore-arm and hand was immediately perceived. In this, as in the last experiment, the animal moisture was sufficient to conduct the Galvanic stimulus without the intervention of salt water.

EXPERIMENT VII.

The short muscles of the thumb were dissected, and submitted to the action of the Galvanic apparatus, which induced a forcible effort to clench the hand.[. . .]

From the preceding narrative it will be easily perceived, that our object in applying the treatment here described was not to produce re-animation, but merely to obtain a practical knowledge how far Galvanism might be employed as an auxiliary to other means in attempts to revive persons under similar circumstances.

In cases when suspended animation has been produced by natural causes, it is found that the pulsations of the heart and arteries become totally imperceptible; therefore, when it is to be restored, it is necessary to re-establish the circulation throughout the whole system. But this cannot be done without re-establishing also the muscular powers which have been suspended, and to these the application of Galvanism gives new energy.

I am far from wishing to raise any objections against the administration of the other remedies which are already known, and which have long been used. I would only recommend Galvanism as the most powerful mean hitherto discovered of *assisting* and increasing the efficacy of every other stimulant.

Volatile alkali, as already observed, produced no effect whatever on the body when applied alone; but, being used conjointly with Galvanism, the power of the latter over the nervous and muscular system was greatly increased: nay, it is possible that volatile alkali, owing to its active powers alone, might convey the Galvanic fluid to the brain with greater facility, by which means its action would become much more powerful in cases of suspended animation. The well known method of injecting atmospheric air ought not to be neglected; but here, likewise, in order that the lungs may be prepared for its reception, it would be proper previously to use Galvanism, to excite the muscular action, and to assist the whole animal system to resume its vital functions. Under this view, the experiments of which I have just given an account, may be of great public utility.

It is with heartfelt gratitude that I recall to mind the politeness and lively interest shown by the members of the College of Surgeons in the prosecution of these experiments. Mr. Keate, the master, in particular proposed to make comparative experiments on animals, in order to give support to the deductions resulting from those on the human body. Mr. Blicke observed that on similar occasions it would be proper to immerse the body in a warm salt bath, in order to ascertain how far it might promote the action of Galvanism on the whole surface of the body. Dr. Pearson recommended oxygen gas to be substituted instead of the atmospheric air blown into the lungs. It gives me great pleasure to have an opportunity of communicating these observations to the public, in justice to the eminent characters who suggested them, and as an inducement to physiologists not to overlook the minutest circumstance which may tend to improve experiments that promise so greatly to relieve the sufferings of mankind.

Mary Wollstonecraft Shelley (1797–1851)

Mary Wollstonecraft Shelley, daughter of Mary Wollstonecraft and William Godwin, was the wife of Percy Bysshe Shelley and the author of one of the most widely read and often redacted novels of the past two centuries. *Frankenstein; or, the Modern Prometheus* was born out of a series of conversations Mary had during the summer of 1816 with Percy Shelley, Lord Byron, and John Polidori. Mary cites conversations between Shelley and Byron about Erasmus Darwin ("They talked of the experiments of Dr. Darwin") and Luigi Galvani ("Perhaps a corpse would be re-animated; galvanism had given token of such things") as sources for her own idea of a reanimated human ("the component parts of a creature might be manufactured, brought together, and endued with vital warmth") in her introduction to the 1831 edition of the novel. The first edition, published in 1818, led to critical acclaim and public controversy. The first play based on the story was staged in 1823.

When asked to explain why he has created a monstrous life form (one that would eventually destroy him), Mary's Victor Frankenstein offers an explanation based on the biological concept of species. "A new species would bless me as its creator," he says to Captain Walton in the opening pages of the novel. Of course, Victor does not really create a new species at all; he creates a hybrid, a being composed of the parts of other humans and other animals. Mary's creature presumably lacks a soul, at least in the minds of most of her 1818 readers. But when Victor considers the "race of demons" that might populate the world if he goes through with his plan to create a female companion for the wretch, he clearly places monster reproductive biology at the center of his own anxieties. As readers, we may well wonder why he does not merely create a sterile female. We may also wonder why he created a fertile male creature in the first place. If he has the power to create life, surely he has the power to create individuals unable to reproduce. Perhaps these textual confusions reflect 18-year-old Mary Shelley's own uncertainties about the precise details of human reproduction, even though she had already given birth to one child that had died only days after it was born. After the death of this child, she wrote a letter in which she said that she dreamt of holding her dead infant to the fire, warming and rubbing the tiny corpse back to life. Of course, Victor Frankenstein's creature does not ever bless him as a creator, much less as a parent. In fact, the wretch turns on his creator and destroys him—as well as everyone he loves—not because the creature is inherently evil but because he never receives love from his creator, or even a name. The human creator, Victor, never shows sufficient concern for the life he has made, much less for the other human (or animate) lives around him. Mary Shelley's novel points toward respect for life—all life—as a crucial aspect of any Romantic natural history.

Included here are passages from the 1818 first edition that suggest the role played by natural philosophy (science) in the creation of Frankenstein's monster, as well as the introduction of 1818 (actually penned by Percy Shelley) and Mary's preface of 1831. All of these texts suggest links between natural history and the mind of Mary Shelley as she imaginatively "conceived" her "hideous progeny."

From Frankenstein; or, the Modern Prometheus [1818]

PREFACE.

The event on which this fiction is founded has been supposed, by Dr. Darwin,[1] and some of the physiological writers of Germany, as not of impossible occurrence. I shall not be supposed as according the remotest degree of serious faith to such an imagination; yet, in assuming it as the basis of a work of fancy, I have not considered myself as merely weaving a series of supernatural terrors. The event on which the interest of the story

---

Mary W. Shelley, *Frankenstein; or, the Modern Prometheus.* London: Lackington, Hughes, 1818.

[1] Erasmus Darwin. [Ed.]

depends is exempt from the disadvantages of a mere tale of spectres or enchantment. It was recommended by the novelty of the situations which it developes; and, however impossible as a physical fact, affords a point of view to the imagination for the delineating of human passions more comprehensive and commanding than any which the ordinary relations of existing events can yield.

I have thus endeavoured to preserve the truth of the elementary principles of human nature, while I have not scrupled to innovate upon their combinations. The *Iliad,* the tragic poetry of Greece, Shakespeare, in the *Tempest* and *Midsummer Night's Dream,* and most especially Milton, in *Paradise Lost,* conform to this rule; and the most humble novelist, who seeks to confer or receive amusement from his labours, may, without presumption, apply to prose fiction a licence, or rather a rule, from the adoption of which so many exquisite combinations of human feeling have resulted in the highest specimens of poetry.

The circumstance on which my story rests was suggested in casual conversation. It was commenced, partly as a source of amusement, and partly as an expedient for exercising any untried resources of mind. Other motives were mingled with these, as the work proceeded. I am by no means indifferent to the manner in which whatever moral tendencies exist in the sentiments or characters it contains shall affect the reader; yet my chief concern in this respect has been limited to the avoiding the enervating effects of the novels of the present day, and to the exhibition of the amiableness of domestic affection, and the excellence of universal virtue. The opinions which naturally spring from the character and situation of the hero are by no means to be conceived as existing always in my own conviction, nor is any inference justly to be drawn from the following pages as prejudicing any philosophical doctrine of whatever kind.

It is a subject also of additional interest to the author, that this story was begun in the majestic region where the scene is principally laid, and in society which cannot cease to be regretted. I passed the summer of 1816 in the environs of Geneva. The season was cold and rainy, and in the evenings we crowded around a blazing wood fire, and occasionally amused ourselves with some German stories of ghosts, which happened to fall into our hands. These tales excited in us a playful desire of imitation. Two other friends (a tale from the pen of one of whom would be far more acceptable to the public than any thing I can ever hope to produce) and myself agreed to write each a story, founded on some supernatural occurrence.

The weather, however, suddenly became serene; and my two friends left me on a journey among the Alps, and lost, in the magnificent scenes which they present, all memory of their ghostly visions. The following tale is the only one which has been completed.

CHAPTER I
[*Victor Frankenstein's childhood and education*]

My brothers were considerably younger than myself; but I had a friend in one of my schoolfellows, who compensated for this deficiency. Henry Clerval was the son of a merchant of Geneva, an intimate friend of my father. He was a boy of singular talent and fancy. I remember, when he was nine years old, he wrote a fairy tale, which was the delight and amazement of all his companions. His favourite study consisted in books of chivalry and romance; and when very young, I can remember, that we used to act plays composed by him out of these favourite books, the principal characters of which were Orlando, Robin Hood, Amadis, and St. George.

No youth could have passed more happily than mine. My parents were indulgent, and my companions amiable. Our studies were never forced; and by some means we always had an end placed in view, which excited us to ardour in the prosecution of them. It was by this method, and not by emulation, that we were urged to application. Elizabeth was not incited to apply herself to drawing, that her companions might not outstrip her; but through the desire of pleasing her aunt, by the representation of some favourite scene done by her own hand. We learned Latin and English, that we might read the writings in those languages; and so far from study being made odious to us through punishment, we loved application, and our amusements would have been the labours of other children. Perhaps we did not read so many books, or learn languages so quickly, as those who are disciplined according to the ordinary methods; but what we learned was impressed the more deeply on our memories.

In this description of our domestic circle I include Henry Clerval; for he was constantly with us. He went to school with me, and generally passed the afternoon at our house; for being an only child, and destitute of companions at home, his father was well pleased that he should find associates at our house; and we were never completely happy when Clerval was absent.

I feel pleasure in dwelling on the recollections of childhood, before misfortune had tainted my mind, and changed its bright visions of extensive usefulness into gloomy and narrow reflections upon self. But, in drawing the picture of my early days, I must not omit to record those events which led, by insensible steps to my after tale of misery: for when I would account to myself for the birth of that passion, which afterwards ruled my destiny, I find it arise, like a mountain river, from ignoble and almost forgotten sources; but, swelling as it proceeded, it became the torrent which, in its course, has swept away all my hopes and joys.

Natural philosophy is the genius that has regulated my fate; I desire therefore, in this narration, to state those facts which led to my predilection for that science. When I was thirteen years of age, we all went on a party of pleasure to the baths near Thonon: the inclemency of the weather obliged us to remain a day confined to the inn. In this house I chanced to find a volume of the works of Cornelius Agrippa.[2] I opened it with apathy; the theory which he attempts to demonstrate, and the wonderful facts which he relates, soon changed this feeling into enthusiasm. A new light seemed to dawn upon my mind; and, bounding with joy, I communicated my discovery to my father. I cannot help remarking here the many opportunities instructors possess of directing the attention of their pupils to useful knowledge, which they utterly neglect. My father looked carelessly at the title-page of my book, and said, "Ah! Cornelius Agrippa! My dear Victor, do not waste your time upon this; it is sad trash."

If, instead of this remark, my father had taken the pains to explain to me, that the principles of Agrippa had been entirely exploded, and that a modern system of science had been introduced, which possessed much greater powers than the ancient, because the powers of the latter were chimerical, while those of the former were real and practical; under such circumstances, I should certainly have thrown Agrippa aside, and, with my imagination warmed as it was, should probably have applied myself to the more rational theory of chemistry which has resulted from modern discoveries. It is even possible, that the train of my ideas would never have received the fatal impulse that led to my ruin. But the cursory glance my father had taken of my volume by no means assured me that he was acquainted with its contents; and I continued to read with the greatest avidity.

When I returned home, my first care was to procure the whole works of this author, and afterwards of Paracelsus[3] and Albertus Magnus.[4] I read and studied the wild fancies of these writers with delight; they appeared to me treasures known to few beside myself; and although I often wished to communicate these secret stores of knowledge to my father, yet his indefinite censure of my favourite Agrippa always withheld me. I disclosed my discoveries to Elizabeth, therefore, under a promise of strict secrecy; but she did not interest herself in the subject, and I was left by her to pursue my studies alone.

It may appear very strange, that a disciple of Albertus Magnus should arise in the eighteenth century; but our family was not scientifical, and

---

[2] Heinrich Cornelius Agrippa (1486–1535), physician and alchemist. [Ed.]

[3] Theophrastus Paracelsus (1493–1541), medical reformer and alchemist. [Ed.]

[4] (1206–1280), scientist and theologian. [Ed.]

I had not attended any of the lectures given at the schools of Geneva. My dreams were therefore undisturbed by reality; and I entered with the greatest diligence into the search of the philosopher's stone and the elixir of life. But the latter obtained my most undivided attention: wealth was an inferior object; but what glory would attend the discovery, if I could banish disease from the human frame, and render man invulnerable to any but a violent death!

Nor were these my only visions. The raising of ghosts or devils was a promise liberally accorded by my favourite authors, the fulfilment of which I most eagerly sought; and if my incantations were always unsuccessful, I attributed the failure rather to my own inexperience and mistake, than to a want of skill or fidelity in my instructors.

The natural phaenomena that take place every day before our eyes did not escape my examinations. Distillation, and the wonderful effects of steam, processes of which my favourite authors were utterly ignorant, excited my astonishment; but my utmost wonder was engaged by some experiments on an airpump, which I saw employed by a gentleman whom we were in the habit of visiting.

The ignorance of the early philosophers on these and several other points served to decrease their credit with me: but I could not entirely throw them aside, before some other system should occupy their place in my mind.

When I was about fifteen years old, we had retired to our house near Belrive, when we witnessed a most violent and terrible thunder-storm. It advanced from behind the mountains of Jura; and the thunder burst at once with frightful loudness from various quarters of the heavens. I remained, while the storm lasted, watching its progress with curiosity and delight. As I stood at the door, on a sudden I beheld a stream of fire issue from an old and beautiful oak, which stood about twenty yards from our house; and so soon as the dazzling light vanished, the oak had disappeared, and nothing remained but a blasted stump. When we visited it the next morning, we found the tree shattered in a singular manner. It was not splintered by the shock, but entirely reduced to thin ribbands of wood. I never beheld any thing so utterly destroyed.

The catastrophe of this tree excited my extreme astonishment; and I eagerly inquired of my father the nature and origin of thunder and lightning. He replied, "Electricity;" describing at the same time the various effects of that power. He constructed a small electrical machine, and exhibited a few experiments; he made also a kite, with a wire and string, which drew down that fluid from the clouds.[5]

---

[5] Benjamin Franklin (1747) and Joseph Priestley (1770) both performed similar electrical experiments. [Ed.]

This last stroke completed the overthrow of Cornelius Agrippa, Albertus Magnus, and Paracelsus, who had so long reigned the lords of my imagination. But by some fatality I did not feel inclined to commence the study of any modern system; and this disinclination was influenced by the following circumstance.

My father expressed a wish that I should attend a course of lectures upon natural philosophy, to which I cheerfully consented. Some accident prevented my attending these lectures until the course was nearly finished. The lecture, being therefore one of the last, was entirely incomprehensible to me. The professor discoursed with the greatest fluency of potassium and boron, of sulphates and oxyds, terms to which I could affix no idea; and I became disgusted with the science of natural philosophy, although I still read Pliny and Buffon with delight, authors, in my estimation, of nearly equal interest and utility.

My occupations at this age were principally the mathematics, and most of the branches of study appertaining to that science. I was busily employed in learning languages; Latin was already familiar to me, and I began to read some of the easiest Greek authors without the help of a lexicon. I also perfectly understood English and German. This is the list of my accomplishments at the age of seventeen; and you may conceive that my hours were fully employed in acquiring and maintaining a knowledge of this various literature.

Another task also devolved upon me, when I became the instructor of my brothers. Ernest was six years younger than myself, and was my principal pupil. He had been afflicted with ill health from his infancy, through which Elizabeth and I had been his constant nurses: his disposition was gentle, but he was incapable of any severe application. William, the youngest of our family, was yet an infant, and the most beautiful little fellow in the world; his lively blue eyes, dimpled cheeks, and endearing manners, inspired the tenderest affection.

Such was our domestic circle, from which care and pain seemed for ever banished. My father directed our studies, and my mother partook of our enjoyments. Neither of us possessed the slightest pre-eminence over the other; the voice of command was never heard amongst us; but mutual affection engaged us all to comply with and obey the slightest desire of each other.

Chapter II

When I had attained the age of seventeen, my parents resolved that I should become a student at the university of Ingolstadt. I had hitherto attended the schools of Geneva; but my father thought it necessary, for the completion of my education, that I should be made acquainted with other customs than those of my native country. My departure was therefore fixed at an early date; but, before the day resolved upon could arrive, the first misfortune of my life occurred—an omen, as it were, of my future misery.

Elizabeth had caught the scarlet fever;[6] but her illness was not severe, and she quickly recovered. During her confinement, many arguments had been urged to persuade my mother to refrain from attending upon her. She had, at first, yielded to our entreaties; but when she heard that her favourite was recovering, she could no longer debar herself from her society, and entered her chamber long before the danger of infection was past. The consequences of this imprudence were fatal. On the third day my mother sickened; her fever was very malignant, and the looks of her attendants prognosticated the worst event. On her death-bed the fortitude and benignity of this admirable woman did not desert her. She joined the hands of Elizabeth and myself: "My children," she said, "my firmest hopes of future happiness were placed on the prospect of your union. This expectation will now be the consolation of your father. Elizabeth, my love, you must supply my place to your younger cousins. Alas! I regret that I am taken from you; and, happy and beloved as I have been, is it not hard to quit you all? But these are not thoughts befitting me; I will endeavour to resign myself cheerfully to death, and will indulge a hope of meeting you in another world."

She died calmly; and her countenance expressed affection even in death. I need not describe the feelings of those whose dearest ties are rent by that most irreparable evil, the void that presents itself to the soul, and the despair that is exhibited on the countenance. It is so long before the mind can persuade itself that she, whom we saw every day, and whose very existence appeared a part of our own, can have departed for ever—that the brightness of a beloved eye can have been extinguished, and the sound of a voice so familiar, and dear to the ear, can be hushed, never more to be heard. These are the reflections of the first days; but when the lapse of time proves the reality of the evil, then the actual bitterness of grief commences. Yet from whom has not that rude hand rent away some dear connexion; and why should I describe a sorrow which all have felt, and must feel? The time at length arrives, when grief is rather an indulgence than a necessity; and the smile that plays upon the lips, although it may be deemed a sacrilege, is not banished. My mother was dead, but we had still duties which we ought to perform; we must continue our course with the rest, and learn to think ourselves fortunate, whilst one remains whom the spoiler has not seized.

---

[6]A form of Streptococcal infection. Epidemics of scarlet fever were common until the early twentieth century. [Ed.]

My journey to Ingolstadt, which had been deferred by these events, was now again determined upon. I obtained from my father a respite of some weeks. This period was spent sadly; my mother's death, and my speedy departure, depressed our spirits; but Elizabeth endeavoured to renew the spirit of cheerfulness in our little society. Since the death of her aunt, her mind had acquired new firmness and vigour. She determined to fulfil her duties with the greatest exactness; and she felt that most imperious duty, of rendering her uncle and cousins happy, had devolved upon her. She consoled me, amused her uncle, instructed my brothers; and I never beheld her so enchanting as at this time, when she was continually endeavouring to contribute to the happiness of others, entirely forgetful of herself.

The day of my departure at length arrived. I had taken leave of all my friends, excepting Clerval, who spent the last evening with us. He bitterly lamented that he was unable to accompany me: but his father could not be persuaded to part with him, intending that he should become a partner with him in business, in compliance with his favourite theory, that learning was superfluous in the commerce of ordinary life. Henry had a refined mind; he had no desire to be idle, and was well pleased to become his father's partner, but he believed that a man might be a very good trader, and yet possess a cultivated understanding.

We sat late, listening to his complaints, and making many little arrangements for the future. The next morning early I departed. Tears gushed from the eyes of Elizabeth; they proceeded partly from sorrow at my departure, and partly because she reflected that the same journey was to have taken place three months before, when a mother's blessing would have accompanied me.

I threw myself into the chaise that was to convey me away, and indulged in the most melancholy reflections. I, who had ever been surrounded by amiable companions, continually engaged in endeavouring to bestow mutual pleasure, I was now alone. In the university, whither I was going, I must form my own friends, and be my own protector. My life had hitherto been remarkably secluded and domestic; and this had given me invincible repugnance to new countenances. I loved my brothers, Elizabeth, and Clerval; these were "old familiar faces;" but I believed myself totally unfitted for the company of strangers. Such were my reflections as I commenced my journey; but as I proceeded, my spirits and hopes rose. I ardently desired the acquisition of knowledge. I had often, when at home, thought it hard to remain during my youth cooped up in one place, and had longed to enter the world, and take my station among other human beings. Now my desires were complied with, and it would, indeed, have been folly to repent.

I had sufficient leisure for these and many other reflections during my journey to Ingolstadt, which was long and fatiguing. At length the high white steeple of the town met my eyes. I alighted, and was conducted to my solitary apartment, to spend the evening as I pleased.

The next morning I delivered my letters of introduction, and paid a visit to some of the principal professors, and among others to M. Krempe, professor of natural philosophy. He received me with politeness, and asked me several questions concerning my progress in the different branches of science appertaining to natural philosophy. I mentioned, it is true, with fear and trembling, the only authors I had ever read upon those subjects. The professor stared: "Have you," he said, "really spent your time in studying such nonsense?"

I replied in the affirmative. "Every minute," continued M. Krempe with warmth, "every instant that you have wasted on those books is utterly and entirely lost. You have burdened your memory with exploded systems, and useless names. Good God! in what desert land have you lived, where no one was kind enough to inform you that these fancies, which you have so greedily imbibed, are a thousand years old, and as musty as they are ancient? I little expected in this enlightened and scientific age to find a disciple of Albertus Magnus and Paracelsus. My dear Sir, you must begin your studies entirely anew."

So saying, he stept aside, and wrote down a list of several books treating of natural philosophy, which he desired me to procure, and dismissed me, after mentioning that in the beginning of the following week he intended to commence a course of lectures upon natural philosophy in its general relations, and that M. Waldman, a fellow-professor, would lecture upon chemistry the alternate days that he missed.

I returned home, not disappointed, for I had long considered those authors useless whom the professor had so strongly reprobated; but I did not feel much inclined to study the books which I procured at his recommendation. M. Krempe was a little squat man, with a gruff voice and repulsive countenance; the teacher, therefore, did not prepossess me in favour of his doctrine. Besides, I had a contempt for the uses of modern natural philosophy. It was very different, when the masters of the science sought immortality and power; such views, although futile, were grand: but now the scene was changed. The ambition of the inquirer seemed to limit itself to the annihilation of those visions on which my interest in science was chiefly founded. I was required to exchange chimeras of boundless grandeur for realities of little worth.

Such were my reflections during the first two or three days spent almost in solitude. But as the ensuing week commenced, I thought of the information which M. Krempe had given me concerning the lectures.

And although I could not consent to go and hear that little conceited fellow deliver sentences out of a pulpit, I recollected what he had said of M. Waldman, whom I had never seen, as he had hitherto been out of town.

Partly from curiosity, and partly from idleness, I went into the lecturing room, which M. Waldman entered shortly after. This professor was very unlike his colleague. He appeared about fifty years of age, but with an aspect expressive of the greatest benevolence; a few gray hairs covered his temples, but those at the back of his head were nearly black. His person was short, but remarkably erect; and his voice the sweetest I had ever heard. He began his lecture by a recapitulation of the history of chemistry and the various improvements made by different men of learning, pronouncing with fervour the names of the most distinguished discoverers. He then took a cursory view of the present state of the science, and explained many of its elementary terms. After having made a few preparatory experiments, he concluded with a panegyric upon modern chemistry, the terms of which I shall never forget:

"The ancient teachers of this science," said he, "promised impossibilities, and performed nothing. The modern masters promise very little; they know that metals cannot be transmuted, and that the elixir of life is a chimera. But these philosophers, whose hands seem only made to dabble in dirt, and their eyes to pour over the microscope or crucible, have indeed performed miracles. They penetrate into the recesses of nature, and shew how she works in her hiding places. They ascend into the heavens; they have discovered how the blood circulates, and the nature of the air we breathe. They have acquired new and almost unlimited powers; they can command the thunders of heaven, mimic the earthquake, and even mock the invisible world with its own shadows."

I departed highly pleased with the professor and his lecture, and paid him a visit the same evening. His manners in private were even more mild and attractive than in public; for there was a certain dignity in his mien during his lecture, which in his own house was replaced by the greatest affability and kindness. He heard with attention my little narration concerning my studies, and smiled at the names of Cornelius Agrippa, and Paracelsus, but without the contempt that M. Krempe had exhibited. He said, that "these were men to whose indefatigable zeal modern philosophers were indebted for most of the foundations of their knowledge. They had left to us, as an easier task, to give new names, and arrange in connected classifications, the facts which they in a great degree had been the instruments of bringing to light. The labours of men of genius, however erroneously directed, scarcely ever fail in ultimately turning to the solid advantage of mankind." I listened to his statement, which was delivered without any presumption or affectation; and then added, that his lecture had removed my prejudices against modern chemists; and I, at the same time, requested his advice concerning the books I ought to procure.

"I am happy," said M. Waldman, "to have gained a disciple; and if your application equals your ability, I have no doubt of your success. Chemistry is that branch of natural philosophy in which the greatest improvements have been and may be made; it is on that account that I have made it my peculiar study; but at the same time I have not neglected the other branches of science. A man would make but a very sorry chemist, if he attended to that department of human knowledge alone. If your wish is to become really a man of science, and not merely a petty experimentalist, I should advise you to apply to every branch of natural philosophy, including mathematics."

He then took me into his laboratory, and explained to me the uses of his various machines; instructing me as to what I ought to procure, and promising me the use of his own, when I should have advanced far enough in the science not to derange their mechanism. He also gave me the list of books which I had requested; and I took my leave.

Thus ended a day memorable to me; it decided my future destiny.

CHAPTER III

From this day natural philosophy, and particularly chemistry, in the most comprehensive sense of the term, became nearly my sole occupation. I read with ardour those works, so full of genius and discrimination, which modern inquirers have written on these subjects. I attended the lectures, and cultivated the acquaintance, of the men of science of the university; and I found even in M. Krempe a great deal of sound sense and real information, combined, it is true, with a repulsive physiognomy and manners, but not on that account the less valuable. In M. Waldman I found a true friend. His gentleness was never tinged by dogmatism; and his instructions were given with an air of frankness and good nature, that banished every idea of pedantry. It was, perhaps, the amiable character of this man that inclined me more to that branch of natural philosophy which he professed, than an intrinsic love for the science itself. But this state of mind had place only in the first steps towards knowledge: the more fully I entered into the science, the more exclusively I pursued it for its own sake. That application, which at first had been a matter of duty and resolution, now became so ardent and eager, that the stars often disappeared in the light of morning whilst I was yet engaged in my laboratory.

As I applied so closely, it may be easily conceived that I improved rapidly. My ardour was indeed the astonishment of the students; and my proficiency, that of the masters. Professor Krempe often asked me, with a sly smile, how Cornelius Agrippa went on? whilst M. Waldman expressed the most heartfelt exultation in my progress. Two years passed in this manner, during which I paid no visit to Geneva, but was engaged, heart and soul, in the pursuit of some discoveries, which I hoped to make. None but those who have experienced them can conceive of the enticements of science. In other studies you go as far as others have gone before you, and there is nothing more to know; but in a scientific pursuit there is continual food for discovery and wonder. A mind of moderate capacity, which closely pursues one study, must infallibly arrive at great proficiency in that study; and I, who continually sought the attainment of one object of pursuit, and was solely wrapt up in this, improved so rapidly, that, at the end of two years, I made some discoveries in the improvement of some chemical instruments, which procured me great esteem and admiration at the university. When I had arrived at this point, and had become as well acquainted with the theory and practice of natural philosophy as depended on the lessons of any of the professors at Ingolstadt, my residence there being no longer conducive to my improvements, I thought of returning to my friends and my native town, when an incident happened that protracted my stay.

One of the phenonema which had peculiarly attracted my attention was the structure of the human frame, and, indeed, any animal endued with life. Whence, I often asked myself, did the principle of life proceed? It was a bold question, and one which has ever been considered as a mystery; yet with how many things are we upon the brink of becoming acquainted, if cowardice or carelessness did not restrain our inquiries. I revolved these circumstances in my mind, and determined thenceforth to apply myself more particularly to those branches of natural philosophy which relate to physiology. Unless I had been animated by an almost supernatural enthusiasm, my application to this study would have been irksome, and almost intolerable. To examine the causes of life, we must first have recourse to death. I became acquainted with the science of anatomy: but this was not sufficient; I must also observe the natural decay and corruption of the human body. In my education my father had taken the greatest precautions that my mind should be impressed with no supernatural horrors. I do not ever remember to have trembled at a tale of superstition, or to have feared the apparition of a spirit. Darkness had no effect upon my fancy; and a church-yard was to me merely the receptacle of bodies deprived of life, which, from being the seat of beauty and strength, had become food for the worm. Now I was led to examine the cause and progress of this decay, and forced to spend days and nights in vaults and charnel houses. My attention was fixed upon every object the most insupportable to the delicacy of the human feelings. I saw how the fine form of man was degraded and wasted; I beheld the corruption of death succeed to the blooming cheek of life; I saw how the worm inherited the wonders of the eye and brain. I paused, examining and analysing all the minutiae of causation, as exemplified in the change from life to death, and death to life, until from the midst of this darkness a sudden light broke in upon me — a light so brilliant and wondrous, yet so simple, that while I became dizzy with the immensity of the prospect which it illustrated, I was surprised that among so many men of genius, who had directed their inquiries towards the same science, that I alone should be reserved to discover so astonishing a secret.

Remember, I am not recording the vision of a madman. The sun does not more certainly shine in the heavens, than that which I now affirm is true. Some miracle might have produced it, yet the stages of the discovery were distinct and probable. After days and nights of incredible labour and fatigue, I succeeded in discovering the cause of generation and life; nay, more, I became myself capable of bestowing animation upon lifeless matter.

The astonishment which I had at first experienced on this discovery soon gave place to delight and rapture. After so much time spent in painful labour, to arrive at once at the summit of my desires, was the most gratifying consummation of my toils. But this discovery was so great and overwhelming, that all the steps by which I had been progressively led to it were obliterated, and I beheld only the result. What had been the study and desire of the wisest men since the creation of the world, was now within my grasp. Not that, like a magic scene, it all opened upon me at once: the information I had obtained was of a nature rather to direct my endeavours so soon as I should point them towards the object of my search, than to exhibit that object already accomplished. I was like the Arabian who had been buried with the dead, and found a passage to life aided only by one glimmering, and seemingly ineffectual, light.

I see by your eagerness, and the wonder and hope which your eyes express, my friend, that you expect to be informed of the secret with which I am acquainted; that cannot be: listen patiently until the end of my story, and you will easily perceive why I am reserved upon that subject. I will not lead you on, unguarded and ardent as I then was, to your destruction and infallible misery. Learn from me, if not by my precepts, at least by my example, how dangerous is the acquirement of knowledge, and how much happier that man is who believes his native town to be the world, than he who aspires to become greater than his nature will allow.

When I found so astonishing a power placed within my hands, I hesitated a long time concerning the manner in which I should employ it. Although I possessed the capacity of bestowing animation, yet to prepare a frame for the reception of it, with all its intricacies of fibres, muscles, and veins, still remained a work of inconceivable difficulty and labour. I doubted at first whether I should attempt the creation of a being like myself or one of simpler organization; but my imagination was too much exalted by my first success to permit me to doubt of my ability to give life to an animal as complex and wonderful as man. The materials at present within my command hardly appeared adequate to so arduous an undertaking; but I doubted not that I should ultimately succeed. I prepared myself for a multitude of reverses; my operations might be incessantly baffled, and at last my work be imperfect: yet, when I considered the improvement which every day takes place in science and mechanics, I was encouraged to hope my present attempts would at least lay the foundations of future success. Nor could I consider the magnitude and complexity of my plan as any argument of its impracticability. It was with these feelings that I began the creation of a human being. As the minuteness of the parts formed a great hindrance to my speed, I resolved, contrary to my first intention, to make the being of a gigantic stature; that is to say, about eight feet in height, and proportionably large. After having formed this determination, and having spent some months in successfully collecting and arranging my materials, I began.

No one can conceive the variety of feelings which bore me onwards, like a hurricane, in the first enthusiasm of success. Life and death appeared to me ideal bounds, which I should first break through, and pour a torrent of light into our dark world. A new species[7] would bless me as its creator and source; many happy and excellent natures would owe their being to me. No father could claim the gratitude of his child so completely as I should deserve their's. Pursuing these reflections, I thought, that if I could bestow animation upon lifeless matter, I might in process of time (although I now found it impossible) renew life where death had apparently devoted the body to corruption.

These thoughts supported my spirits, while I pursued my undertaking with unremitting ardour. My cheek had grown pale with study, and my person had become emaciated with confinement. Sometimes, on the very brink of certainty, I failed; yet still I clung to the hope which the next day or the next hour might realize. One secret which I alone possessed was the hope to which I had dedicated myself; and the moon gazed on my midnight labours, while, with unrelaxed and breathless eagerness, I pursued nature to her hiding places. Who shall conceive the horrors of my secret toil, as I dabbled among the unhallowed damps of the grave, or tortured

---

[7] A new species, of course, would be an impossibility if every biological "type" had been created by divine fiat. [Ed.]

the living animal to animate the lifeless clay? My limbs now tremble, and my eyes swim with the remembrance; but then a resistless, and almost frantic impulse, urged me forward; I seemed to have lost all soul or sensation but for this one pursuit. It was indeed but a passing trance, that only made me feel with renewed acuteness so soon as, the unnatural stimulus ceasing to operate, I had returned to my old habits. I collected bones from charnel houses; and disturbed, with profane fingers, the tremendous secrets of the human frame. In a solitary chamber, or rather cell, at the top of the house, and separated from all the other apartments by a gallery and staircase, I kept my workshop of filthy creation; my eyeballs were starting from their sockets in attending to the details of my employment. The dissecting room and the slaughter-house furnished many of my materials; and often did my human nature turn with loathing from my occupation, whilst, still urged on by an eagerness which perpetually increased, I brought my work near to a conclusion.

The summer months passed while I was thus engaged, heart and soul, in one pursuit. It was a most beautiful season; never did the fields bestow a more plentiful harvest, or the vines yield a more luxuriant vintage: but my eyes were insensible to the charms of nature. And the same feelings which made me neglect the scenes around me caused me also to forget those friends who were so many miles absent, and whom I had not seen for so long a time. I knew my silence disquieted them; and I well remembered the words of my father: "I know that while you are pleased with yourself, you will think of us with affection, and we shall hear regularly from you. You must pardon me, if I regard any interruption in your correspondence as a proof that your other duties are equally neglected."

I knew well therefore what would be my father's feelings; but I could not tear my thoughts from my employment, loathsome in itself, but which had taken an irresistible hold of my imagination. I wished, as it were, to procrastinate all that related to my feelings of affection until the great object, which swallowed up every habit of my nature, should be completed.

I then thought that my father would be unjust if he ascribed my neglect to vice, or faultiness on my part; but I am now convinced that he was justified in conceiving that I should not be altogether free from blame. A human being in perfection ought always to preserve a calm and peaceful mind, and never to allow passion or a transitory desire to disturb his tranquillity. I do not think that the pursuit of knowledge is an exception to this rule. If the study to which you apply yourself has a tendency to weaken your affections, and to destroy your taste for those simple pleasures in which no alloy can possibly mix, then that study is certainly unlawful, that is to say, not befitting the human mind. If this rule were always observed; if no man allowed any pursuit whatsoever to interfere with the tranquillity of his domestic affections, Greece had not been enslaved; Cæsar would have spared his country; America would have been discovered more gradually; and the empires of Mexico and Peru had not been destroyed.

But I forget that I am moralizing in the most interesting part of my tale; and your looks remind me to proceed.

My father made no reproach in his letters; and only took notice of my silence by inquiring into my occupations more particularly than before. Winter, spring, and summer, passed away during my labours; but I did not watch the blossom or the expanding leaves — sights which before always yielded me supreme delight, so deeply was I engrossed in my occupation. The leaves of that year had withered before my work drew near to a close; and now every day shewed me more plainly how well I had succeeded. But my enthusiasm was checked by my anxiety, and I appeared rather like one doomed by slavery to toil in the mines, or any other unwholesome trade, than an artist occupied by his favourite employment. Every night I was oppressed by a slow fever, and I became nervous to a most painful degree; a disease that I regretted the more because I had hitherto enjoyed most excellent health, and had always boasted of the firmness of my nerves. But I believed that exercise and amusement would soon drive away such symptoms; and I promised myself both of these, when my creation should be complete.

Chapter IV

It was on a dreary night of November, that I beheld the accomplishment of my toils. With an anxiety that almost amounted to agony, I collected the instruments of life around me, that I might infuse a spark of being into the lifeless thing that lay at my feet. It was already one in the morning; the rain pattered dismally against the panes, and my candle was nearly burnt out, when, by the glimmer of the half-extinguished light, I saw the dull yellow eye of the creature open; it breathed hard, and a convulsive motion agitated its limbs.

How can I describe my emotions at this catastrophe, or how delineate the wretch whom with such infinite pains and care I had endeavoured to form? His limbs were in proportion, and I had selected his features as beautiful. Beautiful! Great God! His yellow skin scarcely covered the work of muscles and arteries beneath; his hair was of a lustrous black, and flowing; his teeth of a pearly whiteness; but these luxuriances only formed a more horrid contrast with his watery eyes, that seemed almost of the same colour as the dual white sockets in which they were set, his shrivelled complexion, and straight black lips.

The different accidents of life are not so changeable as the feelings of human nature. I had worked hard for nearly two years, for the sole purpose of infusing life into an inanimate body. For this I had deprived myself of rest and health. I had desired it with an ardour that far exceeded moderation; but now that I had finished, the beauty of the dream vanished, and breathless horror and disgust filled my heart. Unable to endure the aspect of the being I had created, I rushed out of the room, and continued a long time traversing my bed-chamber, unable to compose my mind to sleep. At length lassitude succeeded to the tumult I had before endured; and I threw myself on the bed in my clothes, endeavouring to seek a few moments of forgetfulness. But it was in vain: I slept indeed, but I was disturbed by the wildest dreams. [. . .]

From [Introduction to] Frankenstein; or, the Modern Prometheus [1831]

The Publishers of the Standard Novels, in selecting "Frankenstein" for one of their series, expressed a wish that I should furnish them with some account of the origin of the story. I am the more willing to comply, because I shall thus give a general answer to the question, so very frequently asked me — "How I, then a young girl, came to think of, and to dilate upon, so very hideous an idea?" It is true that I am very averse to bringing myself forward in print; but as my account will only appear as an appendage to a former production, and as it will be confined to such topics as have connection with my authorship alone, I can scarcely accuse myself of a personal intrusion.

It is not singular that, as the daughter of two persons of distinguished literary celebrity,[8] I should very early in life have thought of writing. As a child I scribbled; and my favourite pastime, during the hours given me for recreation, was to "write stories." Still I had a dearer pleasure than this, which was the formation of castles in the air — the indulging in waking dreams — the following up trains of thought, which had for their subject the formation of a succession of imaginary incidents. My dreams were at once more fantastic and agreeable than my writings. In the latter I was a close imitator — rather doing as others had done, than putting down the

---

Mary W. Shelley, *Frankenstein; or, the Modern Prometheus.* London: Colburn and Bentley, 1831.

[8]William Godwin and Mary Wollstonecraft. [Ed.]

suggestions of my own mind. What I wrote was intended at least for one other eye — my childhood's companion and friend; but my dreams were all my own; I accounted for them to nobody; they were my refuge when annoyed — my dearest pleasure when free.

I lived principally in the country as a girl, and passed a considerable time in Scotland. I made occasional visits to the more picturesque parts; but my habitual residence was on the blank and dreary northern shores of the Tay, near Dundee. Blank and dreary on retrospection I call them; they were not so to me then. They were the eyry of freedom, and the pleasant region where unheeded I could commune with the creatures of my fancy. I wrote then — but in a most common-place style. It was beneath the trees of the grounds belonging to our house, or on the bleak sides of the wood-less mountains near, that my true compositions, the airy flights of my imagination, were born and fostered. I did not make myself the heroine of my tales. Life appeared to me too common-place an affair as regarded myself. I could not figure to myself that romantic woes or wonderful events would ever be my lot; but I was not confined to my own identity, and I could people the hours with creations far more interesting to me at that age, than my own sensations.

After this my life became busier and reality stood in place of fiction. My husband,[9] however, was from the first, very anxious that I should prove myself worthy of my parentage, and enrol myself on the page of fame. He was for ever inciting me to obtain literary reputation, which even on my own part I cared for then, though since I have become infinitely indifferent to it. At this time he desired that I should write, not so much with the idea that I could produce any thing worthy of notice, but that he might himself judge how far I possessed the promise of better things hereafter. Still I did nothing. Travelling, and the cares of a family, occupied my time; and study, in the way of reading, or improving my ideas in communication with his far more cultivated mind, was all of literary employment that engaged my attention.

In the summer of 1816, we visited Switzerland, and became the neighbours of Lord Byron. At first we spent our pleasant hours on the lake, or wandering on its shores; and Lord Byron, who was writing the third canto of Childe Harold, was the only one among us who put his thoughts upon paper. These, as he brought them successively to us, clothed in all the light and harmony of poetry, seemed to stamp as divine the glories of heaven and earth, whose influences we partook with him.

---

[9]Percy Bysshe Shelley, although Mary and Percy did not marry until December 1816, after the suicide of Shelley's first wife. [Ed.]

But it proved a wet, ungenial summer, and incessant rain often confined us for days to the house. Some volumes of ghost stories, translated from the German into French, fell into our hands. There was the History of the Inconstant Lover, who, when he thought to clasp the bride to whom he had pledged his vows, found himself in the arms of the pale ghost of her whom he had deserted. There was the tale of the sinful founder of his race, whose miserable doom it was to bestow the kiss of death on all the younger sons of his fated house, just when they reached the age of promise. His gigantic, shadowy form, clothed like the ghost in Hamlet, in complete armour, but with the beaver up, was seen at midnight, by the moon's fitful beams, to advance slowly along the gloomy avenue. The shape was lost beneath the shadow of the castle walls; but soon a gate swung back, a step was heard, the door of the chamber opened, and he advanced to the couch of the blooming youths, cradled in healthy sleep. Eternal sorrow sat upon his face as he bent down and kissed the forehead of the boys, who from that hour withered like flowers snapt upon the stalk. I have not seen these stories since then; but their incidents are as fresh in my mind as if I had read them yesterday.

"We will each write a ghost story," said Lord Byron; and his proposition was acceded to. There were four of us. The noble author began a tale, a fragment of which he printed at the end of his poem of Mazeppa. Shelley, more apt to embody ideas and sentiments in the radiance of brilliant imagery, and in the music of the most melodious verse that adorns our language, than to invent the machinery of a story, commenced one founded on the experiences of his early life. Poor Polidori had some terrible idea about a skull-headed lady, who was so punished for peeping through a key-hole—what to see I forget—something very shocking and wrong of course; but when she was reduced to a worse condition than the renowned Tom of Coventry, he did not know what to do with her, and was obliged to despatch her to the tomb of the Capulets, the only place for which she was fitted. The illustrious poets also, annoyed by the platitude of prose, speedily relinquished their uncongenial task.

I busied myself *to think of a story,* a story to rival those which had excited us to this task. One which would speak to the mysterious fears of our nature, and awaken thrilling horror—one to make the reader dread to look round, to curdle the blood, and quicken the beatings of the heart. If I did not accomplish these things, my ghost story would be unworthy of its name. I thought and pondered—vainly. I felt that blank incapability of invention which is the greatest misery of authorship, when dull Nothing replies to our anxious invocations. *Have you thought of a story?* I was asked each morning, and each morning I was forced to reply with a mortifying negative.

Every thing must have a beginning, to speak in Sanchean phrase; and that beginning must be linked to something that went before. The Hindoos give the world an elephant to support it, but they make the elephant stand upon a tortoise. Invention, it must be humbly admitted, does not consist in creating out of void, but out of chaos; the materials must, in the first place, be afforded: it can give form to dark, shapeless substances, but cannot bring into being the substance itself. In all matters of discovery and invention, even of those that appertain to the imagination, we are continually reminded of the story of Columbus and his egg. Invention consists in the capacity of seizing on the capabilities of a subject, and in the power of moulding and fashioning ideas suggested to it.

Many and long were the conversations between Lord Byron and Shelley, to which I was a devout but nearly silent listener. During one of these, various philosophical doctrines were discussed, and among others the nature of the principle of life, and whether there was any probability of its ever being discovered and communicated. They talked of the experiments of Dr. Darwin (I speak not of what the Doctor really did, or said that he did, but, as more to my purpose, of what was then spoken of as having been done by him), who preserved a piece of vermicelli in a glass case, till by some extraordinary means it began to move with voluntary motion.[10] Not thus, after all, would life be given. Perhaps a corpse would be re-animated; galvanism had given token of such things: perhaps the component parts of a creature might be manufactured, brought together, and endued with vital warmth.

Night waned upon this talk, and even the witching hour had gone by, before we retired to rest. When I placed my head on my pillow, I did not sleep, nor could I be said to think. My imagination, unbidden, possessed and guided me, gifting the successive images that arose in my mind with a vividness far beyond the usual bounds of reverie. I saw—with shut eyes, but acute mental vision—I saw the pale student of unhallowed arts kneeling beside the thing he had put together. I saw the hideous phantasm of a man stretched out, and then, on the working of some powerful engine, show signs of life, and stir with an uneasy, half vital motion. Frightful must it be; for supremely frightful would be the effect of any human endeavour to mock the stupendous mechanism of the Creator of the world. His success would terrify the artist; he would rush away from his odious handywork, horror-stricken. He would hope that, left to itself, the slight spark of life which he had communicated would fade; that this thing, which had received such imperfect animation, would subside into dead matter; and he might sleep in the belief that the silence of the grave would quench for ever the transient existence of the hideous corpse which he had looked upon as the cradle of life. He sleeps; but he is awakened; he opens his eyes;

---

[10] Erasmus Darwin actually describes tiny "animalcules" which appear, as if by spontaneous generation, in a "paste composed of flour and water" (*Temple of Nature*, add. notes 3). [Ed.]

behold the horrid thing stands at his bedside, opening his curtains, and looking on him with yellow, watery, but speculative eyes.

I opened mine in terror. The idea so possessed my mind, that a thrill of fear ran through me, and I wished to exchange the ghastly image of my fancy for the realities around. I see them still; the very room, the dark *parquet*, the closed shutters, with the moonlight struggling through, and the sense I had that the glassy lake and white high Alps were beyond. I could not so easily get rid of my hideous phantom; still it haunted me. I must try to think of something else. I recurred to my ghost story, my tiresome unlucky ghost story! O! if I could only contrive one which would frighten my reader as I myself had been frightened that night!

Swift as light and as cheering was the idea that broke in upon me. "I have found it! What terrified me will terrify others; and I need only describe the spectre which had haunted my midnight pillow." On the morrow I announced that I had *thought of a story*. I began that day with the words, *It was on a dreary night of November*,[11] making only a transcript of the grim terrors of my waking dream.

At first I thought but of a few pages — of a short tale; but Shelley urged me to develope the idea at greater length. I certainly did not owe the suggestion of one incident, nor scarcely of one train of feeling, to my husband, and yet but for his incitement, it would never have taken the form in which it was presented to the world. From this declaration I must except the preface. As far as I can recollect, it was entirely written by him.

And now, once again, I bid my hideous progeny go forth and prosper. I have an affection for it, for it was the offspring of happy days, when death and grief were but words, which found no true echo in my heart. Its several pages speak of many a walk, many a drive, and many a conversation, when I was not alone; and my companion was one who, in this world, I shall never see more. But this is for myself; my readers have nothing to do with these associations.

I will add but one word as to the alterations I have made. They are principally those of style. I have changed no portion of the story, nor introduced any new ideas or circumstances. I have mended the language where it was so bald as to interfere with the interest of the narrative; and these changes occur almost exclusively in the beginning of the first volume. Throughout they are entirely confined to such parts as are mere adjuncts to the story, leaving the core and substance of it untouched.

M. W. S.

London, October 15, 1831.

---

[11] The opening line of chap. 4 in the 1818 edition. [Ed.]

Percy Bysshe Shelley (1792–1822)

Percy Shelley exhibited a fascination with natural phenomena from early childhood. Richard Holmes begins his biography of Shelley with family stories about a "Great Tortoise" and "Great Snake" that inhabited the pond and woods of Field Place in Sussex. One of Shelley's teachers at Syon House Academy was Dr. Adam Walker, an itinerant astronomer and inventor who lectured on the possibility of life on other planets and on the links between magnetism and electricity. Shelley's cousin Tom Medwin described looking through Walker's telescopes at the rings of Saturn and through his microscope at a fly's wing, cheese mites, and "vermicular animalculae in vinegar"; Shelley's sister recalled "being placed hand-in-hand round the nursery table to be electrified" (Holmes 16, 17). Shelley was notorious as a school boy and at Oxford for his scientific experiments, many of which resulted in destructive explosions. By 1810, when Shelley left Eton for Oxford, he had translated large sections of Pliny's *Historia Naturalis*. He had additionally experimented with electricity and magnetism as well as with gunpowder and chemical reactions. His rooms at University College, Oxford, contained a wide range of scientific equipment: vials, crucibles, "philosophical instruments," a solar microscope, a galvanic trough, an air pump, a telescope, and an assortment of electrical devices.

By 1812, Shelley had received from his bookseller Hookham copies of *Elements of Chemical Philosophy* by Sir Humphry Davy, as well as *Medical Extracts* and *Hartley on Man*. That same year he ordered Erasmus Darwin's *Zoonomia* and *The Temple of Nature* (*Letters* 1: 342–45) as well as Lazzaro Spallanzani's work on the regeneration of animal body parts. Shelley's notes to *Queen Mab* (1813) contain numerous references to natural philosophers, ancient and modern: Lucretius, Plutarch, Pliny, Cuvier, and d'Holbach. One of Shelley's early fictional characters, in his Gothic novel *St. Irvyne,* possesses characteristics of his undergraduate creator and also of Mary Shelley's Victor Frankenstein in his "desire of unveiling the latent mysteries of nature."

During the Frankenstein summer of 1816, Shelley and Mary visited a natural history "cabinet" at Servox, "like those of Keswick and Bethgelert." Shelley sounds much like a natural historian in his description of "some chamois' horns, and the horns of an exceedingly rare animal called the *Bouctin*" (*Letters* 1: 496). This letter to Thomas Love Peacock also describes the "Cabinet d'Histoire Naturelle at Chamouni" where Shelley purchased "some specimens of minerals and plants" as well as "a large collection of the seeds of rare Alpine plants." This is also the letter in which Shelley says, on his first sight of Mont Blanc, "Nature was the poet whose harmony held our spirits more breathless than the divinest." A parallel link between Shelley's moral thinking and the natural philosophy of his time is evident in his essay "On Love" (1818): "In the motion of the very leaves of spring in the blue air there is then found a secret correspondence with our heart. There is eloquence in the tongueless wind and a melody in the flowing of brooks and the rustling of the reeds beside them which by their inconceivable relation to something within the soul awakens the spirits to a dance of breathless rapture, and bring tears of mysterious tenderness to the eyes" (*Poetry and Prose* 504).

Shelley's Preface to Mary Shelley's *Frankenstein* (1818) refers to the scientific speculations of Erasmus Darwin and "the physiological writers of Germany." His "Mont Blanc" displays an understanding of geology and the fossil record that would not be so well expressed poetically until Tennyson's *In Memoriam*. Poems as diverse as "To a Skylark," "The Cloud," "The Sensitive Plant," "Ode to the West Wind," and *Prometheus Unbound* offer images of interdependence between human and nonhuman realms and of the cyclical and unalterable forces that link animate and inanimate nature. The idea of an essential correspondence between human and natural realms contributes to Shelley's defense of vegetarianism in the note to *Queen Mab* included here. Likewise, the regenerate world of *Prometheus Unbound* presents a picture that we would now call ecological: "Henceforth [. . .] all plants, / And creeping forms, and insects rainbow-winged, / And birds, and beasts, and fish, and human shapes, / [. . .] shall take / And interchange sweet nutriment" (3, 3, 90, 91–93, 95–96). Shelley's work connects natural law directly to social, political, and ethical systems: "I wish no living thing to suffer pain"

(*Prometheus* 1, 305). His metaphors regularly draw on physical science and natural history, and his abstract literary sensibilities are often balanced by a rigorous sense of a material and organic unity that pervades all living things.

From Queen Mab

       The grey morn
Dawns on the mournful scene; the sulphurous smoke
Before the icy wind slow rolls away,
And the bright beams of frosty morning dance
5 Along the spangling snow. There tracks of blood
Even to the forest's depth, and scattered arms,
And lifeless warriors, whose hard lineaments
Death's self could change not, mark the dreadful path
Of the outsallying victors: far behind,
10 Black ashes note where their proud city stood.
Within yon forest is a gloomy glen —
Each tree which guards its darkness from the day,
Waves o'er a warrior's tomb.

         I see thee shrink,
15 Surpassing Spirit! wert thou human else?
I see a shade of doubt and horror fleet
Across thy stainless features: yet fear not;
This is no unconnected misery,
Nor stands uncaused, and irretrievable.
20 Man's evil nature, that apology
Which kings who rule, and cowards who crouch, set up
For their unnumbered crimes, sheds not the blood
Which desolates the discord-wasted land.
From kings, and priests, and statesmen, war arose,
25 Whose safety is man's deep unbettered woe,
Whose grandeur his debasement. Let the axe

Percy Bysshe Shelley, *Queen Mab: A Philosophical Poem.* London, 1813.

Strike at the root, the poison-tree[1] will fall;
And where its venomed exhalations spread
Ruin, and death, and woe, where millions lay
30 Quenching the serpent's famine, and their bones
Bleaching unburied in the putrid blast,
A garden shall arise, in loveliness
Surpassing fabled Eden.

                    Hath Nature's soul,
35 That formed this world so beautiful, that spread
Earth's lap with plenty, and life's smallest chord
Strung to unchanging unison, that gave
The happy birds their dwelling in the grove,
That yielded to the wanderers of the deep
40 The lovely silence of the unfathomed main,
And filled the meanest worm that crawls in dust
With spirit, thought, and love; on Man alone,
Partial in causeless malice, wantonly
Heaped ruin, vice, and slavery; his soul
45 Blasted with withering curses; placed afar
The meteor-happiness, that shuns his grasp,
But serving on the frightful gulph to glare,
Rent wide beneath his footsteps?

                          Nature! no!
50 Kings, priests, and statesmen, blast the human flower
Even in its tender bud; their influence darts
Like subtle poison through the bloodless veins
Of desolate society. The child,
Ere he can lisp his mother's sacred name,
55 Swells with the unnatural pride of crime, and lifts
His baby-sword even in a hero's mood.
This infant-arm becomes the bloodiest scourge
Of devastated earth; whilst specious names,
Learnt in soft childhood's unsuspecting hour,
60 Serve as the sophisms with which manhood dims
Bright reason's ray, and sanctifies the sword
Upraised to shed a brother's innocent blood.
Let priest-led slaves cease to proclaim that man
Inherits vice and misery, when force
65 And falshood hang even o'er the cradled babe,
Stifling with rudest grasp all natural good.

---

[1] Mythical upas tree of Java. [Ed.]

Ah! to the stranger-soul, when first it peeps
From its now tenement, and looks abroad
For happiness and sympathy, how stern
70 And desolate a tract is this wide world!
How withered all the buds of natural good!
No shade, no shelter from the sweeping storms
Of pityless power! On its wretched frame,
Poisoned, perchance, by the disease and woe
75 Heaped on the wretched parent whence it sprung
By morals, law, and custom, the pure winds
Of heaven, that renovate the insect tribes,
May breathe not. The untainting light of day
May visit not its longings. It is bound
80 Ere it has life: yea, all the chains are forged
Long ere its being: all liberty and love
And peace is torn from its defencelessness;
Cursed from its birth, even from its cradle doomed
To abjectness and bondage!

85 Throughout this varied and eternal world
Soul is the only element, the block
That for uncounted ages has remained.
The moveless pillar of a mountain's weight
Is active, living spirit. Every grain
90 Is sentient both in unity and part,
And the minutest atom comprehends
A world of loves and hatreds; these beget
Evil and good: hence truth and falsehood spring;
Hence will and thought and action, all the germs
95 Of pain or pleasure, sympathy or hate,
That variegate the eternal universe.
Soul is not more polluted than the beams
Of heaven's pure orb, ere round their rapid lines
The taint of earth-born atmospheres arise.
100 Man is of soul and body, formed for deeds
Of high resolve, on fancy's boldest wing
To soar unwearied, fearlessly to turn
The keenest pangs to peacefulness, and taste
The joys which mingled sense and spirit yield.
105 Or he is formed for abjectness and woe,
To grovel on the dunghill of his fears,
To shrink at every sound, to quench the flame

Of natural love in sensualism, to know
That hour as blest when on his worthless days
110 The frozen hand of death shall set its seal,
Yet fear the cure, though hating the disease.
The one is man that shall hereafter be;
The other, man as vice has made him now.[...]

Spirit of Nature! all-sufficing Power,
115 Necessity! thou mother of the world!
Unlike the God of human error, thou
Requirest no prayers or praises; the caprice
Of man's weak will belongs no more to thee
Than do the changeful passions of his breast
120 To thy unvarying harmony: the slave,
Whose horrible lusts spread misery o'er the world,
And the good man, who lifts, with virtuous pride,
His being, in the sight of happiness,
That springs from his own works; the poison-tree,
125 Beneath whose shade all life is withered up,
And the fair oak, whose leafy dome affords
A temple where the vows of happy love
Are registered, are equal in thy sight:
No love, no hate thou cherishest; revenge
130 And favoritism, and worst desire of fame
Thou knowest not: all that the wide world contains
Are but thy passive instruments, and thou
Regardst them all with an impartial eye,
Whose joy or pain thy nature cannot feel,
135   Because thou hast not human sense,
Because thou art not human mind.

Yes! when the sweeping storm of time
Has sung its death-dirge o'er the ruined fanes
And broken altars of the almighty fiend,
140 Whose name usurps thy honors, and the blood
Through centuries clotted there, has floated down
The tainted flood of ages, shalt thou live
Unchangeable! A shrine is raised to thee,
    Which, nor the tempest breath of time,
145   Nor the interminable flood,
      Over earth's slight pageant rolling,
        Availeth to destroy,
The sensitive extension of the world.

That wonderous and eternal fane,[2]
150 Where pain and pleasure, good and evil join,
   To do the will of strong necessity,
      And life, in multitudinous shapes,
   Still pressing forward where no term can be,
      Like hungry and unresting flame
155 Curls round the eternal columns of its strength.[. . .]

The habitable earth is full of bliss;
Those wastes of frozen billows that were hurled
By everlasting snow-storms round the poles,
Where matter dared not vegetate or live,
160 But ceaseless frost round the vast solitude
Bound its broad zone of stillness, are unloosed;
And fragrant zephyrs there from spicy isles
Ruffle the placid ocean-deep, that rolls
Its broad, bright surges to the sloping sand,
165 Whose roar is wakened into echoings sweet
To murmur through the heaven-breathing groves
And melodize with man's blest nature there.

Those deserts of immeasurable sand,
Whose age-collected fervors scarce allowed
170 A bird to live, a blade of grass to spring,
Where the shrill chirp of the green lizard's love
Broke on the sultry silentness alone,
Now teem with countless rills and shady woods,
Corn-fields and pastures and white cottages;
175 And where the startled wilderness beheld
A savage conqueror stained in kindred blood,
A tygress sating with the flesh of lambs,
The unnatural famine of her toothless cubs,
Whilst shouts and howlings through the desert rang,
180 Sloping and smooth the daisy-spangled lawn,
Offering sweet incense to the sun-rise, smiles
To see a babe before his mother's door,
      Sharing his morning's meal
   With the green and golden basilisk[3]
185   That comes to lick his feet.

---

[2] A temple. [Ed.]
[3] A mythical lizard. [Ed.]

Those trackless deeps, where many a weary sail
Has seen above the illimitable plain,
Morning on night, and night on morning rise,
Whilst still no land to greet the wanderer spread
190 Its shadowy mountains on the sun-bright sea,
Where the loud roarings of the tempest-waves
So long have mingled with the gusty wind
In melancholy loneliness, and swept
The desert of those ocean solitudes,
195 But vocal to the sea-bird's harrowing shriek,
The bellowing monster, and the rushing storm,
Now to the sweet and many mingling sounds
Of kindliest human impulses respond.

Those lonely realms bright garden-isles begem,
195 With lightsome clouds and shining seas between,
And fertile vallies, resonant with bliss,
Whilst green woods overcanopy the wave,
Which like a toil-worn labourer leaps to shore,
To meet the kisses of the flowrets there.

200 All things are recreated, and the flame
Of consentaneous love inspires all life:
The fertile bosom of the earth gives suck
To myriads, who still grow beneath her care,
Rewarding her with their pure perfectness:
205 The balmy breathings of the wind inhale
Her virtues, and diffuse them all abroad:
Health floats amid the gentle atmosphere,
Glows in the fruits, and mantles on the stream:
No storms deform the beaming brow of heaven,
210 Nor scatter in the freshness of its pride
The foliage of the ever verdant trees;
But fruits are ever ripe, flowers ever fair,
And autumn proudly bears her matron grace,
Kindling a flush on the fair cheek of spring,
215 Whose virgin bloom beneath the ruddy fruit
Reflects its tint and blushes into love.

The lion now forgets to thirst for blood:
There might you see him sporting in the sun
Beside the dreadless kid; his claws are sheathed,
220 His teeth are harmless, custom's force has made
His nature as the nature of a lamb.

Like passion's fruit, the nightshade's tempting bane
Poisons no more the pleasure it bestows:
All bitterness is past; the cup of joy
225 Unmingled mantles to the goblet's brim,
And courts the thirsty lips it fled before. [. . .]

FROM NOTES TO QUEEN MAB

The sun's unclouded orb
Rolled through the black concave.

Beyond our atmosphere the sun would appear a rayless orb of fire in the midst of a black concave. The equal diffusion of its light on earth is owing to the refraction of the rays by the atmosphere, and their reflection from other bodies. Light consists either of vibrations propagated through a subtle medium, or of numerous minute particles repelled in all directions from the luminous body. Its velocity greatly exceeds that of any substance with which we are acquainted: observations on the eclipses of Jupiter's satellites have demonstrated that light takes up no more than 8'7" in passing from the sun to the earth, a distance of 95,000,000 miles. Some idea may be gained of the immense distance of the fixed stars, when it is computed that many years would elapse before light could reach this earth from the nearest of them; yet in one year light travels 5,422,400,000,000 miles, which is a distance 5,707,600 times greater than that of the sun from the earth.

Whilst round the chariot's way
Innumerable systems rolled.

The plurality of worlds, the indefinite immensity of the universe is a most awful subject of contemplation. He who rightly feels its mystery and grandeur, is in no danger of seduction from the falshoods of religious systems, or of deifying the principle of the universe. It is impossible to believe that the Spirit that pervades this infinite machine, begat a son upon the body of a Jewish woman; or is angered at the consequences of that necessity, which is a synonime of itself. All that miserable tale of the Devil, and Eve, and an Intercessor, with the childish mummeries of the God of the Jews, is irreconcileable with the knowledge of the stars. The works of his fingers have borne witness against him.

The nearest of the fixed stars is inconceivably distant from the earth, and they are probably proportionably distant from each other. By a calculation of the velocity of light, Syrius is supposed to be at least

54,224,000,000,000 miles from the earth.[4] That which appears only like a thin and silvery cloud streaking the heaven, is in effect composed of innumerable clusters of suns, each shining with its own light, and illuminating numbers of planets that revolve around them. Millions and millions of suns are ranged around us, all attended by innumerable worlds, yet calm, regular, and harmonious, all keeping the paths of immutable necessity. [. . .]

> No longer now
> He slays the lamb that looks him in the face.

I hold that the depravity of the physical and moral nature of man originated in his unnatural habits of life. The origin of man, like that of the universe of which he is a part, is enveloped in impenetrable mystery. His generations either had a beginning, or they had not. The weight of evidence in favour of each of these suppositions seems tolerably equal; and it is perfectly unimportant to the present argument which is assumed. The language spoken however by the mythology of nearly all religions seems to prove, that at some distant period man forsook the path of nature, and sacrificed the purity and happiness of his being to unnatural appetites. The date of this event seems to have also been that of some great change in the climates of the earth, with which it has an obvious correspondence. The allegory of Adam and Eve eating of the tree of evil, and entailing upon their posterity the wrath of God, and the loss of everlasting life, admits of no other explanation than the disease and crime that have flowed from unnatural diet. Milton was so well aware of this, that he makes Raphael thus exhibit to Adam the consequence of his disobedience.

> ———————————— Immediately a place
> Before his eyes appeared: sad, noisome, dark:
> A lazar-house it seem'd; wherein were laid
> Numbers of all diseased: all maladies
> 5 Of ghastly spasm, or racking torture, qualms
> Of heart-sick agony, all feverous kinds,
> Convulsions, epilepsies, fierce catarrhs,
> Intestine stone and ulcer, cholic pangs,
> Dæmoniac frenzy, moping melancholy,
> 10 And moon-struck madness, pining atrophy,
> Marasmus, and wide-wasting pestilence,
> Dropsies, and asthmas, and joint-racking rheums.

---

[4] See Nicholson's *Encyclopedia.*

And how many thousands more might not be added to this frightful catalogue!

The story of Prometheus is one likewise which, although universally admitted to be allegorical, has never been satisfactorily explained. Prometheus stole fire from heaven, and was chained for this crime to mount Caucasus, where a vulture continually devoured his liver, that grew to meet its hunger. Hesiod says, that, before the time of Prometheus, mankind were exempt from suffering; that they enjoyed a vigorous youth, and that death, when at length it came, approached like sleep, and gently closed their eyes. Again, so general was this opinion, that Horace, a poet of the Augustan age, writes—

> Audax omnia perpeti,
> Gens humana ruit per vetitum nefas;
> Audax Iapeti genus
> Ignem fraude mala gentibus intulit:
> 5   Post ignem ætherià domo
> Subductum, macieset nova febrium
>   Terris incubuit cohors,
> Semotique prius tarda necessitas
>   Lethi corripuit gradum.[5]

How plain a language is spoken by all this. Prometheus (who represents the human race) effected some great change in the condition of his nature, and applied fire to culinary purposes; thus inventing an expedient for screening from his disgust the horrors of the shambles. From this moment his vitals were devoured by the vulture of disease. It consumed his being in every shape of its loathsome and infinite variety, inducing the soul-quelling sinkings of premature and violent death. All vice arose from the ruin of healthful innocence. Tyranny, superstition, commerce, and inequality, were then first known, when reason vainly attempted to guide the wanderings of exacerbated passion. I conclude this part of the subject with an extract from Mr. Newton's *Defence of Vegetable Regimen,* from whom I have borrowed this interpretation of the fable of Prometheus.

"Making allowance for such transposition of the events of the allegory as time might produce after the important truths were forgotten, which

---

[5] "The human race, daring to commit every outrage, rushes headlong into forbidden crime; the descendent of Iapetus (i.e., Prometheus) brought fire to the people through a wicked deception. After fire was stolen from the palace of heaven, a new troop of diseases assailed the Earth, and inevitable death, once distant and slow, quickened its pace." *Odes,* 1.3.25–33 [Ed.]

this portion of the ancient mythology was intended to transmit, the drift of the fable seems to be this: Man at his creation was endowed with the gift of perpetual youth; that is, he was not formed to be a sickly suffering creature as we now see him, but to enjoy health, and to sink by slow degrees into the bosom of his parent earth without disease or pain. Prometheus first taught the use of animal food (primus bovem occidit Prometheus[6]) and of fire, with which to render it more digestible and pleasing to the taste. Jupiter, and the rest of the gods, foreseeing the consequences of these inventions, were amused or irritated at the short-sighted devices of the newly-formed creature, and left him to experience the sad effects of them. Thirst, the necessary concomitant of a flesh diet" (perhaps of all diet vitiated by culinary preparation), "ensued; water was resorted to, and man forfeited the inestimable gift of health which he had received from heaven: he became diseased, the partaker of a precarious existence, and no longer descended slowly to his grave."[7]

> But just disease to luxury succeeds,
> And every death its own avenger breeds;
> The fury passions from that blood began,
> And turned on man a fiercer savage — man.

Man, and the animals whom he has infected with his society, or depraved by his dominion, are alone diseased. The wild hog, the mouflon,[8] the bison, and the wolf, are perfectly exempt from malady, and invariably die either from external violence, or natural old age. But the domestic hog, the sheep, the cow, and the dog, are subject to an incredible variety of distempers; and, like the corrupters of their nature, have physicians who thrive upon their miseries. The supereminence of man is like Satan's, a supereminence of pain; and the majority of his species, doomed to penury, disease and crime, have reason to curse the untoward event, that by enabling him to communicate his sensations, raised him above the level of his fellow animals. But the steps that have been taken are irrevocable. The whole of human science is comprised in one question: How can the advantages of intellect and civilization be reconciled with the liberty and pure pleasures of natural life? How can we take the benefits, and reject the evils of the system, which is now interwoven with all the fibres of our being? I believe that abstinence from animal food and spirituous liquors would in a great measure capacitate us for the solution of this important question.

---

[6] *Plin. Nat. Hist.* lib. vii. sect. 57.

[7] *Return to Nature.* Cadell, 1811.

[8] Breed of Mediterranean sheep. [Ed.]

It is true, that mental and bodily derangement is attributable in part to other deviations from rectitude and nature than those which concern diet. The mistakes cherished by society respecting the connection of the sexes, whence the misery and diseases of unsatisfied celibacy, unenjoying prostitution, and the premature arrival of puberty necessarily spring; the putrid atmosphere of crowded cities; the exhalations of chemical processes; the muffling of our bodies in superfluous apparel; the absurd treatment of infants: all these, and innumerable other causes, contribute their mite to the mass of human evil.

Comparative anatomy teaches us that man resembles frugivorous animals in every thing, and carnivorous in nothing; he has neither claws wherewith to seize his prey, nor distinct and pointed teeth to tear the living fibre. A Mandarin of the first class, with nails two inches long, would probably find them alone inefficient to hold even a hare. After every subterfuge of gluttony, the bull must be degraded into the ox, and the ram into the wether, by an unnatural and inhuman operation, that the flaccid fibre may offer a fainter resistance to rebellious nature. It is only by softening and disguising dead flesh by culinary preparation, that it is rendered susceptible of mastication or digestion; and that the sight of its bloody juices and raw horror does not excite intolerable loathing and disgust. Let the advocate of animal food force himself to a decisive experiment on its fitness, and, as Plutarch recommends, tear a living lamb with his teeth, and plunging his head into its vitals, slake his thirst with the steaming blood; when fresh from the deed of horror, let him revert to the irresistible instincts of nature that would rise in judgment against it, and say, Nature formed me for such work as this. Then, and then only, would he be consistent.

Man resembles no carnivorous animal. There is no exception, unless man be one, to the rule of herbivorous animals having cellulated colons.

The orang-outang perfectly resembles man both in the order and number of his teeth. The orang-outang is the most anthropomorphous of the ape tribe, all of which are strictly frugivorous. There is no other species of animals, which live on different food, in which this analogy exists. In many frugivorous animals, the canine teeth are more pointed and distinct than those of man. The resemblance also of the human stomach to that of the orang-outang, is greater than to that of any other animal.

The intestines are also identical with those of herbivorous animals, which present a larger surface for absorption and have ample and cellulated colons. The caecum also, though short, is larger than that of carnivorous animals; and even here the orang-outang retains its accustomed similarity.

The structure of the human frame then is that of one fitted to a pure vegetable diet, in every essential particular. It is true, that the reluctance to abstain from animal food, in those who have been long accustomed to its stimulus, is so great in some persons of weak minds, as to be scarcely overcome; but this is far from bringing any argument in its favour. A lamb, which was fed for some time on flesh by a ship's crew, refused its natural diet at the end of the voyage. There are numerous instances of horses, sheep, oxen, and even wood-pigeons, having been taught to live upon flesh, until they have loathed their natural aliment. Young children evidently prefer pastry, oranges, apples, and other fruit, to the flesh of animals; until, by the gradual depravation of the digestive organs, the free use of vegetables has for a time produced serious inconveniences; *for a time,* I say, since there never was an instance wherein a change from spirituous liquors and animal food to vegetables and pure water, has failed ultimately to invigorate the body, by rendering its juices bland and consentaneous, and to restore to the mind that cheerfulness and elasticity, which not one in fifty possesses on the present system. A love of strong liquors is also with difficulty taught to infants. Almost every one remembers the wry faces which the first glass of port produced. Unsophisticated instinct is invariably unerring; but to decide on the fitness of animal food, from the perverted appetites which its constrained adoption produces, is to make the criminal a judge in his own cause: it is even worse, it is appealing to the infatuated drunkard in a question of the salubrity of brandy.

What is the cause of morbid action in the animal system? Not the air we breathe, for our fellow denizens of nature breathe the same uninjured; not the water we drink (if remote from the pollutions of man and his inventions,)[9] for the animals drink it too; not the earth we tread upon; not the unobscured sight of glorious nature, in the wood, the field, or the expanse of sky and ocean; nothing that we are or do in common with the undiseased inhabitants of the forest. Something then wherein we differ from them: our habit of altering our food by fire, so that our appetite is no longer a just criterion for the fitness of its gratification. Except in children, there remain no traces of that instinct which determines, in all other animals, what aliment is natural or otherwise; and so perfectly obliterated are they in the reasoning adults of our species, that it has become necessary to urge considerations drawn from comparative anatomy to prove that we are naturally frugivorous.[. . .]

---

[9] The necessity of resorting to some means of purifying water, and the disease which arises from its adulteration in civilized countries, is sufficiently apparent — See Dr. Lambe's *Reports on Cancer.* I do not assert that the use of water is in itself unnatural, but that the unperverted palate would swallow no liquid capable of occasioning disease.

From History of a Six Weeks' Tour
LETTER TO T. P. [THOMAS PEACOCK] ESQ.
St. Martin—Servoz—Chamouni—
Montanvert—Mont Blanc.

Hôtel de Londres, Chamouni,
July 22d, 1816.

Whilst you, my friend, are engaged in securing a home for us, we are wandering in search of recollections to embellish it. I do not err in conceiving that you are interested in details of all that is majestic or beautiful in nature; but how shall I describe to you the scenes by which I am now surrounded? To exhaust the epithets which express the astonishment and the admiration—the very excess of satisfied astonishment, where expectation scarcely acknowledged any boundary, is this, to impress upon your mind the images which fill mine now even till it overflow? I too have read the raptures of travellers; I will be warned by their example; I will simply detail to you all that I can relate, or all that, if related, would enable you to conceive of what we have done or seen since the morning of the 20th, when we left Geneva.

We commenced our intended journey to Chamouni at half-past eight in the morning. We passed through the champain country, which extends from Mont Salêve to the base of the higher Alps. The country is sufficiently fertile, covered with corn fields and orchards, and intersected by sudden acclivities with flat summits. The day was cloudless and excessively hot, the Alps were perpetually in sight, and as we advanced, the mountains, which form their outskirts, closed in around us. We passed a bridge over a stream, which discharges itself into the Arve. The Arve itself, much swollen by the rains, flows constantly to the right of the road.

As we approached Bonneville through an avenue composed of a beautiful species of drooping poplar, we observed that the corn fields on each side were covered with inundation. Bonneville is a neat little town, with no conspicuous peculiarity, except the white towers of the prison, an extensive building overlooking the town. At Bonneville the Alps commence, one of which, clothed by forests, rises almost immediately from the opposite bank of the Arve.

From Bonneville to Cluses the road conducts through a spacious and fertile plain, surrounded on all sides by mountains, covered like those of Mellerie with forests of intermingled pine and chesnut. At Cluses the road

---

Mary Shelley (and Percy Bysshe Shelley), *History of a Six Weeks' Tour.* London: Hookham and Ollier, 1817.

turns suddenly to the right, following the Arve along the chasm, which it seems to have hollowed for itself among the perpendicular mountains. The scene assumes here a more savage and colossal character: the valley becomes narrow, affording no more space than is sufficient for the river and the road. The pines descend to the banks, imitating with their irregular spires, the pyramidal crags which lift themselves far above the regions of forest into the deep azure of the sky, and among the white dazzling clouds. The scene, at the distance of half a mile from Cluses, differs from that of Matlock in little else than in the immensity of its proportions, and in its untameable, inaccessible solitude, inhabited only by the goats which we saw browsing on the rocks.

Near Maglans, within a league of each other, we saw two waterfalls. They were no more than mountain rivulets, but the height from which they fell, at least of *twelve* hundred feet, made them assume a character inconsistent with the smallness of their stream. The first fell from the overhanging brow of a black precipice on an enormous rock, precisely resembling some colossal Egyptian statue of a female deity. It struck the head of the visionary image, and gracefully dividing there, fell from it in folds of foam more like to cloud than water, imitating a veil of the most exquisite woof. It then united, concealing the lower part of the statue, and hiding itself in a winding of its channel, burst into a deeper fall, and crossed our route in its path towards the Arve.

The other waterfall was more continuous and larger. The violence with which it fell made it look more like some shape which an exhalation had assumed, than like water, for it streamed beyond the mountain, which appeared dark behind it, as it might have appeared behind an evanescent cloud.

The character of the scenery continued the same until we arrived at St. Martin (called in the maps Sallanches) the mountains perpetually becoming more elevated, exhibiting at every turn of the road more craggy summits, loftier and wider extent of forests, darker and more deep recesses.

The following morning we proceeded from St. Martin on mules to Chamouni, accompanied by two guides. We proceeded, as we had done the preceding day, along the valley of the Arve, a valley surrounded on all sides by immense mountains, whose rugged precipices are intermixed on high with dazzling snow. Their bases were still covered with the eternal forests, which perpetually grew darker and more profound as we approached the inner regions of the mountains.

On arriving at a small village, at the distance of a league from St. Martin, we dismounted from our mules, and were conducted by our guides to view a cascade. We beheld an immense body of water fall two hundred and fifty feet, dashing from rock to rock, and casting a spray which formed a mist around it, in the midst of which hung a multitude of sunbows, which faded or became unspeakably vivid, as the inconstant sun shone through the clouds. When we approached near to it, the rain of the spray reached us, and our clothes were wetted by the quick-falling but minute particles of water. The cataract fell from above into a deep craggy chasm at our feet, where, changing its character to that of a mountain stream, it pursued its course towards the Arve, roaring over the rocks that impeded its progress.

As we proceeded, our route still lay through the valley, or rather, as it had now become, the vast ravine, which is at once the couch and the creation of the terrible Arve. We ascended, winding between mountains whose immensity staggers the imagination. We crossed the path of a torrent, which three days since had descended from the thawing snow, and torn the road away.

We dined at Servoz, a little village, where there are lead and copper mines, and where we saw a cabinet of natural curiosities, like those of Keswick and Bethgelert. We saw in this cabinet some chamois' horns, and the horns of an exceedingly rare animal called the bouquetin, which inhabits the desarts of snow to the south of Mont Blanc: it is an animal of the stag kind; its horns weigh at least twenty-seven English pounds. It is inconceivable how so small an animal could support so inordinate a weight. The horns are of a very peculiar conformation, being broad, massy, and pointed at the ends, and surrounded with a number of rings, which are supposed to afford an indication of its age: there were seventeen rings on the largest of these horns.

From Servoz three leagues remain to Chamouni. Mont Blanc was before us—the Alps, with their innumerable glaciers on high all around, closing in the complicated windings of the single vale—forests inexpressibly beautiful, but majestic in their beauty—intermingled beech and pine, and oak, overshadowed our road, or receded, whilst lawns of such verdure as I have never seen before occupied these openings, and gradually became darker in their recesses. Mont Blanc was before us, but it was covered with cloud; its base, furrowed with dreadful gaps, was seen above. Pinnacles of snow intolerably bright, part of the chain connected with Mont Blanc, shone through the clouds at intervals on high. I never knew—I never imagined what mountains were before. The immensity of these aerial summits excited, when they suddenly burst upon the sight, a sentiment of extatic wonder, not unallied to madness. And remember this was all one scene, it all pressed home to our regard and our imagination. Though it embraced a vast extent of space, the snowy pyramids which shot into the bright blue sky seemed to overhang our path; the ravine, clothed with gigantic pines, and black with its depth below, so deep that the very roaring of the untameable Arve, which rolled through it, could not be heard above—all was as much our own, as if we had been the creators of such impressions in the minds of others as now occupied our own. Nature was the poet, whose harmony held our spirits more breathless than that of the divinest.

As we entered the valley of Chamouni (which in fact may be considered as a continuation of those which we have followed from Bonneville and Cluses) clouds hung upon the mountains at the distance perhaps of 6000 feet from the earth, but so as effectually to conceal not only Mont Blanc, but the other *aiguilles,* as they call them here, attached and subordinate to it. We were travelling along the valley, when suddenly we heard a sound as of the burst of smothered thunder rolling above; yet there was something earthly in the sound, that told us it could not be thunder. Our guide hastily pointed out to us a part of the mountain opposite, from whence the sound came. It was an avalanche. We saw the smoke of its path among the rocks, and continued to hear at intervals the bursting of its fall. It fell on the bed of a torrent, which it displaced, and presently we saw its tawny-coloured waters also spread themselves over the ravine, which was their couch.

We did not, as we intended, visit the *Glacier de Boisson* to-day, although it descends within a few minutes' walk of the road, wishing to survey it at least when unfatigued. We saw this glacier which comes close to the fertile plain, as we passed, its surface was broken into a thousand unaccountable figures: conical and pyramidical crystalizations, more than fifty feet in height, rise from its surface, and precipices of ice, of dazzling splendour, overhang the woods and meadows of the vale. This glacier winds upwards from the valley, until it joins the masses of frost from which it was produced above, winding through its own ravine like a bright belt flung over the black region of pines. There is more in all these scenes than mere magnitude of proportion: there is a majesty of outline; there is an awful grace in the very colours which invest these wonderful shapes—a charm which is peculiar to them, quite distinct even from the reality of their unutterable greatness.

July 24.

Yesterday morning we went to the source of the Arveiron. It is about a league from this village; the river rolls forth impetuously from an arch of ice, and spreads itself in many streams over a vast space of the valley, ravaged and laid bare by its inundations. The glacier by which its waters are nourished, overhangs this cavern and the plain, and the forests of pine which surround it, with terrible precipices of solid ice. On the other side rises the immense glacier of Montanvert, fifty miles in extent, occupying a chasm among mountains of inconceivable height, and of forms so pointed and abrupt, that they seem to pierce the sky. From this glacier we saw as we sat on a rock, close to one of the streams of the Arveiron, masses of ice detach themselves from on high, and rush with a loud dull noise into the vale. The violence of their fall turned them into powder, which flowed over the rocks in imitation of waterfalls, whose ravines they usurped and filled.

In the evening I went with Ducree, my guide, the only tolerable person I have seen in this country, to visit the glacier of Boisson. This glacier, like that of Montanvert, comes close to the vale, overhanging the green meadows and the dark woods with the dazzling whiteness of its precipices and pinnacles, which are like spires of radiant crystal, covered with a net-work of frosted silver. These glaciers flow perpetually into the valley, ravaging in their slow but irresistible progress the pastures and the forests which surround them, performing a work of desolation in ages, which a river of lava might accomplish in an hour, but far more irretrievably; for where the ice has once descended, the hardiest plant refuses to grow; if even, as in some extraordinary instances, it should recede after its progress has once commenced. The glaciers perpetually move onward, at the rate of a foot each day, with a motion that commences at the spot where, on the boundaries of perpetual congelation, they are produced by the freezing of the waters which arise from the partial melting of the eternal snows. They drag with them from the regions whence they derive their origin, all the ruins of the mountain, enormous rocks, and immense accumulations of sand and stones. These are driven onwards by the irresistible stream of solid ice; and when they arrive at a declivity of the mountain, sufficiently rapid, roll down, scattering ruin. I saw one of these rocks which had descended in the spring, (winter here is the season of silence and safety) which measured forty feet in every direction.

The verge of a glacier, like that of Boisson, presents the most vivid image of desolation that it is possible to conceive. No one dares to approach it; for the enormous pinnacles of ice which perpetually fall, are perpetually reproduced. The pines of the forest, which bound it at one extremity, are overthrown and shattered to a wide extent at its base. There is something inexpressibly dreadful in the aspect of the few branchless trunks, which, nearest to the ice rifts, still stand in the uprooted soil. The meadows perish, overwhelmed with sand and stones. Within this last year, these glaciers have advanced three hundred feet into the valley. Saussure,[10] the naturalist, says, that they have their periods of increase and decay: the people of the country hold an opinion entirely different; but as I judge, more probable. It is agreed by all, that the snow on the summit of Mont Blanc and the

---

[10]H. B. Saussure, Swiss naturalist and physicist (1740–99). [Ed.]

neighbouring mountains perpetually augments, and that ice, in the form of glaciers, subsists without melting in the valley of Chamouni during its transient and variable summer. If the snow which produces this glacier must augment, and the heat of the valley is no obstacle to the perpetual existence of such masses of ice as have already descended into it, the consequence is obvious; the glaciers must augment and will subsist, at least until they have overflowed this vale.

I will not pursue Buffon's sublime but gloomy theory—that this globe which we inhabit will at some future period be changed into a mass of frost by the encroachments of the polar ice, and of that produced on the most elevated points of the earth. Do you, who assert the supremacy of Ahriman,[11] imagine him throned among these desolating snows, among these palaces of death and frost, so sculptured in this their terrible magnificence by the adamantine hand of necessity, and that he casts around him, as the first essays of his final usurpation, avalanches, torrents, rocks, and thunders, and above all these deadly glaciers, at once the proof and symbols of his reign; add to this, the degradation of the human species—who in these regions are half deformed or idiotic, and most of whom are deprived of any thing that can excite interest or admiration. This is a part of the subject more mournful and less sublime; but such as neither the poet nor the philosopher should disdain to regard.

This morning we departed, on the promise of a fine day, to visit the glacier of Montanvert. In that part where it fills a slanting valley, it is called the Sea of Ice. This valley is 950 toises, or 7600 feet above the level of the sea. We had not proceeded far before the rain began to fall, but we persisted until we had accomplished more than half of our journey, when we returned, wet through.

Chamouni, July 25th.

We have returned from visiting the glacier of Montanvert, or as it is called, the Sea of Ice,[12] a scene in truth of dizzying wonder. The path that winds to it along the side of a mountain, now clothed with pines, now intersected with snowy hollows, is wide and steep. The cabin of Montanvert is three leagues from Chamouni, half of which distance is performed on mules, not so sure footed, but that on the first day the one which I rode fell in what the guides call a *mauvais pas,* so that I narrowly escaped being precipitated down the mountain. We passed over a hollow covered with

---

[11] Evil deity in Zoroastrian theology. [Ed.]

[12] The spot where Mary Shelley's fictional creature will confront his creator for the first time. [Ed.]

snow, down which vast stones are accustomed to roll. One had fallen the preceding day, a little time after we had returned: our guides desired us to pass quickly, for it is said that sometimes the least sound will accelerate their descent. We arrived at Montanvert, however, safe.

On all sides precipitous mountains, the abodes of unrelenting frost, surround this vale: their sides are banked up with ice and snow, broken, heaped high, and exhibiting terrific chasms. The summits are sharp and naked pinnacles, whose overhanging steepness will not even permit snow to rest upon them. Lines of dazzling ice occupy here and there their perpendicular rifts, and shine through the driving vapours with inexpressible brilliance: they pierce the clouds like things not belonging to this earth. The vale itself is filled with a mass of undulating ice, and has an ascent sufficiently gradual even to the remotest abysses of these horrible desarts. It is only half a league (about two miles) in breadth, and seems much less. It exhibits an appearance as if frost had suddenly bound up the waves and whirlpools of a mighty torrent. We walked some distance upon its surface. The waves are elevated about 12 or 15 feet from the surface of the mass, which is intersected by long gaps of unfathomable depth, the ice of whose sides is more beautifully azure than the sky. In these regions every thing changes, and is in motion. This vast mass of ice has one general progress, which ceases neither day nor night; it breaks and bursts for ever: some undulations sink while others rise; it is never the same. The echo of rocks, or of the ice and snow which fall from their overhanging precipices, or roll from their aerial summits, scarcely ceases for one moment. One would think that Mont Blanc, like the god of the Stoics, was a vast animal, and that the frozen blood for ever circulated through his stony veins.

We dined (M[ary], C[laire], and I) on the grass, in the open air, surrounded by this scene. The air is piercing and clear. We returned down the mountain, sometimes encompassed by the driving vapours, sometimes cheered by the sunbeams, and arrived at our inn by seven o'clock.

Montalegre, July 28th.

The next morning we returned through the rain to St. Martin. The scenery had lost something of its immensity, thick clouds hanging over the highest mountains; but visitings of sunset intervened between the showers, and the blue sky shone between the accumulated clouds of snowy whiteness which brought them; the dazzling mountains sometimes glittered through a chasm of the clouds above our heads, and all the charm of its grandeur remained. We repassed *Pont Pellisier,* a wooden bridge over the Arve, and the ravine of the Arve. We repassed the pine forests which overhang the defile, the chateau of St. Michel, a haunted ruin, built on the edge of a precipice, and shadowed over by the eternal forest. We repassed the vale of Servoz, a vale more beautiful, because more luxuriant, than that of Chamouni. Mont Blanc forms one of the sides of this vale also, and the other is inclosed by an irregular amphitheatre of enormous mountains, one of which is in ruins, and fell fifty years ago into the higher part of the valley: the smoke of its fall was seen in Piedmont, and people went from Turin to investigate whether a volcano had not burst forth among the Alps. It continued falling many days, spreading, with the shock and thunder of its ruin, consternation into the neighbouring vales. In the evening we arrived at St. Martin. The next day we wound through the valley, which I have described before, and arrived in the evening at our home.

We have bought some specimens of minerals and plants, and two or three crystal seals, at Mont Blanc, to preserve the remembrance of having approached it. There is a cabinet of *Histoire Naturelle* at Chamouni, just as at Keswick, Matlock, and Clifton; the proprietor of which is the very vilest specimen of that vile species of quack that, together with the whole army of aubergistes and guides, and indeed the entire mass of the population, subsist on the weakness and credulity of travellers as leaches subsist on the sick. The most interesting of my purchases is a large collection of all the seeds of rare alpine plants, with their names written upon the outside of the papers that contain them. These I mean to colonize in my garden in England, and to permit you to make what choice you please from them. They are companions which the Celandine—the classic Celandine, need not despise; they are as wild and more daring than he, and will tell him tales of things even as touching and sublime as the gaze of a vernal poet.

Did I tell you that there are troops of wolves among these mountains? In the winter they descend into the vallies, which the snow occupies six months of the year, and devour every thing that they can find out of doors. A wolf is more powerful than the fiercest and strongest dog. There are no bears in these regions. We heard, when we were at Lucerne, that they were occasionally found in the forests which surround that lake. Adieu.

From Poetical Works

Ode to the West Wind[13]

I.

O Wild West Wind, thou breath of Autumn's being,
Thou, from whose unseen presence the leaves dead
Are driven, like ghosts from an enchanter fleeing,

Yellow, and black, and pale, and hectic red,
5 Pestilence-stricken multitudes: O thou,
Who chariotest to their dark wintry bed

The winged seeds, where they lie cold and low,
Each like a corpse within its grave, until
Thine azure sister of the spring shall blow

10 Her clarion o'er the dreaming earth, and fill
(Driving sweet buds like flocks to feed in air)
With living hues and odours plain and hill:

Wild Spirit, which are moving every where;
Destroyer and preserver; hear, oh hear!

II.

15 Thou on whose stream, 'mid the steep sky's commotion,
Loose clouds like earth's decaying leaves are shed,
Shook from the tangled boughs of Heaven and Ocean,

Percy Bysshe Shelley, *Poetical Works.* Ed. Mary Shelley. London: Moxon, 1839.

[13]This poem was conceived and chiefly written in a wood that skirts the Arno, near Florence, and on a day when that tempestuous wind, whose temperature is at once mild and animating, was collecting the vapours which pour down the autumnal rains. They began, as I foresaw, at sunset, with a violent tempest of hail and rain, attended by that magnificent thunder and lightning peculiar to the Cisalpine regions.

The phenomenon alluded to at the conclusion of the third stanza is well known to naturalists. The vegetation at the bottom of the sea, of rivers, and of lakes, sympathises with that of the land in the change of seasons, and is consequently influenced by the winds which announce it.

Angels of rain and lightning: there are spread
On the blue surface of thine airy surge,
20 Like the bright hair uplifted from the head

Of some fierce Mænad, even from the dim verge
Of the horizon to the zenith's height
The locks of the approaching storm. Thou dirge

Of the dying year, to which this closing night
25 Will be the dome of a vast sepulchre,
Vaulted with all thy congregated might

Of vapours, from whose solid atmosphere
Black rain, and fire, and hail, will burst: Oh hear!

III.

Thou who didst waken from his summer dreams
30 The blue Mediterranean, where he lay,
Lulled by the coil of his crystalline streams,

Beside a pumice isle in Baiæ's bay,
And saw in sleep old palaces and towers
Quivering within the wave's intenser day,

35 All overgrown with azure moss and flowers
So sweet, the sense faints picturing them! Thou
For whose path the Atlantic's level powers

Cleave themselves into chasms, while far below
The sea-blooms and the oozy woods which wear
40 The sapless foliage of the ocean, know

Thy voice, and suddenly grow grey with fear,
And tremble and despoil themselves: Oh hear!

IV.

If I were a dead leaf thou mightest bear;
If I were a swift cloud to fly with thee;
45 A wave to pant beneath thy power, and share

The impulse of thy strength, only less free
Than thou, O uncontrollable! If even
I were as in my boyhood, and could be

The comrade of thy wanderings over heaven,
50 As then, when to outstrip thy skyey speed
Scarce seemed a vision, I would ne'er have striven

As thus with thee in prayer in my sore need.
Oh! lift me as a wave, a leaf, a cloud!
I fall upon the thorns of life! I bleed!

55 A heavy weight of hours has chained and bowed
One too like thee: tameless, and swift, and proud.

V.

Make me thy lyre, even as the forest is:
What if my leaves are falling like its own!
The tumult of thy mighty harmonies

60 Will take from both a deep autumnal tone,
Sweet though in sadness. Be thou, spirit fierce,
My spirit! Be thou me, impetuous one!

Drive my dead thoughts over the universe
Like withered leaves to quicken a new birth;
65 And, by the incantation of this verse, .

Scatter, as from an unextinguished hearth
Ashes and sparks, my words among mankind!
Be through my lips to unawakened earth

The trumpet of a prophecy! O wind,
70 If Winter comes, can Spring be far behind?

The Sensitive Plant

Part I

A Sensitive Plant in a garden grew,
And the young winds fed it with silver dew,
And it opened its fan-like leaves to the light,
And closed them beneath the kisses of night.

5 And the Spring arose on the garden fair,
And the Spirit of Love felt every where;
And each flower and herb on Earth's dark breast
Rose from the dreams of its wintry rest.

But none ever trembled and panted with bliss
10 In the garden, the field, or the wilderness,
Like a doe in the noon-tide with love's sweet want,
As the companionless Sensitive Plant.

The snow-drop, and then the violet,
Arose from the ground with warm rain wet,
15 And their breath was mixed with fresh odour, sent
From the turf, like the voice and the instrument.

Then the pied wind-flowers and the tulip tall,
And narcissi, the fairest among them all,
Who gaze on their eyes in the stream's recess,
20 Till they die of their own dear loveliness;

And the Naiad-like lily of the vale,
Whom youth makes so fair and passion so pale,
That the light of its tremulous bells is seen
Through their pavilions of tender green;

25 And the hyacinth purple, and white, and blue,
Which flung from its bells a sweet peal anew
Of music so delicate, soft, and intense,
It was felt like an odour within the sense;

And the rose like a nymph to the bath addrest,
30 Which unveiled the depth of her glowing breast,
Till, fold after fold, to the fainting air
The soul of her beauty and love lay bare:

And the wand-like lily, which lifted up,
As a Mænad, its moonlight-coloured cup,
35 Till the fiery star, which is its eye,
Gazed through clear dew on the tender sky;

And the jessamine faint, and the sweet tuberose,
The sweetest flower for scent that blows;
And all rare blossoms from every clime
40 Grew in that garden in perfect prime.

And on the stream whose inconstant bosom
Was prankt under boughs of embowering blossom,
With golden and green light, slanting through
Their heaven of many a tangled hue,

45 Broad water-lilies lay tremulously,
And starry river-buds glimmered by,

And around them the soft stream did glide and dance
With a motion of sweet sound and radiance.

And the sinuous paths of lawn and of moss,
50 Which led through the garden along and across,
Some open at once to the sun and the breeze,
Some lost among bowers of blossoming trees,

Were all paved with daisies and delicate bells
As fair as the fabulous asphodels,
55 And flowrets which drooping as day drooped too,
Fell into pavilions, white, purple, and blue,
To roof the glow-worm from the evening dew.

And from this undefiled Paradise
The flowers (as an infant's awakening eyes
60 Smile on its mother, whose singing sweet
Can first lull, and at last must awaken it),

When Heaven's blithe winds had unfolded them,
As mine-lamps enkindle a hidden gem,
Shone smiling to Heaven, and every one
65 Shared joy in the light of the gentle sun;

For each one was interpenetrated
With the light and the odour its neighbour shed,
Like young lovers whom youth and love make dear,
Wrapped and filled by their mutual atmosphere.

70 But the Sensitive Plant which could give small fruit
Of the love which it felt from the leaf to the root,
Received more than all, it loved more than ever,
Where none wanted but it, could belong to the giver—

For the Sensitive Plant has no bright flower;
75 Radiance and odour are not its dower;
It loves, even like Love, its deep heart is full,
It desires what it has not, the beautiful!

The light winds which from unsustaining wings
Shed the music of many murmurings;
80 The beams which dart from many a star
Of the flowers whose hues they bear afar;

The plumed insects swift and free,
Like golden boats on a sunny sea,

Laden with light and odour, which pass
85 Over the gleam of the living grass;

The unseen clouds of the dew, which lie
Like fire in the flowers till the sun rides high,
Then wander like spirits among the spheres,
Each cloud faint with the fragrance it bears;

90 The quivering vapours of dim noontide,
Which, like a sea o'er the warm earth glide,
In which every sound, and odour, and beam,
Move, as reeds in a single stream;

Each and all like ministering angels were
95 For the Sensitive Plant sweet joy to bear,
Whilst the lagging hours of the day went by
Like windless clouds o'er a tender sky.

And when evening descended from heaven above,
And the Earth was all rest, and the air was all love,
100 And delight, though less bright, was far more deep,
And the day's veil fell from the world of sleep,

And the beasts, and the birds, and the insects were drowned
In an ocean of dreams without a sound;
Whose waves never mark, though they ever impress
105 The light sand which paves it, consciousness;

(Only over head the sweet nightingale
Ever sang more sweet as the day might fail,
And snatches of its Elysian chant
Were mixed with the dreams of the Sensitive Plant.)

110 The Sensitive Plant was the earliest
Up-gathered into the bosom of rest;
A sweet child weary of its delight,
The feeblest and yet the favourite,
Cradled within the embrace of night.

PART II

115 There was a Power in this sweet place,
An Eve in this Eden; a ruling grace
Which to the flowers, did they waken or dream,
Was as God is to the starry scheme.

A Lady, the wonder of her kind,
120 Whose form was upborne by a lovely mind

Which, dilating, had moulded her mien and motion
Like a sea-flower unfolded beneath the ocean,

Tended the garden from morn to even:
And the meteors of that sublunar heaven,
125 Like the lamps of the air when night walks forth,
Laughed round her footsteps up from the Earth!

She had no companion of mortal race,
But her tremulous breath and her flushing face
Told, whilst the morn kissed the sleep from her eyes,
130 That her dreams were less slumber than Paradise:

As if some bright Spirit for her sweet sake
Had deserted heaven while the stars were awake,
As if yet around her he lingering were,
Though the veil of daylight concealed him from her.

135 Her step seemed to pity the grass it prest;
You might hear, by the heaving of her breast,
That the coming and the going of the wind
Brought pleasure there and left passion behind.

And wherever her airy footstep trod,
140 Her trailing hair from the grassy sod
Erased its light vestige, with shadowy sweep,
Like a sunny storm o'er the dark green deep.

I doubt not the flowers of that garden sweet
Rejoiced in the sound of her gentle feet;
145 I doubt not they felt the spirit that came
From her glowing fingers through all their frame.

She sprinkled bright water from the stream
On those that were faint with the sunny beam;
And out of the cups of the heavy flowers
150 She emptied the rain of the thunder showers.

She lifted their heads with her tender hands,
And sustained them with rods and osier bands;
If the flowers had been her own infants, she
Could never have nursed them more tenderly.

155 And all killing insects and gnawing worms,
And things of obscene and unlovely forms,
She bore in a basket of Indian woof,
Into the rough woods far aloof,

In a basket, of grasses and wild flowers full,
160 The freshest her gentle hands could pull
For the poor banished insects, whose intent,
Although they did ill, was innocent.

But the bee and the beamlike ephemeris,
Whose path is the lightning's, and soft moths that kiss
165 The sweet lips of the flowers, and harm not, did she
Make her attendant angels be.

And many an antenatal tomb,
Where butterflies dream of the life to come,
She left clinging round the smooth and dark
170 Edge of the odorous cedar bark.

This fairest creature from earliest spring
Thus moved through the garden ministering
All the sweet season of summer tide,
And ere the first leaf looked brown—she died!

Part III

175 Three days the flowers of the garden fair,
Like stars when the moon is awakened, were,
Or the waves of Baiæ, ere luminous
She floats up through the smoke of Vesuvius.

And on the fourth, the Sensitive Plant
180 Felt the sound of the funeral chaunt,
And the steps of the bearers, heavy and slow,
And the sobs of the mourners deep and low;

The weary sound and the heavy breath,
And the silent motions of passing death,
185 And the smell, cold, oppressive, and dank,
Sent through the pores of the coffin plank;

The dark grass, and the flowers among the grass,
Were bright with tears as the crowd did pass;
From their sighs the wind caught a mournful tone,
190 And sate in the pines and gave groan for groan.

The garden, once fair, became cold and foul,
Like the corpse of her who had been its soul;
Which at first was lovely as if in sleep,
Then slowly changed, till it grew a heap
195 To make men tremble who never weep.

Swift summer into the autumn flowed,
And frost in the mist of the morning rode,
Though the noon-day sun looked clear and bright,
Mocking the spoil of the secret night.

200 The rose leaves, like flakes of crimson snow
Paved the turf and the moss below.
The lilies were drooping, and white, and wan,
Like the head and the skin of a dying man.

And Indian plants, of scent and hue
205 The sweetest that ever were fed on dew,
Leaf after leaf, day by day,
Were massed into the common clay.

And the leaves, brown, yellow, and grey, and red,
And white with the whiteness of what is dead,
210 Like troops of ghosts on the dry wind past;
Their whistling noise made the birds aghast.

And the gusty winds waked the winged seeds
Out of their birth-place of ugly weeds,
Till they clung round many a sweet flower's stem,
215 Which rotted into the earth with them.

The water-blooms under the rivulet
Fell from the stalks on which they were set;
And the eddies drove them here and there,
As the winds did those of the upper air.

220 Then the rain came down, and the broken stalks
Were bent and tangled across the walks;
And the leafless net-work of parasite bowers
Massed into ruin, and all sweet flowers.

Between the time of the wind and the snow,
225 All loathliest weeds began to grow,
Whose coarse leaves were splashed with many a speck,
Like the water-snake's belly and the toad's back.

And thistles, and nettles, and darnels rank,
And the dock, and henbane, and hemlock dank,
230 Stretch'd out its long and hollow shank,
And stifled the air till the dead wind stank.

And plants, at whose names the verse feels loath,
Filled the place with a monstrous undergrowth,

Prickly, and pulpous, and blistering, and blue,
235 Livid, and starred with a lurid dew.

And agarics and fungi, with mildew and mould,
Started like mist from the wet ground cold;
Pale, fleshy, as if the decaying dead
With a spirit of growth had been animated!

240 Spawn, weeds, and filth, a leprous scum,
Made the running rivulet thick and dumb,
And at its outlet, flags huge as stakes
Dammed it up with roots knotted like water-snakes.

And hour by hour, when the air was still,
245 The vapours arose which have strength to kill:
At morn they were seen, at noon they were felt,
At night they were darkness no star could melt.

And unctuous meteors from spray to spray
Crept and flitted in broad noon-day
250 Unseen; every branch on which they alit
By a venomous blight was burned and bit.

The Sensitive Plant, like one forbid,
Wept, and the tears within each lid
Of its folded leaves, which together grew,
255 Were changed to a blight of frozen glue.

For the leaves soon fell, and the branches soon
By the heavy axe of the blast were hewn;
The sap shrank to the root through every pore,
As blood to a heart that will beat no more.

260 For Winter came: the wind was his whip:
One choppy finger was on his lip:
He had torn the cataracts from the hills,
And they clanked at his girdle like manacles;

His breath was a chain which without a sound
265 The earth, and the air, and the water bound;
He came, fiercely driven in his chariot-throne
By the tenfold blasts of the arctic zone.

Then the weeds which were forms of living death
Fled from the frost to the earth beneath.
270 Their decay and sudden flight from frost
Was but like the vanishing of a ghost!

And under the roots of the Sensitive Plant
The moles and the dormice died for want:
The birds dropped stiff from the frozen air,
275 And were caught in the branches naked and bare.

First there came down a thawing rain,
And its dull drops froze on the boughs again,
Then there steamed up a freezing dew
Which to the drops of the thaw-rain grew;

280 And a northern whirlwind, wandering about
Like a wolf that had smelt a dead child out,
Shook the boughs thus laden, and heavy and stiff,
And snapped them off with his rigid griff.

When winter had gone and spring came back,
285 The Sensitive Plant was a leafless wreck;
But the mandrakes, and toadstools, and docks, and darnels,
Rose like the dead from their ruined charnels.

CONCLUSION

Whether the Sensitive Plant, or that
Which within its boughs like a spirit sat
290 Ere its outward form had known decay,
Now felt this change, I cannot say.

Whether that lady's gentle mind,
No longer with the form combined
Which scattered love, as stars do light,
295 Found sadness, where it left delight,

I dare not guess; but in this life
Of error, ignorance and strife,
Where nothing is, but all things seem,
And we the shadows of the dream,

300 It is a modest creed, and yet
Pleasant, if one considers it,
To own that death itself must be,
Like all the rest, a mockery.

That garden sweet, that lady fair,
305 And all sweet shapes and odours there,
In truth have never passed away:
'Tis we, 'tis ours, are changed; not they.

For love, and beauty, and delight,
There is no death nor change: their might
310 Exceeds our organs, which endure
No light, being themselves obscure.

The Cloud

Horatian ode

I.

I bring fresh showers for the thirsting flowers,
    From the seas and the streams;
I bear light shades for the leaves when laid
    In their noon-day dreams.
5 From my wings are shaken the dews that waken
    The sweet buds every one,
When rocked to rest on their mother's breast,
    As she dances about the sun.
I wield the flail of the lashing hail,
10   And whiten the green plains under,
And then again I dissolve it in rain,
    And laugh as I pass in thunder.

II.

I sift the snow on the mountains below,
    And their great pines groan aghast;
15 And all the night 'tis my pillow white,
    While I sleep in the arms of the blast.
Sublime on the towers of my skiey bowers,
    Lightning my pilot sits,
In a cavern under is fettered the thunder,
20   It struggles and howls at fits;
Over earth and ocean with gentle motion,
    This pilot is guiding me,
Lured by the love of the genii that move
    In the depths of the purple sea;
25 Over the rills, and the crags, and the hills,
    Over the lakes and the plains,
Wherever he dream, under mountain or stream,
    The Spirit he loves remains;
And I all the while bask in heaven's blue smile,
30   Whilst he is dissolving in rains.

III.

The sanguine sunrise, with his meteor eyes,
    And his burning plumes outspread,
Leaps on the back of my sailing rack,
    When the morning star shines dead.
35 As on the jag of a mountain crag,
    Which an earthquake rocks and swings,
An eagle alit one moment may sit
    In the light of its golden wings.
And when sunset may breathe, from the lit sea beneath,
40   Its ardours of rest and of love,
And the crimson pall of eve may fall
    From the depth of heaven above,
With wings folded I rest, on mine airy nest,
    As still as a brooding dove.

IV.

45 That orbed maiden, with white fire laden,
    Whom mortals call the moon,
Glides glimmering o'er my fleece-like floor,
    By the midnight breezes strewn;
And wherever the beat of her unseen feet,
50   Which only the angels hear,
May have broken the woof of my tent's thin roof,
    The stars peep behind her and peer;
And I laugh to see them whirl and flee,
    Like a swarm of golden bees,
55 When I widen the rent in my wind-built tent,
    Till the calm rivers, lakes, and seas,
Like strips of the sky fallen through me on high,
    Are each paved with the moon and these.

V.

I bind the sun's throne with the burning zone,
60   And the moon's with a girdle of pearl;
The volcanoes are dim, and the stars reel and swim,
    When the whirlwinds my banner unfurl.

From cape to cape, with a bridge-like shape,
    Over a torrent sea,
65 Sunbeam-proof, I hang like a roof,
    The mountains its columns be.
The triumphal arch through which I march
    With hurricane, fire, and snow,
When the powers of the air are chained to my chair,
70   Is the million-coloured bow;
The sphere-fire above its soft colours wove,
    While the moist earth was laughing below.

VI.

I am the daughter of earth and water,
    And the nursling of the sky:
75 I pass through the pores of the ocean and shores;
    I change, but I cannot die.
For after the rain, when with never a stain,
    The pavilion of heaven is bare,
And the winds and sunbeams with their convex gleams,
80   Build up the blue dome of air,
I silently laugh at my own cenotaph,
    And out of the caverns of rain,
Like a child from the womb, like a ghost from the tomb,
    I arise and unbuild it again.

To a Skylark

I.

Hail to thee, blithe spirit!
    Bird thou never wert,
    That from heaven, or near it,
      Pourest thy full heart,
5 In profuse strains of unpremeditated art.

II.

Higher still and higher,
    From the earth thou springest

216   BRITISH BIRDS.

THE LARK.

Shelley's skylark. Keats calls this high-flying bird the "sky-searching lark." Shelley says that the lark's song is "a flood of rapture." Before the Romantics, John Milton knew that the lark could "startle the dull night," and Shakespeare put this songster "at heaven's gate." This engraving from Bewick (Newcastle, 1832). Archives and Special Collections, Dickinson College, Carlisle, PA.

Like a cloud of fire;
   The blue deep thou wingest,
10 And singing still dost soar, and soaring ever singest.

III.

In the golden lightning
   Of the sunken sun,
O'er which clouds are brightening,
   Thou dost float and run;
15 Like an unbodied joy whose race is just begun.

IV.

The pale purple even
   Melts around thy flight;

Like a star of heaven,
In the broad day-light
20 Thou art unseen, but yet I hear thy shrill delight,

V.

Keen as are the arrows
Of that silver sphere,
Whose intense lamp narrows
In the white dawn clear,
25 Until we hardly see, we feel that it is there.

VI.

All the earth and air
With thy voice is loud,
As, when night is bare,
From one lonely cloud
30 The moon rains out her beams, and heaven is overflowed.

VII.

What thou art we know not;
What is most like thee?
From rainbow clouds there flow not
Drops so bright to see,
35 As from thy presence showers a rain of melody.

VIII.

Like a poet hidden
In the light of thought,
Singing hymns unbidden,
Till the world is wrought
40 To sympathy with hopes and fears it heeded not:

IX.

Like a high-born maiden
In a palace tower,

Soothing her love-laden
Soul in secret hour
45 With music sweet as love, which overflows her bower:

X.

Like a glow-worm golden
In a dell of dew,
Scattering unbeholden
Its aërial hue
50 Among the flowers and grass, which screen it from the view:

XI.

Like a rose embowered
In its own green leaves,
By warm winds deflowered,
Till the scent it gives
55 Makes faint with too much sweet these heavy-winged thieves.

XII.

Sound of vernal showers
On the twinkling grass,
Rain-awakened flowers,
All that ever was
60 Joyous, and clear, and fresh, thy music doth surpass.

XIII.

Teach us, sprite or bird,
What sweet thoughts are thine:
I have never heard
Praise of love or wine
65 That panted forth a flood of rapture so divine.

XIV.

Chorus hymeneal,
Or triumphal chaunt,

Matched with thine would be all
　　But an empty vaunt —
70　A thing wherein we feel there is some hidden want.

XV.

What objects are the fountains
　　Of thy happy strain?
What fields, or waves, or mountains?
　　What shapes of sky or plain?
75　What love of thine own kind? what ignorance of pain?

XVI.

With thy clear keen joyance
　　Languor cannot be:
Shadow of annoyance
　　Never came near thee:
80　Thou lovest; but ne'er knew love's sad satiety.

XVII.

Waking or asleep,
　　Thou of death must deem
Things more true and deep
　　Than we mortals dream,
85　Or how could thy notes flow in such a crystal stream?

XVIII.

We look before and after,
　　And pine for what is not:
Our sincerest laughter
　　With some pain is fraught;
90　Our sweetest songs are those that tell of saddest thought.

XIX.

Yet if we could scorn
　　Hate, and pride, and fear;

> If we were things born
> Not to shed a tear,
> 95 I know not how thy joy we ever should come near.

XX.

> Better than all measures
> Of delightful sound,
> Better than all treasures
> That in books are found,
> 100 Thy skill to poet were, thou scorner of the ground!

XXI.

> Teach me half the gladness
> That thy brain must know,
> Such harmonious madness
> From my lips would flow,
> 105 The world should listen then, as I am listening now.

Mont Blanc

Lines Written in the Vale of Chamouni.

I.

> The everlasting universe of things
> Flows through the mind, and rolls its rapid waves,
> Now dark—now glittering—now reflecting gloom—
> Now lending splendour, where from secret springs
> 5 The source of human thought its tribute brings
> Of waters, with a sound but half its own,
> Such as a feeble brook will oft assume
> In the wild woods, among the mountains lone,
> Where waterfalls around it leap for ever,
> 10 Where woods and winds contend, and a vast river
> Over its rocks ceaselessly bursts and raves.

II.

Thus thou, Ravine of Arve—dark, deep Ravine—
Thou many-coloured, many-voiced vale,
Over whose pines and crags and caverns sail
15 Fast clouds, shadows and sunbeams; awful scene,
Where Power in likeness of the Arve comes down
From the ice-gulfs that gird his secret throne,
Bursting through these dark mountains like the flame
Of lightning through the tempest; thou dost lie,
20 The giant brood of pines around thee clinging,
Children of elder time, in whose devotion
The chainless winds still come and ever came
To drink their odours, and their mighty swinging
To hear—an old and solemn harmony:
25 Thine earthly rainbows stretched across the sweep
Of the ethereal waterfall, whose veil
Robes some unsculptured image; the strange sleep
Which, when the voices of the desert fail,
Wraps all in its own deep eternity;
30 Thy caverns echoing to the Arve's commotion
A loud, lone sound, no other sound can tame;
Thou art pervaded with that ceaseless motion,
Thou art the path of that unresting sound—
Dizzy Ravine! and when I gaze on thee
35 I seem as in a trance sublime and strange
To muse on my own separate fantasy,
My own, my human mind, which passively
Now renders and receives fast influencings,
Holding an unremitting interchange
40 With the clear universe of things around;
One legion of wild thoughts, whose wandering wings
Now float above thy darkness, and now rest
Where that or thou art no unbidden guest,
In the still cave of the witch Poesy,
45 Seeking among the shadows that pass by
Ghosts of all things that are, some shade of thee,
Some phantom, some faint image; till the breast
From which they fled recals them, thou art there!

III.

Some say that gleams of a remoter world
50 Visit the soul in sleep, that death is slumber,
And that its shapes the busy thoughts outnumber
Of those who wake and live. I look on high;
Has some unknown omnipotence unfurled
The veil of life and death? or do I lie
55 In dream, and does the mightier world of sleep
Speed far around and inaccessibly
Its circles? For the very spirit fails,
Driven like a homeless cloud from steep to steep
That vanishes among the viewless gales!
60 Far, far above, piercing the infinite sky,
Mont Blanc appears, still, snowy, and serene—
Its subject mountains their unearthly forms
Pile around it, ice and rock; broad vales between
Of frozen floods, unfathomable deeps,
65 Blue as the overhanging heaven, that spread
And wind among the accumulated steeps;
A desert peopled by the storms alone,
Save when the eagle brings some hunter's bone,
And the wolf tracks her there—how hideously
70 Its shapes are heaped around! rude, bare, and high,
Ghastly, and scarred, and riven. Is this the scene
Where the old Earthquake-demon taught her young
Ruin? Were these their toys? or did a sea
Of fire envelope once this silent snow?
75 None can reply—all seems eternal now.
The wilderness has a mysterious tongue
Which teaches awful doubt, or faith so mild,
So solemn, so serene, that man may be
But for such faith with nature reconciled;
80 Thou hast a voice, great Mountain, to repeal
Large codes of fraud and woe; not understood,
By all, but which the wise, and great, and good,
Interpret, or make felt, or deeply feel.

IV.

The fields, the lakes, the forests, and the streams,
85 Ocean, and all the living things that dwell
Within the dædal earth; lightning, and rain,
Earthquake, and fiery flood, and hurricane,
The torpor of the year when feeble dreams
Visit the hidden buds, or dreamless sleep
90 Holds every future leaf and flower; the bound
With which from that detested trance they leap;
The works and ways of man, their death and birth,
And that of him and all that his may be;
All things that move and breathe with toil and sound
95 Are born and die, revolve, subside, and swell.
Power dwells apart in its tranquillity
Remote, serene, and inaccessible:
And *this,* the naked countenance of earth,
On which I gaze, even these primæval mountains,
100 Teach the adverting mind. The glaciers creep
Like snakes that watch their prey, from their far fountains,
Slowly rolling on; there, many a precipice
Frost and the Sun in scorn of mortal power
Have piled — dome, pyramid, and pinnacle,
105 A city of death, distinct with many a tower
And wall impregnable of beaming ice.
Yet not a city, but a flood of ruin
Is there, that from the boundaries of the sky
Rolls its perpetual stream; vast pines are strewing
110 Its destined path, or in the mangled soil
Branchless and shattered stand; the rocks, drawn down
From yon remotest waste, have overthrown
The limits of the dead and living world,
Never to be reclaimed. The dwelling-place
115 Of insects, beasts, and birds, becomes its spoil;
Their food and their retreat for ever gone,
So much of life and joy is lost. The race
Of man flies far in dread; his work and dwelling
Vanish, like smoke before the tempest's stream,
120 And their place is not known. Below, vast caves
Shine in the rushing torrent's restless gleam,
Which from those secret chasms in tumult welling

Meet in the vale, and one majestic River,
The breath and blood of distant lands, for ever
125 Rolls its loud waters to the ocean waves,
Breathes its swift vapours to the circling air.

V.

Mont Blanc yet gleams on high: the power is there,
The still and solemn power of many sights
And many sounds, and much of life and death.
130 In the calm darkness of the moonless nights,
In the lone glare of day, the snows descend
Upon that Mountain; none beholds them there,
Nor when the flakes burn in the sinking sun,
Or the star-beams dart through them: Winds contend
135 Silently there, and heap the snow with breath
Rapid and strong, but silently! Its home
The voiceless lightning in these solitudes
Keeps innocently, and like vapour broods
Over the snow. The secret strength of things
140 Which governs thought, and to the infinite dome
Of heaven is as a law, inhabits thee!
And what were thou, and earth, and stars, and sea,
If to the human mind's imaginings
Silence and solitude were vacancy?

Switzerland, *June* 23, 1816.

John Keats (1795–1821)

John Keats had as much sensitivity toward the natural world as any poet of this period. From his earliest lyrical fragments to the great odes of 1819, his poetry and letters incorporate an astonishing array of natural images as well as countless descriptions of animals and plants. His early poetic language was criticized for being too delicate, too flowery, too preoccupied with superfluous lyrical details directed at the ear. But Keats had studied medicine before he turned to poetry, and his language often reflects a keen scientific awareness and an almost clinical observational skill. His medical studies informed his poetry in complex and important ways, as suggested in this passage from his *Anatomical and Physiological Notebook:* "the organ of sight rests in the optic nerve and has the different tunics & humours of the Eye to modify the Medium through which the rays of light pass — A celebrated Italian put out the Eyes of a Bat and turned it loose into a Room and found that it did not strike itself.[. . .] Volition is the contrary of Sensation; it proceeds from the internal to external parts. It does not reside entirely in the Brain but partly in ye spinal Marrow which is seen in the Behaviour of a Frog after having been guillo-teened" (55–56).

Keats can also reveal an awareness of the recent natural discoveries of his own era, as in his description — in *Endymion* (1817) — of long-dead fossils littering the seabed: "skeletons of man, / Of beast, behemoth, and leviathan, / And elephant, and eagle, and huge jaw / Of nameless monster" (3, 133–36). Keats's powers of observation are remarkable not only for their accuracy and intensity but also for their ability to link human activity with the wider animate world: "I go among the Fields and catch a glimpse of a stoat or a fieldmouse peeping out of the withered grass — the creature hath a purpose and its eyes are bright with it — I go amongst the buildings of a city and I see a Man hurrying along—to what? The creature hath a purpose and his eyes are bright with it" (*Letters* 2: 80).

Keats's poems and letters reveal constant attention to precise details of his natural surroundings. From his earliest lyrics—"There the king-fisher saw his plumage bright / Vying with fish of brilliant dye below, / Whose silken fins and golden scalës' light / Cast upward, through the waves, a ruby glow" ("Imitation of Spenser," 1814)—through the Shakespearean cadences of "Ode to a Nightingale," to the naturalistic richness of "To Autumn," Keats seems almost preternaturally aware of forces within nature, of the otherness of the natural world, and of paradoxical links between human sensibility and sensation in all animals, human and otherwise. Keats sometimes treats plants and animals with an almost Renaissance delicacy, a tendency criticized by those—like Byron—who sought more vigorous representations of nature. Keats can then snap back, however, with an image that makes any critical comment superfluous: "How beautiful the season is now—How fine the air. A temperate sharpness about it [...] I never lik'd stubble fields so much as now—Aye better than the chilly green of the spring. Somehow a stubble plain looks warm—in the same way that some pictures look warm.[...] [T]his struck me so much in my [S]unday's walk that I composed upon it" (Letter to Reynolds, 21 September 1819, describing the genesis of "To Autumn").

From Poems

I stood tip-toe upon a little hill

Places of nestling green for Poets made.
—Story of Rimini.[1]

I stood tip-toe upon a little hill,
The air was cooling, and so very still,
That the sweet buds which with a modest pride
Pull droopingly, in slanting curve aside,

John Keats, *Poems*. London: Ollier, 1817.

[1] 1816 poem by Leigh Hunt, based on Dante's legend of Paolo and Francesca. [Ed.]

5   Their scantly leaved, and finely tapering stems,
    Had not yet lost those starry diadems
    Caught from the early sobbing of the morn.
    The clouds were pure and white as flocks new shorn,
    And fresh from the clear brook; sweetly they slept
10 On the blue fields of heaven, and then there crept
    A little noiseless noise among the leaves,
    Born of the very sigh that silence heaves:
    For not the faintest motion could be seen
    Of all the shades that slanted o'er the green.
15 There was wide wand'ring for the greediest eye,
    To peer about upon variety;
    Far round the horizon's crystal air to skim,
    And trace the dwindled edgings of its brim;
    To picture out the quaint, and curious bending
20 Of a fresh woodland alley, never ending;
    Or by the bowery clefts, and leafy shelves,
    Guess where the jaunty streams refresh themselves.
    I gazed awhile, and felt as light, and free
    As though the fanning wings of Mercury
25 Had played upon my heels: I was light-hearted,
    And many pleasures to my vision started;
    So I straightway began to pluck a posey
    Of luxuries bright, milky, soft and rosy.

    A bush of May flowers with the bees about them;
30 Ah, sure no tasteful nook would be without them;
    And let a lush laburnum oversweep them,
    And let long grass grow round the roots to keep them
    Moist, cool and green; and shade the violets,
    That they may bind the moss in leafy nets.

35 A filbert hedge with wild briar overtwined,
    And clumps of woodbine taking the soft wind
    Upon their summer thrones; there too should be
    The frequent chequer of a youngling tree,
    That with a score of light green brethen shoots
40 From the quaint mossiness of aged roots:
    Round which is heard a spring-head of clear waters
    Babbling so wildly of its lovely daughters
    The spreading blue bells: it may haply mourn
    That such fair clusters should be rudely torn
45 From their fresh beds, and scattered thoughtlessly

By infant hands, left on the path to die.

Open afresh your round of starry folds,
Ye ardent marigolds!
Dry up the moisture from your golden lids,
50 For great Apollo bids
That in these days your praises should be sung
On many harps, which he has lately strung;
And when again your dewiness he kisses,
Tell him, I have you in my world of blisses:
55 So haply when I rove in some far vale,
His mighty voice may come upon the gale.

Here are sweet peas, on tip-toe for a flight:
With wings of gentle flush o'er delicate white,
And taper fingers catching at all things,
60 To bind them all about with tiny rings.

Linger awhile upon some bending planks
That lean against a streamlet's rushy banks,
And watch intently Nature's gentle doings:
They will be found softer than ring-dove's cooings.
65 How silent comes the water round that bend;
Not the minutest whisper does it send
To the o'erhanging sallows: blades of grass
Slowly across the chequer'd shadows pass.
Why, you might read two sonnets, ere they reach
70 To where the hurrying freshnesses aye preach
A natural sermon o'er their pebbly beds;
Where swarms of minnows show their little heads,
Staying their wavy bodies 'gainst the streams,
To taste the luxury of sunny beams
75 Temper'd with coolness. How they ever wrestle
With their own sweet delight, and ever nestle
Their silver bellies on the pebbly sand.
If you but scantily hold out the hand,
That very instant not one will remain;
80 But turn your eye, and they are there again.
The ripples seem right glad to reach those cresses,
And cool themselves among the em'rald tresses;
The while they cool themselves, they freshness give,
And moisture, that the bowery green may live:
85 So keeping up an interchange of favours,
Like good men in the truth of their behaviours

Sometimes goldfinches one by one will drop
From low hung branches; little space they stop;
But sip, and twitter, and their feathers sleek;
90 Then off at once, as in a wanton freak:
Or perhaps, to show their black, and golden wings,
Pausing upon their yellow flutterings.
Were I in such a place, I sure should pray
That nought less sweet, might call my thoughts away,
95 Than the soft rustle of a maiden's gown
Fanning away the dandelion's down;
Than the light music of her nimble toes
Patting against the sorrel as she goes.
How she would start, and blush, thus to be caught
100 Playing in all her innocence of thought.
O let me lead her gently o'er the brook,
Watch her half-smiling lips, and downward look;
O let me for one moment touch her wrist;
Let me one moment to her breathing list;
105 And as she leaves me may she often turn
Her fair eyes looking through her locks auburne.
What next? A tuft of evening primroses,
O'er which the mind may hover till it dozes;
O'er which it well might take a pleasant sleep,
110 But that 'tis ever startled by the leap
Of buds into ripe flowers; or by the flitting
Of diverse moths, that aye their rest are quitting;
Or by the moon lifting her silver rim
Above a cloud, and with a gradual swim
115 Coming into the blue with all her light.
O Maker of sweet poets, dear delight
Of this fair world, and all its gentle livers;
Spangler of clouds, halo of crystal rivers,
Mingler with leaves, and dew and tumbling streams,
120 Closer of lovely eyes to lovely dreams,
Lover of loneliness, and wandering,
Of upcast eye, and tender pondering!
Thee must I praise above all other glories
That smile us on to tell delightful stories.
125 For what has made the sage or poet write
But the fair paradise of Nature's light?
In the calm grandeur of a sober line,
We see the waving of the mountain pine;

And when a tale is beautifully staid,
130 We feel the safety of a hawthorn glade:
When it is moving on luxurious wings,
The soul is lost in pleasant smotherings:
Fair dewy roses brush against our faces,
And flowering laurels spring from diamond vases;
135 O'er head we see the jasmine and sweet briar,
And bloomy grapes laughing from green attire:
While at our feet, the voice of crystal bubbles
Charms us at once away from all our troubles:
So that we feel uplifted from the world,
140 Walking upon the white clouds wreath'd and curl'd.
So felt he, who first told, how Psyche went
On the smooth wind to realms of wonderment;
What Psyche felt, and Love, when their full lips
First touch'd; what amorous, and fondling nips
145 They gave each other's cheeks; with all their sighs,
And how they kist each other's tremulous eyes:
The silver lamp, the ravishment, the wonder —
The darkness, loneliness, the fearful thunder;
Their woes gone by, and both to heaven upflown,
150 To bow for gratitude before Jove's throne.
So did he feel, who pull'd the boughs aside,
That we might look into a forest wide,
To catch a glimpse of Fawns, and Dryades
Coming with softest rustle through the trees;
155 And garlands woven of flowers wild, and sweet,
Upheld on ivory wrists, or sporting feet:
Telling us how fair, trembling Syrinx fled
Arcadian Pan, with such a fearful dread.
Poor nymph, poor Pan, how he did weep to find,
160 Nought but a lovely sighing of the wind
Along the reedy stream; a half heard strain,
Full of sweet desolation — balmy pain.

What first inspired a bard of old to sing
Narcissus pining o'er the untainted spring?
165 In some delicious ramble, he had found
A little space, with boughs all woven round;
And in the midst of all, a clearer pool
Than e'er reflected in its pleasant cool,
The blue sky here, and there, serenely peeping

170 Through tendril wreaths fantastically creeping.
And on the bank a lonely flower he spied,
A meek and forlorn flower, with naught of pride,
Drooping its beauty o'er the watery clearness,
To woo its own sad image into nearness:
175 Deaf to light Zephyrus it would not move;
But still would seem to droop, to pine, to love.
So while the Poet stood in this sweet spot,
Some fainter gleamings o'er his fancy shot;
Nor was it long ere he had told the tale
180 Of young Narcissus, and sad Echo's bale.

Where had he been, from whose warm head out-flew
That sweetest of all songs, that ever new,
That aye refreshing, pure deliciousness,
Coming ever to bless
185 The wanderer by moonlight? to him bringing
Shapes from the invisible world, unearthly singing
From out the middle air, from flowery nests,
And from the pillowy silkiness that rests
Full in the speculation of the stars.
190 Ah! surely he had burst our mortal bars;
Into some wond'rous region he had gone,
To search for thee, divine Endymion!

He was a Poet, sure a lover too,
Who stood on Latmus' top, what time there blew
195 Soft breezes from the myrtle vale below;
And brought in faintness solemn, sweet, and slow
A hymn from Dian's temple; while upswelling,
The incense went to her own starry dwelling.
But though her face was clear as infant's eyes,
200 Though she stood smiling o'er the sacrifice,
The Poet wept at her so piteous fate,
Wept that such beauty should be desolate:
So in fine wrath some golden sounds he won,
And gave meek Cynthia her Endymion.

205 Queen of the wide air; thou most lovely queen
Of all the brightness that mine eyes have seen!
As thou exceedest all things in thy shine,
So every tale, does this sweet tale of thine.
O for three words of honey, that I might
210 Tell but one wonder of thy bridal night!

Where distant ships do seem to show their keels,
Phœbus awhile delayed his mighty wheels,
And turned to smile upon thy bashful eyes,
Ere he his unseen pomp would solemnize.
215 The evening weather was so bright, and clear,
That men of health were of unusual cheer;
Stepping like Homer at the trumpet's call,
Or young Apollo on the pedestal:
And lovely women were as fair and warm,
220 As Venus looking sideways in alarm.
The breezes were ethereal, and pure,
And crept through half closed lattices to cure
The languid sick; it cool'd their fever'd sleep,
And soothed them into slumbers full and deep.
225 Soon they awoke clear eyed: nor burnt with thirsting,
Nor with hot fingers, nor with temples bursting:
And springing up, they met the wond'ring sight
Of their dear friends, nigh foolish with delight;
Who feel their arms, and breasts, and kiss and stare,
230 And on their placid foreheads part the hair.
Young men, and maidens at each other gaz'd
With hands held back, and motionless, amaz'd
To see the brightness in each others' eyes;
And so they stood, fill'd with a sweet surprise,
235 Until their tongues were loos'd in poesy.
Therefore no lover did of anguish die:
But the soft numbers, in that moment spoken,
Made silken ties, that never may be broken.
Cynthia! I cannot tell the greater blisses,
240 That follow'd thine, and thy dear shepherd's kisses:
Was there a Poet born? but now no more,
My wand'ring spirit must no further soar.

To Some Ladies

What though while the wonders of nature exploring,
    I cannot your light, mazy footsteps attend;
Nor listen to accents, that almost adoring,
    Bless Cynthia's face, the enthusiast's friend:

5 Yet over the steep, whence the mountain stream rushes,
    With you, kindest friends, in idea I rove;
Mark the clear tumbling crystal, its passionate gushes,
    Its spray that the wild flower kindly bedews.

Why linger you so, the wild labyrinth strolling?
10   Why breathless, unable your bliss to declare?
Ah! you list to the nightingale's tender condoling,
    Responsive to sylphs, in the moon beamy air.

'Tis morn, and the flowers with dew are yet drooping,
    I see you are treading the verge of the sea:
15 And now! ah, I see it—you just now are stooping
    To pick up the keep-sake intended for me.

If a cherub, on pinions of silver descending,
    Had brought me a gem from the fret-work of heaven;
And smiles, with his star-cheering voice sweetly blending,
20   The blessings of Tighe[2] had melodiously given;

It had not created a warmer emotion
    Than the present, fair nymphs, I was blest with from you,
Than the shell, from the bright golden sands of the ocean
    Which the emerald waves at your feet gladly threw.

25 For, indeed, 'tis a sweet and peculiar pleasure,
    (And blissful is he who such happiness finds,)
To possess but a span of the hour of leisure,
    In elegant, pure, and aerial minds.

---

[2]Mary Tighe, author of *Psyche; or, The Legend of Love* (1805). [Ed.]

On Receiving a Curious Shell and a Copy of Verses, from the Same Ladies

Hast thou from the caves of Golconda,[3] a gem
    Pure as the ice-drop that froze on the mountain?
Bright as the humming-bird's green diadem,
    When it flutters in sun-beams that shine through a fountain?

5 Hast thou a goblet for dark sparkling wine?
    That goblet right heavy, and massy, and gold?
And splendidly mark'd with the story divine
    Of Armida the fair, and Rinaldo the bold?[4]

Hast thou a steed with a mane richly flowing?
10 Hast thou a sword that thine enemy's smart is?
Hast thou a trumpet rich melodies blowing?
    And wear'st thou the shield of the fam'd Britomartis?[5]

What is it that hangs from thy shoulder, so brave,
    Embroidered with many a spring peering flower?
15 Is it a scarf that thy fair lady gave?
    And hastest thou now to that fair lady's bower?

Ah! courteous Sir Knight, with large joy thou art crown'd;
    Full many the glories that brighten thy youth!
I will tell thee my blisses, which richly abound
20 In magical powers to bless, and to sooth.

On this scroll thou seest written in characters fair
    A sun-beamy tale of a wreath, and a chain;
And, warrior, it nurtures the property rare
    Of charming my mind from the trammels of pain.

25 This canopy mark: 'tis the work of a fay;
    Beneath its rich shade did King Oberon languish,
When lovely Titania was far, far away,
    And cruelly left him to sorrow, and anguish.

There, oft would he bring from his soft sighing lute
30 Wild strains to which, spell-bound, the nightingales listened;
The wondering spirits of heaven were mute,
    And tears 'mong the dewdrops of morning oft glistened.

---

[3] Ancient fort near Hyderabad, India. [Ed.]
[4] In Tasso's *Gerusalemme Liberata*. [Ed.]
[5] Warrior maiden in Spenser's *Fairie Queene*. [Ed.]

In this little dome, all those melodies strange,
    Soft, plaintive, and melting, for ever will sigh;
35 Nor e'er will the notes from their tenderness change;
    Nor e'er will the music of Oberon die.

So, when I am in a voluptuous vein,
    I pillow my head on the sweets of the rose,
And list to the tale of the wreath, and the chain,
40   Till its echoes depart; then I sink to repose.

Adieu, valiant Eric! with joy thou art crown'd;
    Full many the glories that brighten thy youth,
I too have my blisses, which richly abound
    In magical powers, to bless and to sooth.

To a Friend Who Sent Me Some Roses

As late I rambled in the happy fields,
    What time the sky-lark shakes the tremulous dew
    From his lush clover covert; when anew
Adventurous knights take up their dinted shields:
5 I saw the sweetest flower wild nature yields,
    A fresh-blown musk-rose; 'twas the first that threw
    Its sweets upon the summer: graceful it grew
As is the wand that queen Titania wields.
And, as I feasted on its fragrancy,
10   I thought the garden-rose it far excell'd:
But when, O Wells! thy roses came to me
    My sense with their deliciousness was spell'd:
Soft voices had they, that with tender plea
    Whisper'd of peace, and truth, and friendliness unquell'd.

On the Grasshopper and Cricket

The poetry of earth is never dead:
    When all the birds are faint with the hot sun,
    And hide in cooling trees, a voice will run
From hedge to hedge about the new-mown mead;
5 That is the Grasshopper's—he takes the lead
    In summer luxury, he has never done

With his delights; for when tired out with fun
He rests at ease beneath some pleasant weed.
The poetry of earth is ceasing never:
10   On a lone winter evening, when the frost
      Has wrought a silence, from the stove there shrills
The Cricket's song, in warmth increasing ever,
    And seems to one in drowsiness half lost,
      The Grasshopper's among some grassy hills.

December 30, 1816.

From Endymion

Amid his toil thou[6] gav'st Leander breath;
Thou leddest Orpheus through the gleams of death;
Thou madest Pluto bear thin element;
And now, O winged Chieftain! thou hast sent
5 A moon-beam to the deep, deep water-world,
To find Endymion.

           On gold sand impearl'd
With lily shells, and pebbles milky white,
Poor Cynthia greeted him, and sooth'd her light
10 Against his pallid face: he felt the charm
To breathlessness, and suddenly a warm
Of his heart's blood: 'twas very sweet; he stay'd
His wandering steps, and half-entranced laid
His head upon a tuft of straggling weeds,
15 To taste the gentle moon, and freshening beads,
Lashed from the crystal roof by fishes' tails.
And so he kept, until the rosy veils
Mantling the east, by Aurora's peering hand
Were lifted from the water's breast, and fann'd
20 Into sweet air; and sober'd morning came
Meekly through billows: when like taper-flame
Left sudden by a dallying breath of air,
He rose in silence, and once more 'gan fare
Along his fated way.

John Keats. *Endymion.* London: Taylor and Hessey, 1818.
[6]Love [Ed.]

25   Far had he roam'd,
With nothing save the hollow vast, that foam'd
Above, around, and at his feet; save things
More dead than Morpheus' imaginings:
Old rusted anchors, helmets, breast-plates large
30 Of gone sea-warriors; brazen beaks and targe;
Rudders that for a hundred years had lost
The sway of human hand; gold vase emboss'd
With long-forgotten story, and wherein
No reveller had ever dipp'd a chin
35 But those of Saturn's vintage; mouldering scrolls,
Writ in the tongue of heaven, by those souls
Who first were on the earth; and sculptures rude
In ponderous stone, developing the mood
Of ancient Nox; then skeletons of man,
40 Of beast, behemoth, and leviathan,
And elephant, and eagle, and huge jaw
Of nameless monster. A cold leaden awe
These secrets struck into him; and unless
Dian had chaced away that heaviness,
45 He might have died: but now, with cheered feel,
He onward kept; wooing these thoughts to steal
About the labyrinth in his soul of love.

    "What is there in thee, Moon! that thou shouldst move
My heart so potently? When yet a child
50 I oft have dried my tears when thou hast smil'd.
Thou seem'dst my sister: hand in hand we went
From eve to morn across the firmament.
No apples would I gather from the tree,
Till thou hadst cool'd their cheeks deliciously:
55 No tumbling water ever spake romance,
But when my eyes with thine thereon could dance:
No woods were green enough, no bower divine,
Until thou liftedst up thine eyelids fine:
In sowing time ne'er would I dibble take,
60 Or drop a seed, till thou wast wide awake;
And, in the summer tide of blossoming,
No one but thee hath heard me blithly sing
And mesh my dewy flowers all the night.
No melody was like a passing spright
65 If it went not to solemnize thy reign.

Yes, in my boyhood, every joy and pain
By thee were fashion'd to the self-same end;
And as I grew in years, still didst thou blend
With all my ardours: thou wast the deep glen;
70 Thou wast the mountain-top—the sage's pen—
The poet's harp—the voice of friends—the sun;
Thou wast the river—thou wast glory won;
Thou wast my clarion's blast—thou wast my steed—
My goblet full of wine—my topmost deed:
80 Thou wast the charm of women, lovely Moon!
O what a wild and harmonized tune
My spirit struck from all the beautiful!
On some bright essence could I lean, and lull
Myself to immortality: I prest
85 Nature's soft pillow in a wakeful rest."[. . .]

"Goddess! I love thee not the less: from thee
By Juno's smile I turn not—no, no, no—
While the great waters are at ebb and flow.
I have a triple soul! O fond pretence—
90 For both, for both my love is so immense,
I feel my heart is cut in twain for them."

    And so he groan'd, as one by beauty slain.
The lady's heart beat quick, and he could see
Her gentle bosom heave tumultuously.
95 He sprang from his green covert: there she lay,
Sweet as a muskrose upon new-made hay;
With all her limbs on tremble, and her eyes
Shut softly up alive. To speak he tries.
"Fair damsel, pity me! forgive that I
100 Thus violate thy bower's sanctity!
O pardon me, for I am full of grief—
Grief born of thee, young angel! fairest thief!
Who stolen hast away the wings wherewith
I was to top the heavens. Dear maid, sith
105 Thou art my executioner, and I feel
Loving and hatred, misery and weal,
Will in a few short hours be nothing to me,
And all my story that much passion slew me;
Do smile upon the evening of my days:
110 And, for my tortur'd brain begins to craze,
Be thou my nurse; and let me understand

How dying I shall kiss that lily hand.
Dost weep for me? Then should I be content.
Scowl on, ye fates! until the firmament
115 Outblackens Erebus, and the full-cavern'd earth
Crumbles into itself. By the cloud girth
Of Jove, those tears have given me a thirst
To meet oblivion." As her heart would burst
The maiden sobb'd awhile, and then replied:
120 "Why must such desolation betide
As that thou speakest of? Are not these green nooks
Empty of all misfortune? Do the brooks
Utter a gorgon voice? Does yonder thrush,
Schooling its half-fledg'd little ones to brush
125 About the dewy forest, whisper tales?
Speak not of grief, young stranger, or cold snails
Will slime the rose to night. Though if thou wilt,
Methinks 'twould be a guilt—a very guilt—
Not to companion thee, and sigh away
130 The light—the dusk—the dark—till break of day!"
"Dear lady," said Endymion, " 'tis past:
I love thee! and my days can never last.
That I may pass in patience still speak:
Let me have music dying, and I seek
135 No more delight—I bid adieu to all.
Didst thou not after other climates call,
And murmur about Indian streams?" Then she,
Sitting beneath the midmost forest tree,
For pity sang this roundelay—

140   "O Sorrow,
        Why dost borrow
The natural hue of health, from vermeil lips?
        To give maiden blushes
        To the white rose bushes?
145 Or is it thy dewy hand the daisy tips?

        "O Sorrow,
        Why dost borrow
The lustrous passion from a falcon-eye?
        To give the glow-worm light?
150   Or, on a moonless night,
To tinge, on syren shores, the salt sea-spry?

"O Sorrow,
Why dost borrow
The mellow ditties from a mourning tongue?
155   To give at evening pale
Unto the nightingale,
That thou mayst listen the cold dews among?

"O Sorrow,
Why dost borrow
160 Heart's lightness from the merriment of May?
A lover would not tread
A cowslip on the head,
Though he should dance from eve till peep of day—
Nor any drooping flower
165   Held sacred for thy bower,
Wherever he may sport himself and play.

"To Sorrow,
I bade good-morrow,
And thought to leave her far away behind;
170   But cheerly, cheerly,
She loves me dearly;
She is so constant to me, and so kind:
I would deceive her
And so leave her,
175 But ah! she is so constant and so kind.

"Beneath my palm trees, by the river side,
I sat a weeping: in the whole world wide
There was no one to ask me why I wept,
And so I kept
180 Brimming the water-lily cups with tears
Cold as my fears.

"Beneath my palm trees, by the river side,
I sat a weeping: what enamour'd bride,
Cheated by shadowy wooer from the clouds,
185   But hides and shrouds
Beneath dark palm trees by a river side?

"And as I sat, over the light blue hills
There came a noise of revellers: the rills
Into the wide stream came of purple hue—
190   'Twas Bacchus and his crew!
The earnest trumpet spake, and silver thrills

From kissing cymbals made a merry din —
    'Twas Bacchus and his kin!
Like to a moving vintage down they came,
195 Crown'd with green leaves, and faces all on flame;
All madly dancing through the pleasant valley,
    To scare thee, Melancholy!
O then, O then, thou wast a simple name!
And I forgot thee, as the berried holly
200 By shepherds is forgotten, when, in June,
Tall chesnuts keep away the sun and moon:
    I rush'd into the folly!

"Within his car, aloft, young Bacchus stood,
Trifling his ivy-dart, in dancing mood,
205   With sidelong laughing;
And little rills of crimson wine imbrued
His plump white arms, and shoulders, enough white
    For Venus' pearly bite:
And near him rode Silenus on his ass,
210 Pelted with flowers as he on did pass
    Tipsily quaffing.

"Whence came ye, merry Damsels! whence came ye!
So many, and so many, and such glee?
Why have ye left your bowers desolate,
215   Your lutes, and gentler fate?
 'We follow Bacchus! Bacchus on the wing,
    A conquering!
Bacchus, young Bacchus! good or ill betide,
We dance before him thorough kingdoms wide:
220 Come hither, lady fair, and joined be
    To our wild minstrelsy!'

"Whence came ye, jolly Satyrs! whence came ye!
So many, and so many, and such glee?
Why have ye left your forest haunts, why left
225   Your nuts in oak-tree cleft?
 'For wine, for wine we left our kernel tree;
For wine we left our heath, and yellow brooms,
    And cold mushrooms;
For wine we follow Bacchus through the earth;
230 Great God of breathless cups and chirping mirth!
come hither, lady fair, and joined be
    To our mad minstrelsy!'

"Over wide streams and mountains great we went,
And, save when Bacchus kept his ivy tent,
235 Onward the tiger and the leopard pants,
　　With Asian elephants:
Onward these myriads—with song and dance,
With zebras striped, and sleek Arabians' prance,
Web-footed alligators, crocodiles,
240 Bearing upon their scaly backs, in files,
Plump infant laughers mimicking the coil
Of seamen, and stout galley-rowers' toil:
With toying oars and silken sails they glide,
　　Nor care for wind and tide.

245 "Mounted on panthers' furs and lions' manes,
From rear to van they scour about the plains;
A three days' journey in a moment done:
And always, at the rising of the sun,
About the wilds they hunt with spear and horn,
250　　On spleenful unicorn.

"I saw Osirian Egypt kneel adown
　　Before the vine-wreath crown!
I saw parch'd Abyssinia rouse and sing
　　To the silver cymbals' ring!
255 I saw the whelming vintage hotly pierce
　　Old Tartary the fierce!
The kings of Inde their jewel-sceptres vail,
And from their treasures scatter pearled hail;
Great Brahma from his mystic heaven groans,
260　　And all his priesthood moans;
Before young Bacchus' eye-wink turning pale.
Into these regions came I following him,
Sick hearted, weary—so I took a whim
To stray away into these forests drear
265　　Alone, without a peer:
And I have told thee all thou mayest hear.
　　"Young stranger!
　　I've been a ranger
In search of pleasure throughout every clime:
270　　Alas, 'tis not for me!
　　Bewitch'd I sure must be,
To lose in grieving all my maiden prime.

"Come then, Sorrow!
Sweetest Sorrow!
275 Like an own babe I nurse thee on my breast:
      I thought to leave thee
      And deceive thee,
But now of all the world I love thee best.

      "There is not one,
280   No, no, not one
But thee to comfort a poor lonely maid;
      Thou art her mother,
      And her brother,
Her playmate, and her wooer in the shade."

From Lamia, Isabella, The Eve of St. Agnes, and Other Poems

Ode to a Nightingale

1.

My heart aches, and a drowsy numbness pains
      My sense, as though of hemlock I had drunk,
Or emptied some dull opiate to the drains
      One minute past, and Lethe-wards had sunk:
5 'Tis not through envy of thy happy lot,
      But being too happy in thine happiness,
            That thou, light-winged Dryad of the trees,
                  In some melodious plot
      Of beechen green, and shadows numberless,
10   Singest of summer in full-throated ease.

2.

O, for a draught of vintage! that hath been
      Cool'd a long age in the deep-delved earth,
Tasting of Flora and the country green,
      Dance, and Provençal song, and sunburnt mirth!

John Keats, *Lamia, Isabella, The Eve of St. Agnes, and Other Poems.* London:
Taylor and Hessey, 1820.

15 O for a beaker full of the warm South,
  Full of the true, the blushful Hippocrene,
   With beaded bubbles winking at the brim,
    And purple-stained mouth;
  That I might drink, and leave the world unseen,
20   And with thee fade away into the forest dim:

3.

Fade far away, dissolve, and quite forget
  What thou among the leaves hast never known,
The weariness, the fever, and the fret
  Here, where men sit and hear each other groan;
25 Where palsy shakes a few, sad, last gray hairs,
  Where youth grows pale, and spectre-thin, and dies;
   Where but to think is to be full of sorrow
    And leaden-eyed despairs,
  Where Beauty cannot keep her lustrous eyes,
30   Or new Love pine at them beyond to-morrow.

4.

Away! away! for I will fly to thee,
  Not charioted by Bacchus and his pards,
But on the viewless wings of Poesy,
  Though the dull brain perplexes and retards:
35 Already with thee! tender is the night,
  And haply the Queen-Moon is on her throne,
   Cluster'd around by all her starry Fays;[7]
    But here there is no light,
  Save what from heaven is with the breezes blown
40   Through verdurous glooms and winding mossy ways.

5.

I cannot see what flowers are at my feet,
  Nor what soft incense hangs upon the boughs,
But, in embalmed darkness, guess each sweet
  Wherewith the seasonable month endows

---

[7] Fairies. [Ed.]

45 The grass, the thicket, and the fruit-tree wild;
   White hawthorn, and the pastoral eglantine;
    Fast fading violets cover'd up in leaves;
      And mid-May's eldest child,
   The coming musk-rose, full of dewy wine,
50   The murmurous haunt of flies on summer eves.

6.

Darkling I listen; and, for many a time
   I have been half in love with easeful Death,
Call'd him soft names in many a mused rhyme,
   To take into the air my quiet breath;
55   Now more than ever seems it rich to die,
To cease upon the midnight with no pain,
   While thou art pouring forth thy soul abroad
      In such an ecstasy!
Still wouldst thou sing, and I have ears in vain —
60   To thy high requiem become a sod.

7.

Thou wast not born for death, immortal Bird!
   No hungry generations tread thee down;
The voice I hear this passing night was heard
   In ancient days by emperor and clown:
65 Perhaps the self-same song that found a path
   Through the sad heart of Ruth, when, sick for home,
    She stood in tears amid the alien corn;
      The same that oft-times hath
Charm'd magic casements, opening on the foam
70   Of perilous seas, in faery lands forlorn.

8.

Forlorn! the very word is like a bell
   To toll me back from thee to my sole self!
Adieu! the fancy cannot cheat so well
   As she is fam'd to do, deceiving elf.

75 Adieu! adieu! thy plaintive anthem fades
      Past the near meadows, over the still stream,
        Up the hill-side; and now 'tis buried deep
          In the next valley-glades:
      Was it a vision, or a waking dream?
80   Fled is that music: Do I wake or sleep?

To Autumn

1.

Season of mists and mellow fruitfulness,
      Close bosom-friend of the maturing sun;
Conspiring with him how to load and bless
      With fruit the vines that round the thatch-eves run;
5 To bend with apples the moss'd cottage-trees,
      And fill all fruit with ripeness to the core;
        To swell the gourd, and plump the hazel shells
With a sweet kernel; to set budding more,
      And still more, later flowers for the bees,
10   Until they think warm days will never cease,
      For Summer has o'er-brimm'd their clammy cells.

2.

Who hath not seen thee oft amid thy store?
      Sometimes whoever seeks abroad may find
Thee sitting careless on a granary floor,
15   Thy hair soft-lifted by the winnowing wind;
Or on a half-reap'd furrow sound asleep,
      Drows'd with the fume of poppies, while thy hook
        Spares the next swath and all its twined flowers:
And sometimes like a gleaner thou dost keep
20   Steady thy laden head across a brook;
      Or by a cyder-press, with patient look,
        Thou watchest the last oozings hours by hours.

3.

Where are the songs of Spring? Ay, where are they?
Think not of them, thou hast thy music too,
25 While barred clouds bloom the soft-dying day,
And touch the stubble-plains with rosy hue;
Then in a wailful choir the small gnats mourn
Among the river sallows, borne aloft
Or sinking as the light wind lives or dies;
30 And full-grown lambs loud bleat from hilly bourn;
Hedge-crickets sing; and now with treble soft
The red-breast whistles from a garden-croft;
And gathering swallows twitter in the skies.

William Kirby (1759–1850) and
William Spence (1783–1860)

Kirby and Spence were the leading entomologists in England during the early years of the nineteenth century. Kirby claimed to have derived his interest in natural history from his mother. He took holy orders in 1782 and remained, like Gilbert White, a country parson for the rest of his life. He began his career as a botanist, but he shifted to the study of insects after the discovery of one particularly beautiful specimen. Kirby was among the founders of the Linnaean Society in 1788, and by 1802 he had published an important study of English bees. He collected over 150 specimens in and around his own parish in Suffolk. He met William Spence in 1805, and Spence soon agreed to assist Kirby in producing *An Introduction to Entomology,* a project that included four volumes and took over a decade (1815–26). Spence engaged in research in the extensive library of Sir Joseph Banks and traveled widely in Europe. Kirby and Spence were elected as the only honorary British members of the Entomological Society of London in 1833. In addition to his entomological researches, Spence wrote numerous works on the relationship between agriculture and political economy. Kirby also wrote *On the History, Habits, and Instincts of Animals* (London: Pickering, 1835), a work that set out to offer a natural theological explanation for the wonders of the insect world but ended up arguing for a stronger version of mindless, mechanical instinct than even Charles Darwin was willing to accept.

Thoreau cites their work—"I find it in Kirby and Spence—that 'some insects in their perfect state, though furnished with organs of feeding, make no use of them'"(*Walden,* chap. 11)—as does Charles Darwin: "Kirby has remarked (and I have observed the same fact) that the anterior tarsi, or feet, of many male dung-feeding beetles are very often broken off" (*Origin 135*). Darwin also annotated his copy of their work with extensive comments on the subject of animal instinct. The accurate observations and descriptions recorded by Kirby and Spence remained standard scientific texts throughout the nineteenth century. Miriam Allott, in her edition of Keats's poems, notes the echo of their language in Keats's "To Autumn" (653): "Then in a wailful choir the small gnats mourn / Among the river sallows, borne aloft / Or sinking as the light wind lives or dies" (ll. 27–29). The selections below offer a clear sense of the way that the discourse of natural history in this era contributed to a wider scientific, as well as artistic, sensibility.

From An Introduction to Entomology

MOTIONS OF INSECTS

I now come to motions whose object seems to be *sport* and amusement rather than locomotion. They may be considered as of three kinds—hovering—gyrations—and dancing.

You have often in the woods and other places seen flies suspended as it were in the air, their wings all the while moving so rapidly as to be almost invisible. This hovering, which seems peculiar to the aphidivorous flies, has been also noticed by De Geer. I have often amused myself with watching them; but when I have endeavoured to entrap them with my forceps, they have immediately shifted their quarters, and resumed their amusement elsewhere. The most remarkable insects in this respect are the sphinxes, and from this they doubtless took their name of hawk-moths. When they unfold their long tongue, and wipe its sweets from any nectariferous flower, they always keep upon the wing, suspending themselves over it till they have exhausted them, when they fly away to another. The species called by collectors the humming-bird (*S. Stellatarum*, L.), and by some persons mistaken for a real one, is remarkable for this, and the motion of its wings is inconceivably rapid.

The gyrations of insects take place either when they are reposing, or when they are flying or swimming. I was once much amused by observing

William Kirby and William Spence, *An Introduction to Entomology: or Elements of the Natural History of Insects: with Plates*. London: Longman, 1817.

the actions of a minute moth (*Tinea*) upon a leaf on which it was stationed. Making its head the centre of its revolutions, it turned round and round with considerable rapidity, as if it had the vertigo, for some time. I did not, however, succeed in my attempts to take it. Scaliger noticed a similar motion in the book-crab (*Chelifer cancroides*).

Reaumur describes in a very interesting and lively way the gyrations of the Ephemerae before noticed, round a lighted flambeau. It is singular, says he, that moths which fly only in the night, and shun the day, should be precisely those that come to seek the light in our apartments. It is still more extraordinary that these Ephemeræ—which appearing after sun-set, and dying before sun-rise, are destined never to behold the light of that orb— should have so strong an inclination for any luminous object. To hold a flambeau when they appeared was no very pleasant office; for he who filled it, in a few seconds had his dress covered with the insects, which rushed from all quarters to him. The light of the flambeau exhibited a spectacle which enchanted every one that beheld it. All that were present, even the most ignorant and stupid of his domestics, were never satisfied with looking at it. Never had any armillary sphere so many zones, as there were here circles, which had the light for their centre. There was an infinity of them—crossing each other in all directions, and of every imaginable inclination—all of which were more or less eccentric. Each zone was composed of an unbroken string of Ephemeræ, resembling a piece of silver lace formed into a circle deeply notched, and consisting of equal triangles placed end to end (so that one of the angles of that which followed touched the middle of the base of that which preceded), and moving with astonishing rapidity. The wings of the flies, which was all of them that could then be distinguished, formed this appearance. Each of these creatures, after having described one or two orbits, fell upon the earth or into the water, but not in consequence of being burned. Reaumur was one of the most accurate of observers; and yet I suspect that the appearance he describes was a visual deception, and for the following reason. I was once walking in the day-time with a friend[1], when our attention was caught by myriads of small flies, which were dancing under every tree; viewed in a certain light they appeared a concatenated series of insects (as Reaumur has here described his Ephemeræ) moving in a spiral direction upwards; but each series, upon close examination, we found was produced by the astonishingly rapid movement of a single fly. Indeed when we consider the space that a fly will pass through in a second, it is not wonderful that the eye should be unable to trace its gradual progress, or that it should appear

---

[1] The persons observing the appearance here related were the authors of this work.

present in the whole space at the same instant. The fly we saw was a small male Ichneumon.

Other circular motions of sportive insects take place in the waters. Linné,[2] in his Lapland tour, noticed a black Tipula which ran over the water, and turned round like a Gyrinus. This last insect I have often mentioned; it seems the merriest and most agile of all the inhabitants of the waves. Wonderful is the velocity with which they turn round and round, as it were, pursuing each other in incessant circles, sometimes moving in oblique, and indeed in every other direction. Now and then they repose on the surface, as if fatigued with their dances, and desirous of enjoying the full effect of the sun-beam: if you approach, they are instantaneously in motion again. Attempt to entrap them with your net, and they are under the water and dispersed in a moment. When the danger ceases they reappear and resume their vagaries. Covered with lucid armour, when the sun shines they look like little dancing masses of silver or brilliant pearls.

But the motions of this kind to which I particularly wish to call your attention, are the choral dances of males in the air; for the dancing sex amongst insects is the masculine, the ladies generally keeping themselves quiet at home. These dances occur at all seasons of the year, both in winter and summer, though in the former season they are confined to the hardy Tipulidae. In the morning before twelve, the *Hopliæ*, root-beetles before mentioned, have their dances in the air, and the solstitial and common cockchafer appear in the evening—the former generally coming forth at the summer solstice—and fill the air over the trees and hedges with their myriads and their hum. Other dancing insects resemble moving columns—each individual rising and falling in a vertical line a certain space, and which will follow the passing traveller—often intent upon other business, and all-unconscious of his aërial companions—for a considerable distance.

Towards sun-set the common Ephemeræ(*E.vulgata*, L.), distinguished by their spotted wings and three long tails *(Caudulæ)*, commence their dances in the meadows near the rivers. They assemble in troops, consisting sometimes of several hundreds, and keep rising and falling continually, usually over some high tree. They rise, beating the air rapidly with their wings, till they have ascended five or six feet above the tree; then they descend to it with their wings extended and motionless, sailing like hawks, and having their three tails elevated, and the lateral ones so separated as to form nearly a right angle with the central one. These tails seem given them to balance their bodies when they descend, which they do in a horizontal position. This motion continues two or three hours without ceasing, and commences in fine clear weather about an hour before sun-set, lasting till

---

[2]Linnaeus. [Ed.]

the copious falling of the dew compels them to retire to their nocturnal station. Our most common species, which I have usually taken for the *E. vulgata,* varies from that of De Geer in its proceedings. I found them at the end of May dancing over the meadows, not over the trees, at a much earlier hour — at half-past three — rising in the way just described, about a foot, and then descending, at the distance of about four or five feet from the ground. Another species, common here, rises seven or eight feet. I have also seen Ephemeræ flying over the water in a horizontal direction. The females are sometimes in the air, when the males seize them, and they fly paired. These insects seem to use their fore legs to break the air; they are applied together before the head, and look like antennæ. *Empis maura,* a little beaked fly, I have observed rushing in infinite numbers like a shower of rain driven by the wind, as before observed, over waters, and then returning back.

It is remarkable that the smaller *Tipulidæ* will fly unwetted in a heavy shower of rain, as I have often observed. How keen must be their sight, and how rapid their motions, to enable them to steer between drops bigger than their own bodies, which, if they fell upon them, must dash them to the ground!

Amidst this infinite variety of motions, for purposes so numerous and diversified, and performed by such a multiplicity of instruments and organs, who does not discern and adore the Great First Mover? From him all proceed, by him all are endowed, in him all move: and it is to accomplish his ends, and to go on his errands, that these little, but not insignificant beings are thus gifted; since it is by them that he maintains this terraqueous globe in order and beauty, thus rendering it fit for the residence of his creature man.[. . .]

On The Noises Produced By Insects

That insects, though they fill the air with a variety of sounds, have no voice, may seem to you a paradox, and you may be tempted to exclaim with the Roman naturalist, What, amidst this incessant diurnal hum of bees; this evening boom of beetles; this nocturnal buz of gnats; this merry chirp of crickets and grasshoppers; this deafening drum of Cicadæ, have insects no voice! If by voice we understand sounds produced by the air expelled from the lungs, which, passing through the larynx, is modified by the tongue, and emitted from the mouth, it is even so. For no insect, like the larger animals, uses its mouth for utterance of any kind: in this respect they are all perfectly mute; and though incessantly noisy, are everlastingly silent. Of this fact the Stagyrite[3] was not ignorant, since, denying them a voice, he

---

[3] Aristotle, born in Stagira in Macedon. [Ed.]

attributes the sounds emitted by insects to another cause. But if we feel disposed to give a larger extent to this word; if we are of opinion that all sounds, however produced, by means of which animals determine those of their own species to certain actions, merit the name of voice; then I will grant that insects have a voice. But, decide this question as we will, we all know that by some means or other, at certain seasons and on various occasions, these little creatures make a great din in the world. I must therefore now bespeak your attention to this department of their history.

In discussing this subject, I shall consider the noises insects emit — during their motions — when they are feeding, or otherwise employed — when they are calling or commanding — or when they are under the influence of the passions; of fear, of anger, of sorrow, joy, or love.

The only kind of locomotion during which these animals produce sounds, is flying: for though the hill-ants (*Formica rufa,* L.), as I formerly observed, make a rustling noise with their feet when walking over dry leaves, I know of no other insect the tread of which is accompanied by sound — except indeed the flea, whose steps, a lady assures me, she always hears when it paces over her night-cap, and that it clicks as if it was walking in pattens!! That the flight of numbers of insects is attended by a humming or booming is known to almost every one; but that the great majority move through the air in silence, has not perhaps been so often observed. Generally speaking, those that fly with the most force and rapidity, and with wings seemingly motionless, make the most noise: while those that fly gently and leisurely, and visibly fan the air with their wings, yield little or no sound.

Amongst the beetle tribes (*Coleoptera*), none is more noticed, or more celebrated for "wheeling its droning flight," than the common dung-chafer (*Scarabœus stercorarius,* L.) and its affinities. Linné affirms — but the prognostic sometimes fails — that when these insects fly in numbers, it indicates a subsequent fine day. The truth is, they only fly in fine weather. Mr. White[4] has remarked, that in the dusk of the evening beetles begin to buz, and that partridges begin to call exactly at the same time. The common cockchafer, and that which appears at the summer solstice (*Melolonthavulgaris* and *solstitialis,* F.), when they hover over the summits of trees in numbers, produce a hum somewhat resembling that of bees swarming. Perhaps some insect of this kind may occasion the humming in the air mentioned by Mr. White, and which you and I have often heard in other places. "There is," says he, "a natural occurrence to be met with in the highest part of our down on the hot summer days, which always amuses me much, without giving me any satisfaction with respect to the cause of it; and that is a loud

---

[4]Gilbert White. [Ed.]

audible humming of bees in the air, though not one insect is to be seen. Any person would suppose that a large swarm of bees was in motion, and playing about over his head."

> Resounds the living surface of the ground—
> Nor undelightful is the ceaseless hum
> To him who muses through the woods at noon,
> Or drowsy shepherd as he lies reclin'd.

The hotter the weather, the higher insects will soar; and it is not improbable that the sound produced by numbers may be heard, when those that produce it are out of sight. The burying-beetle (*Necrophorus Vespillo,* F.), whose singular history so much amused you, as well as *Cicindela sylvatica* of the same order, flies likewise, as I have more than once witnessed, with a considerable hum.

Whether the innumerable locust armies, to which I have so often called your attention, make any noise in their flight, I have not been able to ascertain; the mere impulse of the wings of myriads and myriads of these creatures upon the air, must, one would think, produce some sound. In the symbolical locusts mentioned in the Apocalypse, this is compared to the sound of chariots rushing to battle: an illustration which the inspired author of that book would scarcely have had recourse to, if the real locusts winged their way in silence.

Amongst the *Hemiptera,* I know only a single species that is of noisy flight; though doubtless, were the attention of entomologists directed to that object, others would be found exhibiting the same peculiarity. The insect I allude to (*Coreus marginatus,* F.) is one of the numerous tribe of bugs; when flying, especially when hovering together in a sunny sheltered spot, they emit a hum as loud as that of the hive-bee.

From the magnitude and strength of their wings, it might be supposed that many *lepidopterous* insects would not be silent in their flight; and indeed many of the hawk-moths (*Sphinx,* F.), and some of the larger moths (*Bombyx,* F.), are not so; *B. Cossus,* for instance, is said to emulate the booming of beetles by means of its large stiff wings; whence in Germany it is called the humming-bird (*Brumm-Vogel*). But the great body of these numerous tribes, even those that fan the air with "sail-broad vans," produce little or no sound by their motion. I must therefore leave them, as well as the *Trichoptera* and *Neuroptera,* which are equally barren of insects of sounding wing—and proceed to an order, the *Hymenoptera,* in which the insects that compose it are, many of them, of more fame for this property.

The indefatigable hive-bee, as she flies from flower to flower, amuses the observer with her hum, which, though monotonous, pleases by exciting the idea of happy industry, that wiles the toils of labour with a song. When she alights upon a flower, and is engaged in collecting its sweets, her hum ceases; but it is resumed again the moment that she leaves it. The wasp and hornet also are strenuous hummers; and when they enter our apartments, their hum often brings terror with it. But the most sonorous fliers of this order are the larger humble-bees, whose bombination, booming, or bombing, may be heard from a considerable distance, gradually increasing as the animal approaches you, and when, in its wheeling flight, it rudely passes close to your ear, almost stunning you by its sharp, shrill, and deafening sound. Many genera, however, of this order fly silently.

But the noisiest wings belong to insects of the *dipterous* order, a majority of which, probably, give notice of their approach by the sound of their trumpets. Most of those, however, that have a slender body, the gnat genus (*Culex*) excepted, explore the air in silence. Of this description are the *Tipulidæ*, the *Asilidæ*, the genus *Empis*, and their affinities. The rest are more or less insects of a humming flight; and with respect to many of them, their hum is a sound of terror and dismay to those who hear it. To man, the trumpet of the gnat or mosquito; and to beasts, that of the gad-fly; the various kinds of horse flies (*Tabanus, Stomoxys, Hippobosca*); and of the Ethiopian zimb, as I have before related at large, is the signal of intolerable annoyance. Homer, in his *Batrachomyomachia*, long ago celebrated the first of these as a trumpeter —

For their sonorous trumpets far renown'd,
Of battle the dire charge mosquitos sound.

Mr. Pope, in his translation, with his usual inaccuracy, thinking no doubt to improve upon his author, has turned the old bard's gnats into hornets. In Guiana these animals are distinguished by a name still more tremendous, being called the devil's trumpeters. I have observed that early in the spring, before their thirst for blood seizes them, gnats when flying emit no sound. At this moment (Feb. 18th) two females are flying about my windows in perfect silence.[. . .]

But love is the soul of song with those that may be esteemed the most musical insects, the grasshopper tribes (*Gryllidae*), and the long celebrated Cicada (*Tettigonia*, F.). You would suppose, perhaps, that the ladies would bear their share in these amatory strains. But here you would be mistaken — female insects are too intent upon their business, too coy and reserved to tell their love even to the winds. The males alone

Formosam resonare docent Amaryllida sylvas.[5]

---

[5] "You teach the forest to resound with the name Amyrillis." Virgil, *Eclogues* 1.5. [Ed.]

With respect to the *Cicadæ*, this was observed by Aristotle; and Pliny, as usual, has retailed it after him. The observation also holds good with respect to the *Gryllidæ* and other insects, probably, whose love is musical. Olivier however has noticed an exception to this doctrine; for he relates, that in a species of beetle (*Pimelia striata*, F.), the female has a round granulated spot in the middle of the second segment of the abdomen, by striking which against any hard substance, she produces a rather loud sound, and that the male, obedient to this call, soon attends her, and they pair.

As I have nothing to communicate to you with respect to the love-songs of other insects, my further observations will be confined to the two tribes lately mentioned, the *Gryllidæ* and the *Cicadæ*.

No sound is to me more agreeable than the chirping of most of the Gryllidæ; it gives life to solitude, and always conveys to my mind the idea of a perfectly happy being. As these creatures are now very properly divided into several genera, I shall say a few words upon the song of such as are known to be vocal, separately.

The remarkable genus *Pneumora*—whose pellucid abdomen is blown up like a bladder, on which account they are called Blaazops by the Dutch colonists at the Cape—in the evening, for they are silent in the day, make a tremulous and tolerably loud noise, which is sometimes heard on every side. How their sound is produced is not stated.

The cricket tribe are a very noisy race, and their chirping is caused by the friction of the bases of their elytra against each other. For this purpose there is something peculiar in their structure, which I shall describe to you. The elytra[6] of both sexes are divided longitudinally into two portions; a vertical or lateral one, which covers the sides; and a horizontal or dorsal one, which covers the back. In the female both these portions resemble each other in their nervures;[7] which running obliquely in two directions, by their intersection form numerous small lozenge-shaped or rhomboidal meshes or areolets. The elytra also of these have no elevation at their base. In the males the vertical portion does not materially differ from that of the females; but in the horizontal the base of each elytrum is elevated so as to form a cavity underneath. The nervures also, which are stronger and more prominent, run here and there very irregularly with various inflexions, describing curves, spirals, and other figures difficult and tedious to describe, and producing a variety of areolets of different size and shape, but generally larger than those of the female: particularly towards the

---

[6] Forewings of beetles. [Ed.]

[7] Veins of an insect's wing. [Ed.]

extremity of the wing you may observe a space nearly circular, surrounded by one nervure, and divided into two areolets by another. The friction of the nervures of the upper or convex surface of the base of the left-hand elytrum—which is the undermost—against those of the lower or concave surface of the base of the right-hand—which is the uppermost one—will communicate vibrations to the areas of membrane, more or less intense in proportion to the rapidity of the friction, and thus produce the sound for which these creatures are noted.

The merry inhabitant of our dwellings, the house-cricket (*Acheta domestica,* F.), though it is often heard by day, is most noisy in the night. As soon as it grows dusk, their shrill note increases till it becomes quite an annoyance, and interrupts conversation. When the male sings, he elevates the elytra so as to form an acute angle with the body, and then rubs them against each other by a horizontal and very brisk motion. The learned Scaliger is said to have been particularly delighted with the chirping of these animals, and was accustomed to keep them in a box for his amusement. We are told that they have been sold in Africa at a high price, and employed to procure sleep. If they could be used to supply the place of laudanum, and lull the restlessness of busy thought in this country, the exchange would be beneficial. Like many other noisy persons, crickets like to hear nobody louder than themselves. Ledelius relates that a woman, who had tried in vain every method she could think of to banish them from her house, at last got rid of them by the noise made by drums and trumpets, which she had procured to entertain her guests at a wedding. They instantly forsook the house, and she heard of them no more.[8]

The field-cricket (*Acheta campestris,* F.) makes a shrilling noise—still more sonorous than that of the house-cricket—which may be heard at a great distance. Mouffet tells us, that their sound may be imitated by rubbing their elytra, after they are taken off, against each other. "Sounds," says Mr. White, "do not always give us pleasure according to their sweetness and melody; nor do harsh sounds always displease. Thus the shrilling of the field-cricket, though sharp and stridulous, yet marvellously delights some hearers, filling their minds with a train of summer ideas of every thing that is rural, verdurous, and joyous." One of these crickets, when confined in a paper cage and set in the sun, and supplied with plants moistened with water—for if they are not wetted it will die—will feed, and thrive, and become so merry and loud, as to be irksome in the same room where a person is sitting.

---

[8] Goldsmith's *Animated Nature,* 6. 28.

Having never seen a female of that extraordinary animal the mole-cricket (*Gryllotalpa vulgaris*, Latr.), I cannot say what difference obtains in the reticulation of the elytra of the two sexes. The male varies in this respect from the other male crickets, for they have no circular area, nor do the nervures run so irregularly; the areolets, however, toward their base are large, with very tense membrane. The base itself also is scarcely at all elevated. Circumstances these, which demonstrate the propriety of considering them distinct from the other crickets. This creature is not however mute. Where they abound they may be heard about the middle of April singing their love-ditty in a low, dull, jarring, uninterrupted note, not unlike that of the goat-sucker (*Caprimulgus europæus*, L.), but more inward. I remember once tracing one by its shrilling to the very hole, under a stone, in the bank of my canal, in which it was concealed.

Another tribe of grasshoppers (*Locusta*, F.)—the females of which are distinguished by their long ensi-form ovipositor—like the crickets, make their noise by the friction of the base of their elytra. And the chirping they thus produce is long, and seldom interrupted, which distinguishes it from that of the common grasshoppers (*Gryllas*, F.). What is remarkable, the grasshopper lark (*Alauda trivialis*, L.), which preys upon them, makes a similar noise. Professor Lichtenstein in the *Linnean Transactions* has called the attention of naturalists to the eye-like area in the right wing of the males of this genus; but he seems not to have been aware that De Geer had noticed it before him as a sexual character; who also, with good reason, supposes it to assist these animals in the sounds they produce. Speaking of *Locusta viridissima*—common with us—he says "In our male grasshoppers, in that part of the right elytrum which is folded horizontally over the trunk, there is a round plate made of very fine transparent membrane, resembling a little mirror or piece of talc, of the tension of a drum. This membrane is surrounded by a strong and prominent nervure, and is concealed under the fold of the left elytrum, which has also several prominent nervures answering to the margin of the membrane or ocellus. There is," he further remarks, "every reason to believe that the brisk movement with which the grasshopper rubs these nervures against each other, produces a vibration in the membrane augmenting the sound. The males in question sing continually in the hedges and trees during the months of July and August, especially towards sun-set and part of the night. When any one approaches they immediately cease their song."

The last description of singers that I shall notice amongst the Gryllidæ, are those that are more commonly denominated grasshoppers (*Gryllus*, F.). To this genus belong the little chirpers that we hear in every sunny bank, and which make vocal every heath. They begin their song—which is a short chirp regularly interrupted, in which it differs from that of the *Locusta*—long before sun-rise. In the heat of the day it is intermitted, and resumed in the evening. This sound is thus produced: Applying its posterior shank to the thigh, the animal rubs it briskly against the elytrum, doing this alternately with the right and left legs, which causes the regular breaks in the sound. But this is not their whole apparatus of song—since, like the Tettigoniae, they have also a tympanum or drum." De Geer, who examined the insects he describes with the eye of an anatomist, seems to be the only entomologist that has noticed this organ. "On each side of the first segment of the abdomen," says he, "immediately above the origin of the posterior thighs, there is a considerable and deep aperture of rather an oval form, which is partly closed by an irregular flat plate or operculum of a hard substance, but covered by a wrinkled flexible membrane. The opening left by this operculum is semi-lunar, and at the bottom of the cavity is a white pellicle of considerable tension, and shining like a little mirror. On that side of the aperture which is towards the head, there is a little oval hole, into which the point of a pin may be introduced without resistance. When the pellicle is removed, a large cavity appears. In my opinion this aperture, cavity, and above all the membrane in tension, contribute much to produce and augment the sound emitted by the grasshopper." This description, which was taken from the migratory locust (*G. migratorius*, L.), answers tolerably well to the tympanum of our common grasshoppers, only in them the aperture seems to be rather semicircular, and the wrinkled plate—which has no marginal hairs—is clearly a continuation of the substance of the segment. This apparatus so much resembles the drum of the Cicadæ, that there can be little doubt as to its use. The vibrations caused by the friction of the thighs and elytra striking upon this drum, are reverberated by it, and so intenseness is given to the sound. In Spain, we are told that people of fashion keep these animals—called there *Grillo*—in cages, which they name *Grilleria*, for the sake of their song.

I shall conclude this diatribe upon the noises of insects, with a tribe that have long been celebrated for their musical powers; I mean the *Cicadæ*, including the two genera *Fulgora*, L. and *Tettigonia*, F. The *Fulgoræ* appear to be night-singers, while the *Cicadæ* sing usually in the day. The great lantern-fly (*Fulgora laternaria*, L.), from its noise in the evening—nearly resembling the sound of a cymbal, or razorgrinder when at work—is called *Scare-sleep* by the Dutch in Guiana. It begins regularly at sun-set. Perhaps an insect mentioned by Ligon as making a great noise in the night in Barbadoes, may belong to this tribe. "There is a kind of animal in the woods," says he, "that I never saw, which lie all day in holes and hollow trees, and as soon as the sun is down begin their tunes, which are neither singing nor crying, but the shrillest voices I ever heard: nothing can be so nearly resembled to it as the mouths of a pack of small beagles at a distance; and so lively and chirping the noise is, as nothing can be more delightful to the ears, if there were not too much of it; for the music hath no intermission till morning, and then all is husht."

The species of the other genus, *Tettigonia,* F., called by the ancient Greeks—by whom they were often kept in cages for the sake of their song— *Tettix,* seem to have been the favourites of every Grecian bard from Homer and Hesiod to Anacreon and Theocritus. Supposed to be perfectly harmless, and to live only upon the dew, they were addressed by the most endearing epithets, and were regarded as all but divine. One bard entreats the shepherds to spare the innoxious Tettix, that nightingale of the Nymphs, and to make those mischievous birds the thrush and blackbird their prey. Sweet prophet of the summer, says Anacreon, addressing this insect, the Muses love thee, Phœbus himself loves thee, and has given thee a shrill song; old age does not wear thee; thou art wise, earth-born, musical, impassive, without blood; thou art almost like a god. So attached were the Athenians to these insects, that they were accustomed to fasten golden images of them in their hair, implying at the same time a boast that they themselves, as well as the Cicadæ, were *Terrae filii.* They were regarded indeed by all as the happiest as well as the most innocent of animals—not, we will suppose, for the reason given by the saucy Rhodian Xenarchus, when he says,

Happy the Cicadas' lives,
Since they all have voiceless wives.

If the Grecian *Tettix* or *Cicada* had been distinguished by a harsh and deafening note, like those of some other countries, it would hardly have been an object of such affection. That it was not, is clearly proved by the connection which was supposed to exist between it and music. Thus the sound of this insect and of the harp were called by one and the same name. A Cicada sitting upon a harp was a usual emblem of the science of music, which was thus accounted for: When two rival musicians, Eunomus and Ariston, were contending upon that instrument, a Cicada flying to the former and sitting upon his harp, supplied the place of a broken string, and so secured to him the victory. To excel this animal in singing seems to have been the highest commendation of a singer; and even the eloquence of Plato was not thought to suffer by a comparison with it. At Surinam the noise of the *Tettigonia Tibicen* is still supposed so much to resemble the sound of a harp or lyre, that they are called there harpers (*Lierman*).

Whether the Grecian Cicadæ maintain at present their ancient character for music, travellers do not tell us.

Those of other countries, however, have been held in less estimation for their powers of song; or rather have been execrated for the deafening din that they produce. Virgil accuses those of Italy of bursting the very shrubs with their noise; and Dr. Smith observes that this species, which is very common, makes a most disagreeable dull chirping.[. . .]

William Lawrence (1783–1867)

W illiam Lawrence was a surgeon and comparative anatomist whose lectures produced widespread discussion and controversy in the early years of the nineteenth century. He was among the first to use the phrase "natural history" in relation to the study of human beings and to use the term *biology* to refer to the life sciences (*OED*). His *Lectures on Physiology, Zoology, and the Natural History of Man* (1819) were deemed so controversial that Lord Eldon refused copyright on the grounds that they undermined religion by contradicting Biblical authority. These lectures, from which the following extracts are taken, were also attacked for taking the idea of evolution seriously, for frankly discussing human sexuality and inbreeding, and for setting forth views that increasingly came to be seen as racist. Lawrence had been apprenticed to John Abernethy in 1799, although the two would later become prime antagonists in a debate between materialists and vitalists at the Royal College of Surgeons. Marilyn Butler notes that Lawrence served as Percy Shelley's personal physician. She adds that Mary Shelley's *Frankenstein* "to some degree acts out the debate between Abernethy and Lawrence" ("Radical Science" 307). According to Butler, Lawrence's position was important because it "was above all *natural history*—the early evolutionists' non-scriptural and for some minds anti-scriptural narrative of the life of animal species" (305).

Mechanists, like Lawrence, believed that the physical body of an organism, plus a mechanical and chemical explanation of its processes, was all that was needed to account for life, including even activities such as reproduction, dreaming, and complex mental states. In short, there was no "soul." Vitalists like Abernethy, by contrast, believed that something more than the physical body (a vital force, an *elan vital*) had to be posited in order to account for life. This debate, and Lawrence's presentation of the materialist view, contributed to an even wider controversy about physical nature and natural history during the Romantic period. On the one hand, naturalists were beginning to ascribe birdsong to a purely mechanistic instinct. In addition, they came increasingly to see all human beings and the history of the human species as parts of animate nature, subject to the same physical laws and organic operations as orangutans, lizards, and bacteria. On the other hand, even skeptical poets remained willing to imagine the songs of nightingales and skylarks as directly connected to human life in important ways. In this regard, nature continued to hold powerful secrets that might be discoverable by humans, even if these secrets were now imagined in increasingly secular and scientific terms.

From Lectures on Physiology, Zoology, and the Natural History of Man

FROM LECTURE III, ON THE STUDY OF PHYSIOLOGY

In physiology, as in the physical sciences, we quickly reach the boundaries of knowledge whenever we attempt to penetrate the first causes of the phenomena. The most we can accomplish is to make gradual conquests from the territories of ignorance and doubt; and to leave under their dominion those objects only, which our reason has not reached, or is not able to reach. The great end of observation and experiment is to discover, among the various phenomena, those which are the most general. When these are well ascertained, they serve as principles, from which other facts may be déduced. The Newtonian theory of gravitation is a most splendid example. The only object of uncertainty, which then remains, is the first cause of a small number of facts. The phenomena succeed each other, like the generations of men, in an order which we observe, but of which we can neither determine nor conceive the commencement. We follow the links of an endless chain: and, by holding fast to it, we may ascend from one link to another; but the point of suspension is not within the reach of our feeble powers.

To call life a property of organisation would be unmeaning: it would be nonsense. The primary or elementary animal structures are endued with

William Lawrence, *Lectures on Physiology, Zoology, and the Natural History of Man*. London: J. Callow, 1819.

vital properties; their combinations compose the animal organs, in which, by means of the vital properties of the component elementary structures, the animal functions are carried on. The state of the animal, in which the continuance of these processes is evidenced by obvious external signs, is called life.

The striking differences between living and inorganic bodies, and the strong contrast of their respective properties, naturally excited curiosity respecting the causes of this diversity, and endeavours to shew the mode in which it was effected. Here we quit the path of observation, and wander into the regions of imagination and conjecture. It is the poetic ground of physiology; but the union is unnatural, and, like other unnatural unions, unproductive. The fiction spoils the science, and the admixture of science is fatal to inspiration. The fictitious beings of poetry are generally interesting in themselves, and are brought forwards to answer some useful purpose; but the genii and spirits of physiology are awkward and clumsy, and do nothing at last, which could not be accomplished just as well without them: they literally incumber us with their help.

For those, who think it impossible that the living organic structures should have vital properties without some extrinsic aid; although they require no such assistance for the equally wonderful affinities of chemistry, for gravity, elasticity, or the other properties of matter, a great variety of explanations, suited to all tastes and comprehensions, has been provided.

Some are contented with stating that the properties of life arise from a vital principle. This explanation has the merit of simplicity, whatever we may think of its profoundness: and it has the advantage of being transferable and equally applicable to any other subject. Some hold that an immaterial principle, and others, that a material, but invisible and very subtle agent is superadded to the obvious structure of the body, and enables it to exhibit vital phenomena. The former explanation will be of use to those who are conversant with immaterial beings, and who understand how they are connected with and act on matter. But I know no description of persons likely to benefit by the latter. For subtle matter is still matter; and if this fine stuff can possess vital properties, surely they may reside in a fabric which differs only in being a little coarser.

Mr. Hunter has a good substantial sort of living principle; he seems to have had no taste for immaterial agents, or for subtle matters. His materia vitæ is something tangible; he describes it as a substance like that of the brain, diffused all over the body, and entering into the composition of every part. He conceives even the blood to have its share.[1] We may smile at

---

[1] That the author of the *Physiological Lectures* should have published two books, principally for the purpose of explaining, illustrating, and confirming Mr. Hunter's "*Theory of*

these fancies, without any disrespect to a name that we all revere, without any insensibility to the merits of a surgeon and physiologist, whose genius and labours have reflected honour on our profession and our country. If the father of poetry sometimes falls asleep, a physiologist may be allowed to dream a little: but they who are awake, need not shut their eyes, and endeavour to follow his example, need not exhibit another instance of the perverted taste, which led the disciples of an ancient philosopher to drink spinach-juice, that they might look pale like their master.

Plato made the vital principle to be an emanation of the anima mundi, or soul of the world; an explanation, no doubt, quite satisfactory to those who know what the soul of the world is, and how other souls emanate from it.

The Brahmins of the East hold a similar notion; but they make the soul after death pass on into other bodies or into animals, according to its behaviour; admitting, however, that those of the good are immediately reabsorbed into the Divinity. Some of the Greeks adopted a distinct vital, sensitive, and rational principle in man.

These are merely specimens; a few articles, as patterns, selected from a vast assortment. If you do not like either of them, there are plenty more to choose from. As these and a hundred other such hypotheses are all supported by equally good proof; which is neither more nor less, in each instance, than the thorough conviction of the inventor; and, as they are inconsistent with each other, and, therefore, mutually destructive, we need not trouble ourselves further until their respective advocates can agree together in selecting some one for their patronage, and discarding the rest. For of these, as of the numerous religions in the world, only one can be true.

What is comparative anatomy? The expression is rather vague and indefinite. You naturally inquire what is compared? what is the object of comparison? The structure of animals may be compared to that of man. To lay down the laws of the animal economy from facts furnished by the

---

Life," without shewing us in either what that theory was, without a single citation or reference to identify this doctrine, thus boldly baptised with the name of Hunter, as the literary offspring of its alleged parent, appears strange and suspicious. It is easily explained; for this *Hunterian* theory of life, which its real author so stoutly maintains to be not only probable and rational, but also verifiable, is no where to be found in the published writings of Mr. Hunter; and does not even resemble the speculations on the same subject, which occur in the posthumous work on the *Blood, Inflammation, &c.* part i. chap. i. sec. 5, *on the living Principle of the Blood.* In perusing the writings of Mr. Hunter, we should always remember his unfortunate want of early education, the difficulty he felt in conveying his notions clearly by words, and the mutilation which his thoughts must have suffered in passing through the press, both from the causes just mentioned, and from the revision and correction to which some of his writings were subjected.

human subject only, would be like writing the natural history of our species from observing the inhabitants of a single town or village.

Repeated observations and multiplied experiments on the various tribes of animated nature have cleared up many obscure and doubtful phenomena in the economy of man; a continuation of this method will place physiology on the solid basis of experience, and build up science on ground hitherto occupied by fancy and conjecture.

The physiologist, who is conversant with natural history in general, is fortified against uncertain opinions, and the showy but flimsy textures of verbal sophistry. An hypothesis, which to others appears perfectly adequate to the object in view, is not convincing to him. He rises above the particular object to which it is accommodated, in order to appreciate its value; as we ascend an eminence to gain a commanding view of a district, to distinguish its features, to ascertain the number and bearings of its parts, and their relations to the surrounding country.

There are three points of view, in which comparative anatomy has an important bearing on human physiology.

In the infancy of science, physiology, such as it was, owed its origin to zootomy, which was practised by physicians and naturalists eighteen centuries before human dissections began. The *Anatomia Partium Corporis humani* of Mondini, written in the beginning of the fourteenth century, was the first compendium of human anatomy composed from actual dissection. It is easy to shew that even the osteology of Galen was not drawn from the human skeleton: and many parts of the body still bear names derived from animals, which names are in some instances not correctly applicable to the human structure; for example, the epithets right and left as applied to the cavities of the heart.

Although human anatomy, after its first scientific development by Berengar of Carpi, was so quickly brought to a high pitch of perfection by the great triumvirate, Vesalius, Fallopius, and Eustachius, yet the most important discoveries, those of greatest weight in physiology considered as the basis of medicine, were made in animals. No period has been so fruitful in these discoveries, nor so distinguished in the literary history of our science, as the seventeenth century, in which the anatomy of brutes was most zealously cultivated, and most of the great anatomical facts were found out, which, by unveiling the hidden springs and movements of the animal machine, have furnished the principles, on which rational pathology and practical medicine have been established.

These comparative researches render the most important service by affording a criterion in doubtful cases for determining the uses of parts; which, as the main object of this fundamental medical science, has been well chosen by Galen for the title of his classical work on physiology.

Hence Haller observes that the situation, figure, and size of parts ought to be learned from man; their uses and motions must be drawn from animals.

I shall adduce a few particulars for the purpose of exemplifying the preceding remarks.

A serpent swallows an animal larger than itself, which fills its aesophagus, as well as stomach, and of which the digestion occupies several days or even weeks. We open the reptile during this process, and find that part of the animal which remained in the aesophagus, sound and natural, while the portion which had descended into the stomach, though still retaining its figure, is semi-liquefied, reduced into so soft a state, as to break down under the slightest pressure. How effectually does this simple fact refute the notions of digestion being mechanical trituration; or solution by heat (for the animal is cold-blooded); or the effect of fermentation, or putrefaction, or coction![2]

The slow and languid motion of the blood in cold-blooded animals, has enabled us to demonstrate in them the circulation, which in man can only be proved by argument.

Physiologists have been much perplexed to find out a common centre in the nervous system, in which all sensations may meet, and from which all acts of volition may emanate; a central apartment for the superintendent of the human panopticon; or, in its imposing Latin name, a sensorium commune. That there must be such a point they are well convinced, having satisfied themselves that the human mind is simple and indivisible, and therefore capable of dwelling only in one place. The pineal gland, the corpus callosum, the pons Varolii, and other parts, have been successively suggested.[3] Now, there are many orders of animals with sensation and volition, who have none of these parts. And this assumed unity of the sentient principle becomes very doubtful, when we see other animals, possessed of nervous systems, which, after being cut in two, form again two perfect animals. Is the immaterial principle divided by the knife, as well as the body?

The heart has been regarded by many physiologists as the prime mover in the animal machine; the origin of vital motion in the embryo, the chief agent in forming and maintaining the fabric, and the main-spring for keeping the whole machinery in action. There are whole classes of living beings, and some of complicated structure, which have no heart.

Some have regarded the spleen as a spunge; soaking up the blood when the stomach is empty, and allowing it to be squeezed out again by the pressure of this bag when distended. In many animals the spleen is neither

---

[2] Boiling, the action of heat. [Ed.]

[3] Lawrence lists only physical structures of the human brain in this discussion of the soul. [Ed.]

cellular, nor so situated as to be compressible by the stomach. This is the case, generally speaking, with birds and reptiles.

The office of conveying away fluids from the stomach has been assigned to it, making it a kind of waste-pipe to prevent the liquid contents of the digestive cistern from rising above a certain level. But it exists in reptiles and fishes, where neither the figure of the stomach, nor the known habits of the animals, in respect to food and digestion, admit of this explanation. In the camel, which retains the water in its stomach, and in the horse, where it passes very rapidly into the caecum, the spleen is as large as in other animals. In beasts of prey, which hardly drink at all, it is as large and cellular as in the herbivorous ruminant animals. Its size and its cells are particularly conspicuous in the latter: yet the fluids which they swallow, go into the paunch, and not into the true digestive stomach.

Although arguments from analogy are of great service in physiology, and other departments of natural history, although they throw light on obscure points, and give an interest to many discussions, their employment requires caution, and they should rather be resorted to for illustration than relied on for direct proof. Organs corresponding in situation and name are not always constructed alike; hence a part is sometimes employed in one class of animals for a different purpose from that which the instrument of the same name and of analogous position in the body executes in another. The gizzards of the gallinæ have a prodigious triturating power; and those, who first ascertained by experiment the extent of their power, were disposed to infer that digestion is effected in man by mechanical attrition. Now, the gizzard, although the corresponding part to our stomach, is in structure and action the instrument of mastication; and, as birds have no teeth, it is the only instrument for dividing the hard grain on which they feed. Further inquiry shews, that even in this stomach, which is covered by a thick insensible cuticle, capable of bearing the friction of grain and siliceous pebbles, digestion is really effected, as in the stomach of man, by solution; the solvent juice being secreted by the large collection of glands at the cardiac end of the œsophagus, and having an operation similar to that of the gastric fluid of quadrupeds.

It has been argued, that the arteries of the mammalia must have a contractile power, because, in some worms without a heart, these vessels carry on the circulation alone. The whole economy is too different in the two instances to admit of inferences from analogy; the circulating apparatus, in particular, is formed on plans altogether different in the two cases; and the structure and actions of the vessels of worms, are, in fact, very little known.

Because the vesiculæ seminales in some animals do not communicate with the vasa deferentia, and therefore cannot receive the fluid secreted in the testicles, it has been inferred that they do not serve the purpose of reservoirs for the seminal secretion in man, where, however, they have so free a communication with the vasa deferentia, that any fluids pass into and even distend the former, before they go on into the urethra. The organic arrangement is different in the two instances; and this difference leads us to expect a modification in the function, instead of authorising us to infer that the same office is executed in exactly the same manner in both cases. If we met with animals, in whom the cystic duct opened into the small intestines separately from the hepatic, shall we therefore infer that the human gall-bladder is not a receptacle for the hepatic bile?

Again, animals may be compared to each other. Each organ must be examined in all the gradations of living beings; its modifications compared and surveyed in relation to the varieties of other parts, before a just notion of its functions can be formed. This kind of examination of the animal kingdom, leads to what may be called general anatomy, the basis of general physiology; the objects of which are to determine the organisation, and unfold the vital laws of the whole system of living beings.

In the physical sciences we have the power of insulating the various objects of our research; of analysing them into their component elements, of subtracting these successively, and thus determining beforehand all the conditions of the problem we may be studying. It would be desirable to employ the same proceeding in natural history; and it is resorted to, when the objects are sufficiently simple. But they are for the most part too complicated, and connected too closely by mutual influences. We cannot analyse an animal of the higher orders, and observe the simple result of each organ by itself; for, if we destroy one part, the motion of the whole machine is stopped. The phenomena come before us under conditions not regulated by our own choice; and in a state of complication requiring close attention and careful discrimination to search out and determine the precise share of each component part.

In this difficulty, comparative observations afford some assistance. The animals of inferior classes are so many subjects of experiment ready prepared for us; where any organ may be observed under every variety of simplicity and complication in its own structure: of existence alone, or in combination with others.

LECTURE IV

Nature of Life; Methodical Arrangement of living
Beings; Species, Varieties, Genera, Orders, &c.
Progressive Simplification of Organisation, and of
Functions. Intellectual Functions of the Brain, in the
natural and disordered State, explained on the same
Principles as the Offices of other Organs.

The notion of life is too complicated, embraces too many particulars, to admit of a short definition. It varies in the different kinds of animals, as their structure and functions vary; so that a description drawn from one would not be applicable to others differently situated in the animal series. If we include in the description those circumstances only, which are common to the whole animal kingdom, we must direct our view to beings of the most simple structure, where the phenomenon is reduced to its essential features, and these are not obscured or confused by accessary circumstances.

The distinguishing characters of living beings will be found in their texture or organisation; in their component elements; in their form; in their peculiar manifestations or phenomena; and in the limits, that is, in the origin and termination of their vital existence.

Their body is composed of solids and fluids; the former arranged in fibres and laminae,[4] so as to intercept spaces, which are occupied by the latter. The solids give the form to the body, and are contractile. The fluids are generally in motion.

The component elements, of which nitrogen is a principal one, united in numbers of three, four, or more, easily pass into new combinations; and are, for the most part, readily convertible into fluid or gas.

Such a kind of composition, and such an arrangement of the constituent parts, is called organisation; and, as the vital phenomena are only such motions as are consistent with these material arrangements, life, so far as our experience goes (and we have no other guide in these matters), is necessarily connected with organisation. Life presupposes organisation, as the movements of a watch presuppose the wheels, levers, and other mechanism of the instrument.

The organisation assumes certain definite forms in each kind of animals; not merely in the external arrangement of the whole, but in each part, and in all the details of each. On this depends the kind of motion

---

[4]Connective tissues. [Ed.]

which each part can exercise, the share which it is capable of contributing to the general vital movement; which latter, or, in short, life, is the result of the mutual actions and reactions of all parts.

Living bodies exhibit a constant internal motion, in which we observe an uninterrupted admission and assimilation of new, and a correspondent separation and expulsion of old particles. The form remains the same, the component particles are continually changing. While this motion lasts, the body is said to be alive; when it has irrecoverably ceased, to be dead. The organic structure then yields to the chemical affinities of the surrounding agents, and is speedily destroyed.

All living beings have, in the first place, formed part of a body like their own; have been attached to a parent before the period of their independent existence. The new animal, while thus connected, is called a germ: its separation constitutes generation or birth. After this it increases in size according to certain fixed laws for each species and each part.

The duration of existence is limited in all animals: after a longer or shorter period the vital movements are arrested, and their cessation or death seems to occur as a necessary consequence of life.

Thus, then, absorption, assimilation, exhalation, generation, and growth, are functions common to all living beings; birth and death the universal limits of their existence; a reticular contractile tissue, with fluids in its interstices, the general essence of their structure; substances easily convertible into the state of liquid or gas, and combinations readily changing, the basis of their chemical composition. Fixed forms, perpetuated by generation, distinguish their species, determine the combination of secondary functions peculiar to each, and assign to them their respective situations in the system of the universe.

After forming this general notion of living beings, we proceed to examine the animal kingdom in detail. The first glance discovers to us an infinite variety of forms; diversities so numerous, that the attempt to observe and register the whole seems almost hopeless. We find, however, that these forms, at first view so infinitely various, admit of being classed together, of being formed into groups, each of which is distinguished by certain essential characters. In the latter all the animals comprehended in each group agree; while they differ from each other in particulars of minor importance.

I have already mentioned that a fixed external form belongs to each animal, and that it is continued by generation. Certain forms, the same as those existing in the world at the present moment, have existed from time immemorial. Such, at least, is the result of the separate and combined proofs furnished by our own observation and experience respecting the laws of the animal kingdom, by the voice of tradition and of history, by the remains of antiquity, and by every kind of collateral evidence.

All the animals belonging to one of these forms constitute what zoologists call a species. This resemblance must not be understood in a rigorous sense; for every being has its individual characters of size, figure, colour, proportions. In this sense the character of variety is stamped on all nature's works. She has made it a fundamental law, that no two of her productions shall be exactly alike; and this law is invariably observed through the whole creation. Each tree, each flower, each leaf, exemplifies it; every animal has its individual character; each human being has something distinguishing in form, proportions, countenance, gesture, voice; in feelings, thought, and temper; in mental as well as corporeal physiognomy. This variety is the source of every thing beautiful and interesting in the external world; the foundation of the whole moral fabric of the universe.

I cannot help pointing out to you how strongly the voice of nature, so clearly expressed in this obvious law, opposes all attempts at making mankind act or think alike. Yet the legislators and rulers of the world have persisted for centuries in endeavouring to reduce the opinions, the belief of their subjects, to certain fancied standards of perfection; to impress on human thought that dreary sameness, and dull monotony, which all the discipline and all the rigour of a religious sect have been hardly able to maintain in the outward garb of its followers. The mind, however, cannot be drilled, cannot be made to move at the word of command; it scorns all shackles; and rises with fresh energy from every new attempt to bind it down on this bed of Procrustes.

All the oppression and persecution, all the bloodshed and misery, which the attempts to produce uniformity have occasioned, are, however, a less evil than the success of these mad efforts would be, were it possible for them to succeed in opposition to the natural constitution of the human mind, to the general scheme and plain design of nature.

The most powerful monarch of modern history, who exhibited the rare example of a voluntary retreat from the cares of empire, while still fully able to wield the sceptre, was rendered sensible of the extreme folly he had been guilty of in attempting to produce uniformity of opinion among the numerous subjects of his extensive dominions, by finding himself unable to make even two watches go alike, although every part of this simple mechanism was constructed, formed, and adjusted by himself. The dear experience and the candid confession of Charles V. were thrown away on his bigoted son; who repeated on a still grander scale, with fresh horrors and cruelties, the bloody experiment of dragooning his subjects into uniformity, only to instruct the world by a still more memorable failure.

The increasing light of reason has destroyed many of these remnants of ignorance and barbarism; but much remains to be done, before the final accomplishment of the grand purpose, which, however delayed, cannot be ultimately defeated; I mean the complete emancipation of the mind, the destruction of all creeds and articles of faith, and the establishment of full freedom of opinion and belief. I cannot doubt that a day will arrive, when the attempts at enforcing uniformity of opinion will be deemed as irrational, and as little desirable, as to endeavour at producing sameness of face and stature.[5]

In the mean time, no efforts capable of accelerating a consummation so beneficial to mankind should be omitted; and I have therefore attempted to shew you that, on this point, the analogies of natural history accord with the dictates of reason and the invariable instructions of experience.

Certain external circumstances, as food, climate, mode of life, have the power of modifying the animal organisation, so as to make it deviate from that of the parent. But this effect terminates in the individual. Thus, a fair Englishman, if exposed to the sun, becomes dark and swarthy in Bengal; but his offspring, if from an Englishwoman, are born just as fair as he himself was originally: and the children, after any number of generations, that we have yet observed, are still born equally fair, provided there has been no intermixture of dark blood.

Moreover, under certain circumstances, with which we are not well acquainted, a more important change of organisation occurs. A new character springs up, and is propagated by generation: this constitutes a variety, in the language of naturalists. The number and degree of these variations are confined within narrow limits; they occur chiefly in the domesticated animals, and have not interfered with the transmission and continuation of those forms which constitute species. They will be more particularly considered hereafter.

---

[5] These opinions do not need the support of names, or I might cite Locke, in whose *Letters on Toleration* all the great principles on which the freedom of the human mind rests are fully developed, and unanswerably established. This may be called speculation, theory, or other bad names; I have therefore pleasure in referring to the authority of a practical statesman and enlightened magistrate. See Jefferson's *Notes on Virginia*, p. 261–270. Also, the Appendix, No. 3, containing *"An Act for establishing religious Freedom passed in the Assembly of Virginia in the Beginning of the Year 1786"*; an admirable model, which has been perfectly successful, and hitherto adopted in no other part of the world.

John Clare (1793–1864)

John Clare has been described as the quintessential nature poet of the Romantic era. He was acclaimed as a "natural poet" from the time his first volume, *Poems Descriptive of Rural Life and Scenery,* appeared in 1820. Unlike Robert Burns, whose education undercut claims for his status as a primitive or rustic, Clare was an uneducated field laborer who produced direct, sensuous lyrics that described the natural world around his native village of Helpston in Northamptonshire. Many of his most powerful poems derive directly from the memories of his childhood, recorded with an immediacy and naturalness that has rarely been achieved in English verse before or since. Although influenced by his reading of Thomson, Cowper, Wordsworth, and Byron, Clare's poetic style and manuscript idiosyncrasies reveal a voice that is unique among the poets of his era:

> While ground larks on a sweeing clump of rushes
> Or on the top twigs of the oddling bushes
> Chirp their "cree creeing" note that sounds of spring
> And sky larks meet the sun wi' flittering wing
> 5 Soon as the morning opes its brightning eye
> Large clouds of sturnels blacken thro the sky
> From oizer holts about the rushy fen
> And reedshaw borders by the river Nen.
> (From "March," *The Shepherd's Calendar.*)

Clare's unselfconsciousness came at a price, however. By 1837 he was committed to an asylum at Epping Forest and later to the Northampton Asylum for the remainder of his life. Some of his most powerful and moving lyrics were written during his periods of "insanity."

From Poems Descriptive
of Rural Life and Scenery

Address to a Lark

Singing in Winter

Ay, little Larky! what's the reason,
Singing thus in winter season?
Nothing, surely, can be pleasing
    To make thee sing;
5 For I see nought but cold and freezing,
    And feel its sting.

Perhaps, all done with silent mourning,
Thou think'st that Summer is returning,
And this the last, cold, frosty morning,
10   To chill thy breast;
  If so, I pity thy discerning:
    And so I've guess'd.

Poor, little Songster! vainly cheated;
Stay, leave thy singing uncompleted;
15 Drop where thou wast beforehand seated,
    In thy warm nest;
Nor let vain wishes be repeated,
    But sit at rest.

'Tis Winter; let the cold content thee:
20 Wish after nothing till it's sent thee,
For disappointments will torment thee,
    Which will be thine:
I know it well, for I've had plenty
    Misfortunes mine.

25 Advice, sweet Warbler! don't despise it:
None knows what's what, but he that tries it;
And then he well knows how to prize it,
    And so do I:
Thy case, with mine I sympathise it,
30   With many a sigh.

John Clare, *Poems Descriptive of Rural Life and Scenery*. London: Taylor and Hessey, 1821.

Vain Hope! of thee I've had my portion;
Mere flimsy cobweb! changing ocean!
That flits the scene at every motion,
    And still eggs on,
35 With sweeter view, and stronger notion
      To dwell upon:

Yes, I've dwelt long on idle fancies,
Strange and uncommon as romances,
On future luck my noddle[1] dances,
40   What I would be;
But, ah! when future time advances,
      All's blank to me.

Now twenty years I've pack'd behind me,
Since Hope's deluding tongue inclin'd me
45 To fuse myself. But, Warbler, mind me,
    It's all a sham;
And twenty more's as like to find me
      Just as I am.

I'm poor enough, there's plenty knows it;
50 Obscure; how dull, my scribbling shews it:
Then sure 'twas madness to suppose it,
    What I was at,
To gain preferment! there I'll close it:
      So mum for that.

55 Let mine, sweet Bird, then be a warning:
Advice in season, don't be scorning;
But wait till Spring's first days are dawning
    To glad and cheer thee;
And then, sweet Minstrel of the morning,
60   I'd wish to hear thee.

Evening

Now grey-ey'd hazy Eve's begun
    To shed her balmy dew,
Insects no longer fear the sun,
    But come in open view.

---

[1] The head, in this sense describing "the seat of the mind or thought" (*OED*). [Ed.]

5 Now buzzing, with unwelcome din,
     The heedless beetle bangs,
  Against the cow-boy's dinner-tin,
     That o'er his shoulder hangs.

  And on he keeps in heedless pat,
10   Till, quite enrag'd, the boy
  Pulls off his weather-beaten hat,
     Resolving to destroy.

  Yet thoughtless that he wrongs the clown,
     By blows he'll not be driven,
15 But buzzes on, till batter'd down
     For unmeant injury given.

  Now from each hedge-row fearless peep
     The slowly-pacing snails,
  Betraying their meand'ring creep,
20   In silver-slimy trails.

  The dew-worms too in couples start,
     But leave their holes in fear;
  For in a moment they will part,
     If aught approaches near.

25 The owls mope out, and scouting bats
     Begin their giddy round;
  While countless swarms of dancing gnats
     Each water pudge[2] surround.

  And 'side yon pool, as smooth as glass,
30   Reflecting every cloud,
  Securely hid among the grass,
     The crickets chirrup loud.

  That rural call, *"Come mulls! come mulls!"*[3]
     From distant pasture-grounds,
35 All noises now to silence lulls,
     In soft and ushering sounds;

  While echoes weak, from hill to hill
     Their dying sounds deplore,
  That whimper faint and fainter still,
40   Till they are heard no more.

---

[2] Puddle. [Ed.]

[3] "Come cows!" [Ed.]

The breezes, once so cool and brief,
    At Eve's approach all died;
None's left to make the aspen leaf
    Twirl up its hoary side.

45 But breezes all are useless now;
    The hazy dun, that spreads
Her moist'ning dew on every bough,
    Sufficient coolness sheds.

The flowers, reviving from the ground,
50   Perk up again and peep,
While many different tribes around
    Are shutting up to sleep.

Now let me, hid in cultur'd plain,
    Pursue my evening walk,
55 Where each way beats the nodding grain,
    Aside the narrow balk;

While fairy visions intervene,
    Creating dread surprize,
From distant objects dimly seen,
60   That catch the doubtful eyes.

And fairies now, no doubt, unseen,
    In silent revels sup;
With dew-drop bumpers toast their queen,
    From crow-flower's golden cup.

65 Although about these tiny things
    Folks make so much ado;
I never heed the darksome rings,
    Where they are said to go:

But Superstition still deceives;
70   And fairies still prevail;
While stooping Genius e'en believes
    The customary tale.

Oh, loveliest time! oh, sweetest hours
    The musing soul can find!
75 Now, Evening, let thy soothing powers
    At freedom fill the mind.

A Reflection in Autumn

Now Autumn's come, adieu the pleasing greens,
    The charming landscape, and the flow'ry plains!
All have deserted from these motley scenes,
    With blighted yellow ting'd, and russet stains.

5 Though Desolation seems to triumph here,
    Yet this is Spring to what we still shall find:
The trees must all in nakedness appear,
    'Reft of their foliage by the blustry wind.

Just so 'twill fare with me in Autumn's Life;
10   Just so I'd wish: but may the trunk and all
Die with the leaves; nor taste that wintry strife,
    When sorrows urge, and fear impedes the fall.

The Robin

Now the snow hides the ground, little birds leave the wood,
And fly to the cottage to beg for their food;
While the Robin, domestic, more tame than the rest,
With its wings drooping down, and its feathers undrest,
5 Comes close to our windows, as much as to say,
"I would venture in, if I could find a way:
I'm starv'd, and I want to get out of the cold;
Oh! make me a passage, and think me not bold."
Ah, poor little creature! thy visits reveal
10 Complaints such as these, to the heart that can feel:
Nor shall such complainings be urged in vain;
I'll make thee a hole, if I take out a pane.
Come in, and a welcome reception thou'lt find;
I keep no grimalkin[4] to murder inclin'd.
15 But oh, little Robin! be careful to shun
That house, where the peasant makes use of a gun;
For if thou but taste of the seed he has strew'd,
Thy life as a ransom must pay for the food:
His aim is unerring, his heart is as hard;
20 And thy race, though so harmless, he'll never regard.

---

[4]A fiendish cat. [Ed.]

Distinction with him, boy, is nothing at all;
Both the Wren, and the Robin, with Sparrows must fall.
For his soul (though he outwardly looks like a man,)
Is in nature a wolf of the Apennine clan;
25 Like them his whole study is bent on his prey:
Then be careful, and shun what is meant to betray.
Come, come to my cottage; and thou shalt be free
To perch on my finger, and sit on my knee:
Thou shalt eat of the crumbles of bread to thy fill,
30 And have leisure to clean both thy feathers and bill.
Then come, little Robin! and never believe
Such warm invitations are meant to deceive:
In duty I'm bound to show mercy on thee,
Since God don't deny it to sinners like me.

To an Insignificant Flower

Obscurely Blooming in a Lonely Wild

And though thou seem'st a weedling wild,
    Wild and neglected like to me,
Thou still art dear to Nature's child,
    And I will stoop to notice thee.

5 For oft, like thee, in wild retreat,
    Array'd in humble garb like thee,
There's many a seeming weed proves sweet,
    As sweet as garden-flowers can be.

And, like to thee, each seeming weed
10   Flowers unregarded; like to thee,
Without improvement, runs to seed,
    Wild and neglected like to me.

And, like to thee, when Beauty's cloth'd
    In lowly raiment like to thee,
15 Disdainful Pride, by Beauty loath'd,
    No beauties there can ever see.

For, like to thee, my Emma blows.
    A Flower like thee I dearly prize;
And, like to thee, her humble clothes
20   Hide every charm from prouder eyes.

But though, like thee, a lowly flower,
    If fancied by a polish'd eye,
She soon would bloom beyond my power,
    The finest flower beneath the sky.

25 And, like to thee, lives many a swain
    With genius blest; but, like to thee,
So humble, lowly, mean, and plain,
    No one will notice them, or me.

So, like to thee, they live unknown,
30   Wild weeds obscure; and, like to thee,
Their sweets are sweet to them alone:
    The only pleasure known to me.

Yet when I'm dead, let's hope I have
    Some friend in store, as I'm to thee,
35 That will find out my lowly grave,
    And heave a sigh to notice me.

To the Glow-Worm

Tasteful Illumination of the night,
    Bright scatter'd, twinkling star of spangled earth!
Hail to the nameless colour'd dark-and-light,
    The witching nurse of thy illumin'd birth.
5 In thy still hour how dearly I delight
    To rest my weary bones, from labour free;
In lone spots, out of hearing, out of sight,
    To sigh day's smother'd pains; and pause on thee
    Bedecking dangling brier and ivied tree,
10 Or diamonds tipping on the grassy spear;
    Thy pale-fac'd glimmering light I love to see,
Gilding and glistering in the dew-drop near:
    O still-hour's mate! my easing heart sobs free,
While tiny bents low bend with many an added tear.

The Ant

Thou little Insect, infinitely small,
    What curious texture marks thy minute frame!
How seeming large thy foresight, and withal,

   Thy labouring talents not unworthy fame,
5 To raise such monstrous hills along the plain,
     Larger than mountains, when compar'd with thee;
   To drag the crumb dropp'd by the village swain,
     Huge size to thine, is strange indeed to me.
   But that great Instinct which foretels the cold,
10   And bids to guard 'gainst winter's wasteful power,
   Endues this mite with cheerfulness to hold
     Its toiling labours through the sultry hour:
   So that same soothing power, in misery,
   Cheers the poor Pilgrim to Eternity.

From The Shepherd's Calendar and Other Poems

June

   Now Summer is in flower, and Nature's hum
   Is never silent round her bounteous bloom;
   Insects, as small as dust, have never done
   With glitt'ring dance, and reeling in the sun;
5 And green wood-fly, and blossom-haunting bee,
   Are never weary of their melody.
   Round field and hedge, flowers in full glory twine,
   Large bind-weed bells, wild hop, and streak'd wood-bine,
   That lift athirst their slender throated flowers,
10 Agape for dew-falls, and for honey showers;
   These o'er each bush in sweet disorder run,
   And spread their wild hues to the sultry sun.
   The mottled spider, at eve's leisure, weaves
   His webs of silken lace on twigs and leaves,
15 Which ev'ry morning meet the poet's eye,
   Like fairies' dew-wet dresses hung to dry.
   The wheat swells into ear, and hides below
   The May-month wild flowers and their gaudy show,

John Clare, *The Shepherd's Calendar and Other Poems*. London: John Taylor, 1827.

Leaving, a school-boy's height, in snugger rest,
20 The leveret's seat, and lark, and partridge nest.

The mowers now bend o'er the beaded grass,
Where oft the gipsy's hungry journeying ass
Will turn his wishes from the meadow paths,
List'ning the rustle of the falling swaths.
25 The ploughman sweats along the fallow vales,
And down the sun-crack'd furrow slowly trails;
Oft seeking, when athirst, the brook's supply,
Where, brushing eagerly the bushes by
For coolest water, he disturbs the rest
30 Of ring-dove, brooding o'er its idle nest.
The shepherd's leisure hours are over now;
No more he loiters 'neath the hedge-row bough,
On shadow-pillowed banks and lolling stile;
The wilds must lose their summer friend awhile.

35 With whistle, barking dogs, and chiding scold,
He drives the bleating sheep from fallow fold
To wash-pools, where the willow shadows lean,
Dashing them in, their stained coats to clean;
Then, on the sunny sward, when dry again,
40 He brings them homeward to the clipping pen,
Of hurdles form'd, where elm or sycamore
Shut out the sun—or to some threshing-floor.
There with the scraps of songs, and laugh, and tale,
He lightens annual toil, while merry ale
45 Goes round, and glads some old man's heart to praise
The threadbare customs of his early days:
How the high bowl was in the middle set
At breakfast time, when clippers yearly met,
Fill'd full of furmety, where dainty swum
50 The streaking sugar and the spotting plum.
The maids could never to the table bring
The bowl, without one rising from the ring
To lend a hand; who, if 'twere ta'en amiss,
Would sell his kindness for a stolen kiss.
55 The large stone pitcher in its homely trim,
And clouded pint-horn with its copper rim,
Were there; from which were drunk, with spirits high,
Healths of the best the cellar could supply;

While sung the ancient swains, in uncouth rhymes,
60 Songs that were pictures of the good old times.
Thus will the old man ancient ways bewail,
Till toiling shears gain ground upon the tale,
And break it off—for now the timid sheep,
His fleece shorn off, starts with a fearful leap,
65 Shaking his naked skin with wond'ring joys,
While others are brought in by sturdy boys.

Though fashion's haughty frown hath thrown aside
Half the old forms simplicity supplied,
Yet there are some pride's winter deigns to spare,
70 Left like green ivy when the trees are bare.
And now, when shearing of the flocks is done,
Some ancient customs, mix'd with harmless fun,
Crown the swain's merry toils. The timid maid,
Pleased to be praised, and yet of praise afraid,
75 Seeks the best flowers; not those of woods and fields,
But such as every farmer's garden yields—
Fine cabbage-roses, painted like her face;
The shining pansy, trimm'd with golden lace;
The tall topp'd larkheels, feather'd thick with flowers;
80 The woodbine, climbing o'er the door in bowers;
The London tufts, of many a mottled hue;
The pale pink pea, and monkshood darkly blue:
The white and purple gilliflowers, that stay
Ling'ring, in blossom, summer half away;
85 The single blood-walls, of a luscious smell,
Old-fashion'd flowers which housewives love so well;
The columbines, stone-blue, or deep night-brown,
Their honeycomb-like blossoms hanging down,
Each cottage-garden's fond adopted child,
90 Though heaths still claim them, where they yet grow wild;
With marjoram knots, sweet-brier, and ribbon-grass,
And lavender, the choice of ev'ry lass,
And sprigs of lad's-love—all familiar names,
Which every garden through the village claims.
95 These the maid gathers with a coy delight,
And ties them up, in readiness for night;
Then gives to ev'ry swain, 'tween love and shame,
Her "clipping posies" as his yearly claim.
He rises, to obtain the custom'd kiss:

100 With stifled smiles, half hankering after bliss,
   She shrinks away, and blushing, calls it rude;
   Yet turns to smile, and hopes to be pursued;
   While one, to whom the hint may be applied,
   Follows to gain it, and is not denied.
105 The rest the loud laugh raise, to make it known,
   She blushes silent, and will not disown!
   Thus ale, and song, and healths, and merry ways,
   Keep up a shadow still of former days;
   But the old beechen bowl, that once supplied
110 The feast of furmety,[5] is thrown aside;
   And the old freedom that was living then,
   When masters made them merry with their men;
   When all their coats alike were russet brown,
   And his rude speech was vulgar as their own—
115 All this is past, and soon will pass away
   The time-torn remnant of the holiday.

October

   Nature now spreads around, in dreary hue,
   A pall to cover all that summer knew;
   Yet, in the poet's solitary way,
   Some pleasing objects for his praise delay;
5 Something that makes him pause and turn again,
   As every trifle will his eye detain:
   The free horse rustling through the stubble field;
   And cows at lair in rushes, half conceal'd;
   With groups of restless sheep who feed their fill,
10 O'er clear'd fields rambling wheresoe'er they will;
   The hedger stopping gaps, amid the leaves,
   Which time, o'er-head, in every colour weaves;
   The milkmaid pausing with a timid look,
   From stone to stone, across the brimming brook;
15 The cotter journeying with his noisy swine,
   Along the wood-side where the brambles twine,
   Shaking from mossy oaks the acorns brown,
   Or from the hedges red haws dashing down;

---

[5] Wheat boiled in milk and seasoned with cinnamon and sugar. [Ed.]

The nutters, rustling in the yellow woods,
20 Who teaze the wild things in their solitudes;
The hunters, from the thicket's avenue,
In scarlet jackets, startling on the view,
Skimming a moment o'er the russet plain,
Then hiding in the motley woods again;
25 The plopping gun's sharp, momentary shock,
Which echo bustles from her cave to mock;
The bawling song of solitary boys,
Journeying in rapture o'er their dreaming joys,
Haunting the hedges in their reveries,
30 For wilding fruit that shines upon the trees;
The wild wood music from the lonely dell,
Where merry Gipseys o'er their raptures dwell,
Haunting each common's wild and lonely nook,
Where hedges run as crooked as the brook,
35 Shielding their camps beneath some spreading oak,
And but discovered by the circling smoke
Puffing, and peeping up, as wills the breeze,
Between the branches of the coloured trees:
Such are the pictures that October yields,
40 To please the poet as he walks the fields;
While Nature—like fair woman in decay,
Whom pale consumption hourly wastes away—
Upon her waning features, winter chill,
Wears dreams of beauty that seem lovely still.
45 Among the heath-furze still delights to dwell,
Quaking, as if with cold, the harvest bell;
And mushroom-buttons each moist morning brings,
Like spots of snow-shine in dark fairy rings.
Wild shines each hedge in autumn's gay parade;
50 And, where the eldern trees to autumn fade,
The glossy berry picturesquely cleaves
Its swarthy bunches 'mid the yellow leaves,
On which the tootling robin feeds at will,
And coy hedge-sparrow stains its little bill.
55 The village dames, as they get ripe and fine,
Gather the bunches for their "eldern wine;"
Which, bottled up, becomes a rousing charm,
To kindle winter's icy bosom warm;
And, with its merry partner, nut-brown beer,
60 Makes up the peasant's Christmas-keeping cheer.

    Like to a painted map the landscape lies;
    And wild above, shine the cloud-thronged skies,
    That chase each other on with hurried pace,
    Like living things, as if they ran a race.
65 The winds, that o'er each sudden tempest brood,
    Waken like spirits in a startled mood;
    Flirting the sear leaves on the bleaching lea,
    That litter under every fading tree;
    And pausing oft, as falls the patting rain;
70 Then gathering strength, and twirling them again,
    Till drops the sudden calm: the hurried mill
    Is stopt at once, and every noise is still;
    Save crows, that from the oak trees quawking spring,
    Dashing the acorns down with beating wing,
75 Waking the wood's short sleep in noises low,
    Patting the crimpt brakes withering brown below;
    And whirr of starling crowds, that dim the light
    With mimic darkness, in their numerous flight;
    Or shrilly noise of puddocks' feeble wail,
80 As in slow circles round the woods they sail;
    While huge black beetles, revelling alone,
    In the dull evening hum their heavy drone.
    These trifles linger through the shortening day,
    To cheer the lone bard's solitary way;
85 Till surly Winter comes with biting breath,
    And strips the woods, and numbs the scene with death;
    Then all is still o'er wood and field and plain,
    As nought had been, and nought would be again.

To the Cowslip

    Once more, thou flower of childish fame,
       Thou meet'st the April wind;
    The self-same flower, the very same
       As those I used to find.
5 Thy peeps, tipt round with ruddy streak,
       Again attract mine eye,
    As they were those I used to seek
       Full twenty summers by.

But I'm no more akin to thee,
10   A partner of the Spring;
For Time has had a hand with me,
    And left an alter'd thing:
A thing that's lost thy golden hours,
    And all I witness'd then,
15 Mix'd in a desert, far from flowers,
    Among the ways of men.

Thy blooming pleasures, smiling, gay,
    The seasons still renew;
But mine were doom'd a stinted stay,
20   Ah, they were short and few!
The every hour that hurried by,
    To eke the passing day,
Lent restless pleasures wings to fly
    Till all were flown away.

25 Blest flower! with spring thy joys begun,
    And no false hopes are thine;
One constant cheer of shower and sun
    Makes all thy stay divine.
But my May-morning quickly fled,
30   And dull its noon came on,
And Happiness is past and dead
    Ere half that noon is gone.

Ah! smile and bloom, thou lovely thing!
    Though May's sweet days are few,
35 Still coming years thy flowers shall bring,
    And bid them bloom anew.
Man's Life, that bears no kin to them,
    Past pleasures well may mourn:
No bud clings to its withering stem —
40   No hope for Spring's return.

Poesy

Oh! I have been thy lover long,
    Soul-soothing Poesy;
If 'twas not thou inspired the song,
    I still owe much to thee:

5 And still I feel the cheering balm
     Thy heavenly smiles supply,
That keeps my struggling bosom calm
     When life's rude storms are high.

Oh! in that sweet romance of life
10   I loved thee, when a boy,
And ever felt thy gentle strife
     Awake each little joy:
To thee was urged each nameless song,
     Soul-soothing Poesy;
15 And as my hopes wax'd warm and strong,
     My love was more for thee.

'Twas thou and Nature bound, and smil'd,
     Rude garlands round my brow,
Those dreams that pleased me when a child,
20   Those hopes that warm me now.
Each year with brighter blooms return'd,
     Gay visions danced along,
And, at the sight, my bosom burn'd,
     And kindled into song.

25 Springs came not, as they yearly come
     To low and vulgar eyes,
With here and there a flower in bloom,
     Green trees, and brighter skies:
Thy fancies flush'd my boyish sight,
30   And gilt its earliest hours,
And Spring came wrapt in beauty's light,
     An angel dropping flowers.

Oh! I have been thy lover long,
     Soul-soothing Poesy,
35 And sung to thee each simple song,
     With witching ecstasy,
Of flowers, and things that claim'd from thee
     Of life an equal share,
And whisper'd soft their tales to me
40   Of pleasure or of care.

With thee, life's errand all perform,
     And feel its joy and pain;
Flowers shrink, like me, from blighting storm,
     And hope for suns again:

45 The bladed grass, the flower, the leaf,
    Companions seem to be,
That tell their tales of joy and grief,
    And think and feel with me.

A spirit speaks in every wind,
50   And gives the storm its wings;
With thee all nature owns a mind,
    And stones are living things;
The simplest weed the Summer gives
    Smiles on her as a mother,
55 And, through the little day it lives,
    Owns sister, friend, and brother.

Oh! Poesy, thou heavenly flower,
    Though mine a weed may be,
Life feels a sympathising power,
60   And wakes inspired with thee;
Thy glowing soul's enraptured dreams
    To all a beauty give,
While thy impassion'd warmth esteems
    The meanest things that live.

65 Objects of water, earth, or air,
    Are pleasing to thy sight;
All live thy sunny smiles to share,
    Increasing thy delight;
All Nature in thy presence lives
70   With new creative claims,
And life to all thy fancy gives
    That were but shades and names.

Though cheering praise and cold disdain
    My humble songs have met,
75 To visit thee I can't refrain,
    Or cease to know thee yet;
Though simple weeds are all I bring,
    Soul-soothing Poesy,
They share the sunny smiles of Spring,
80   Nor are they scorn'd by thee.

John Leonard Knapp (1767–1845)

John Leonard Knapp is an example of a natural historian whose literary style and tone contributed as much to his importance as his scientific observations did. He is part of the tradition of poetic naturalists that began with Gilbert White and continues, through Henry David Thoreau in America, down to the present day: Annie Dillard, Barry Lopez, David Quammen, and Terry Tempest Williams. Inspired by White's *Natural History of Selborne*, Knapp claimed that every careful observer of the natural world could contribute new information that would be useful to our understanding as well as emotional responses that might be pleasing to readers. He was a botanical expert on British grasses, although he also published an anonymous poem, "Arthur, or the Pastor of the Village" (1818). His *Journal of a Naturalist* (1829) recorded his observations and speculations based on rambles around his home near Bristol. It went through several editions before Knapp's death and was widely distributed in America up through the 1850 edition from which the following prose selections are taken.

Knapp is among the first English nature writers to record the decline of certain species and to suggest likely explanations. He describes how numerous birds have been diminished or destroyed by an increase in the human population, enclosures and clearances of land, and the "noise of our fire-arms." He similarly records how many nonpoisonous snakes have been killed because of the "ignorance and cruelty" of human beings. In these observations he is a precursor of a whole line of subsequent writers and environmentalists who argue that links between the natural world and the human world do not exist merely for the benefit of the "superior" species.

From **The Journal of a Naturalist**

The Progress of a Naturalist

To Flora

'Tis said that poets, if they'd muse,
Must first a fancied object choose,
And, by imagination's aid,
Picture some visionary maid,
5   To hear the wand'rings of their brain —
Sigh to their transports, or their pain.

     Then may a fond adorer, too,
Muse on the maid he's loved so true —
The first dear idol of his praise,
10   And faithful still in calmer days.

     Time's finger, perhaps, has rased from view
Some fancies that he early knew;
But, Nymph, the love for thee profess'd
Has ne'er been rifled from his breast.

15   The aged spaniel in his lair
Pursues in sleep the timid hare;
Too old his ferny hills to trace,
In slumbers still he leads the chace.
So, Flora, in the vale of time
20   I trace the pleasures of my prime,
And find my heart beats calm and true
To the first mistress that my fancy knew.

     Deep in the mist of years, I see,
Rambling alone the woodland lea,
25   A musing, slender, happy child,
Snatching in haste his flowers wild:
Twined in a wreath, with rushes green,
Cowslips and violets are seen;
Now both his hands he stoops to fill,

John Leonard Knapp, *The Journal of a Naturalist*. London: John Murray, 1829–30.

30 Then shouts, and smiles, and gathers still:
　　He seems the very king of joy —
　　This young, this gleeful, slender boy.

　　　　The wild bee sees, and murmurs round,
　　To scare him from her fav'rite ground,
35 In fear, lest he should gather more,
　　And rob her of her honied store.

　　　　In little garden see him toil,
　　Planting these natives of the soil:
　　Though tended by his daily care,
40 The sickly nurslings languish there.

　　　　A dusky cloud is come between—
　　This musing child's no longer seen.

　　　　By table now, with blossoms spread,
　　A pallid youth bends low his head;
45 Some ancient volume poring o'er,
　　A dark bound herbal on the floor.
　　The tawny page he reads with care,
　　Yet finds a something wanting there;
　　Then lifts his face with thoughtful look,
50 And calmly shuts his musty book.

　　　　I trace him still on Scotia's hills,
　　By craggy steeps, by mossy rills,
　　In heathy vale, o'er ferny lands,
　　'Long dusky shelves, on granite bands;
55 Each nook, each cranny, close explore,
　　And half the island's sandy shore;
　　The mead, the woodland, and the plain:
　　And now the wand'rer's home again.

　　　　I see, upon a wide-spread board,
60 This rambler's rare and cherish'd hoard:
　　Mysterious grasses scatter'd o'er,
　　A glass, a press, and books of lore;
　　With grave, consid'rate care and thought,
　　Compares the species he has brought;
65 Then, ranging out each sep'rate race,
　　He bids their form the pencil trace.

　　　　Ah, Vulcan! that thy hateful rage
　　Should moulder half his studious page.

How wav'ring is the mind of man!
70 A fickle thing since time began —
Hates this to-day, to-morrow loves,
Neglecting what he most approves —

Thy votarist can his errors see,
And, Flora, owns his slights to thee;
75 E'en he could once unsteady prove,
A wand'rer from his fair one's love.

In silent ev'ning's balmy hour,
He sought Phalaena in her shady bower;
And oft his morning walks prolong,
80 To hear the syren Sylvia's song;
And then he'd seek the azure main,
Where dwelt fair Doris and her train.

The mystic nymph by Nilus' shore,[1]
From thrice-fam'd Hermes named of yore,
85 With meteor flames beguiled his heart;
Seduced the man, and ruled by art.
And as her veil she coyly drew;
Combined beauties met his view;
But soon the subtle lady fled,
90 To beam her lights on Davie's head —
And other fancies too there are
Which turn'd him from his early fair,
Yet, not forgetful of the joy
Thy smiles in spring-time gave the boy,
95 He seeks — these little wand'rings o'er,
His former love, nor quits her more.

There, mark him now in Cambria's shades,
Panting up steeps through forest glades,
To woo thee in thy humblest seat,
100 Rarely disturb'd by mortal feet,
To view thee on thy mossy bed,
Where changeful agarics lift their head,

---

[1] This is rather a shadowy fair one — yet the Egyptian Minerva has ever been considered as the patroness of the liberal arts, the Hermetic, or mystic science; and then we have such veracious relations as those of Borrichius and Zosimus, as quoted by Scaliger, that a son of heaven was expelled his seat for instructing an earthly nymph in metallurgy and alchemical secrets.

And riveted in rock, the oak
Scarcely has heard the woodman's stroke;
105 Whilst his grey lichen, pendent there,
Looks like some hoary peasant's hair.
The staring woodcock wakes in fright
From leafy bed on alpine height,
And flutt'ring from her foliage sere,
110 Steals to some silent valley near;
The squirrel peeps beside the tree,
Th' intruder on his haunts to see;
Then darts with agile leaps away
To watch him from some mossy spray.
115 The dark owl glares with moony eye,
As the lone wand'rer passes by,
And wonders what could bring him there,
To wake her in her beechen lair.

But time a change to all must bring,
120 And wear the form of mortal thing,
The ardour of the fire decay
As its best fuel wastes away,
And things are lost, and heeded not —
This is forsaken, that forgot.

125 And where is he, that infant, fled,
Which wreath'd the wild flower round his head?

That aged man reposing there,
On cushion soft in elbow chair,
Was he, the slender, musing boy,
130 Which play'd with Flora, as his toy,
And to his early passion true,
Fair nymph! still often thinks on you!
He sits in silent humble bower,
And marks the border's varied flower;
135 Exulting to his neighbour shows
The bright Geranium's vivid glows;
Some new Carnation from its bed
Lifts by his care her speckled head;
And other simple pretty things
140 As harmless recreation brings;
Tells of the seasons that are flown,
And waits in patient hope — his own.

Yet one spray more — one wreath would crave,
Such palmy boughs as angels wave;
145 In that fair pasture he would stray,
Where faith, where virtue, point the way,
With amaranthine crown to sing
Hosannas sweet to Flora's King.

Birds

Some of our birds are annually diminishing in numbers; others have been entirely destroyed, or no longer visit the shores of Britain. The increase of our population, inclosure, and clearage of rude and open places, and the drainage of marshy lands, added to the noise of our fire-arms, have driven them away, or rendered their former breeding and feeding stations no longer eligible to many, especially to the waders and aquatic birds. The great Swan Pool, near the city of Lincoln, on which I have seen at one time forty of these majestic creatures sailing in all their dignity, is, I am told, no longer a pool; the extensive marshes of Glastonbury, which have afforded me the finest snipe shooting, are now luxuriant corn farms; and multitudes of other cases of such subversions of harbor for birds are within memory. An ornithological list made no longer ago than the days of Elizabeth would present the names of multitudes now aliens to our shores. The nightingale was common with us here a few years past; the rival songs of many were heard every evening during the season, and in most of our shady lanes we were saluted by the harsh warning note of the parent to its young; but from the assiduity of bird-catchers, or some local change that we are not sensible of, a solitary vocalist or so now only delights our evening walk. The egg of this bird is rather singularly colored, and not commonly to be obtained. Our migrating small birds incur from natural causes great loss in their transits; birds of prey, adverse winds, and fatigue, probably reduce their numbers nearly as much as want, and the severity of the winter season, does those that remain; and in some summers the paucity of such birds is strikingly manifest. Even the hardy rook is probably not found in such numbers as formerly, its haunts having been destroyed or disturbed by the felling of trees, in consequence of the increased value of timber, and the changes in our manners and ideas. Rooks love to build near the habitation of man: but their delight, the long avenue, to caw as it

John Leonard Knapp, *The Journal of a Naturalist*. Philadelphia: Gihon, 1850.

were in perspective from end to end, is no longer the fashion; and the poor birds have been dispersed to settle on single distant trees, or in the copse, and are captured and persecuted.

Old-fashioned halls, dull aunts, and croaking rooks,[2]

a modern Zephalinda would scarcely find now to anticipate with dread. In many counties very few rookeries remain, where once they were considered as a necessary appendage, and regularly pointed out the abbey, the hall, the court-house, and the grange.

The starling (sturnus vulgaris) breeds with us, as in most villages in England. Towards autumn the broods unite, and form large flocks; but those prodigious flights, with which, in some particular years, we are visited, especially in parts of those districts formerly called the "fen counties," are probably an accumulation from foreign countries. We have seldom more than a pair, or two, which nestle under the tiling of an old house, in the tower of the church, the deserted hole of the wood-pecker, or some such inaccessible place. The flights probably migrate to this country alone, as few birds could travel long, and continue such a rapid motion as the starling. The Royston crow, the only migrating bird with which it forms an intimate association, is infinitely too heavy of wing to have journeyed with the stare. The delight of these birds in society is a predominant character; and to feed they will associate with the rook, the pigeon, or the daw; and sometimes, but not cordially, with the fieldfare: but they chiefly roost with their own families, preferring some reedy, marshy situation. These social birds are rarely seen alone, and should any accident separate an individual from the companions of its flight, it will sit disconsolate on an eminence, piping and plaining, till some one of its congeners join it. Even in small parties they keep continually calling and inviting associates to them, with a fine clear note, that, in particular states of the air, may be heard at a considerable distance. This love of society seems to be innate; for I remember one poor bird, that had escaped from domestication, in which it had entirely lost, or probably never knew, the language or manners of its race, and acquired only the name of its mistress; disliked and avoided by its congeners, it would sit by the hour together, sunning on some tall elm, calling in a most plaintive strain, Nanny, Nanny, but no Nanny came; and our poor solitary either pined itself to death, or was killed, as its note ceased. They vastly delight, in a bright autumnal morning, to sit basking and preening themselves on the summit of a tree, chattering all together in a

---

[2]Alexander Pope, "Epistle to Miss Blount" (1717). [Ed.]

low song-like note. There is something singularly curious and mysterious in the conduct of these birds previous to their nightly retirement, by the variety and intricacy of the evolutions they execute at that time. They will form themselves perhaps into a triangle, then shoot into a long, pear-shaped figure, expand like a sheet, wheel into a ball, as Pliny observes, each individual striving to get into the centre, &c., with a promptitude more like parade movements, than the actions of birds. As the breeding season advances, these prodigious flights divide, and finally separate into pairs, and form their summer settlements; but probably the vast body of them leaves the kingdom. Travellers tell us, that starlings abound in Persia and the regions of Caucasus.

No birds, except sparrows, congregate more densely than stares. They seem continually to be running into clusters, if ever so little scattered; and the stopping of one, to peck at a worm, immediately sets all its companions hastening to partake. This habit in the winter season brings on them death, and protracted sufferings, as every village popper notices these flocks, and fires at the poor starlings. Their flesh is bitter and rank, and thus useless when obtained; but the thickness of the flights, the possibility of killing numbers, and manifesting his skill, encourages the trial. The flight of these birds, whether from feeding to roost, or on their return to feed, is so rapid, that none with any impediment can keep company; and in consequence we see many, which have received slight wing or body wounds, lingering about the pastures long into spring, and pining after companions they cannot associate with.

These birds are very assiduous in their attentions to their young, and in continual progress to collect worms and insects for them. However strong parental affection may be in all creatures, yet the care which birds manifest in providing for their nestlings is more obvious than that of other animals. The young of beasts sleep much; some are hidden in lairs and thickets nearly all the day, others take food only at intervals or stated periods, the parent ruminating, feeding, or reposing too: but birds, the young of which remain in their nests, as most of them do, excepting the gallinaceous and aquatic tribes, have no cessation of labor from early morning till the close of eve, till the brood can provide for themselves. What unceasing toil and perseverance are manifest in the rooks, and what distances do they travel to obtain nourishment for their clamorous brood! It is a very amusing occupation for a short time, to attend to the actions of a pair of swallows, or martens, the family of which have left the nest, and settled upon some naked spray, or low bush in the field, the parents cruising around, and then returning with their captures to their young: the constant supply which they bring, the celerity with which it is given and received, and the activity and evolutions of the elder birds, present a pleasing example of industry and affection. I have observed a pair of starlings for several days in constant progress before me, having young ones in the hole of a neighboring poplar tree, and they have been probably this way in action from the opening of the morning—thus persisting in this labor of love for twelve or thirteen hours in the day! The space they pass over in their various transits and returns must be very great, and the calculation vague; yet, from some rude observations it appears probable that this pair in conjunction do not travel less than fifty miles in the day, visiting and feeding their young about a hundred and forty times, which consisting of five in number, and admitting only one to be fed each time, every bird must receive in this period eight-and-twenty portions of food or water! This excessive labor seems entailed upon most of the land birds, except the gallinaceous tribes, and some of the marine birds, which toil with infinite perseverance in fishing for their broods; but the very precarious supply of food to be obtained in dry seasons by the terrestrial birds renders theirs a labor of more unremitting hardship than that experienced by the piscivorous tribes, the food of which is probably little influenced by season, while our poor land birds find theirs to be nearly annihilated in some cases. The gallinaceous birds have nests on the ground; the young leave them as soon as they escape from the shell, are led immediately from the hatch to fitting situations for food and water, and all their wants are most admirably attended to; but the constant journeyings of those parent birds that have nestlings unable to move away, the speed with which they accomplish their trips, the anxiety they manifest, and the long labor in which they so gaily persevere, is most remarkable and pleasing, and a duty consigned but to a few.

We have no bird more assiduous in attentions to their young, than the red-start, (*steort,* Saxon, a tail,) one or other of the parents being in perpetual action, conveying food to the nest, or retiring in search of it; but as they are active, quick-sighted creatures, they seem to have constant success in their transits. They are the most restless and suspicious of birds during this season of hatching and rearing their young; for when the female is sitting, her mate attentively watches over her safety, giving immediate notice of the approach of any seemingly hostile thing, by a constant repetition of one or two querulous notes, monitory to her or menacing to the intruder: but when the young are hatched, the very appearance of any suspicious creature sets the parents into an agony of agitation, and perching upon some dead branch or a post, they persevere in one unceasing clamor till the object of their fears is removed; a magpie near their haunts, with some reason, excites their terror greatly, which is expressed with unremitting vociferation. All this parental anxiety, however, is no longer in operation than during the helpless state of their offspring, which, being enabled to

provide their own requirements, gradually cease to be the objects of solic-
itude and care: they retire to some distant hedge, become shy and timid
things, feeding in unobtrusive silence.[. . .]

Voices of Birds

Rural sounds, the voices, the language of the wild creatures, as heard by the
naturalist, belong to, and are in concord with the country only. Our sight,
our smell, may perhaps be deceived for an interval by conservatories, hor-
ticultural arts, and bowers of sweets; but our hearing can in no way be
beguiled by any semblance of what is heard in the grove or the field. The
hum, the murmur, the medley of the mead, is peculiarly its own, admits of
no imitation, and the voices of our birds convey particular intimation, and
distinctly notify the various periods of the year, with an accuracy as certain
as they are detailed in our calendars. The season of spring is always
announced as approaching by the notes of the rookery, by the jangle or
wooing accents of the dark frequenters of its trees; and that time having
passed away, these contentions and cadences are no longer heard. The
cuckoo then comes, and informs us that spring has arrived; that he has
journeyed to us, borne by gentle gales in sunny days; that fragrant flowers
are in the copse and the mead, and all things telling of gratulation and of
joy: the children mark this well-known sound, spring out, and cuckoo!
cuckoo! as they gambol down the lane: the very plow-boy bids him welcome in the early morn. It is hardly spring without the cuckoo's song; and
having told his tale, he has voice for no more—is silent or away. Then
comes the dark, swift-winged marten, glancing through the air, that seems
afraid to visit our uncertain clime: he comes, though late, and hurries
through his business here, eager again to depart, all day long in agitation
and precipitate flight. The bland zephyrs of the spring have no charms with
them; but basking and careering in the sultry gleams of June and July, they
associate in throngs, and, screaming, dash round the steeple or the ruined
tower, to serenade their nesting mates; and glare and heat are in their train.
When the fervor of summer ceases, this bird of the sun will depart. The
evening robin from the summit of some leafless bough, or projecting
point, tells us that autumn is come, and brings matured fruits, chilly airs,
and sober hours, and he, the lonely minstrel now that sings, is understood
by all. These four birds thus indicate a separate season, have no interference
with the intelligence of the other, nor could they be transposed without
the loss of all the meaning they convey, which no contrivance of art could

supply; and, by long association, they have become identified with the period, and in peculiar accordance with the time.

We note birds in general more from their voices than their plumage; for the carols of spring may be heard involuntarily, but to observe the form and decoration of these creatures, requires an attention not always given. Yet we have some native birds beautifully and conspicuously feathered; the goldfinch, the chaffinch, the wagtails, are all eminently adorned, and the fine gradations of sober browns in several others are very pleasing. Those sweet sounds, called the song of birds, proceed only from the male; and, with a few exceptions, only during the season of incubation. Hence the comparative quietness of our summer months, when this care is over, except from accidental causes, where a second nest is formed; few of our birds bringing up more than one brood in the season. The redbreast, blackbird, and thrush, in mild winters will continually be heard, and form exceptions to the general procedure of our British birds; and we have one little bird, the woodlark (alunda arborea), that in the early parts of the autumnal months delights us with its harmony, and its carols may be heard in the air commonly during the calm sunny mornings of this season. They have a softness and quietness perfectly in unison with the sober, almost melancholy, stillness of the hour. The skylark also sings now, and its song is very sweet, full of harmony, cheerful as the blue sky and gladdening beam in which it circles and sports, and known and admired by all; but the voice of the woodlark is local, not so generally heard, from its softness must almost be listened for, to be distinguished, and has not any pretensions to the hilarity of the former. This little bird sings likewise in the spring; but, at that season, the contending songsters of the grove, and the variety of sound proceeding from every thing that has utterance, confuse and almost render inaudible the placid voice of the woodlark. It delights to fix its residence near little groves and copses, or quiet pastures, and is a very unobtrusive bird, not uniting in companies, but associating in its own little family parties only, feeding in the woodlands on seeds and insects. Upon the approach of man it crouches close to the ground, then suddenly darts away, as if for a distant flight, but settles again almost immediately. This lark will often continue its song, circle in the air, a scarcely visible speck, by the hour together; and the vast distance from which its voice reaches us in a calm day is almost incredible. In the scale of comparison, it stands immediately below the nightingale in melody and plaintiveness; but compass of voice is given to the linnet, a bird of very inferior powers. The strength of the larynx and of the muscles of the throat in birds is infinitely greater than in the human race. The loudest shout of the peasant is but a feeble cry, compared with that of the golden-eyed duck, the wild goose, or even this lark. The sweet song of this poor little bird, with a fate like that of the nightingale, renders it an object of capture and confinement, which few of them comparatively survive. I have known our country birdcatchers take them by a very simple but effectual method. Watching them to the ground, the wings of a hawk, or of the brown owl, stretched out, are drawn against the current of air by a string, as a paper kite, and made to flutter and librate like a kestrel over the place where the woodlark has lodged; which so intimidates the bird that it remains crouching and motionless as a stone on the ground; a hand-net is brought over it, and it is caught.

From various little scraps of intelligence scattered through the sacred and ancient writings, it appears certain, as it was reasonable to conclude, that the notes now used by birds, and the voices of animals, are the same as uttered by their earliest progenitors. The language of man, without any reference to the confusion accomplished at Babel, has been broken into innumerable dialects, created or compounded as his wants occurred, or his ideas prompted; or obtained by intercourse with others, as mental enlargement or novelty necessitated new words to express new sentiments. Could we find a people from Japan or the Pole, whose progress in mind has been stationary, without increase of idea, from national prejudice or impossibility of communication with others, we probably should find little or no alteration in the original language of that people; so, by analogy of reasoning, the animal having no idea to prompt, no new want to express, no converse with others, (for a note caught and uttered merely is like a boy mocking the cuckoo,) so no new language is acquired. With civilized man, every thing is progressive; with animals, where there is no mind, all is stationary. Even the voice of one species of birds, except in particular cases, seems not to be attended to by another species. That peculiar call of the female cuckoo, which assembles so many contending lovers, and all the various amatorial and caressing language of others, excites no influence generally, that I am aware of; with all but the individual species, it is a dialect unknown. I know but one note, which animals make use of, that seems of universal comprehension, and this is the signal of danger. The instant that it is uttered, we hear the whole flock, though composed of various species, repeat a separate moan, and away they all scuttle into the bushes for safety. The reiterated "twink, twink" of the chaffinch, is known by every little bird as information of some prowling cat or weasel. Some give the maternal hush to their young, and mount to inquire into the jeopardy announced. The wren, that tells of perils from the hedge, soon collects about her all the various inquisitive species within hearing, to survey and ascertain the object, and add their separate fears. The swallow, that shrieking darts in devious flight through the air when a hawk appears, not only calls up all the hirundines of the village, but is instantly understood by every finch and sparrow, and its warning attended to. As Nature, in all her ordinations, had a fixed design and foreknowledge, it may be that each species had a separate voice assigned it, that each might continue as created, distinct and unmixed: and the very few deviations and admixtures that have taken place, considering the lapse of time, association, and opportunity, united with the prohibition of continuing accidental deviations, are very remarkable, and indicate a cause and original motive. That some of the notes of birds are as language designed to convey a meaning, is obvious from the very different sounds uttered by these creatures at particular periods: the spring voices become changed as summer advances, and the requirements of the early season have ceased; the summer excitements, monitions, informations, are not needed in autumn, and the notes conveying such intelligences are no longer heard. The periodical calls of animals, croaking of frogs, &c., afford the same reasons for concluding that the sound of their voices by elevation, depression, or modulation, conveys intelligence equivalent to an uttered sentence. The voices of birds seem applicable in most instances to the immediate necessities of their condition; such as the sexual call, the invitation to unite when dispersed, the moan of danger, the shriek of alarm, the notice of food. But there are other notes, the designs and motives of which are not so obvious. One sex only is gifted with the power of singing, for the purpose, as Buffon supposed, of cheering his mate during the period of incubation; but this idea, gallant as it is, has such slight foundation in probability, that it needs no confutation: and after all, perhaps, we must conclude, that listened to, admired, and pleasing, as the voices of many birds are, either for their intrinsic melody, or from association, we are uncertain what they express, or the object of their song. The singing of most birds seems entirely a spontaneous effusion produced by no exertion, or occasioning no lassitude in muscle, or relaxation of the parts of action. In certain seasons and weather, the nightingale sings all day, and most part of the night; and we never observe that the powers of song are weaker, or that the notes become harsh and untunable, after all these hours of practice. The song-thrush, in a mild moist April, will commence his tune early in the morning, pipe unceasingly through the day, yet, at the close of eve, when he retires to rest, there is no obvious decay of his musical powers, or any sensible effort required to continue his harmony to the last. Birds of one species sing in general very like each other, with different degrees of execution. Some counties may produce finer songsters, but without great variation in the notes. In the thrush, however, it is remarkable, that there seem to be no regular notes, each individual piping a voluntary of his own. Their voices may always be distinguished amid the choristers of the copse, yet some one performer will more particularly engage attention by a peculiar modulation or tune; and should several stations of these birds be visited in the same morning, few or none probably will be found to preserve the same round of notes; whatever is uttered seeming the effusion of the moment. At times a strain will break out perfectly unlike any preceding utterance, and we may wait a long time without noticing any repetition of it. During one spring an individual song-thrush, frequenting a favorite copse, after a certain round of tune, trilled out most regularly some notes that conveyed so clearly the words, lady-bird! lady-bird! that every one remarked the resemblance. He survived the winter, and in the ensuing season the lady-bird! lady-bird! was still the burden of our evening song; it then ceased, and we never heard this pretty modulation more. Though merely an occasional strain, yet I have noticed it elsewhere—it thus appearing to be a favorite utterance. Harsh, strained, and tense, as the notes of this bird are, yet they are pleasing from their variety. The voice of the blackbird is infinitely more mellow, but has much less variety, compass, or execution; and he too commences his carols with the morning light, persevering from hour to hour without effort, or any sensible faltering of voice. The cuckoo wearies us throughout some long May morning with the unceasing monotony of its song; and, though there are others as vociferous, yet it is the only bird I know that seems to suffer from the use of the organs of voice. Little exertion as the few notes it makes use of seem to require, yet, by the middle or end of June, it loses its utterance, becomes hoarse, and ceases from any further essay of it. The croaking of the nightingale in June, or the end of May, is not apparently occasioned by the loss of voice, but a change of note, a change of object; his song ceases when his mate has hatched her brood; vigilance, anxiety, caution, now succeed to harmony, and his croak is the hush, the warning of danger or suspicion to the infant charge and the mother bird.

But here I must close my notes of birds, lest their actions and their ways, so various and so pleasing, should lure me on to protract

My tedious tale through many a page;

for I have always been an admirer of these elegant creatures, their notes, their nests, their eggs, and all the economy of their lives; nor have we, throughout the orders of creation, any beings that so continually engage our attention as these our feathered companions. Winter takes from us all the gay world of the meads, the sylphs that hover over our flowers, that steal our sweets, that creep, or gently wing their way in glittering splendor around us; and of all the miraculous creatures that sported their hour in the sunny beam, the winter gnat (tipula hiemalis) alone remains to frolic in some rare and partial gleam. The myriads of the pool are dormant, or hidden from our sight; the quadrupeds, few and wary, veil their actions in the glooms of night, and we see little of them; but birds are with us always, they give a character to spring, and are identified with it; they enchant and amuse us all summer long with their sports, animation, hilarity, and glee; they cluster round us, suppliant in the winter of our year, and, unrepining through cold and want, seek their scanty meal amidst the refuse of the barn, the stalls of the cattle, or at the doors of our house; or, flitting hungry from one denuded and bare spray to another, excite our pity and regard; their lives are patterns of gaiety, cleanliness, alacrity, and joy.

The Glow-Worm, Snakes, and Ants

In all our pursuits we shall find in nature, wheresoever we can penetrate, a formation, a faculty adapted to all the wants and comforts of the creature, yet the objects of infinite wisdom in the creation of this world of matter, animate and inanimate, will probably never be made known to mankind; for though knowledge is in a constant progressive state, and the attainments of science in latter years have been comparatively prodigious, yet these acquirements are in fact but entanglements: they lead us deeper into surprise and perplexity, and the little perceptions of light which we obtain serve to show how hopeless any attempt must be to penetrate the secrets of infinity, a conviction, if we "dwell deep in the valley of humility," that will in no manner discourage our pursuits, but rather incite our ardor to investigate so exhaustless a store, which will lead us, from contemplation, to admiration, to devotion.

That pretty sparkler of our summer evenings, so often made the plowboy's prize, the only brilliant that glitters in the rustic's hat, the glow-worm (lampyris noctiluca), is not found in such numbers with us, as in many other places, where these signal tapers glimmer upon every grassy bank; yet, in some seasons, we have a reasonable sprinkling of them. Every body probably knows, that the male glow-worm is a winged, erratic animal, yet may not have seen him. He has ever been a scarce creature to me, meeting perhaps with one or two in a year; and, when found, always a subject of admiration. Most creatures have their eyes so placed as to be enabled to see about them; or, as Hook says of the house-fly, to be "circumspect animals;" but this male glow-worm has a contrivance by which any upward [. . .] vision is prevented. Viewed when at rest, no portion of his eyes is visible, but the head is margined with a horny band, or plate, being a character of one of the genera of the order coleoptera, under which the eyes are situate. This prevents all upward vision; and blinds, or winkers, are so fixed at the sides of his eyes as greatly to impede the view of all lateral objects. The chief end of this creature in his nightly peregrinations is to seek his mate, always beneath him on the earth; and hence this apparatus appears designed to facilitate his search, confining his view entirely to what is before or below him. The first serves to direct his flight, the other presents the object of his pursuit: and as we commonly, and with advantage, place our hand over the brow, to obstruct the rays of light falling from above, which enables us to see clearer an object on the ground, so must the projecting hood of this creature converge the visual rays to a point beneath. This is a very curious provision for the purposes of the insect, if my conception of its design be reasonable. Possibly the same ideas may have been brought forward by others; but, as I have not seen them, I am not guilty of any undue appropriation, and no injury can be done to the cause I wish to promote, by detailing again such beautiful and admirable contrivances.

Glow-worms emit light only for a short period in the year; and I have but partially observed it after the middle of July. I have collected many of these pretty creatures on a bank before my house, into which they retire during the winter, to shine out again when revived by the summer's warmth; but in this latter season, I have frequently missed certain of my little protegés, and have reason to apprehend that they formed the banquet of a toad, that frequented the same situation.

Observing above, that the glow-worm does not emit light after the 14th of July, I mean thereby that clear, steady light, which has rendered this creature so remarkable to all persons; for I have repeatedly noticed, deep in the herbage, a faint evanescent light proceeding from these creatures, even as late as August and September. This was particularly manifested September the 28th, 1826. The evening was warm and dewy, and we observed on the house-bank multitudes of these small evanescent sparks in the grass. The light displayed was very different from that which they exhibit in the warm summer months. Instead of the permanent green glow that illumines all the blades of the surrounding herbage, it was a pale transient spot, visible for a moment or two, and then so speedily hidden that we were obliged, in order to capture the creature, to employ the light of a candle. The number of them, and their actions, creeping away from our sight, contrary to that half-lifeless dullness observed in summer, suggested the idea that the whole body had availed themselves of this warm, moist evening, to migrate to their winter station. A single spark or so was to be seen some evenings after this, but no such large moving parties were discovered again. If we conclude, that the summer light of the glow-worm is displayed as a signal taper, the appearance of this autumnal light can have no such object in view, nor can we rationally assign any use of it to the creature itself, unless, indeed, it serves as a point of union in these supposed migrations, like the leading call in the flight of night-moving birds. The activity and numbers of these insects, in the above-mentioned evening, enabled me to observe the frequent presence and disappearance of the light of an individual, which did not seem to be the result of will, but produced by situation. During the time the insect crawled along the ground, or upon the fine grass, the glow was hidden; but on its mounting any little blade, or sprig of moss, it turned round and presented the luminous caudal spot, which, on its falling or regaining its level, was hidden again.

My laborer this day, July the 18th, in turning over some manure, laid open a mass of snake's eggs (coluber natrix), fifteen only, and they must have been recently deposited, the manure having very lately been placed where they were found. They were larger than the eggs of a sparrow, obtuse at each end, of a very pale yellow color, feeling tough and soft like little bags of some gelatinous substance. The interior part consisted of a glareous matter like that of the hen, enveloping the young snake, imperfect, yet the eyes and form sufficiently defined. Snakes must protrude their eggs singly, but probably all at one time, as they preserve no regular disposition of them, but place them in a promiscuous heap. At the time of protrusion they appear to be surrounded with a clammy substance, which, drying in the air, leaves the mass of eggs united wherever they touch each other. I have heard of forty eggs being found in these deposits; yet, notwithstanding such provision for multitudes, the snake, generally speaking, is not a very common animal. The kite, the buzzard, and the raven, which prey on it occasionally, are too seldom found greatly to reduce the race; and its deep retirement in the winter seems to secure it from fatal injures by the severity of the weather: yet in the warm days of spring, when it awakens from its torpidity and basks upon our sunny banks, the numbers that appear are not proportionate to what might be expected from the number of eggs produced. Few creatures can assail it in its dormitory, yet its paucity proves that it is not exempt from mortality and loss. The mole may follow it in its retirement, but would hardly attempt to seize so large an animal. The polecat and the weasel too can enter its runs; are sufficiently bold and strong to attempt the conquest; and not improbably in the winter season resort to such food, the poor snake having no power of defending itself, or of avoiding the assault. The common snake of this country is a very harmless, unobtrusive creature; so timid, as to avoid the presence of man whenever he appears, hiding itself as much as possible in bushes and rugged places from his sight. At times a strong fetor proceeds from it; but this appears to be sexual, or made use of as the means of annoying its enemies. It possesses no power to commit injury, and has apparently no inclination to molest any thing beyond its requirements for food, as frogs and mice. When a young man, I have repeatedly handled it with impunity; and though often bitten, a temporary swelling, with slight inflammation, was the only result; but in these experiments the viper must not be mistaken for the common snake. Yet this poor creature, under the curse of ignorance and cruelty, never escapes unscathed from power and opportunity. All the snake tribe, innocuous and pernicious, seem to be viewed with horror and aversion by mankind. This horror, from the knowledge of their power of inflicting harm in countries where such kinds are found, is natural, and often preservative of life; but the aversion generally felt, and that shuddering occasionally noticed at the sight of our harmless snake, is like a deep-rooted principle. We imbibe in infancy, and long retain in remembrance the impression of injuries from the wiles of the serpent; and the "enmity between it and the seed of the woman" appears still in full operation, and is possibly more extensively and insensibly diffused among mankind than we are aware of. The harmless nature of our snake seems to be fully known to the little birds of the hedge, as they in no way give intimation of its presence by any warning of avoidance to their young, or that insulting vociferation so observable when any really injurious creature is perceived, but hop and sport about the basking snake without fear or notice.

All the human race seem to have inherited the original anathema against this creature; for though the capricious cruelty of man is very frequently exerted to the injury of many that his power enables him to tyrannize over, yet the serpent appears to be a peculiar object of his enmity, as if it was understood to be an absolute duty to "bruise his head," whenever the opportunity should be afforded.

It is very remarkable how few noxious creatures, animals which annoy man, inhabit with us; beasts and birds we have none, for the petty depredations occasionally made on his property are undeserving of attention. The gnat, and perhaps a few insects, may at times puncture our skin, but the period of action is brief, the injury only temporary. The wasp and the hornet, I believe, very rarely use their weapons wantonly, only in self-defence and when persecuted; thus leaving the balance incalculably in favor of innocency and harmlessness. But of all the guiltless beings which are met with, we have none less chargeable with criminality than the poor slow-worm (anguis fragilis), yet none are more frequently destroyed than it— included as it is in the general and deep-rooted prejudice attached to the serpent race. The viper and the snake, though they experience no mercy, escape often by activity of action; but this creature, from the slowness of his movements, falls at more frequent victim. We call it a "blind worm," possibly from the supposition that as it makes little effort to escape, it sees badly; but its eyes, though rather small, are clear and lively, with no apparent defect of vision. The natural habits of the slow-worm are obscure; but living in the deepest foliage, and the roughest banks, he is generally secreted from observation; and loving warmth, like all his race, he creeps half torpid from his hole, to bask in spring-time in the rays of the sun, and is, if seen, inevitably destroyed. Exquisitely formed as all these gliding creatures are, for rapid and uninterrupted transit through herbage and such impediments, it is yet impossible to examine a slow-worm without admiration at the peculiar neatness and fineness of the scales with which it is covered. All separate as they are, yet they lap over, and close upon each other with such exquisite exactitude, as to appear only as faint markings upon the skin, requiring a magnifier to ascertain their separations; and, to give him additional facility of proceeding through rough places, these are all highly polished, appearing lustrous in the sun, the animal looking like a thick piece of tarnished copper wire. When surprised in his transit from the hedge, contrary to the custom of the snake or viper, which writhe themselves away into the grass in the ditch, he stops, as if fearful of proceeding, or to escape observation by remaining motionless, but if touched he makes some effort to escape: this habit of the poor slow-worm becomes frequently the cause of his destruction.

Of all the active, vigilant creatures that animate our paths, we have none superior to the little, bee-like bombylius (bombylius medius); but this creature is to be seen only in the mornings of a few bright days in spring, seeming to delight in the hot, windy gleams of that season, presenting an emblem of that portion of our year, fugitive and violent. It is, I believe, plentiful nowhere. Particularly solicitous of warmth, it seeks the dry sunny reflection of some sheltered gravel-walk, or ditch-bank in a warm lane; and here it darts and whisks about, in seeming continual suspicion or danger; starting away with angry haste, yet returning immediately to the spot it had left; buffeting and contending with every winged fly that approaches, with a jealous, pugnacious fury, that keeps it in constant agitation. This action, its long projecting proboscis, and its pretty, spotted wings, placed at right angles with its body, distinguish our bombylius from every other creature. It appears singularly cautious of settling on the ground. After long hovering over and surveying some open spot, with due deliberation and the utmost gentleness it commits its long, delicate feet to the earth; but on the approach of any winged insect, or on the least alarm, is away again to combat or escape. Associates it has none: the approach even of its own race excites its ire, and, darting at them with the celerity of thought, it drives them from its haunts. When a captive it becomes tame and subdued, and loses all its characteristic bustling and activity, the inspiration of freedom.

The great black ant (formica fuliginosa) is commonly found in all little copses, animating by its numbers those large heaps of vegetable fragments, which it collects and is constantly increasing with unwearied industry and perseverance as a receptacle for its eggs. The game-fowl, the woodpecker, the wryneck, and all the birds that feed upon the little red ant, and soon depopulate the hillocks which they select, do not seem equally to annoy this larger species. These systematic creatures appear always to travel from and return to their nests in direct lines, from which no trifling obstacle will divert them; and any interruption on this public highway they resent, menacing the intruder with their vengeance. A neighbor related to me an instance of this unyielding disposition, which he witnessed in one of our lanes. Two parties of these black ants were proceeding from different nests upon a foraging expedition, when the separate bodies happened to meet each other. Neither would give way; and a violent contest for the passage ensued. After a time the combat ceased, and all animosity subsided, each party retiring to its nest, carrying with it its dead and maimed companions. This encounter seemed quite accidental, and the disposition to move in a uniform line, which their meeting prevented, the sole cause of their hostility, combat, and injury. The strength of some creatures, especially insects, considering the smallness of their size, is in several instances prodigious. Man, by his reason and power, calls to his aid mechanical means, and other agents, to effect his objects; but unreasoning beings accomplish their purposes by contrivance and bodily powers. The strength of these black ants is manifested by the quantity and magnitude of the materials which they collect for their heaps; but the common little red ant (formica rubea), a much smaller creature, gives daily proofs of its abilities to remove heavy substances, equal to any that we meet with. One of these little creatures, thirty-six of which only weigh a single grain, I have seen bear away the great black fly as its prize, equal to a grain in weight, with considerable ease; and even the wasp, which exceeds forty times its own weight, will be dragged away by the labor and perseverance of an individual emmet. These little ants are occasionally and profusely deprived of their lives by some unknown visitation. In the year 1826, in particular, and again in the following year, I observed, in the month of August, a lane strewed with their bodies. They had bred during the summer in an adjoining bank; but some fatality had overwhelmed them when absent from their nests, and nearly annihilated the fraternity, as only a few scattered survivors were to be seen feebly inspecting the bodies of their associates. The task of removal, however, with all their industry, appeared beyond their powers to accomplish, as on the ensuing day few had been taken away. Had these creatures been destroyed in combat by rival contention, the animosity must have been excessive; but it is more probably that they met their death by some other infliction.[. . .]

Alfred, Lord Tennyson (1809–1892)

Tennyson was not the last Romantic, but he may have been the last poet of the nineteenth century to fully capture the lyrical spirit of his powerful predecessors. His early poems echo the naturalistic cadences of Byron and Wordsworth while also resonating with the voice of the Victorian bard-sage that Tennyson would become. His attitude toward the natural world, like that of his well-known precursors, is hard to represent in singular or unified terms. Whatever consolation nature offers in his poems is almost always overshadowed by a sense that nature does not care about human beings or that nature swallows up petty human concerns in its vastness and impersonal timelessness. By the time Tennyson decided, after years of anxious delay and revision, to publish his masterpiece, *In Memoriam* (1850), he had become as much the producer as the recorder of numerous widespread Victorian sentiments.

Tennyson had a lifelong interest in popular as well as experimental science. *In Memoriam,* the elegy for his friend Arthur Henry Hallam written between 1833 and 1850, offers clear indications of powerful cultural influences produced by the catastrophism of Cuvier, the geological speculations of Sir Charles Lyell, and the protoevolutionary thinking of Chambers, Lamarck, von Humboldt, and Étienne Geoffroy St. Hilaire. Hallam Tennyson recorded two sentiments voiced by his father that suggest the challenges to orthodoxy posed by some of Tennyson's ideas: "An Omnipotent Creator who could make such a painful world is to me *sometimes* as hard to believe in as to believe in blind matter behind everything. The lavish profusion too in the natural world appals me, from the growths of the tropical forest to the capacity of man to multiply, the torrent of babies"; or "If we look at Nature alone, full of perfection and imperfection, she tells us that God is disease, murder, and rapine" (*Memoir* 1: 314). The selections from *In Memoriam* included here are the stanzas that seemed most disturbing to many of Tennyson's contemporary readers, but these famous lines of poetry also capture the heart of the scientific revolution that was about to take place. In the closing stanzas of the poem, Tennyson argues for a hopeful and progressive view of evolution, but it is nonetheless a view surprisingly close to Charles Darwin's. *In Memoriam* was published nine years before Darwin's *On the Origin of Species,* yet the poem reveals how many of these ideas were already in circulation among an educated public during the middle years of the century.

From In Memoriam

XXXIV.

My own dim life should teach me this,
    That life shall live for evermore,
    Else earth is darkness at the core,
And dust and ashes all that is;

5 This round of green, this orb of flame,
    Fantastic beauty; such as lurks
    In some wild Poet, when he works
Without a conscience or an aim.

What then were God to such as I?
10   'Twere hardly worth my while to choose
    Of things all mortal, or to use
A little patience ere I die;

'Twere best at once to sink to peace,
    Like birds the charming serpent draws,
15   To drop head-foremost in the jaws
Of vacant darkness and to cease.[. . .]

Alfred, Lord Tennyson, *In Memoriam*. London: Moxon, 1850.

LIII.

Oh yet we trust that somehow good
  Will be the final goal of ill,
  To pangs of nature, sins of will,
20 Defects of doubt, and taints of blood;

That nothing walks with aimless feet;
  That not one life shall be destroy'd,
  Or cast as rubbish to the void,
When God hath made the pile complete;

25 That not a worm is cloven in vain;
  That not a moth with vain desire
  Is shrivel'd in a fruitless fire,
Or but subserves another's gain.

Behold! we know not anything;
30 I can but trust that good shall fall
  At last—far off—at last, to all,
And every winter change to spring.

So runs my dream: but what am I?
  An infant crying in the night:
35 An infant crying for the light:
And with no language but a cry.

LIV.

The wish, that of the living whole
  No life may fail beyond the grave;
  Derives it not from what we have
40 The likest God within the soul?

Are God and Nature then at strife,
  That Nature lends such evil dreams?
  So careful of the type she seems,
So careless of the single life;

45 That I, considering everywhere
  Her secret meaning in her deeds,
  And finding that of fifty seeds
She often brings but one to bear;

I falter where I firmly trod,
50   And falling with my weight of cares
        Upon the great world's altar-stairs
That slope thro' darkness up to God;

I stretch lame hands of faith, and grope,
        And gather dust and chaff, and call
55   To what I feel is Lord of all,
And faintly trust the larger hope.

LV.

"So careful of the type?" but no.
        From scarped cliff and quarried stone
        She cries "a thousand types are gone:
60 I care for nothing, all shall go.

"Thou makest thine appeal to me:
        I bring to life, I bring to death:
        The spirit does but mean the breath:
I know no more." And he, shall he,

65 Man, her last work, who seem'd so fair,
        Such splendid purpose in his eyes,
        Who roll'd the psalm to wintry skies,
Who built him fanes of fruitless prayer,

Who trusted God was love indeed
70   And love Creation's final law —
        Tho' Nature, red in tooth and claw
With ravine, shriek'd against his creed —

Who loved, who suffer'd countless ills,
        Who battled for the True, the Just,
75   Be blown about the desert dust,
Or seal'd within the iron hills?

No more? A monster then, a dream,
        A discord. Dragons of the prime,
        That tare each other in their slime,
80 Were mellow music match'd with him.

O life as futile, then, as frail!
        O for thy voice to soothe and bless!
        What hope of answer, or redress?
Behind the veil, behind the veil.

LVI.

85 Peace, come away: the song of woe
    Is after all an earthly song:
    Peace, come away; we do him wrong
To sing so wildly; let us go.

Come, let us go, your cheeks are pale,
90   But half my life I leave behind;
    Methinks my friend is richly shrined,
But I shall pass; my work will fail.

Yet in these ears till hearing dies,
    One set slow bell will seem to toll
95   The passing of the sweetest soul
That ever looked with human eyes.

I hear it now, and o'er and o'er,
    Eternal greetings to the dead;
    And "Ave, Ave, Ave," said,
100 "Adieu, adieu" for evermore!

LVII.

In those sad words I took farewell:
    Like echoes in sepulchral halls,
    As drop by drop the water falls
In vaults and catacombs, they fell;

105 And, falling, idly broke the peace
    Of hearts that beat from day to day,
    Half-conscious of their dying clay,
And those cold crypts where they shall cease.

The high Muse answer'd: "Wherefore grieve
110   Thy brethren with a fruitless tear?
    Abide a little longer here,
And thou shalt take a nobler leave."[. . .]

CXXI.

There rolls the deep where grew the tree.
    O earth, what changes hast thou seen!
115   There where the long street roars, hath been
The stillness of the central sea.

The hills are shadows, and they flow
    From form to form, and nothing stands;
    They melt like mist, the solid lands,
120 Like clouds they shape themselves and go.

But in my spirit will I dwell,
    And dream my dream, and hold it true;
    For tho' my lips may breathe adieu,
I cannot think the thing farewell.

CXXII.

125 That which we dare invoke to bless;
    Our dearest faith, our ghastliest doubt;
    He, They, One, All; within, without;
The Power in darkness whom we guess;

I found Him not in world or sun,
130   Or eagle's wing, or insect's eye;
    Nor thro' the questions men may try,
The petty cobwebs we have spun:

If e'er when faith had fall'n asleep,
    I heard a voice "believe no more"
135   And heard an ever-breaking shore
That tumbled in the Godless deep;

A warmth within the breast would melt
    The freezing reason's colder part,
    And like a man in wrath the heart
140 Stood up and answer'd "I have felt."

No, like a child in doubt and fear:
    But that blind clamour made me wise;
    Then was I as a child that cries,
But, crying, knows his father near;

145 And what I seem beheld again
    What is, and no man understands;
    And out of darkness came the hands
That reach thro' nature, moulding men.

Charles Darwin (1809–1882)

Charles Darwin was the naturalist most responsible for altering humanity's view of nature (and human nature) over the past two centuries. Darwin's main ideas were not new, nor were they complete, but his account of the way species evolve over time by means of natural selection has had a profound influence on our world. His writings, and the works of his successors, have also had a direct impact on biology, ecology, paleontology, and social theory. In addition, his ideas continue to influence religious thinkers, literary and visual artists, psychologists, and politicians. Darwin was a mediocre student and a young adult with no clear sense of an occupation. After *wasting* (Darwin's word) his time as a student of medicine and theology, he was invited to sail on H.M.S. *Beagle* in 1831. He returned five years later as a seasoned collector and recorder of scientific information. His own research, along with the work of Lyell, Sir John Herschel, and Whewell, led him directly into the species question, then being widely debated by naturalists.

The evidence of Darwin's voyages and observations made it seem impossible that existing creatures were not directly related to previous forms of life and thus to each other. So traumatized was Darwin by the implications of his emerging theory, that he refused to publish his findings for two decades. The letter in which he may have committed his conclusion to paper for the first time conveys Darwin's sense of the dangerous power of his insight: "I am almost convinced (quite contrary to opinion [sic] I started with) that species are not (it is like confessing a murder) immutable" (11 January 1844, *Letters* 81). Many earlier writers and investigators (including Darwin's own grandfather Erasmus) had suggested the possibility of organic evolution. No one before Darwin had provided an explanation for the means by which evolution took place. Natural selection, however, was not a complete idea as expressed by Darwin. His account lacked the insights of Mendelian genetics, which would not be available to the scientific community until 1900. Nevertheless, Darwin's powerful views have affected all those who have sought to understand nature from his day until our own.

In his *Autobiography,* Darwin recounts his childhood proclivity for solitary walks. He also describes his fondness for Shakespeare, Thomson's *Seasons,* Byron, and Scott, affections which he claims to have lost later in life. He makes a suggestive comment that links a youthful interest in poetry to the lifelong appeal of natural scenery: "in connection with pleasure from poetry, I may add that in 1822 a vivid delight in scenery was first awakened in my mind, during a riding tour on the borders of Wales, and which has lasted longer than any other aesthetic pleasure" (44). Darwin also notes that he read evolutionary ideas in his grandfather's *Zoonomia,* but adds, surprisingly, that they entered his thinking "without producing any effect on me"; he also criticized Erasmus Darwin for the "proportion of speculation being so large to the facts given" (49). Darwin's own scientific successes resulted from his ability to offer observable facts that could outweigh speculation.

In one sense, Charles Darwin's ideas are responsible for the end of Romantic natural history, insofar as they provide a systematic explanation for natural processes that had previously seemed enigmatic, cryptic, and mysterious. His work also reminds us that great leaps in human understanding can be fostered by imaginative metaphors and analogical thinking. Darwin often described the animals and plants he studied in a language that rose to the rhetorical pitch of poetry. Here is a Coleridgean-sounding Darwin on a ship in South America in 1832, on a voyage to collect beetles, butterflies, and finches: "such a strange scene as it is. Every thing is in flames, the sky with lightning, the water with luminous particles, & even the very masts are pointed with a blue flame" (*Letters* 23). Even his more strictly scientific insights rely on mental constructions that have as much to do with what he can imagine as with what he can prove: "Therefore I should infer from analogy that probably all the organic beings which have ever lived on this earth have descended from some one primordial form" (*Origin* 484). In Darwin's case—like Copernicus, Newton, and Einstein—many of his analogical inferences have turned out to be true. Included here are extracts from the *Beagle Journal* and *On the Origin of Species* that reveal Darwin's intensity of observation and his willingness to engage in imagined possibilities in order to advance his observational conclusions.

From Journal of H.M.S. Beagle

PATAGONIA

December 6th, 1833.—The Beagle sailed from the Rio Plata, never again to enter its muddy stream. Our course was directed to Port Desire, on the coast of Patagonia. Before proceeding any further, I will here put together a few observations made at sea.

Several times when the ship has been some miles off the mouth of the Plata, and at other times when off the shores of Northern Patagonia, we have been surrounded by insects. One evening, when we were about ten miles from the Bay of San Blas, vast numbers of butterflies, in bands or flocks of countless myriads, extended as far as the eye could range. Even by the aid of a glass it was not possible to see a space free from butterflies. The seamen cried out "it was snowing butterflies," and such in fact was the appearance. More species than one were present, but the main part belonged to a kind very similar to, but not identical with, the common English *Colias edusa*.[1] Some moths and hymenoptera accompanied the butterflies; and a fine Calosoma flew on board. Other instances are known of this beetle having been caught far out at sea; and this is the more remarkable, as the greater number of the Carabidæ seldom or never take wing. The day had been fine and calm, and the one previous to it equally so, with light and variable airs. Hence we cannot suppose that the insects were blown off the land, but we must conclude that they voluntarily took flight. The great bands of the Colias seem at first to afford an instance like those on record of the migrations of *Vanessa cardui;* but the presence of other insects makes the case distinct, and not so easily intelligible. Before sunset, a strong breeze sprung up from the north, and this must have been the cause of tens of thousands of the butterflies and other insects having perished.

On another occasion, when seventeen miles off Cape Corrientes, I had a net overboard to catch pelagic animals. Upon drawing it up, to my surprise I found a considerable number of beetles in it, and although in the

---

Charles Darwin, *Journal of Researches into the Geology and Natural History of the Various Countries Visited by H.M.S. Beagle.* London: Henry Colburn, 1839.

[1] I am indebted to Mr. Waterhouse for naming these and other insects.

open sea, they did not appear much injured by the salt water. I lost some of the specimens, but those which I preserved, belonged to the genera, colymbetes, hydroporus, hydrobius (two species), notaphus, cynucus, adimonia, and scarabæus. At first, I thought that these insects had been blown from the shore; but upon reflecting that out of the eight species, four were aquatic, and two others partly so in their habits, it appeared to me most probable that they were floated into the sea, by a small stream which drains a lake near Cape Corrientes. On any supposition, it is an interesting circumstance to find insects, quite alive, swimming in the open ocean, seventeen miles from the nearest point of land. There are several accounts of insects having been blown off the Patagonian shore. Captain Cook observed it, as did more lately Captain King in the Adventure. The cause probably is due to the want of shelter, both of trees and hills, so that an insect on the wing with an off-shore breeze, would be very apt to be blown out to sea. The most remarkable instance I ever knew of an insect being caught far from the land, was that of a large grasshopper (*Acrydium*), which flew on board, when the Beagle was to windward of the Cape de Verd Islands, and when the nearest point of land, not directly opposed to the trade-wind, was Cape Blanco on the coast of Africa, 370 miles distant. [2]

On several occasions, when the vessel has been within the mouth of the Plata, the rigging has been coated with the web of the Gossamer Spider. One day (November 1st, 1832) I paid particular attention to the phenomenon. The weather had been fine and clear, and in the morning the air was full of patches of the flocculent web, as on an autumnal day in England. The ship was sixty miles distant from the land, in the direction of a steady though light breeze. Vast numbers of a small spider, about one-tenth of an inch in length, and of a dusky red colour were attached to the webs. There must have been, I should suppose, some thousands on the ship. The little spider when first coming in contact with the rigging, was always seated on a single thread, and not on the flocculent mass. This latter seems merely to be produced by the entanglement of the single threads. The spiders were all of one species, but of both sexes, together with young ones. These latter were distinguished by their smaller size, and more dusky colour. I will not give the description of this spider, but merely state that it does not appear to me to be included in any of Latreille's genera. The little aeronaut as soon as it arrived on board, was very active, running about; sometimes letting itself fall, and then reascending the same thread; sometimes employing itself in making a small and very irregular mesh in the corners between the ropes. It could run with facility on the surface of water. When disturbed it

---

[2] The flies which frequently accompany a ship for some days on its passage from harbour to harbour, wandering from the vessel, are soon lost, and all disappear.

lifted up its front legs, in the attitude of attention. On its first arrival it appeared very thirsty, and with exserted maxillæ drank eagerly of the fluid; this same circumstance has been observed by Strack: may it not be in consequence of the little insect having passed through a dry and rarefied atmosphere? Its stock of web seemed inexhaustible. While watching some that were suspended by a single thread, I several times observed that the slightest breath of air bore them away out of sight, in a horizontal line. On another occasion (25th) under similar circumstances, I repeatedly observed the same kind of small spider, either when placed, or having crawled, on some little eminence, elevate its abdomen, send forth a thread, and then sail away in a lateral course, but with a rapidity which was quite unaccountable. I thought I could perceive that the spider before performing the above preparatory steps, connected its legs together with the most delicate threads, but I am not sure, whether this observation is correct.

One day, at St. Fe, I had a better opportunity of observing some similar facts. A spider which was about three-tenths of an inch in length, and which in its general appearance resembled a Citigrade (therefore quite different from the gossamer), while standing on the summit of a post, darted forth four or five threads from its spinners. These glittering in the sunshine, might be compared to rays of light; they were not, however, straight, but in undulations like a film of silk blown by the wind. They were more than a yard in length, and diverged in an ascending direction from the orifices. The spider then suddenly let go its hold, and was quickly borne out of sight. The day was hot and apparently quite calm; yet under such circumstances the atmosphere can never be so tranquil, as not to affect a vane so delicate as the thread of a spider's web. If during a warm day we look either at the shadow of any object cast on a bank, or over a level plain at a distant landmark, the effect of an ascending current of heated air will almost always be evident. And this probably would be sufficient to carry with it so light an object as the little spider on its thread. The circumstances of spiders of the same species but of different sexes and ages, being found on several occasions at the distance of many leagues from the land, attached in vast numbers to the lines, proves that they are the manufacturers of the mesh, and that the habit of sailing through the air, is probably as characteristic of some tribe, as that of diving is of the Argyroneta. We may then reject Latreille's supposition, that the gossamer owes its origin to the webs of the young of several genera, as Epeira or Thomisa: although, as we have seen that the young of other spiders to possess the power of performing serial voyages.

During our different passages south of the Plata, I often towed astern a net made of bunting, and thus caught many curious animals. The structure of the Beroe (a kind of jelly fish) is most extraordinary, with its rows of vibratory ciliae, and complicated though an irregular system of circulation. Of Crustacea, there were many strange and undescribed genera. One, which in some respects is allied to the Notopods (or those crabs which have their posterior legs placed almost on their backs, for the purpose of adhering to the under side of ledges), is very remarkable from the structure of its hind pair of legs. The penultimate joint, instead of being terminated by a simple claw, ends in three bristle-like appendages of dissimilar lengths, the longest equalling that of the entire leg. These claws are very thin, and are serrated with teeth of an excessive fineness, which are directed towards the base. The curved extremities are flattened, and on this part five most minute cups are placed, which seem to act in the same manner as the suckers on the arms of the cuttle-fish. As the animal lives in the open sea, and probably wants a place of rest, I suppose this beautiful structure is adapted to take hold of the globular bodies of the Medusae, and other floating marine animals.

In deep water, far from the land, the number of living creatures is extremely small: south of the latitude 35°, I never succeeded in catching any thing besides some beroe, and a few species of minute crustacea belonging to the Entomostraca. In shoaler water, at the distance of a few miles from the coast, very many kinds of crustacea and some other animals were numerous, but only during the night. Between latitudes 56° and 57° south of Cape Horn the net was put astern several times; it never, however, brought up any thing besides a few of two extremely minute species of Entomostraca. Yet whales and seals, petrels and albatross, are exceedingly abundant throughout this part of the ocean. It has always been a source of mystery to me, on what the latter, which live far from the shore, can subsist. I presume the albatross, like the condor, is able to fast long; and that one good feast on the carcass of a putrid whale lasts for a long siege of hunger. It does not lessen the difficulty to say, they feed on fish; for on what can the fish feed? It often occurred to me, when observing how the waters of the central and intertropical parts of the Atlantic,[3] swarmed with Pteropoda, Crustacea, and Radiata, and with their devourers the flying-fish, and again with *their* devourers the bonitos and albicores, that the lowest of these pelagic animals perhaps possess the power of decomposing carbonic acid gas, like the members of the vegetable kingdom.

While sailing in these latitudes on one very dark night, the sea presented a wonderful and most beautiful spectacle. There was a fresh breeze, and every part of the surface, which during the day is seen as foam, now glowed

---

[3] From my experience, which has been but little, I should say that the Atlantic was far more prolific than the Pacific, at least, than in that immense open area, between the west coast of America and the extreme eastern isles of Polynesia.

with a pale light. The vessel drove before her bows two billows of liquid phosphorus, and in her wake she was followed by a milky train. As far as the eye reached, the crest of every wave was bright, and the sky above the horizon, from the reflected glare of these livid flames, was not so utterly obscure, as over the rest of the heavens.

As we proceed further southward, the sea is seldom phosphorescent; and off Cape Horn, I do not recollect more than once having seen it so, and then it was far from being brilliant. This circumstance probably has a close connection with the scarcity of organic beings in that part of the ocean. After the elaborate paper by Ehrenberg,[4] on the phosphorescence of the sea, it is almost superfluous on my part to make any observations on the subject. I may however add, that the same torn and irregular particles of gelatinous matter, described by Ehrenberg, seem in the southern as well as in the northern hemisphere, to be the common cause of this phenomenon. The particles were so minute as easily to pass through fine gauze; yet many were distinctly visible by the naked eye. The water when placed in a tumbler and agitated gave out sparks, but a small portion in a watch-glass, scarcely ever was luminous. Ehrenberg states, that these particles all retain a certain degree of irritability. My observations, some of which were made directly after taking up the water, would give a different result. I may also mention, that having used the net during one night I allowed it to become partially dry, and having occasion twelve hours afterwards, to employ it again, I found the whole surface sparkled as brightly as when first taken out of the water. It does not appear probable in this case, that the particles could have remained so long alive. I remark also in my notes, that having kept a Medusa of the genus Dianaea, till it was dead, the water in which it was placed became luminous. When the waves scintillate with bright green sparks, I believe it is generally owing to minute crustacea. But there can be no doubt that very many other pelagic animals, when alive, are phosphorescent.

On two occasions I have observed the sea luminous at considerable depths beneath the surface. Near the mouth of the Plata some circular and oval patches, from two to four yards in diameter, and with defined outlines, shone with a steady, but pale light; while the surrounding water only gave out a few sparks. The appearance resembled the reflection of the moon, or some luminous body; for the edges were sinuous from the undulation of the surface. The ship, which drew thirteen feet water, passed over, without disturbing, these patches. Therefore we must suppose that some

---

[4]Christian Gottfried Ehrenberg (1795–1876), zoologist who isolated bioluminescent dinoflagellates. [Ed.]

animals were congregated together at a greater depth than the bottom of the vessel.

Near Fernando Noronha the sea gave out light in flashes. The appearance was very similar to that which might be expected from a large fish moving rapidly through a luminous fluid. To this cause the sailors attributed it; at the time, however, I entertained some doubts, on account of the frequency and rapidity of the flashes. With respect to any general observations, I have already stated that the display is very much more common in warm than in cold countries. I have sometimes imagined that a disturbed electrical condition of the atmosphere was most favourable to its production. Certainly I think the sea is most luminous after a few days of more calm weather than ordinary, during which time it has swarmed with various animals. Observing that the water charged with gelatinous particles is in an impure state, and that the luminous appearance in all common cases is produced by the agitation of the fluid in contact with the atmosphere, I have always been inclined to consider that the phosphorescence was the result of the decomposition of the organic particles, by which process (one is tempted almost to call it a kind of respiration) the ocean becomes purified.[. . .]

The law of the succession of types, although subject to some remarkable exceptions, must possess the highest interest to every philosophical naturalist, and was first clearly observed in regard to Australia, where fossil remains of the large and extinct species of Kangaroo and other marsupial animals were discovered buried in a cave. In America the most marked change among the mammalia has been the loss of several species of Mastodon, of an elephant, and of the horse. These Pachydermata appear formerly to have had a range over the world, like that which deer and antelopes now hold. If Buffon had known of these gigantic armadilloes, llamas, great rodents, and lost pachydermata, he would have said with a greater semblance of truth, that the creative force in America had lost its vigour, rather than that it had never possessed such powers.

It is impossible to reflect without the deepest astonishment, on the changed state of this continent. Formerly it must have swarmed with great monsters, like the southern parts of Africa, but now we find only the tapir, guanaco, armadillo, and capybara; mere pigmies compared to the antecedent races. The greater number, if not all, of these extinct quadrupeds lived at a very recent period; and many of them were contemporaries of the existing molluscs. Since their loss, no very great physical changes can have taken place in the nature of the country. What then has exterminated so many living creatures? In the Pampas, the great sepulchre of such remains, there are no signs of violence, but on the contrary, of the most quiet and scarcely sensible changes. At Bahia Blanca I endeavoured to show the probability that the ancient Edentata, like the present species, lived in a dry and sterile country, such as now is found in that neighbourhood. With respect to the camel-like llama of Patagonia, the same grounds which, before knowing more than the size of the remains, perplexed me, by not allowing any great changes of climate, now that we can guess the habits of the animal, are strangely confirmed. What shall we say of the death of the fossil horse? Did those plains fail in pasture, which afterwards were overrun by thousands and tens of thousands of the successors of the fresh stock introduced with the Spanish colonist? In some countries, we may believe, that a number of species subsequently introduced, by consuming the food of the antecedent races, may have caused their extermination; but we can scarcely credit that the armadillo has devoured the food of the immense Megatherium, the capybara of the Toxodon, or the guanaco of the camel-like kind. But granting that all such changes have been small, yet we are so profoundly ignorant concerning the physiological relations, on which the life, and even health (as shown by epidemics) of any existing species depends, that we argue with still less safety about either the life or death of any extinct kind.

One is tempted to believe in such simple relations, as variation of climate and food, or introduction of enemies, or the increased numbers of other species, as the cause of the succession of races. But it may be asked whether it is probable than any such cause should have been in action during the same epoch over the whole northern hemisphere, so as to destroy the *Elephas primigenus,* on the shores of Spain, on the plains of Siberia, and in Northern America; and in a like manner, the *Bos urus,* over a range of scarcely less extent? Did such changes put a period to the life of *Mastodon angustidens,* and of the fossil horse, both in Europe and on the Eastern slope of the Cordillera in Southern America? If they did, they must have been changes common to the whole world; such as gradual refrigeration, whether from modifications of physical geography, or from central cooling. But on this assumption, we have to struggle with the difficulty that these supposed changes, although scarcely sufficient to affect molluscous animals either in Europe or South America, yet destroyed many quadrupeds in regions now characterized by frigid, temperate, and warm climates! These cases of extinction forcibly recall the idea (I do not wish to draw any close analogy) of certain fruit-trees, which, it has been asserted, though grafted on young stems, planted in varied situations, and fertilized by the richest manures, yet at one period, have all withered away and perished. A fixed and determined length of life has in such cases been given to thousands and thousands of buds (or individual germs), although produced in long succession. Among the greater number of animals, each individual appears nearly independent of its kind; yet all of one kind may be bound together by common laws, as well as a certain number of individual buds in the tree, or polypi in the Zoophyte.

I will add one other remark. We see that whole series of animals, which have been created with peculiar kinds of organization, are confined to certain areas; and we can hardly suppose these structures are only adaptations to peculiarities of climate or country; for otherwise, animals belonging to a distinct type, and introduced by man, would not succeed so admirably, even to the extermination of the aborigines. On such grounds it does not seem a necessary conclusion, that the extinction of species, more than their creation, should exclusively depend on the nature (altered by physical changes) of their country. All that at present can be said with certainty, is that, as with the individual, so with the species, the hour of life has run its course, and is spent.[. . .]

From On the Origin of Species

INTRODUCTION

When on board H.M.S. "Beagle," as naturalist, I was much struck with certain facts in the distribution of the inhabitants of South America, and in the geological relations of the present to the past inhabitants of that continent. These facts seemed to me to throw some light on the origin of species—that mystery of mysteries, as it has been called by one of our greatest philosophers. On my return home, it occurred to me, in 1837, that something might perhaps be made out on this question by patiently accumulating and reflecting on all sorts of facts which could possibly have any bearing on it. After five years' work I allowed myself to speculate on the subject, and drew up some short notes; these I enlarged in 1844 into a sketch of the conclusions, which then seemed to me probable: from that period to the present day I have steadily pursued the same object. I hope that I may be excused for entering on these personal details, as I give them to show that I have not been hasty in coming to a decision.

My work is now nearly finished; but as it will take me two or three more years to complete it, and as my health is far from strong, I have been urged to publish this Abstract. I have more especially been induced to do this, as

Charles Darwin, On the Origin of Species by Means of Natural Selection. London: John Murray, 1859.

Mr. Wallace,[5] who is now studying the natural history of the Malay archipelago, has arrived at almost exactly the same general conclusions that I have on the origin of species. Last year he sent to me a memoir on this subject, with a request that I would forward it to Sir Charles Lyell, who sent it to the Linnean Society, and it is published in the third volume of the Journal of that Society. Sir C. Lyell and Dr. Hooker, who both knew of my work—the latter having read my sketch of 1844—honoured me by thinking it advisable to publish, with Mr. Wallace's excellent memoir, some brief extracts from my manuscripts.

This Abstract, which I now publish, must necessarily be imperfect. I cannot here give references and authorities for my several statements; and I must trust to the reader reposing some confidence in my accuracy. No doubt errors will have crept in, though I hope I have always been cautious in trusting to good authorities alone. I can here give only the general conclusions at which I have arrived, with a few facts in illustration, but which, I hope, in most cases will suffice. No one can feel more sensible than I do of the necessity of hereafter publishing in detail all the facts, with references, on which my conclusions have been grounded; and I hope in a future work to do this. For I am well aware that scarcely a single point is discussed in this volume on which facts cannot be adduced, often apparently leading to conclusions directly opposite to those at which I have arrived. A fair result can be obtained only by fully stating and balancing the facts and arguments on both sides of each question; and this cannot possibly be here done.

I much regret that want of space prevents my having the satisfaction of acknowledging the generous assistance which I have received from very many naturalists, some of them personally unknown to me. I cannot, however, let this opportunity pass without expressing my deep obligations to Dr. Hooker, who for the last fifteen years has aided me in every possible way by his large stores of knowledge and his excellent judgment.

In considering the Origin of Species, it is quite conceivable that a naturalist, reflecting on the mutual affinities of organic beings, on their embryological relations, their geographical distribution, geological succession, and other such facts, might come to the conclusion that each species had not been independently created, but had descended, like varieties, from other species. Nevertheless, such a conclusion, even if well founded, would be unsatisfactory, until it could be shown how the innumerable species inhabiting this world have been modified, so as to acquire that perfection of structure and coadaptation which most justly excites our admira-

---

[5] Alfred Russel Wallace, whose conclusions about evolution and natural selection closely paralleled Darwin's. [Ed.]

tion. Naturalists continually refer to external conditions, such as climate, food, &c., as the only possible cause of variation. In one very limited sense, as we shall hereafter see, this may be true; but it is preposterous to attribute to mere external conditions, the structure, for instance, of the woodpecker, with its feet, tail, beak, and tongue, so admirably adapted to catch insects under the bark of trees. In the case of the misseltoe, which draws its nourishment from certain trees, which has seeds that must be transported by certain birds, and which has flowers with separate sexes absolutely requiring the agency of certain insects to bring pollen from one flower to the other, it is equally preposterous to account for the structure of this parasite, with its relations to several distinct organic beings, by the effects of external conditions, or of habit, or of the volition of the plant itself.

The author[6] of the "Vestiges of Creation" would, I presume, say that, after a certain unknown number of generations, some bird had given birth to a woodpecker, and some plant to the misseltoe, and that these had been produced perfect as we now see them; but this assumption seems to me to be no explanation, for it leaves the case of the coadaptations of organic beings to each other and to their physical conditions of life, untouched and unexplained.

It is, therefore, of the highest importance to gain a clear insight into the means of modification and coadaptation. At the commencement of my observations it seemed to me probable that a careful study of domesticated animals and of cultivated plants would offer the best chance of making out this obscure problem. Nor have I been disappointed; in this and in all other perplexing cases I have invariably found that our knowledge, imperfect though it be, of variation under domestication, afforded the best and safest clue. I may venture to express my conviction of the high value of such studies, although they have been very commonly neglected by naturalists.

From these considerations, I shall devote the first chapter of this Abstract to Variation under Domestication. We shall thus see that a large amount of hereditary modification is at least possible; and, what is equally or more important, we shall see how great is the power of man in accumulating by his Selection successive slight variations. I will then pass on to the variability of species in a state of nature; but I shall, unfortunately, be compelled to treat this subject far too briefly, as it can be treated properly only by giving long catalogues of facts. We shall, however, be enabled to discuss what circumstances are most favourable to variation. In the next chapter the Struggle for Existence amongst all organic beings throughout the world, which inevitably follows from their high geometrical powers of increase, will be treated of. This is the doctrine of Malthus, applied to the whole

---

[6] Robert Chambers. [Ed.]

animal and vegetable kingdoms. As many more individuals of each species are born than can possibly survive; and as, consequently, there is a frequently recurring struggle for existence, it follows that any being, if it vary however slightly in any manner profitable to itself, under the complex and sometimes varying conditions of life, will have a better chance of surviving, and thus be *naturally selected*. From the strong principle of inheritance, any selected variety will tend to propagate its new and modified form.

This fundamental subject of Natural Selection will be treated at some length in the fourth chapter; and we shall then see how Natural Selection almost inevitably causes much Extinction of the less improved forms of life, and induces what I have called Divergence of Character. In the next chapter I shall discuss the complex and little known laws of variation and of correlation of growth. In the four succeeding chapters, the most apparent and gravest difficulties on the theory will be given: namely, first, the difficulties of transitions, or in understanding how a simple being or a simple organ can be changed and perfected into a highly developed being or elaborately constructed organ; secondly, the subject of Instinct, or the mental powers of animals; thirdly, Hybridism, or the infertility of species and the fertility of varieties when intercrossed; and fourthly, the imperfection of the Geological Record. In the next chapter I shall consider the geological succession of organic beings throughout time; in the eleventh and twelfth, their geographical distribution throughout space; in the thirteenth, their classification or mutual affinities, both when mature and in an embryonic condition. In the last chapter I shall give a brief recapitulation of the whole work, and a few concluding remarks.

No one ought to feel surprise at much remaining as yet unexplained in regard to the origin of species and varieties, if he makes due allowance for our profound ignorance in regard to the mutual relations of all the beings which live around us. Who can explain why one species ranges widely and is very numerous, and why another allied species has a narrow range and is rare? Yet these relations are of the highest importance, for they determine the present welfare, and, as I believe, the future success and modification of every inhabitant of this world. Still less do we know of the mutual relations of the innumerable inhabitants of the world during the many past geological epochs in its history. Although much remains obscure, and will long remain obscure, I can entertain no doubt, after the most deliberate study and dispassionate judgment of which I am capable, that the view which most naturalists entertain, and which I formerly entertained — namely, that each species has been independently created — is erroneous. I am fully convinced that species are not immutable; but that those belonging to what are called the same genera are lineal descendants of some other and generally extinct species, in the same manner as the acknowledged varieties of any one species are the descendants of that species. Furthermore, I am convinced that Natural Selection has been the main but not exclusive means of modification.[. . .]

Illustrations of the action of Natural Selection

In order to make it clear how, as I believe, natural selection acts, I must beg permission to give one or two imaginary illustrations. Let us take the case of a wolf, which preys on various animals, securing some by craft, some by strength, and some by fleetness; and let us suppose that the fleetest prey, a deer for instance, had from any change in the country increased in numbers, or that other prey had decreased in numbers, during that season of the year when the wolf is hardest pressed for food. I can under such circumstances see no reason to doubt that the swiftest and slimmest wolves would have the best chance of surviving, and so be preserved or selected, provided always that they retained strength to master their prey at this or at some other period of the year, when they might be compelled to prey on other animals. I can see no more reason to doubt this, than that man can improve the fleetness of his greyhounds by careful and methodical selection, or by that unconscious selection which results from each man trying to keep the best dogs without any thought of modifying the breed.

Even without any change in the proportional numbers of the animals on which our wolf preyed, a cub might be born with an innate tendency to pursue certain kinds of prey. Nor can this be thought very improbable; for we often observe great differences in the natural tendencies of our domestic animals; one cat, for instance, taking to catch rats, another mice; one cat, according to Mr. St. John, bringing home winged game, another hares or rabbits, and another hunting on marshy ground and almost nightly catching woodcocks or snipes. The tendency to catch rats rather than mice is known to be inherited. Now, if any slight innate change of habit or of structure benefited an individual wolf, it would have the best chance of surviving and of leaving offspring. Some of its young would probably inherit the same habits or structure, and by the repetition of this process, a new variety might be formed which would either supplant or coexist with the parent-form of wolf. Or, again, the wolves inhabiting a mountainous district, and those frequenting the lowlands, would naturally be forced to hunt different prey; and from the continued preservation of the individuals best fitted for the two sites, two varieties might slowly be formed. These varieties would cross and blend where they met; but to this subject of intercrossing we shall soon have to return. I may add, that, according to Mr. Pierce, there are two varieties of the wolf inhabiting the Catskill Mountains in the United States, one with a light greyhound-like form, which pursues deer, and the other more bulky, with shorter legs, which more frequently attacks the shepherd's flocks.

Let us now take a more complex case. Certain plants excrete a sweet juice, apparently for the sake of eliminating something injurious from their sap: this is effected by glands at the base of the stipules in some Leguminosæ, and at the back of the leaf of the common laurel. This juice, though small in quantity, is greedily sought by insects. Let us now suppose a little sweet juice or nectar to be excreted by the inner bases of the petals of a flower. In this case insects in seeking the nectar would get dusted with pollen, and would certainly often transport the pollen from one flower to the stigma of another flower. The flowers of two distinct individuals of the same species would thus get crossed; and the act of crossing, we have good reason to believe (as will hereafter be more fully alluded to), would produce very vigorous seedlings, which consequently would have the best chance of flourishing and surviving. Some of these seedlings would probably inherit the nectar-excreting power. Those individual flowers which had the largest glands or nectaries, and which excreted most nectar, would be oftenest visited by insects, and would be oftenest crossed; and so in the long-run would gain the upper hand. Those flowers, also, which had their stamens and pistils placed, in relation to the size and habits of the particular insects which visited them, so as to favour in any degree the transportal of their pollen from flower to flower, would likewise be favoured or selected. We might have taken the case of insects visiting flowers for the sake of collecting pollen instead of nectar; and as pollen is formed for the sole object of fertilisation, its destruction appears a simple loss to the plant; yet if a little pollen were carried, at first occasionally and then habitually, by the pollen-devouring insects from flower to flower, and a cross thus effected, although nine-tenths of the pollen were destroyed, it might still be a great gain to the plant; and those individuals which produced more and more pollen, and had larger and larger anthers, would be selected.

When our plant, by this process of the continued preservation or natural selection of more and more attractive flowers, had been rendered highly attractive to insects, they would, unintentionally on their part, regularly carry pollen from flower to flower; and that they can most effectually do this, I could easily show by many striking instances. I will give only one—not as a very striking case, but as likewise illustrating one step in the separation of the sexes of plants, presently to be alluded to. Some holly-trees bear only male flowers, which have four stamens producing rather a small quantity of pollen, and a rudimentary pistil; other holly-trees bear only female flowers; these have a full-sized pistil, and four stamens with shrivelled anthers, in which not a grain of pollen can be detected. Having found a female tree exactly sixty yards from a male tree, I put the stigmas of twenty flowers, taken from different branches, under the microscope, and on all, without exception, there were pollen-grains, and on some a profusion of pollen. As the wind had set for several days from the female to the male tree, the pollen could not thus have been carried. The weather had been cold and boisterous, and therefore not favourable to bees, nevertheless every female flower which I examined had been effectually fertilised by the bees, accidentally dusted with pollen, having flown from tree to tree in search of nectar. But to return to our imaginary case: as soon as the plant had been rendered so highly attractive to insects that pollen was regularly carried from flower to flower, another process might commence. No naturalist doubts the advantage of what has been called the "physiological division of labour"; hence we may believe that it would be advantageous to a plant to produce stamens alone in one flower or on one whole plant, and pistils alone in another flower or on another plant. In plants under culture and placed under new conditions of life, sometimes the male organs and sometimes the female organs become more or less impotent; now if we suppose this to occur in ever so slight a degree under nature, then as pollen is already carried regularly from flower to flower and as a more complete separation of the sexes of our plant would be advantageous on the principle of the division of labour, individuals with this tendency more and more increased, would be continually favoured or selected, until at last a complete separation of the sexes would be effected.

Let us now turn to the nectar-feeding insects in our imaginary case: we may suppose the plant of which we have been slowly increasing the nectar by continued selection, to be a common plant; and that certain insects depended in main part on its nectar for food. I could give many facts, showing how anxious bees are to save time; for instance, their habit of cutting holes and sucking the nectar at the bases of certain flowers, which they can, with a very little more trouble, enter by the mouth. Bearing such facts in mind, I can see no reason to doubt that an accidental deviation in the size and form of the body, or in the curvature and length of the proboscis, &c., far too slight to be appreciated by us, might profit a bee or other insect, so that an individual so characterised would be able to obtain its food more quickly, and so have a better chance of living and leaving descendants. Its descendants would probably inherit a tendency to a similar slight deviation of structure. The tubes of the corollas of the common red and incarnate clovers (Trifolium pratense and incarnatum) do not on a hasty glance appear to differ in length; yet the hive-bee can easily suck the nectar out of the incarnate clover, but not out of the common red clover, which is visited by humble-bees alone; so that whole fields of the red clover offer in vain an abundant supply of precious nectar to the hive-bee. Thus it might be a great advantage to the hive-bee to have a slightly longer or differently constructed proboscis. On the other hand, I have found by experiment that the fertility of clover greatly depends on bees visiting and moving parts of the corolla, so as to push the pollen on to the stigmatic surface. Hence, again, if humble-bees were to become rare in any country, it might be a great advantage to the red clover to have a shorter or more deeply divided tube to its corolla, so that the hive-bee could visit its flowers. Thus I can understand how a flower and a bee might slowly become, either simultaneously or one after the other, modified and adapted in the most perfect manner to each other, by the continued preservation of individuals presenting mutual and slightly favourable deviations of structure.

I am well aware that this doctrine of natural selection, exemplified in the above imaginary instances, is open to the same objections which were at first urged against Sir Charles Lyell's noble views on "the modern changes of the earth, as illustrative of geology"; but we now very seldom hear the action, for instance, of the coast-waves, called a trifling and insignificant cause, when applied to the excavation of gigantic valleys or to the formation of the longest lines of inland cliffs. Natural selection can act only by the preservation and accumulation of infinitesimally small inherited modifications, each profitable to the preserved being; and as modern geology has almost banished such views as the excavation of a great valley by a single diluvial wave, so will natural selection, if it be a true principle, banish the belief of the continued creation of new organic beings, or of any great and sudden modification in their structure.[. . .]

On Extinction

We have as yet spoken only incidentally of the disappearance of species and of groups of species. On the theory of natural selection the extinction of old forms and the production of new and improved forms are intimately connected together. The old notion of all the inhabitants of the earth having been swept away at successive periods by catastrophes, is very generally given up, even by those geologists, as Elie de Beaumont, Murchison, Barrande, &c., whose general views would naturally lead them to this conclusion. On the contrary, we have every reason to believe, from the study of the tertiary formations, that species and groups of species gradually disappear, one after another, first from one spot, then from another, and finally from the world. Both single species and whole groups of species last for very unequal periods; some groups, as we have seen, having endured from the earliest known dawn of life to the present day; some having disappeared before the close of the palæozoic period. No fixed law seems to determine the length of time during which any single species or any single genus endures. There is reason to believe that the complete extinction of the species of a group is generally a slower process than their production: if the appearance and disappearance of a group of species be represented, as before, by a vertical line of varying thickness, the line is found to taper more gradually at its upper end, which marks the progress of extermination, than at its lower end, which marks the first appearance and increase in numbers of the species. In some cases, however, the extermination of whole groups of beings, as of ammonites towards the close of the secondary period, has been wonderfully sudden.

The whole subject of the extinction of species has been involved in the most gratuitous mystery. Some authors have even supposed that as the individual has a definite length of life, so have species a definite duration. No one I think can have marvelled more at the extinction of species, than I have done. When I found in La Plata the tooth of a horse embedded with the remains of Mastodon, Megatherium, Toxodon, and other extinct monsters, which all co-existed with still living shells at a very late geological period, I was filled with astonishment; for seeing that the horse, since its introduction by the Spaniards into South America, has run wild over the whole country and has increased in numbers at an unparalleled rate, I asked myself what could so recently have exterminated the former horse under conditions of life apparently so favourable. But how utterly groundless was my astonishment! Professor Owen soon perceived that the tooth, though so like that of the existing horse, belonged to an extinct species. Had this horse been still living, but in some degree rare, no naturalist would have felt the least surprise at its rarity; for rarity is the attribute of a vast number of species of all classes, in all countries. If we ask ourselves why this or that species is rare, we answer that something is unfavourable in its conditions of life; but what that something is, we can hardly ever tell. On the supposition of the fossil horse still existing as a rare species, we might have felt certain from the analogy of all other mammals, even of the slow-breeding elephant, and from the history of the naturalisation of the domestic horse in South America, that under more favourable conditions it would in a very few years have stocked the whole continent. But we could not have told what the unfavourable conditions were which checked its increase, whether some one or several contingencies, and at what period of the horse's life, and in what degree, they severally acted. If the conditions had gone on, however slowly, becoming less and less favourable, we assuredly should not have perceived the fact, yet the fossil horse would certainly have become rarer and rarer, and finally extinct; its place being seized on by some more successful competitor.

It is most difficult always to remember that the increase of every living being is constantly being checked by unperceived injurious agencies; and that these same unperceived agencies are amply sufficient to cause rarity, and finally extinction. We see in many cases in the more recent tertiary formations, that rarity precedes extinction; and we know that this has been the progress of events with those animals which have been exterminated, either locally or wholly, through man's agency. I may repeat what I published in 1845, namely, that to admit that species generally become rare before they become extinct—to feel no surprise at the rarity of a species, and yet to marvel greatly when it ceases to exist, is much the same as to admit that sickness in the individual is the forerunner of death—to feel no surprise at sickness, but when the sick man dies, to wonder and to suspect that he died by some unknown deed of violence.

The theory of natural selection is grounded on the belief that each new variety, and ultimately each new species, is produced and maintained by having some advantage over those with which it comes into competition: and the consequent extinction of less-favoured forms almost inevitably follows. It is the same with our domestic productions: when a new and slightly improved variety has been raised, it at first supplants the less improved varieties in the same neighbourhood; when much improved it is transported far and near, like our short-horn cattle, and takes the place of other breeds in other countries. Thus the appearance of new forms and the disappearance of old forms, both natural and artificial, are bound together. In certain flourishing groups, the number of new specific forms which have been produced within a given time is probably greater than that of the old forms which have been exterminated; but we know that the number of species has not gone on indefinitely increasing, at least during the later geological periods, so that looking to later times we may believe that the production of new forms has caused the extinction of about the same number of old forms.

The competition will generally be most severe, as formerly explained and illustrated by examples, between the forms which are most like each other in all respects. Hence the improved and modified descendants of a species will generally cause the extermination of the parent-species; and if many new forms have been developed from any one species, the nearest allies of that species, *i.e.* the species of the same genus, will be the most liable to extermination. Thus, as I believe, a number of new species descended from one species, that is a new genus, comes to supplant an old genus, belonging to the same family. But it must often have happened that a new species belonging to some one group will have seized on the place occupied by a species belonging to a distinct group, and thus caused its extermination; and if many allied forms be developed from the successful intruder, many will have to yield their places; and it will generally be allied forms, which will suffer from some inherited inferiority in common. But whether it be species belonging to the same or to a distinct class, which yield their places to other species which have been modified and improved, a few of the sufferers may often long be preserved, from being fitted to some peculiar line of life, or from inhabiting some distant and isolated station, where they have escaped severe competition. For instance, a single species of Trigonia, a great genus of shells in the secondary formations, survives in the Australian seas; and a few members of the great and almost extinct group of Ganoid fishes still inhabit our fresh waters. Therefore the utter extinction of a group is generally, as we have seen, a slower process than its production.

With respect to the apparently sudden extermination of whole families or orders, as of Trilobites at the close of the palæozoic period and of Ammonites at the close of the secondary period, we must remember what has been already said on the probable wide intervals of time between our consecutive formations; and in these intervals there may have been much slow extermination. Moreover, when by sudden immigration or by unusually rapid development, many species of a new group have taken possession of a new area, they will have exterminated in a correspondingly rapid manner many of the old inhabitants; and the forms which thus yield their places will commonly be allied, for they will partake of some inferiority in common.

Thus, as it seems to me, the manner in which single species and whole groups of species become extinct, accords well with the theory of natural selection. We need not marvel at extinction; if we must marvel, let it be at our presumption in imagining for a moment that we understand the many complex contingencies, on which the existence of each species depends. If we forget for an instant, that each species tends to increase inordinately, and that some check is always in action, yet seldom perceived by us, the whole economy of nature will be utterly obscured. Whenever we can precisely say why this species is more abundant in individuals than that; why this species and not another can be naturalised in a given country; then, and not till then, we may justly feel surprise why we cannot account for the extinction of this particular species or group of species.[. . .]

[From] Conclusion

It may be asked how far I extend the doctrine of the modification of species. The question is difficult to answer, because the more distinct the forms are which we may consider, by so much the arguments fall away in force. But some arguments of the greatest weight extend very far. All the members of whole classes can be connected together by chains of affinities, and all can be classified on the same principle, in groups subordinate to groups. Fossil remains sometimes tend to fill up very wide intervals between existing orders. Organs in a rudimentary condition plainly show that an early progenitor had the organ in a fully developed state; and this in some instances necessarily implies an enormous amount of modification in the descendants. Throughout whole classes various structures are formed on the same pattern, and at an embryonic age the species closely resemble each other. Therefore I cannot doubt that the theory of descent with modification embraces all the members of the same class. I believe that animals have descended from at most only four or five progenitors, and plants from an equal or lesser number.

Analogy would lead me one step further, namely, to the belief that all animals and plants have descended from some one prototype. But analogy may be a deceitful guide. Nevertheless all living things have much in common, in their chemical composition, their germinal vesicles, their cellular structure, and their laws of growth and reproduction. We see this even in so trifling a circumstance as that the same poison often similarly affects plants and animals; or that the poison secreted by the gall-fly produces monstrous growths on the wild rose or oak-tree. Therefore I should infer from analogy that probably all the organic beings which have ever lived on this earth have descended from some one primordial form, into which life was first breathed.

When the views entertained in this volume on the origin of species, or when analogous views are generally admitted, we can dimly foresee that there will be a considerable revolution in natural history. Systematists will be able to pursue their labours as at present; but they will not be incessantly haunted by the shadowy doubt whether this or that form be in essence a species. This I feel sure, and I speak after experience, will be no slight relief. The endless disputes whether or not some fifty species of British brambles are true species will cease. Systematists will have only to decide (not that this will be easy) whether any form be sufficiently constant and distinct from other forms, to be capable of definition; and if definable, whether the differences be sufficiently important to deserve a specific name. This latter point will become a far more essential consideration than it is at present; for differences, however slight, between any two forms, if not blended by intermediate gradations, are looked at by most naturalists as sufficient to raise both forms to the rank of species. Hereafter we shall be compelled to acknowledge that the only distinction between species and well-marked varieties is, that the latter are known, or believed, to be connected at the present day by intermediate gradations, whereas species were formerly thus connected. Hence, without quite rejecting the consideration of the present existence of intermediate gradations between any two forms, we shall be led to weigh more carefully and to value higher the actual amount of difference between them. It is quite possible that forms now generally acknowledged to be merely varieties may hereafter be thought worthy of specific names, as with the primrose and cowslip; and in this case scientific and common language will come into accordance. In short, we shall have to treat species in the same manner as those naturalists treat genera, who admit that genera are merely artificial combinations made for convenience. This may not be a cheering prospect; but we shall at least be freed from the vain search for the undiscovered and undiscoverable essence of the term species.

The other and more general departments of natural history will rise greatly in interest. The terms used by naturalists of affinity, relationship, community of type, paternity, morphology, adaptive characters, rudimentary and aborted organs, &c., will cease to be metaphorical, and will have a plain signification. When we no longer look at an organic being as a savage looks at a ship, as at something wholly beyond his comprehension; when we regard every production of nature as one which has had a history; when we contemplate every complex structure and instinct as the summing up of many contrivances, each useful to the possessor, nearly in the same way as when we look at any great mechanical invention as the summing up of the labour, the experience, the reason, and even the blunders of numerous workmen; when we thus view each organic being, how far more interesting, I speak from experience, will the study of natural history become!

A grand and almost untrodden field of inquiry will be opened, on the causes and laws of variation, on correlation of growth, on the effects of use and disuse, on the direct action of external conditions, and so forth. The study of domestic productions will rise immensely in value. A new variety raised by man will be a far more important and interesting subject for study than one more species added to the infinitude of already recorded species. Our classifications will come to be, as far as they can be so made, genealogies; and will then truly give what may be called the plan of creation. The rules for classifying will no doubt become simpler when we have a definite object in view. We possess no pedigrees or armorial bearings; and we have to discover and trace the many diverging lines of descent in our natural genealogies, by characters of any kind which have long been inherited. Rudimentary organs will speak infallibly with respect to the nature of long-lost structures. Species and groups of species; which are called aberrant, and which may fancifully be called living fossils, will aid us in forming a picture of the ancient forms of life. Embryology will reveal to us the structure, in some degree obscured, of the prototypes of each great class.

When we can feel assured that all the individuals of the same species, and all the closely allied species of most genera, have within a not very remote period descended from one parent, and have migrated from some one birthplace; and when we better know the many means of migration, then, by the light which geology now throws, and will continue to throw, on former changes of climate and of the level of the land, we shall surely be enabled to trace in an admirable manner the former migrations of the inhabitants of the whole world. Even at present, by comparing the differences of the inhabitants of the sea on the opposite sides of a continent, and the nature of the various inhabitants of that continent in relation to their apparent means of immigration, some light can be thrown on ancient geography.

The noble science of Geology loses glory from the extreme imperfection of the record. The crust of the earth with its embedded remains must not be looked at as a well-filled museum, but as a poor collection made at hazard and at rare intervals. The accumulation of each great fossiliferous formation will be recognised as having depended on an unusual concurrence of circumstances, and the blank intervals between the successive stages as having been of vast duration. But we shall be able to gauge with some security the duration of these intervals by a comparison of the preceding and succeeding organic forms. We must be cautious in attempting to correlate as strictly contemporaneous two formations, which include few identical species, by the general succession of their forms of life. As species are produced and exterminated by slowly acting and still existing causes, and not by miraculous acts of creation and by catastrophes; and as the most important of all causes of organic change is one which is almost independent of altered and perhaps suddenly altered physical conditions, namely, the mutual relation of organism to organism, the improvement of one being entailing the improvement or the extermination of others; it follows, that the amount of organic change in the fossils of consecutive formations probably serves as a fair measure of the lapse of actual time. A number of species, however, keeping in a body might remain for a long period unchanged, whilst within this same period, several of these species, by migrating into new countries and coming into competition with foreign associates, might become modified; so that we must not overrate the accuracy of organic change as a measure of time. During early periods of the earth's history, when the forms of life were probably fewer and simpler, the rate of change was probably slower; and at the first dawn of life, when very few forms of the simplest structure existed, the rate of change may have been slow in an extreme degree. The whole history of the world, as at present known, although of a length quite incomprehensible by us, will hereafter be recognised as a mere fragment of time, compared with the ages which have elapsed since the first creature, the progenitor of innumerable extinct and living descendants, was created.

In the distant future I see open fields for far more important researches. Psychology will be based on a new foundation, that of the necessary acquirement of each mental power and capacity by gradation. Light will be thrown on the origin of man and his history.

Authors of the highest eminence seem to be fully satisfied with the view that each species has been independently created. To my mind it accords better with what we know of the laws impressed on matter by the Creator, that the production and extinction of the past and present inhabitants of the world should have been due to secondary causes, like those determining the birth and death of the individual. When I view all beings not as special creations, but as the lineal descendants of some few beings which lived long before the first bed of the Silurian system was deposited, they seem to me to become ennobled. Judging from the past, we may safely infer that not one living species will transmit its unaltered likeness to a distant futurity. And of the species now living very few will transmit progeny of any kind to a far distant futurity; for the manner in which all organic beings are grouped, shows that the greater number of species of each genus, and all the species of many genera, have left no descendants, but have become utterly extinct. We can so far take a prophetic glance into futurity as to foretel that it will be the common and widely-spread species, belonging to the larger and dominant groups, which will ultimately prevail and procreate new and dominant species. As all the living forms of life are the lineal descendants of those which lived long before the Silurian epoch, we may feel certain that the ordinary succession by generation has never once been broken, and that no cataclysm has desolated the whole world. Hence we may look with some confidence to a secure future of equally inappreciable length. And as natural selection works solely by and for the good of each being, all corporeal and mental endowments will tend to progress towards perfection.

It is interesting to contemplate an entangled bank, clothed with many plants of many kinds, with birds singing on the bushes, with various insects flitting about, and with worms crawling through the damp earth, and to reflect that these elaborately constructed forms, so different from each other, and dependent on each other in so complex a manner, have all been produced by laws acting around us. These laws, taken in the largest sense, being Growth with Reproduction; Inheritance which is almost implied by reproduction; Variability from the indirect and direct action of the external conditions of life, and from use and disuse; a Ratio of Increase so high as to lead to a Struggle for Life, and as a consequence to Natural Selection, entailing Divergence of Character and the Extinction of less-improved forms. Thus, from the war of nature, from famine and death, the most exalted object which we are capable of conceiving, namely, the production of the higher animals, directly follows. There is grandeur in this view of life, with its several powers, having been originally breathed into a few forms or into one; and that, whilst this planet has gone cycling on according to the fixed law of gravity, from so simple a beginning endless forms most beautiful and most wonderful have been, and are being, evolved.

WORKS CITED

Aikin, Anna. See Barbauld.

Aikin, John. *An Essay on the Application of Natural History to Poetry.* Warrington: W. Eyres for J. Johnson of London, 1777.

―――. *The Natural History of the Year.* Ed. Arthur Aikin. London: J. Johnson, 1798.

Aldini, Giovanni. *An Account of the Late Improvements in Galvanism.* London: Cuthell and Martin, Middle-Row, Holborn, John Murray, 1803.

―――. *General Views on the Application of Galvanism to Medical Purposes; principally in cases of suspended animation.* London: J. Callow, 1819.

[Barbauld, Anna Letitia]. *Poems.* 4th ed. London: J. Johnson, 1774.

Barbauld, Anna Letitia. *The Poems of Anna Letitia Barbauld.* Ed. William McCarthy and Elizabeth Kraft. Athens: U of Georgia P, 1994.

―――. *The Works of Anna Letitia Barbauld.* With a memoir by Lucy Aikin. 2 vols. London: Longman, Hurst, Rees, Orme, 1825.

Barbauld, Anna Letitia, and John Aikin. *Evenings at Home; or, the Juvenile Budget Opened, consisting of a Variety of Miscellaneous Pieces for the Instruction and Amusement of Young Persons.* London: J. Johnson, 1794.

Barber, Lynn. *The Heyday of Natural History: 1820–1870.* London: Cape, 1980.

Bartram, William. *Travels Through North and South Carolina, Georgia, East and West Florida.* Philadelphia: James and Johnson, 1791.

Bate, Jonathan. *Romantic Ecology: Wordsworth and the Environmental Tradition.* London: Routledge, 1991.

Bewick, Thomas. *A General History of Quadrupeds.* Newcastle: S. Hodgson, Beilby, and Bewick, 1790.

———. *History of British Birds.* 2 vols. London: Longman. 1816. [Newcastle: Hodgson, 1797].

———. *The New Museum of Natural History.* Edinburgh: Oliver and Boyd, 1810.

Blake, William. "Auguries of Innocence." Ed. Dante Gabriel Rossetti. *Life of William Blake, Pictor Ignotus.* Alexander Gilchrist. 2 vols. London: Macmillan, 1863.

———. *Complete Writings.* Ed. Geoffrey Keynes. Oxford: Oxford UP, 1976.

———. *Songs of Innocence and of Experience.* London: W. Blake, 1794.

Brontë, Charlotte. *Jane Eyre.* Ed. Beth Newman. Boston: St. Martin's, 1996.

Buffon, Georges Louis Leclerc, Comte de. *Histoire naturelle, générale et particulière.* 44 vols. Paris: De l'Imprimerie royale, 1749–1804.

———. *The Natural History of Insects, compiled from Swammerdam, Brookes, Goldsmith.* Perth: Morison, 1792 [bound together with Buffon, *System,* 1791].

———. *The System of Natural History.* Ed. R. Morison. Edinburgh: Mudie, 1791.

———. Trans. J. S. Barr. *Barr's Buffon: Buffon's Natural History; containing a theory of the Earth.* 10 vols. London: J. S. Barr, 1792.

Butler, Marilyn. "Frankenstein and Radical Science," *TLS,* 4 April 1993. *Frankenstein.* Ed. J. Paul Hunter. New York: Norton, 1996. 302–12.

Byron, George Gordon, Lord. *The Complete Poetical Works of Byron.* Ed. Paul E. More. Boston: Houghton Mifflin, 1933.

[Chambers, Robert]. *Vestiges of the Natural History of Creation.* London: Churchill, 1844.

Clare, John. *Poems Descriptive of Rural Life and Scenery.* London: Taylor and Hessey, 1821.

———. *The Rural Muse.* London: Whittaker, 1835.

———. *The Shepherd's Calendar and Other Poems.* London: John Taylor, 1827.

Coleridge, Samuel Taylor. *Anima Poetae.* Ed. E. H. Coleridge. London: Heinemann, 1895.

———. *Biographia Literaria*. Ed. James Engell and W. J. Bate. Princeton: Princeton UP, 1983.

———. *Lyrical Ballads*. London: J. and A. Arch, 1798.

———. *Poems on Various Subjects*. London: Robinson and Cottle, 1796.

———. *Poetical Works*. Ed. E. H. Coleridge. Oxford: Oxford UP, 1969 [1912].

———. *Sibylline Leaves*. London: Rest Fenner, 1817.

Crook, Nora, and Derek Guiton. *Shelley's Venomed Melody*. Cambridge: Cambridge UP, 1986.

Darwin, Charles. *The Autobiography of Charles Darwin*. New York: Norton, 1969.

———. *Charles Darwin's Letters: A Selection*. Ed. Frederick Burkhardt. Cambridge: Cambridge UP, 1996.

———. *Journal of Researches into the Geology and Natural History of the Various Countries Visited by H.M.S. Beagle*. London: Henry Colburn, 1839.

———. *On the Origin of Species by Means of Natural Selection*. London: John Murray, 1859.

Darwin, Erasmus. *The Botanic Garden; A Poem, in Two Parts: The Economy of Vegetation, The Loves of the Plants*. London: J. Johnson, 1791–94.

———. *The Letters of Erasmus Darwin*. Ed. Desmond King-Hele. Cambridge: Cambridge UP, 1981.

———. *Phytologia*. London: J. Johnson, 1800.

———. *The Temple of Nature; or, the Origin of Society*. London: J. Johnson, 1803.

———. *Zoonomia; or, the Laws of Organic Life*. 2 vols. London: J. Johnson, 1794–96.

[Davy, Sir Humphry]. *Salmonia: or Days of Fly Fishing, by an Angler*. London: John Murray, 1828.

Davy, Sir Humphry. *The Annual Anthology*. Ed. Robert Southey. London: Longman and Rees, 1799–1800.

———. *Collected Works*. Ed. John Davy. 9 vols. London: Smith and Elder, 1839–40.

———. *A Discourse, introductory to a course of lectures on Chemistry, delivered in the Theatre of the Royal Institution, 21 January 1802*. London: J. Johnson, 1802.

————. *Elements of Chemical Philosophy*. Philadelphia: Bradford and Inskeep. London: J. Johnson, 1812.

————. "An Essay on the Generation of Phosoxygen (Oxygen Gas) and on the Causes of Colours of Organic Beings." *Contributions to Physical and Medical Knowledge*. Ed. Thomas Beddoes. Bristol: Biggs and Cottle, 1799.

————. *Fragmentary remains, literary and scientific*. Ed. John Davy. London: John Churchill, 1858.

Descriptive Poetry; being a selection from the best modern authors; principally having reference to subjects in Natural History. London, 1807. [Works by Burns, Coleridge, Charlotte Smith, Southey, Moore, Mrs. Opie, Spenser, Blair, etc.]

Galvani, Luigi. *Commenatry on the effects of electricity on muscular motion. With a facsimile of De viribus electricitatis in motu musculari commentarius* (1791). Trans. Margaret G. Foley. Norwalk, Conn.: Burndy Library, 1953.

Goethe, Johann Wolfgang von. *Goethe on Science*. Ed. Jeremy Naydler. Edinburgh: Floris, 1996.

Goldsmith, Oliver. *An History of the Earth and Animated Nature*. 8 vols. Dublin: James Williams, 1782 [London, 1774].

Holmes, Richard. *Shelley: The Pursuit*. New York: Dutton, 1975.

Irmscher, Christoph. *The Poetics of Natural History: From John Bartram to William James*. New Brunswick: Rutgers UP, 1999.

Kastner, Joseph. *A Species of Eternity*. New York: Knopf, 1977.

Keats, John. *Anatomical and Physiological Notebook*. Ed. M. Buxton Forman. New York: Haskell House, 1970 [1934].

————. *The Complete Poems*. Ed. Miriam Allott. New York: Longman, 1970.

————. *Endymion*. London: Taylor and Hessey, 1818.

————. *Lamia, Isabella, The Eve of St. Agnes, and Other Poems*. London: Taylor and Hessey, 1820.

————. *The Letters of John Keats*. Ed. Edward Hyder Rollins. 2 vols. Cambridge: Harvard UP, 1976 [1958].

————. *Poems*. London: Ollier, 1817.

King-Hele, Desmond. *Erasmus Darwin*. New York: Scribner's, 1963.

————. *Erasmus Darwin and the Romantic Poets.* New York: St. Martin's, 1986.

————. *Erasmus Darwin: A Life of Unequalled Achievement.* London: Giles de la Mare, 1999.

Kirby, William, and William Spence. *An introduction to entomology: or Elements of the natural history of insects: with plates.* 4 vols. London: Longman, 1815–26 [1 (1815), 2 (1817), 3 and 4 (1826)].

Knapp, John Leonard. *The Journal of a Naturalist.* London: John Murray, 1829–30.

————. *The Journal of a Naturalist.* Philadelphia: Gihon, 1850.

La Mettrie, Julien Offray de. *Man a Machine and Man a Plant.* Trans. Richard A. Watson and Maya Rybalka. Indiana: Hackett, 1994.

Lawrence, William. *An Introduction to Comparative Anatomy, being two introductory lectures delivered at the Royal College of Surgeons.* London: J. Callow, 1816.

————. *Lectures on Physiology, Zoology, and the Natural History of Man.* London: J. Callow, 1819.

Linnaeus, Carolus. *A Dissertation on the Sexes of Plants.* Trans. James Edward Smith. London: George Nicol, 1786.

————. *Lapland Journey (Lachesis Lapponica).* Trans. Carl Troilius. Ed. James Edward Smith. London, 1792.

————. *A Selection of the Correspondence of Linnaeus and Other Naturalists.* Ed. James Edward Smith. London, 1821.

————. *Systema Naturae.* Stockholm: Laurentii Salvii Holmiae, 1735. [10th ed. 1758].

Mellor, Anne. *Mary Shelley: Her Life, Her Fictions, Her Monsters.* New York: Methuen, 1988.

Pennant, Thomas. *British Zoology.* 4th ed. 4 vols. London: Benjamin White, 1777.

Priestley, Joseph. *Disquisitions Relating to Matter and Spirit.* London: J. Johnson, 1777.

————. *Experiments and Observations on Different Kinds of Air.* London: J. Johnson, 1774.

————. *The History and Present State of Electricity.* London: Dodsley, Johnson, Davenport and Cadell, 1767.

———. *The History and Present State of Electricity, with Original Experiments*. 3rd edition. London: Bathurst, J. Johnson, 1775.

———. *Memoirs of Dr. Joseph Priestley to the Year 1795*. 2 vols. London: J. Johnson, 1806.

———. "Observations and experiments relating to equivocal, or spontaneous, generation." *Transactions of the American Philosophical Society*. London and Philadelphia: Conrad and Mawman, 1804.

Ritterbush, Philip C. *Overtures to Biology: The Speculations of Eighteenth-Century Naturalists*. New Haven: Yale UP, 1964.

[Shelley, Mary W.]. *Frankenstein; or, the Modern Prometheus*. 3 vols. London: Lackington, Hughes, 1818.

[Shelley, Mary W. (and Percy Bysshe Shelley)]. *History of a Six Weeks' Tour*. London: Hookham and Ollier, 1817.

Shelley, Mary W. *Frankenstein; or, the Modern Prometheus*. London: Colburn and Bentley, 1831.

———. *The Frankenstein Notebooks*. Ed. Charles E. Robinson. Vol. 9: *The Manuscripts of the Younger Romantics*. New York: Garland, 1996.

Shelley, Percy Bysshe. *Letters*. Ed. Frederick L. Jones. 2 vols. Oxford: Clarendon, 1964.

———. *Queen Mab: A Philosophical Poem*. London: Author, 1813.

———. *Poetical Works*. Ed. Mary W. Shelley. London: Moxon, 1839.

———. *Shelley's Poetry and Prose*. Ed. Donald H. Reiman and Neil Fraistat. 2nd ed. New York: Norton, 2002.

[Smith, Charlotte]. *Conversations Introducing Poetry, Chiefly on Subjects of Natural History for the Use of Young Persons*. London: Whittingham and Arliss, 1819 [1804].

Smith, Charlotte. *Marchmont*. London: Low, 1796.

———. *The Poems of Charlotte Smith*. Ed. Stuart Curran. Oxford: Oxford University Press, 1993.

Tennyson, Alfred, Lord. *In Memoriam*. London: Moxon, 1850.

———. *Tennyson: A Selected Edition*. Ed. Christopher Ricks. Berkeley: U of California P, 1989.

Tennyson, Hallam, Lord. *Alfred, Lord Tennyson: A Memoir*. 2 vols. New York: Macmillan, 1897.

Volta, Alessandro. "Account of some discoveries made by Mr. Galvani, of Bologna." *Philosophical Transactions* 83 (1793): 10–44.

Wardle, Ralph M. *Oliver Goldsmith*. Lawrence: U of Kansas P, 1957.

Wells, William Charles. "Observations and Experiments on the Colour of Blood, read before the Royal Society July 6, 1797." *Philosophical Transactions* 87 (1797).

———. *An Essay on Dew, and several appearances connected with it*. London: Taylor and Hessey, 1814.

White, Gilbert. *The Natural History and Antiquities of Selborne*. London: T. Bensley, 1789.

———. *A Naturalist's Calendar, with Observations on Various Branches of Natural History*. London: B. and J. White, 1795.

———. *The Natural History of Selborne, to which are added The Naturalist's Calendar, Miscellaneous Observations, and Poems*. London: Longman, 1813.

———. *The Works in Natural History of the Late Gilbert White, comprising The Natural History of Selborne; The Naturalist's Calendar; and miscellaneous observations*. Ed. William Markwick. London: J. White, 1802.

Wordsworth, Dorothy. *Journals of Dorothy Wordsworth*. Ed. Mary Moorman. Oxford: Oxford UP, 1971.

Wordsworth, William. *The Excursion*. London: Longman, 1814.

———. *Lyrical Ballads*. London: J. and A. Arch, 1798.

———. *Poems in Two Volumes*. London: Longman, 1807.

———. *The Prelude: 1799, 1805, 1850*. Ed. Jonathan Wordsworth, M. H. Abrams, and Stephen Gill. New York: Norton, 1979.

———. *William Wordsworth* (Oxford Authors). Ed. Stephen Gill. Oxford: Oxford UP, 1984.

FOR FURTHER READING

Abernethy, John. *An Enquiry into the Probability and Rationality of Mr Hunter's "Theory of Life."* London: Longman, 1814.

Agassiz, Louis. "On the succession and development of organized beings at the surface of the terrestrial globe." *New Philosophical Journal* 23 (1842): 388–99.

Anonymous. *A Philosophical Essay on Fecundation; or, an impartial inquiry into the first rudiments of progression and perfection of animal generation, particularly of the human species.* 1742.

Audubon, John James. *The Original Water-Color Paintings by John James Audubon for the Birds of America.* New York: American Heritage, 1966.

———. *Ornithological Biography; or, an account of the habits of the birds of the United States of America.* Edinburgh: Adam Black, 1831.

Baine, Rodney M. *The Scattered Portions: William Blake's Biological Symbolism.* Athens, Ga.: Author, 1986.

Barber, L. *The Heyday of Natural History: 1820–1870.* London: Jonathan Cape, 1980.

Bartram, John. *A Description of East Florida with a Journal kept by John Bartram, of Philadelphia, Botanist to His Majesty for the Floridas.* London, 1766.

———. *Observations on the inhabitants, climate, soil, rivers, productions worthy of notice, made by John Bartram in his travels from Pennsylvania to Onondaga, Oswego, and the Lake Ontario in Canada.* London: J. Whiston and B. White, 1751.

Bate, Jonathan. *The Song of the Earth.* Cambridge: Harvard UP, 2000.

Bell, Thomas. *A History of British Reptiles.* London: J. Van Voorst, 1839.

Bichat, Marie François Xavier. *Physiological Researches on Life and Death.* Trans. F. Gold. London: Longman, 1815.

Brown, William Rust. *The Emerson Museum: Practical Romanticism and the Pursuit of the Whole.* Cambridge, Mass.: Harvard UP, 1997.

Bruce, James. *Travels to Discover the Source of the Nile.* London, 1790.

Buckland, William. *Geology and Mineralogy Considered with Reference to Natural Theology.* 2 vols. London: William Pickering, 1836.

Catesby, Mark. *The Natural History of the Carolinas, Florida, and the Bahamas.* London: George Edwards, 1754.

Cochrane, Archibald. *A Treatise shewing the intimate connection that subsists between agriculture and chemistry.* London: J. Murray and S. Hoghley, 1795.

Coletta, W. John. "'Writing Larks': John Clare's Semiosis of Nature." *The Wordsworth Circle* 28.3 (1997): 192–200.

Collins, Samuel. *Paradise Retriev'd, plainly and fully demonstrating the most beautiful, durable and beneficial method of managing and improving fruit-trees.* London: J. Collins, 1717.

Conybeare, W. D. "On the Discovery of an almost perfect skeleton of the Plesiosaurus." *Transactions of the Geological Society of London* 1 (1824): 381–89.

Cook, James, and James King. *A Voyage to the Pacific Ocean* (1776–80). Dublin: Chamberlaine, 1784.

Cunningham, Andrew, and Nicholas Jardine, eds. *Romanticism in the Sciences.* Cambridge: Cambridge UP, 1990.

Cuvier, Georges L. C. F. D. *Essay on the Theory of the Earth.* Trans. R. Kerr. Edinburgh: Blackwood, 1813.

———. *Lectures on Comparative Anatomy.* Trans. William Ross. 2 vols. London: Longman and Rees, 1802.

Darwin, Robert Waring. *Principia Botanica; or, a Concise and Easy Introduction to the Sexual Botany of Linnaeus.* Newark: M. Hage, 1810.

De Almeida, Hermione. *Romantic Medicine and John Keats.* Oxford: Oxford UP, 1991.

A Dictionary of Natural History; or, Complete Summary of Zoology, containing a full and succinct description of all the animated beings in nature. London: Whittingham, 1802.

Dramatic Romances: containing "The Poison Tree" and "The Torrid Zone." London: John Murray, 1809.

Drummond, William Hamilton. *The Giant's Causeway: A Poem.* Belfast, 1811.

————. *The Rights of Animals, and Man's Obligation to Treat them with Humanity.* London: J. Mardon, 1838.

Ellis, John. "A botanical description of the Dionaea muscipula, or Venus's fly-trap. A newly-discovered sensitive plant: in a letter to Sir Charles Linnaeus." *Directions for bringing over seeds and plants from the East-Indies and other distant countries.* London: L. Davis, 1770. 35–41.

————. "On the nature of the Gorgonia; that it is a real marine animal, and not of a mixed nature, between animal and vegetable." *Philosophical Transactions* 66 (1776): 1–17.

Fontana, Felix. *Treatise on the Venom of the Viper; on the American poisons; and on the Cherry Laurel; and some other Vegetable Poisons, to which are annexed, observations on the primitive structure of the animal body; different experiments on the reproduction of the nerves; and a description of a new canal of the eye.* Trans. Joseph Skinner. 2 vols. London: J. Murray, 1807 [Florence, 1781].

Fothergill, Charles. *An Essay on the Philosophy, Study, and Use of Natural History.* London: White and Cochran, 1813.

Fulford, Tim. "Coleridge, Darwin, Linnaeus: The Sexual Politics of Botany." *The Wordsworth Circle* 28.3 (Summer 1997): 124–30.

Garden, Alexander. "An account of the Gymnotus electricus or electrical eel." *Philosophical Transactions* 65 (1775): 102–110.

Gaull, Marilyn. "Natural History and Its Illusion." *English Romanticism: The Human Context.* New York: Norton, 1988.

Gemmil, James Fairlie. *Natural History in the Poetry of Robert Burns.* Glasgow: N. Adshead, 1928.

Geoffroy Saint-Hillaire, Étienne *Philosophie Anatomique.* Paris: Mequignon-Marvis, 1818.

Godman, John D. *American Natural History.* Philadelphia: Carey and Lea, 1828.

Grabo, Carl. *The Magic Plant: The Growth of Shelley's Thought.* Chapel Hill: U of North Carolina P, 1936.

————*A Newton Among Poets: Shelley's Use of Science.* Chapel Hill: U of North Carolina P, 1930.

Gray, Thomas. *The Poet Gray as Naturalist* (1903). Boston: Goodspeed, 1903.

Gronovius, J. F. "Concerning a water insect, which, being cut into several pieces, becomes so many perfect animals." *Philosophical Transactions* 466 (1742): 218–20.

Haley, William. *Ballads, founded on anecdotes relating to animals, with prints designed and engraved by Wm. Blake.* London: R. Phillips, 1805.

Hanley, Wayne. *Natural History in America: From Mark Catesby to Rachel Carson.* New York: Quadrangle, 1977.

Herschel, J. F. W. *Preliminary Discourse on the Study of Natural Philosophy.* London: Longman, 1831.

Hoage, R. J., and William A. Deiss, eds. *New Worlds, New Animals: From Menagerie to Zoological Park in the Nineteenth Century.* Baltimore: Johns Hopkins UP, 1996.

Hooke, R. *Micrographia: or some Physiological Descriptions of Minute Bodies Made by Magnifying Glasses, with Observations and Inquiries thereupon.* London, 1665.

Hunter, John. "Experiments on animals and vegetables, with respect to the power of producing heat." *Philosophical Transactions* 65 (1775): 446–58.

———. *Observations on Certain Parts of the Animal Oeconomy.* London, 1786.

Hutton, James. "Theory of the Earth; or an investigation of the laws observable in the composition, dissolution, and restoration of land upon the globe." *Transactions of the Royal Society of Edinburgh* 1 (1788): 209–304.

Irmscher, Christoph. *The Poetics of Natural History: From John Bartram to William James.* New Brunswick: Rutgers UP, 1999.

Jardine, Nicholas, J.A. Secord, and E.C. Spary. *Cultures of Natural History.* Cambridge: Cambridge UP, 1996.

Jardine, Sir William. *The Natural History of Monkeys.* Edinburgh: Lizars, 1833.

Jones, Christine Kenyon. *Kindred Brutes: Animals in Romantic Period Writing.* Hampshire: Ashgate, 2001.

Kalm, Peter. *Travels in North America.* Ed. Carl Adolph Benson. New York, 1937.

Keegan, Bridget, and James C. McKusick. *Literature and Nature: Four Centuries of Nature Writing.* Upper Saddle River, N.J.: Prentice-Hall, 2000.

Kerr, Robert. *A General History and Collection of Voyages and Travels.* Edinburgh: Ramsay, 1811.

Kroeber, Karl. *Ecological Literary Criticism: Romantic Imagining and the Biology of Mind.* New York: Columbia UP, 1994.

———. "Proto-Evolutionary Bards and Post-Ecological Critics." *Keats-Shelley Journal* 48 (1999): 157–72.

Lamarck, Jean-Baptiste de. *Philosophie Zoologique.* Paris: Chez Dentu, 1809.

The Law of Java; or, the Poison Tree, a play in three acts. London: J. L. Marks, 1816.

Loudon, Jane Webb. *The Entertaining Naturalist.* London: Henry Bohn, 1843.

Lussier, Mark. "Blake's Deep Ecology." *Studies in Romanticism* 35 (1996): 393–408.

Lyell, Charles. *Life, Letters, and Journals of Sir Charles Lyell.* New York: AMS, 1881.

———. *Principles of Geology: Being an Attempt to Explain the Former Changes of the Earth's Surface by References to Causes Now in Operation.* 3 vols. London, 1830–33.

Mabey, Richard, ed. *The Oxford Book of Nature Writing.* Oxford: Oxford UP, 1995.

Macgillivray, William. *A History of British Birds.* London: Scott, Webster and Geary, 1837.

Malthus, Thomas. R. *An Essay on the Principle of Population.* London: Johnson, 1826 [1798].

Marshall, Tim. *Murdering to Dissect: Grave-robbing, Frankenstein and the Anatomy Literature.* Manchester: Manchester UP, 1995.

Martyn, William Frederic. *A New Dictionary of Natural History; or, Compleat Universal Display of Animated Nature with accurate representations of the most curious and beautiful animals.* 2 vols. London: Harrison, 1785.

McKusick, James C. "Coleridge and the Economy of Nature." *Studies in Romanticism* 35 (1996): 375–90.

———. ed. "Romanticism & Ecology." *Romantic Circles Praxis Series.* College Park: U of Maryland, 2001. http://www.rc.umd.edu/praxis/ecology/index.html.

Miller, John. *An Illustration of the Sexual System of Linnaeus.* London: Miller, 1799.

Morton, Timothy. *The Poetics of Spice*. Cambridge: Cambridge UP, 2001.

──── . "Shelley's Green Desert." *Studies in Romanticism* 35 (1996): 409–30.

──── . *Shelley and the Revolution in Taste: The Body and the Natural World*. Cambridge: Cambridge UP, 1994.

Murchison, Sir Roderick Impey. *The Silurian System*. London, 1839.

Nichols, Ashton. "The Anxiety of Species: Toward a Romantic Natural History." *The Wordsworth Circle* 28.3 (1997): 130–36.

Norton, Charles Eliot. *The Poet Gray as Naturalist: with selections from his notes on the* Systemma Naturae *of Linnaeus*. Boston: Charles Goodspeed, 1903.

Oerlemans, Onno Dag. "'The Meanest Thing that Feels': Anthropomorphizing Animals in Romanticism." *Mosaic* 27.4 (1994): 1–32.

──── . "Romanticism and the Metaphysics of Species." *The Wordsworth Circle* 28.3 (1997): 136–47.

Paley, William. *Natural Theology: or, Evidences of the Existence and Attributes of the Deity collected from the appearances of nature*. 4th ed. London: L. Faulder, 1803.

Parsons, James. *Philosophical Observations on the Analogy Between the Propagation of Animals and that of Vegetables: In which are answered some Objections against the indivisibility of the Soul, which have been inadvertently drawn from the late curious and useful Experiments upon the Polypus and other Animals, with an Explanation of the Manner in which each Piece of a divided Polypus becomes another perfect animal of the same species*. London: C. Davis, 1752.

Percival, Thomas. *Natural History and Poetry; miscellaneous observations on the alliance of natural history, and philosophy, with poetry*. Warrington: W. Eyres for J. Johnson of London, 1784.

A Philosophical Essay on Fecundation; or, an Impartial Inquiry into the first rudiments of progression of animal generation, particularly of the human species, by a member of the Society for Propagating Human Nature and Knowledge. London: J. Roberts, 1742.

Prichard, J. C. *Researches into the Physical History of Mankind*. London: J. & A. Arch, 1813.

Priestman, Martin. *Romantic Atheism*. Cambridge: Cambridge UP, 2000.

Ray, John. *The Wisdom of God Manifested in Works of Creation*. London: Samuel Smith, 1691.

————. *Miscellaneous Discourses Concerning the Dissolution and Changes of the World*. London: Samuel Smith, 1692.

Reed, Edward S. *From Soul to Mind: The Emergence of Psychology from Erasmus Darwin to William James*. New Haven: Yale UP, 1997.

Rice, Tony. *Voyages of Discovery: Three Centuries of Natural History Exploration*. New York: Clarkson Potter, 1999.

Richardson, Alan. *British Romanticism and the Science of the Mind*. Cambridge: Cambridge UP, 2001.

Ritterbush, Philip C. *Overtures to Biology: The Speculations of Eighteenth-Century Naturalists*. New Haven: Yale UP, 1964.

Roe, Nicholas, ed. *Samuel Taylor Coleridge and the Sciences of Life*. Oxford: Oxford UP, 2002.

Rudwick, M. J. S. *The Meaning of Fossils: Episodes in the History of Paleontology*. Chicago: U of Chicago P, 1985.

Rush, Benjamin. *An Inquiry Into the Natural History of Medicine Among the Indians* [originally read before the American Philosophical Society in 1774]. Philadelphia, 1789.

————. *Three Lectures Upon Animal Life*. Philadelphia: Budd and Bartram, 1799.

Scrope, G. P. *Memoir on the Geology of Central France, including the Volcanic Formations of Auvergne, the Velay and the Vivarais*. London, 1827.

Sebright, John Saunders. *The Art of Improving the Breeds of Domestic Animals, in a Letter Addressed to the Right Hon. Sir Joseph Banks, K. B.* London: J. Harding, 1809.

Sharrock, Robert. *The History of the Propagation and Improvement of Vegetables by the Concurrence of Art and Nature*. Oxford: T. Robinson, 1660.

Sims, Michael. *Darwin's Orchestra: An Analysis of Nature in History and the Arts*. New York: Henry Holt, 1997.

Slaughter, Thomas P. *The Natures of John and William Bartram*. New York: Knopf, 1996.

Smellie, William. *The Philosophy of Natural History*. Edinburgh: Elliot, 1790.

Smith, Samuel Stanhope. *An Essay on the Causes of the Variety of Complexion and Figure in Human Species*. New Brunswick: J. Simpson, 1810.

Smith, W. *Strata Identified by Organised Fossils.* London, 1816.

Sterling, Keir B. *Natural Science in America.* New York: Arno, 1974.

Temkin, O. "Basic Science, Medicine, and the Romantic Era." *The Double Face of Janus.* Baltimore: Johns Hopkins UP, 1977.

Thorpe, T. E. *Humphry Davy: Poet and Philosopher.* London: Cassell, 1896.

Tyson, E. *Orang-Outang, sive Homo Sylvestris* ["Man of the Woods"]. London, 1699.

Valli, Eusebius. *Experiments on Animal Electricity, with their application to physiology, and some pathological and medical observations.* London: J. Johnson, 1793.

Weissmann, Gerald. *Darwin's Audubon: Science and the Liberal Imagination.* New York: Plenum, 1998.

Wilson, Eric. *Emerson's Sublime Science.* New York: St. Martin's, 1999.

———. *Romantic Turbulence: Chaos, Ecology, and American Space.* New York: St. Martin's, 2000.

Worster, Donald. *Nature's Economy: A History of Ecological Ideas.* Cambridge: Cambridge UP, 1994 [1977].

Wylie, Ian. *Young Coleridge and the Philosophers of Nature.* Oxford: Clarendon, 1989.

Young, David. *The Discovery of Evolution.* Cambridge: Cambridge UP, 1992.